The Battle for Butte

The Battle for Butte

MINING AND POLITICS
ON THE NORTHERN FRONTIER, 1864–1906

by Michael P. Malone

Montana Historical Society Press
Helena

Cover photograph: Anaconda Hill, Butte, Montana, circa 1900 (Montana Historical Society Photograph Archives)

Cover design: Finstad Visual Design, Helena, Montana

Printed by Thomson-Shore, Inc., Dexter, Michigan

Montana Historical Society Press
225 N. Roberts St.
P. O. Box 201201
Helena, Montana 59620-1201

Reprinted 1995 by the Montana Historical Society Press by arrangement with University of Washington Press

03 02 01   8 7 6 5 4 3

Library of Congress Cataloging-in-Publication Data

Malone, Michael P.
 The battle for Butte : mining and politics on the northern frontier, 1864–1906 / by Michael P. Malone.
  p.   cm.
 Originally published: Seattle : University of Washington Press, 1981, in series: Emil and Kathleen Sick lecture-book series in western history and biography.
  Includes bibliographical references and index.
  ISBN 0-917298-34-9 (pbk : alk. paper)
  1. Mineral industries—Montana—Butte—History. 2. Mines and mineral resources—Montana—Butte—History. 3. Butte (Mont.)—Politics and government. I. Title.
 HD9506.U63B875 1995   95-14591
 338.2'74'0978668—dc20   CIP

For John Thomas and Molly Christine, my beloved children, . . . whose maternal ancestors were and are a part of Butte and its history.

Contents

Illustrations

Preface to the 1995 Edition

It is good, indeed, to have the Montana Historical Society Press bring out a new, reprint edition of my book *The Battle for Butte,* which was first published by the University of Washington Press in 1981. This is doubly gratifying to me. Naturally, I am delighted to have the Society Press reprint and distribute the book because, frankly, it does both tasks exceptionally well. But in addition to that, I am also pleased because of my long association with the Montana Historical Society, an association that included long service on its Board of Trustees. It is an organization that means a lot to me, as it does to most everyone who cares about Montana and the West.

Of the books I have written over the years, this one was the most fun both to research and to write. Looking back from the perspective of fifteen years, I think it has weathered reasonably well. It appeared at a climatic time, amidst the series of closures in which ARCO was shutting down its unrewarding investment in the old Anaconda Company, a series of closures that fell like hammer blows upon the communities of Butte, Anaconda, and Great Falls. I am relieved now that I did not deliver any prophecies about the future at that time, for neither I nor most other people could or would have foreseen the remarkable renaissance of Butte mining that occurred a few years later.

As with all books looked back upon in perspective, one wishes that he had been able to use, in preparing it, research by others that appeared subsequently. Two prime cases regarding this book are Jerry W. Calvert's *The Gibraltar: Socialism and Labor in Butte, Montana, 1895–1920,* published in 1988 by the Montana Historical Society Press, and David M. Emmons's

The Butte Irish: Class and Ethnicity in an American Mining Town, 1875–1925, published in 1989 by the University of Illinois Press.

Certainly, with the further convolutions now taking place in the regional mining industry, Butte faces more uncertainty both regarding mining and regarding its own future. Given the resiliency of the community and its inhabitants, I believe that the great old "camp" will make the best of whatever hand is dealt it. And I hope that the reissue of *The Battle for Butte* by the Montana Historical Society Press assists in this process, for it is only by coming to terms with the past that we can hope to come to terms with present and future challenges.

In addition to the acknowledgments given in the original 1981 edition, I wish to express my sincere thanks to Editor Charles E. Rankin, Assistant Editor Glenda Bradshaw, and the entire Publications staff of the Montana Historical Society.

Michael P. Malone
Bozeman, Montana
March 1995

Preface

This is not, first of all, a history of Butte, Montana, although such a history is admittedly needed. Neither is it a history of Butte mining, Butte labor, or Butte ethnicity, though all of these are parts of the story. Rather, it is a study of the rise of the Butte mining district to supremacy among western metal mining centers and, more to the point, a study of the economic-political struggle to win supremacy over and consolidation of the great Butte Hill. The story is a fascinating one, and more than once I regretted that the title *War of the Copper Kings* had been preempted by C. B. Glasscock back in 1935. But perhaps that is just as well, for I have tried here to avoid that heroic, personalized approach which Glasscock's racy title implies. Some might charge that this task involves merely a retelling of the earlier accounts by C. P. Connolly and by Glasscock, both of whom knew and interviewed some of the participants. In response, I would say that both men relied heavily on oral history and that neither attempted to approach the subject with the detached objectivity that relies upon thorough research in primary and secondary sources. Needless to say, many such sources are available now which were not then.

Thus this book attempts, for the first time, to depict an epic chapter in the history of the mining West from the vantage of modern historical analysis. As the reader will see, I have dwelt less upon good and bad copper kings than upon the institutions and the economic-political forces which they created, and which created them. W. A. Clark probably emerges here as less of a villain than in earlier accounts, and certainly

F. Augustus Heinze emerges as less than a hero. Both, along with Marcus Daly, are seen as vitally important, but as less important than the institutions which outlasted them—the Anaconda Company, the city of Butte, the heritage of political nastiness. In any case, it is an incredible story, and it is hoped that the attempt to deal with its real substance will not tarnish its real drama.

One always accumulates many debts in such undertakings. Many good people helped me in this task, and without them I would not have gotten far. A heartfelt thanks to Research Vice President John Jutila of Montana State University for helping to finance research travel; to historians Merrill Burlingame, Duane Hampton, Rodman Paul, and Richard Roeder for advice and support; to Minnie Paugh and Ilah Shriver at the Montana State University Library; to Robert Clark, Brian Cockhill, Jeff Cuniff, William Lang, Lory Morrow, and David Walter at the Montana Historical Society; to Dale Johnson and Claire Rhein at the University of Montana Archives; to Jack Brennan and his staff at the University of Colorado Archives; and to the staffs of the National Archives, the Library of Congress, and the Bancroft Library. A number of friends helped me in many ways. They include Martha Edsall, Alan Goddard, Toni Hamilton, Al Hooper, Sammi Keith, Mrs. Dan Kinsella, John Montagne, Terry McGlynn, Eric Myhre, Henry Parsons, Paul Schmechel, Marlene Short, Ann Smith, William Walker, and Lester Zeihen. I owe a special debt to Neil Lynch, who assisted me in many ways, most notably by giving me free access to his valuable Butte collection. Three fine Butte men, now deceased, guided me in distinct ways: Dan Harrington, E. E. MacGilvra, and W. J. Wilcox.

I am especially indebted to Dianne Dougherty, who assisted me at great length with research in the *Engineering and Mining Journal* and in legal sources, and to Eileen Harrington, my former mother-in-law.

Michael P. Malone
Bozeman, Montana
Winter, 1981

The Battle for Butte

1. Gold Camp:
The Rise and Fall of Butte City

Nestled high in the northern Rocky Mountains of southwestern Montana is the small alpine basin drained by Silver Bow Creek, one of the headwaters of the west-flowing Clark Fork of the Columbia. In terms of geography this handsome little valley, carpeted with sage and mountain grasses, flanked by towering peaks on the east and south and by rugged ridges on the west and north, is unexceptional. Its northern latitude and mile-high elevation bring severe winters and springs, and its location well to the east of the major Rocky Mountain summits means diminished rainfalls and parched summers and autumns. The basin lies directly in the cornice of the continental divide, walled on the east and south by this great line of division beween the river flows of America. Tightly enclosed by mountain walls, the remote little valley seemed unlikely to witness much of the commerce of history, which flowed naturally to the east along the Jefferson and Boulder rivers, and to the west through the open and lovely Deer Lodge Valley.

It was geology, not geography, that made this isolated valley such a remarkable place. At the northern end of the basin stands a russet, furrowed hill, which slopes southward onto the valley floor. This incredible hill, which took its name from the pointed rise named "Big Butte" on its western side, covers one of the greatest mineral formations on earth. Almost beyond measure in their value, these mineral riches would lure thousands of people and millions of dollars in investments to this spot, and one day the valley would be denuded of vegetation and smothered in clouds of sulfurous smoke. One of the world's greatest mining centers and most colorful cities would arise here. The millions in profits yielded by the great hill would swell some of the world's greatest fortunes and would find their way, like a seeping pollution, into the political waters of state and nation.

The experienced prospectors who first entered the valley knew at once, from its appearance, that it was an area of rich and complex mineralization. Typically, they were looking for surface, or placer, gold, which could be washed from gravels or diggings along streambeds and banks with relative ease. Silver Bow Creek and its tributary gulches did indeed yield such gold; but the gold was heavily alloyed with silver, which lessened its value, and the placer deposits here were not particularly rich or extensive in any case. They could not compare with the fabled "poor man's diggings" of nearby Alder Gulch, where the placer gold was both plentiful and easy to wash and work.

Here, as at the great Comstock Lode of Nevada, the big bonanza lay in the puzzling quartz veins, which surfaced atop and along the southeasterly slopes of the Butte hill. The mineralized outcrops ran profusely from the brow of the hill in a general direction of north-west-to-southeast toward the "flats" below. Along the great Original and Parrot lodes, where the first hard rock mining centered, were long stretches of ground where mineralization caused a lack of vegetation and where the earth bore unmistakable signs of a metal presence: green and blue carbonates of copper, the rusty brown discoloration of iron, the brown and black stains of zinc and manganese. Even more alluring were the "conspicuous quartz-ledges, rising prominent above the surface," whose obvious metal content caused them to thrust beckoningly above the eroding country rock surrounding them.[1] As Butte's argonauts wondered at what might lay below such a remarkable surface, their pulses quickened with excitement.

Below lay one of the greatest prizes that man has ever found on this planet. The Butte ore deposits lie along the southern periphery of the Boulder Batholith, a geological region which extends northward nearly to Helena. The veins were intensively fractured, a source of many engineering and legal headaches in working them. Nearer the surface, the quartz was richest in silver; but due to the leaching process of erosion, copper in the form of sulphides prevailed at depths of a few hundred feet. The "central" or "Anaconda Hill" zone of the Butte district formed the prized core of the big bonanza. Interlaced throughout the country rock of quartz and altered granite in this core zone ran seams and veinlets of copper glance (or chalcocite, a sulphide of copper) and enargite (a copper-arsenic sulphide), compounded with iron pyrites, silver, and gold. In the intermediate zone, which surrounds the now hollowed-out central mining district, the copper content dwindles significantly. Zinc and manganese become more prevalent. In the third or outer zone, copper is even more sparse, and manganese, along with zinc, is the dominant metal.

Such were the hidden outlines of Butte's complex geology. Montana's pioneer quartz miners, experienced mainly with California's free milling gold, which could be easily freed through amalgamation with mercury, found the Butte ores impossibly "refractory" or "rebellious." They could not reduce them. Only after much experimentation and the importing of the world's most advanced mining technology would the great boom begin. Until roughly 1920, the close of the prosperity surrounding World War I, Butte mining focused almost exclusively in the rich central zone. Beginning about 1910, large-scale operations opened in the intermediate zone; and mining in the outer zone started only during the war itself, in 1918.[2]

The gold rush which descended upon Silver Bow Creek in 1864 was a small part of a much larger historical mosaic. Beginning in 1848–49, the epic mining rush to California brought a sudden influx of population from the ends of the earth to the west slopes of the Sierra Nevada. For the next decade, California remained the center of western mining. Drawing from Spanish-Mexican as well as from older European traditions, the California miners of the 1850s set the styles in technology, government, law, and social life which later mining frontier would follow.[3] The 49ers, "Old Californians," or "Yon-Siders," as they were variously known, appeared and reappeared on each successive mining frontier, including Montana's.

As the California placers declined after the mid–1850s, the gold frontier surged suddenly inward toward midcontinent, opening such new areas as Nevada, Colorado, Arizona, British Columbia, and Idaho during the period of 1857–61. The greatest of these new frontiers were those that opened in the Colorado Rockies and at the remarkable Comstock Lode in the eastern slopes of the Sierra Nevada. Each of these frontiers bore a direct relationship to what later happened in Montana. In Colorado, beginning with the ill-fated "Pike's Peak Rush" of 1859 and continuing through later bonanzas, a sizable population of Americans inhabited the Rocky Mountains for the first time. Many of these Colorado miners would end up in Montana, bringing with them valuable metallurgical and engineering experience.

Even more important was the mighty Comstock, where so much of American deep mining technology was hammered out by hard experience. Indeed, when the Comstock finally faded out in the 1880s, first Leadville, Colorado, and then Butte, Montana, succeeded it as America's premier metal mining centers, absorbing thousands of its seasoned miners.[4] Interestingly, the careers of Butte's two greatest developers typify the effects which these two mining frontiers had upon Montana. William A. Clark came to Montana from Colorado and played the key role in applying the lessons of Colorado smelting to Butte. Marcus Daly, who came from Nevada via Utah, learned the arts of mining first in California and then at the Comstock Lode.

If California, Nevada, and Colorado served as the matrices of Montana mining, Idaho served as the conduit. The gold rushes into the Clearwater, Salmon, and Boise tributaries of the Snake River during 1860–62 brought the mining frontier directly into the western reaches of the Northern Rockies. When Congress created the territory of Idaho in 1863, its boundaries included all of present Idaho and Montana, and nearly all of Wyoming. The polyglot population of Idaho miners, drawn heavily from earlier mining frontiers, stood poised on the doorstep of what was about to become Montana.

Montana's earliest recorded gold discoveries date from the 1850s, but its first major bonanza came with the opening of the Grasshopper Creek diggings in the upper Jefferson River drainage during the summer of 1862. Here arose Montana's first boom town, Bannack City. Bannack's surplus population of miners, most of whom had simply crossed the continental divide from present-day Idaho, soon found more bonanzas. To the east at Alder Gulch, they discovered in 1863 Montana's greatest placer deposits. Virginia City and its sister towns in Alder Gulch housed over 10,000 inhabitants by 1864–65; and from this base of population, dozens of prospecting parties quickly opened new camps throughout the upper Missouri and Clark Fork drainages.

During 1864, the year in which Montana Territory was carved out of Idaho, came many new discoveries, the most notable being Last Chance Gulch (Helena), Confederate Gulch (Diamond City), Emigrant on the upper Yellowstone, and the diggings on Silver Bow Creek. The Montana gold rush crested in 1866, by which time the territory was home to roughly 28,000 people and ranked second only to California in gold production. Soon, however, the Montana placers, like all others, fell into steep decline. Montana's surface gold deposits never approached those of California in richness; and her intriguing quartz veins were too refractory and too demanding of high cost machinery and transportation to promise much for the near future.

By 1870 the gold boom had collapsed. The census of that year recorded only 29,595 isolated Montanans. These "Montanians," as they called themselves in those days, knew that their mining-based economy could never thrive again until railroads and outside investors came to develop the quartz mines which clearly held the area's mineral future. Impatiently, they would have to wait for most of a decade. A severe nationwide depression, the Panic of 1873, deadened the economy of the region; and the Black Hills gold rush of 1875–76 robbed the territory of much of its restless population.[5] Inevitably, the boom had fallen into a bust.

The first recorded acknowledgment of the Butte hill and its peculiarities predates the mining frontier. Caleb E. Irvine, an associate of the famous Major John Owen, who ran a trading establishment in the Bitterroot Valley, often frequented these areas enroute to trade with Crow and Shoshoni Indians. In the spring of 1856, Irvine and a trading party camped along what became known as Town Gulch, later renamed Dublin Gulch. Nearby, they found a "trench" which had been dug into exposed quartz on the soon-to-be-famous Original Lode. Elk antlers found lying nearby had evidently been used as gads to dig the hole. Whether this excavation was the work of Indians or of wandering whites remains an unanswerable question; but few ever doubted Irvine's story, as he lived in Butte for many years and enjoyed a solid reputation. The Irvine party had little time to explore further, for an approaching band of Blackfeet Indians forced them to hurry away to the north.[6]

Irvine's discovery is not especially noteworthy, except as a "first," for it led to nothing. The real opening of Silver Bow Creek came, as noted, in direct consequence of the great gold rush to Virginia City in 1863–64. As Alder Gulch's population scattered in all directions, prospectors arrived on the Silver Bow, which is about seventy miles northwest of Virginia City, in the warm season of 1864. Evidently, the first discoverers, a small group including Bud (or Budd) Parker, William Allison, Pete McMahon, and others, found their placers along the big bend of the clear, cold creek a few miles below and west of the present city of Butte. McMahon named the creek, which impressed him in its meanderings as a succession of little silver bows.[7]

When the discoverers returned to Virginia City for supplies, the news of their find immediately brought more miners to the Silver Bow. William Allison, for instance, returned with his friend G. O. Humphreys. They came to the Butte hill itself this time, to the site they smartly named Baboon Gulch. These two men thus rank as the real first miners of Butte. They were soon joined by three other men, including Dennis Leary, who had followed them.[8] As others arrived, the "old town" of Butte took shape in the autumn of 1864 in "Town Gulch," adjacent to the present city. It was not, by any standard, much of a town—a cluster of cabins and hovels inhabited by a few dozen people, some of them stalwarts like Leary, Henry Porter, and Humphreys, but most of them drifters. The early group included Butte's one female resident, Mrs. Green Weathers, who reportedly "reigned supreme."[9]

In the meantime, more and more groups of gold miners moved into the area. Nearby German Gulch opened in the autumn of 1864 and boasted a sizable population by the following spring. The main action centered downstream from Butte along the middle course of Silver Bow Creek. Silver Bow City, about seven miles west of Butte, arose as the real placer mining center. It became the first seat of Deer Lodge County and the hub of the Summit Mountain Mining District. According to reports, about 150 people, most of them frozen-out placer miners, wintered there during 1864–65.[10]

The gold boom crested during the next two to three years. During the warm seasons of 1865–67, thousands of placer miners toiled along the banks of Silver Bow Creek and its gulches. "By 1866," according to Harry Freeman, "the entire creek channel from Silver Bow to Butte was worked by a company of four or more men to every two-hundred-foot claim." Due to the scarcity of water, the placer men faced severe problems. Often, they had to haul gravel down to the creek for washing with rockers and sluices. Efforts to build long ditches and flumes to bring the water to the diggings, led by Allison, Humphreys, and John Noyes, proved expensive and extremely difficult. Still, with new finds of surface gold and with wages soaring to $6.00 and even $7.00 per day, both owners and workers did well; and by 1867, as many as 5,000 people may have inhabited the general area.[11]

A typical air of optimism and boosterism surrounded the Silver Bow gold boom. Writing from Butte in early 1865, Joe Bowers told Virginia City newspaper readers: "Water and timber are in the greatest abundance and convenient to the lodes. The hills and vales are covered with the best vegetation. Stock of all kinds browse thereon, getting fat and saucy too." Bowers reassured his audience that he was not exaggerating: "In fact, I dare not tell the whole truth, because I know the story would be read and regarded as the emanation of a heated brain."[12]

In actual truth, the Silver Bow camps were rough and unattractive places. Silver Bow led the district, at one time boasting a population of perhaps a thousand. At its peak in 1867, Butte's population probably reached 350–500. In that same year, a new townsite was laid out, just to the west of Town Gulch. Both towns were typical gold camps: heavily male in population, slovenly in appearance with dirt-mud streets, and log or rough-cut lumber buildings, many of them bearing false frame fronts. Early observers described Butte as a "deplorable" place, filled with men armed with guns and knives and enlivened by "hurdy-gurdy houses and the 'wide-open' gambling dens." Although "Colonel" J. G. Wood managed to open a school in 1866, the town had no newspaper and showed little interest in religion or culture.[13]

Everyone knew that the placers must soon fade, and soon they did. By 1868, Butte was in noticeable decline; and, with the severe drought of 1869, so was Silver Bow. Nearby French and Highland gulches still registered some gains, as did the little camp of Rocker, midway along the creek.[14] In simple truth, though, Silver Bow Creek was no Alder Gulch. It lacked both the richness of eroded, surface gold and the ready availability of sufficient water. If the area was to prosper, vein mining was the key.

Among the thousands of miners who came in the Silver Bow gold rush, some from the very beginning attempted to work the quartz leads on the Butte hill. They knew that these black quartz reefs, stained by manganese and rich with silver, held some combination of precious and base metals; but they had no idea how to work them. Along the clearly defined and fabulously rich Parrott (later shortened to Parrot) Lode, a determined foursome—Joseph Ramsdell, Billy Parks, Dennis Leary, and Charles Porter—erected a crude blast furnace with a jerry-built bellows to work the puzzling cuprous ores they extracted. Ramsdell, a freighter from Ohio who is often considered the "father" of Butte quartz mining, knew that the ore was rich in copper, but he could not "flux" it for smelting. In other words, he could not figure out how to mix the various ores in such a way as to smelt out the valuable metals. Thus, even though some of the Parrot ore exceeded 50 percent in copper content, it proved too refractory to reduce. Ramsdell and his associates rebuilt their furnace with a fan-blast in 1868 and even sent four tons of matte to either St. Louis or Swansea in Wales for smelting. (Matte is the product which emerges from the initial stages of smelting copper sulphide ore. It is heavily composed of concentrated metals and is thus more easily transported for final smelting and refining.) But they finally gave up, realizing that they had neither the technology nor the transportation facilities to succeed.[15]

In the meantime, other experimenters met the same fate. William

L. Farlin, who would one day play a key role in Butte's rise, resolutely worked his Asteroid claim, which was later renamed the Travona. Farlin sent high-grade ore all the way to New Jersey via the Missouri River and eastern railroads for smelting. He also tried, without much luck, to roast his silver-bearing ores and then to free the precious metal through mercury amalgamation. In 1868, Charles Hendrie and Harvey Bay erected a crude, California gold quartz mill, the first such device to appear in Butte. It failed, because most of the gold-silver ores simply washed through it. Several others duplicated such experiments, and a few had some luck crushing higher grade gold and silver ores using arrastras. (An arrastra is a Mexican ore crusher. Horses or mules simply pull a rotating beam in a circle; the beam draws large stones across a rock floor, crushing the ore. Sometimes mercury is used to amalgamate the precious metals.)[16] Soon, however, almost all of them gave up and moved away. Some, like Farlin, remembered the mysterious black "reefs" of Butte and eventually returned. A few others stayed steadfastly on. For years, Billy Parks dug bravely away at his "glory hole" on the Parrot Lode, convinced that he had a copper mine while his neighbors drank up his whiskey and chuckled at his obstinacy.

In retrospect, the failure of these early quartz miners seems to have been clearly inevitable. Not only did they lack technology and scientific expertise: more importantly, they were looking in vain for free milling gold like that of California. The compounding of Butte's gold with silver, copper, manganese, zinc, and lead perplexed them and also lowered the value of the product. Small wonder, then, that they joined the armies of disheartened placer miners in abandoning the Silver Bow diggings. In 1870, the first census takers to visit Montana found only 241 people remaining in Butte City, and most of these would leave soon thereafter. That first Butte census registered 142 white residents, 1 lone Negro, and, interestingly, 98 Chinese. As any miner knew, the presence of so many Chinese showed beyond any doubt that the whites no longer considered the diggings worthy of their efforts.[17]

With the close of the 1860s, then, Butte sank into lethargy, looking like any of the hundreds of other played out mining towns of the Mountain West. Like the rest of Montana, its future seemed dim. Railheads still lay hundreds of miles away, and hopes for economic improvement were practically nonexistent. The era of the gold boom was over, but not forgotten.

2. Clark, Daly, and the Anaconda: 1872–84

The hard times of the early 1870s brought great frustration to western out-of-the-way places like Butte, Montana. For the few quartz miners who continued to work the veins along the hill, there appeared little hope of success in the near future, especially after the onset of the 1873 Panic. Rail builders and eastern capitalists now seemed farther away than ever. But, then as now, times of depression can be good times for opportunistic investors. In fact, as Richard H. Peterson has recently demonstrated in his study of *The Bonanza Kings*, what happened in the rebirth of Butte City was typical of the general pattern in frontier mining. Control of the major mines soon rested in the hands, not of the pioneers who opened them, but of the shrewd merchant-financiers who moved in during the hard times, bought them up cheaply, and had the capital and the ability to develop them.[1] The two men who personified this trend at Butte were William Andrews Clark and Andrew Jackson Davis.

A. J. Davis (1819–90) seems a near perfect example of the shrewd and calculating Yankee merchant in the frontier West. In his young manhood, he migrated from Massachusetts to Iowa, where he established himself as a merchant-farmer. By the time he followed the frontier to Montana in 1864, the modest and soft-spoken Davis was already middle-aged. He invested wisely and successfully in a number of enterprises, including merchandising, freighting, and flour mills. Most importantly, he developed a close friendship and business relationship with Samuel T. Hauser of Helena, a young Missourian capitalist and one of the shrewdest investors and toughest political manipulators in the West. During the 1860s and 1870s, the cynical and hard-nosed Hauser wielded greater business and political

11

power than any other man in Montana, manipulating banks, railroads, livestock ventures, and politicians with effortless aplomb. Davis bought a sizable share of Hauser's First National Bank of Helena; and the two men joined in numerous other ventures, including the famous DHS Ranch of central Montana and several investments at Butte.[2]

Passing through the camp on his business travels, Davis became excited about the possibilities of Butte. He began financing the Hendrie Mill as early as 1868; and sometime between 1872 and 1876, he acquired the fabulous Lexington Mine, which under his direction would become one of Butte's great silver producers. One may doubt the old tale that Davis picked up the Lexington in a horse trade, but it is still true that he acquired this property and other mines and mills at ridiculously low prices. As Davis's Butte holdings increased, he took up residence there in 1875, managing his mines and importing and selling heavy machinery. He sold $80,000 worth of mining machinery at Butte in 1876 alone. Things went so well that Davis, Hauser, and associates opened the Butte banking house of S. T. Hauser and Company in 1877. Despite Hauser's name on the masthead, Davis was actually the principal owner. The firm eventually became the First National of Butte, with Davis its sole owner. As a banker and mining investor, laconic A. J. Davis wielded a strong influence in the rise of Butte and soon won recognition as Montana's first millionaire.[3]

The arrival of William Andrews Clark (1839–1925) at Butte in 1872 truly signaled the great changes that were about to occur. This grim little man, so uninspiring in appearance, would dominate the life of Butte and of Montana to a larger extent than any other figure of his generation. Spare and somewhat pinched in features, Clark stood a short five feet, seven inches in height and weighed a trim 140 pounds. Austere in personality and obviously vain in his mannerisms, he was a man of few friends but a man who commanded and demanded respect. To understand the remarkable personality and career of W. A. Clark, one must fathom his two prime traits: a genius at business affairs, and a relentless, all-consuming ambition.

Anyone who ever looked into the cold, penetrating eyes of Clark, or whoever witnessed his incredibly self-taxing work habits, or whoever made a deal with him knew that he was a capitalist *par excellence.* He combined a remarkable intelligence and attention to detail with a plunger's genius for comprehending the rewards to be had in gambling on a large scale. His naked ambition recalls J. B. Bury's old adage: "There is no force in nature more terrible than a young Scotsman on the make." A jaundiced observer once said: ". . . his heart is frozen and his instincts are those of the fox: there is craft in his stereotyped smile and icicles in his handshake. He is about as magnetic as last year's bird's nest."[4] Few loved him, but many courted him. And despite his aloofness, thousands came to follow his lead. Clark's business acumen and his mighty compulsion would one day make him one of the world's richest men and would carry him to the United States Senate. The same traits, however, would also lead to his disgrace and to the disgrace of his adopted state. His tempestuous life seemed an embodiment of raw, unrestrained frontier capitalism.

William A. Clark well represents two prominent stereotypes of the American past: the Protestant "work-ethic," and the Horatio Alger-style, rags-to-riches success story. The descendants of Scots-Irish and French Huguenot immigrant families, John and Mary Clark scratched out a meager living as dirt farmers in Fayette County, Pennsylvania. Their son, William Andrews, was born there on 8 January 1839. Even as a young schoolboy, this son of a Presbyterian elder seemed determined to better his lot in life. Having stumbled at mathematics, for instance, young Clark drove himself to master the subject, just as he would later refuse to interrupt his long working hours when ill, or would force himself as an old man to learn French and German.

The Clarks pulled up roots in 1856 and moved west to Van Buren County, Iowa. Now approaching manhood, their son had acquired a good schooling by frontier standards, and he continued his studies with two years of law at Iowa Wesleyan College. He taught school for a few years in Missouri, until the turmoil of the Civil War and the lure of a gold rush in Colorado sent him westward in the early 1860s.[5] Like so many of the aspiring capitalists of his generation, Clark avoided the call to arms to seek his fortune in a time of great opportunity. Along with most of the young midwesterners who flocked to Colorado, Clark had little luck; and with most of the others, he soon moved on again. With a party of friends, he traveled to the booming gold camp of Bannack in 1863, the year before Montana was carved out of Idaho Territory. Clark and one of his Colorado pals took up placering at Horse Prairie Creek near Bannack, building a log cabin and sluices, to which they hauled their paydirt for washing. They did quite well. After a year of placering, they sold their claim and each pocketed roughly $2,000. This bankroll, tidy for its day, formed the embryo of the fabled Clark fortune.[6]

In the rough and wide open gold camps of early Montana, Clark found his element. One cannot deny his courage, for even amidst the frenzy of murders by the notorious Henry Plummer Gang, he traveled alone and invested freely. In fact, Clark knew both Plummer himself and his violent associate Buck Stinson. On one trip home, he saw the frozen corpse of road agent "Dutch John" Wagner swaying at the end of a vigilante rope. Nor can one deny the remarkable shrewdness and initiative that Clark demonstrated as a young frontier merchant. As he turned from back-breaking manual labor to broad-based investing, everything he touched seemed to turn to gold.

Gambling against the weather, the environment, the outlaws, and the unpredictable markets of the mining camps, Clark made huge profits by buying up large stocks of goods and freighting them to the right places at the right times. Clark and his occasional partners loaded their wagons at points as far away as Salt Lake City. The comely Mormon lasses there caught his eye, as women always did. Despite the terrible hardships of winter travel—on one occasion their oxen were frozen in the yokes—they usually made it, selling everything from tools to frozen eggs for Tom and Jerry's. Clark hauled Salt Lake City cargoes to Bannack and Virginia City, huge lots of tobacco from Boise City to Helena, even large tonnages of goods from the Pacific Coast to Elk City. He nearly always prospered under the most trying circumstances.[7] People learned that the busy little man was tough and conniving, but that he kept his word and his commitments.

One success led to another. Unlike many of his contemporaries, who stayed on the raw frontier just long enough to make a "pile," Clark remained to "grow with the country." He returned triumphantly home to Iowa in 1867, proving his success to an adoring family, and traveled on eastward to consign more goods for shipment to Montana. On a similar trip in 1869, he married childhood friend Kate Stauffer at his old home in Pennsylvania. She bore him six children, of whom four grew to maturity.[8] Back in Montana, he procured the profitable mail contract between Walla Walla, Washington, and Missoula, Montana. Then he established a store on Bridge Street in Helena. In order to secure futher capital, Clark formed a partnership first with R. W. Donnell of New York and then also with S. E. Larabie of Deer Lodge. At Helena and increasingly at Deer Lodge, where Clark soon made his home, the partners specialized in wholesale and retail merchandising and in the lucrative practice of buying gold dust for resale to eastern banks. Clark acted as a purchasing agent for several Helena merchants and began extending loans to these and other men at rates of up to 2 percent monthly.

The loans and the gold purchasing led naturally into banking. In 1872 the partners formed the First National Bank of Deer Lodge, capitalized at $50,000. This prosperous little bank, which as the base of the burgeoning Clark empire later became one of the strongest financial institutions in the country, passed through several reorganizations. In 1879 the partners surrendered their national charter, which was no longer necessary, and the firm became Donnell, Clark, and Larabie. When Clark bought out his old associates and added his brother J. Ross Clark as a partner, the title changed to Clark and Larabie and finally to W. A. Clark and Brother, with its main branch at Butte.[9]

As a prospering banker-merchant with a sharp eye for investments and ready access to credit, W. A. Clark inevitably came to fasten his attention upon the near-dormant mining camp of Butte, a mere forty miles east of Deer Lodge. He visited the moribund camp in the summer of 1872, and the few dozen men still working the mines showed them off with an unquenchable enthusiasm. Realizing the tremendous potential value of such cheap investments, the thirty-three-year-old banker bought four major claims. All of them would one day become giant producers: the Original, Colusa, Mountain Chief, and Gambetta mines. With astounding audacity, Clark quickly shifted his career focus to vein mining. He could now free up valuable time because his businesses were on such a regularized basis; and since his $150,000 per year gold buying trade was in decline, he needed to make the transition. Taking ore samples with him, he journeyed to New York for a cram course in geological and mineralogical studies at the great Columbia University School of Mines.[10] Within a decade and a half, he would be one of the world's richest and most powerful men.

W. A. Clark and A. J. Davis played key roles in the rebirth of Butte by bringing large-scale capital and astute business management to bear upon the unproductive mines of the hill. But the man who really touched off the big boom was William L. Farlin, a veteran hard rock miner. A Pennsylvanian who had followed the mining frontier to Idaho and then to Virginia City, Farlin had tried without success to work the puzzling black quartz reefs of Butte during the 1860s and early 1870s. When he finally abandoned the camp, he took ore samples with him; and when he eventually managed to get a reliable test of them at Owyhee, Idaho, the assay showed the specimens to be rich in silver and copper. The restless promoter, now fired with enthusiasm, returned to Butte. According to the then recently revised federal mining law, any claim owner who allowed one year to lapse without working his ground must forfeit it. Since the law took effect on 1 January 1875, Farlin relocated his old Asteroid (Travona) claim and twelve other plots on the last day of 1874.[11]

The oldtimers of Butte credited Bill Farlin's perseverance with "sav-

ing" the camp, even though its salvation seems in hindsight to have
been inevitable. With financing from the bank of W. A. Clark, Farlin
began construction of his 10-stamp Dexter Mill to reduce the silver
ores of the Travona Mine. The success of the Travona galvanized the
camp into a frenzied activity. Rolla Butcher located the Alice, a fine
silver mine, in January of 1875. John How, a veteran Montana quartz
man, started work on his aptly named Centennial Mill; and Giles
Olin, pathetically crippled due to the amputation of his frozen legs,
labored at building a concentrator downstream on Silver Bow Creek.
(A concentrator is a pre-smelting device which crushes and removes
much of the waste material from mid- and low-grade ore. The heavily
mineralized "concentrates" produced by this process are then ready
for efficient smelting.) A. J. Davis acquired full control of the old
Hendrie Mill and rebuilt it to work the ores of the Lexington.[12]

Early in 1876 Billy Parks, who had toiled for years with an excavation bucket and a crude windlass to dig into the Parrot Lode, found
the copper bonanza he had so long envisioned. At a depth of 150 feet,
he hit a four-foot-wide vein of copper glance (ore which glistens due
to its high metallic content). Parks and two employees were soon
extracting a ton of ore per day, concentrating and sacking it at Olin's
works, and shipping it to Baltimore by wagon and rail for a "handsome
profit"[13] If Farlin had proven Butte to be a silver camp, Parks had
likewise demonstrated its copper potential.

By the centennial year of 1876, Butte was basking in the glow of a
major quartz mining boom. Both Farlin's Dexter Mill and How's
Centennial cranked up in mid-year, and Davis's mill started operations early in 1877. Experienced miners were moving in, bringing
families with them; and respectable frame houses sprang up amidst
the scattering of cabins which had been "Old Butte." New businesses
moved in, including numerous saloons and "hurdy-gurdy" dance
halls, two breweries, and a newspaper called the *Butte Miner*, whose
first issue announced to the world that "there is more daylight on
more good ore here than in all the other camps of Montana."[14]

Butte City numbered 1,000 inhabitants by the close of 1876, and
nearly 3,400 four years later. To the north of town, near the brow of
the hill, a settlement soon to be known as Walkerville began to ger-
minate around the Alice and Lexington silver mines. Another cluster
of two dozen dwellings adjoined the Travona, southwest of town.
Merchants from nearby Deer Lodge and Virginia City started running
daily expresses into Butte; and a visiting newspaperman warned
Helena that, if she wished to hold her hegemony over the territory,
she had better improve her tortuous road over the mountains to the

lusty boom town. Meanwhile, the old placer camp of Silver Bow, once the center of the district, faded into insignificance.[15]

Thus Butte had special reason to join in the great national celebration of America's 100th birthday on 4 July 1876. Rising again like the phoenix from the ashes, Butte and its boomers knew that, in contrast to Montana's other depression-racked towns, their future prosperity was assured. July 4 at Butte began with a thirteen-gun salute and a twenty-seven-entry parade, which attracted so many male participants that almost all the onlookers were women and children. Following numerous orations and festivities, the day closed with an awe-inspiring fireworks display. Unfortunately, the day's big event failed to materialize. Professor B. Pettit, "noted aeronaut of the Northwest," was to fly a balloon from Butte to Deer Lodge. Furthermore, as the *Butte Miner* announced: "At 8:45 Grand Balloon 'Gem City of Montana' will be let loose from moorings. Copies of the *BUTTE MINER*, orations and Historical addresses will be part of her cargo. This balloon is expected to land at the foot of Bunker Hill monument. (Boston papers please copy)." Alas, the balloons caught fire, and Professor Pettit was "deeply mortified" at the failure.[16] But no matter, for the rosy future promised many more such grand celebrations.

Soon after the festivities of mid–1876, several of the men who had made them possible passed from the scene. Poor Giles Olin, who had great difficulty moving about on his self-made artificial legs, died only a year later. Rolla Butcher sold the Alice Mine to Utah developers only weeks after July 4, and Billy Parks later sold his Parrot No. 1 mine for a mere $10,000. It later yielded millions, but Parks died in obscurity.[17] Even Bill Farlin soon came to grief. W. A. Clark, who had been shipping his own high-grade ore out of Montana for treatment, took an ever increasing hand in managing the Dexter Mill as Farlin passed deeper into his debt. According to Butte tradition, Clark may well have hoodwinked his unsophisticated client and cheated him. Be that as it may, when Farlin proved unable to make his payments, Clark took over his properties and soon had them turning handsome profits. Bill Farlin stayed on at Butte for many years, well liked and respected, but he never again came as close to success as he had been in 1876. At Butte, as at most mining camps, the discoverers thus lost out to the men of finance.[18]

As noted previously, Rolla Butcher's sale of the Alice Mine in the autumn of 1876 closely fit this pattern of small speculators selling out to larger ones. The sale of the Alice, however, bore a special significance. Indeed, it marked a turning point in the rise of Butte; for the developers of the Alice, Marcus Daly and the Walker brothers of Salt

Lake City, first brought major outside capital and expertise into the area. As recently as 1874, Commissioner of Mining Statistics Rossiter Raymond had lamented the backwardness of industrial mining in Montana: "This territory has not been fruitful of inventions and improvements in mining. Its isolated and remote position has caused it rather to lag behind other mining regions of the country, even in the adoption of improvements already known."[19] Daly and the Walkers rapidly changed this situation.

Marcus Daly (1841–1900) was undoubtedly one of the greatest practical miners and mine developers who ever lived. He was a man of the earth, whose stocky frame, stooping shoulders, brusque mannerisms, simple tastes, and open and unpretentious personality all bore evidence of his Irish peasant roots. So unlike his great rival Clark, Daly was a hearty and likable man who never pretended to be anything more than he really was, a working miner who had made it big. This unaffected simplicity made him a popular favorite in the democratic, hairy-chested mining camp of Butte. Actually, Daly's ready wit and relaxed charm masked a keen and ruthless intelligence and an explosive temper. He loved his friends with enduring loyalty, but he hated his enemies implacably and never forgot a grudge. He was a simple man of intense likes and dislikes, of warm compassion and bitter hatred, of towering achievement and low rascality.[20]

He was born in "an obscure rural hamlet" near Ballyjamesduff in County Cavan, Ireland, on 5 December 1841. His typical Irish Catholic parents, Luke and Mary Daly, had six children and could never offer them much more than bare subsistence. So "Mark" received very little education; and for the rest of his life, even when testifying before a committee of the U. S. Senate, his crude and faltering speech testified to his early lack of opportunity. Faced with few opportunities and the pall which the potato famine cast over Ireland, the boy joined the thousands of his countrymen who came to America, arriving at New York, alone in the world, at age fifteen in 1856. He worked at various jobs in New York for two years, principally as a longshoreman and a telegraph operator; and then with money he had saved, he headed for California by sea and the isthmus of Panama.[21]

These early years on the frontier he would later recall as "rough ones, and the hard knocks brought with them quite a bit of common sense." He worked for a while on farms and ranches. Then he and his Irish pal Thomas Murray, whom he later made yard superintendent at the Anaconda smelter, decided to head for Calaveras County to take up mining. Here and then at Grass Valley, he did some prospecting on his own; but mainly he worked in established mines, learning well the many skills of the hard rock miner. By 1862 he had drifted to Virginia City, Nevada, where the Comstock Lode was booming. John Mackay, the greatest of the quartet of capitalists who developed the "Big Bonanza" of the Comstock, liked Daly and made him a mine foreman. He held this position for six years, and here at the center of American mining development he became a widely recognized expert in his profession, a master at assessing vein structures, at tunneling, timbering, and blasting. Here, too, he struck up a lasting friendship with newspaperman Mark Twain, like Daly a fun-loving fellow who appreciated the raucous life of the mining camps.[22]

Daly remained at the Comstock until 1868 and then moved on, first to White Pine and then to the boom town of Mineral Hill, Nevada. Here he met Jeremiah Kelley, who became his lifelong friend and whose son Cornelius would for many years manage the company which Daly founded. Also at Mineral Hill, if not earlier on the Comstock, he met George Hearst, with whom he later struck up a remarkably lucrative business relationship. With each move, Daly's reputation as an expert mine manager and appraiser grew. His greatest advance came in 1870, when the powerful Walker brothers hired him as foreman of their Emma Mine at Alta, Utah. The four Walker brothers—Joseph R., Samuel Sharp, Matthew H., and David F.— were British immigrants who had come to Utah years earlier with their widowed mother. They prospered first with a drygoods store and then with the famous bank which they founded at Salt Lake City in 1857 and which still thrives today. By the 1870s Joseph was the dominant brother, and the family's banking-mining empire had grown to major proportions.[23]

The famous Emma Mine was a mighty producer, and under Daly's management it did much to boom the silver industry of Utah. Continuing his mutually rewarding relationship with the Walkers, the Irishman moved on to manage their Lion Hill property in the Ophir District, about fifty-six miles south of Salt Lake City. While at Ophir, rough-hewn but highly regarded Marcus Daly met Margaret Evans, the daughter of a local mine manager, and a romance soon developed. The two were married at Joseph Walker's Salt Lake City home in 1872, and two years later, Daly became a United States citizen. Marcus and Margaret Daly forever remained a close and devoted couple; they raised four children.[24]

The Walkers continued steadily to expand their mining operations. After seeing Butte ores sent to them for processing, they sent Daly to look over the camp in August of 1876. He took the train to its terminus at Franklin, Idaho, and then boarded the stage for the hot and dirty remainder of the journey. One of Butte's favorite bits of Daly lore recalls how he arrived there dressed in the tattered canvas clothes of the working miner, and how he stayed at a cheap boarding house while clandestinely checking out the camp's best claims without disclosing his identity and purpose. In fact, he did no such thing. Daly made no secret of who he was or what he was doing.[25]

In late September, he returned to Butte, this time accompanied by two of the Walkers and a mine appraiser. Butte folks welcomed the Utah group with open arms, the *Miner* heralding their arrival as "the most auspicious event" in the town's brief history. In partnership with Daly, the Walkers negotiated several purchases, all of them along the extended series of ledges then known as the Rainbow lode. They bought 800 feet along the Alice lode from Rolla Butcher and his partner, 1,050 feet of the Magna Charter [sic] from the veteran Porter brothers and their partner, and a further 400-foot extension of the Alice from the banking firm of W. A. Clark. It is interesting to note, parenthetically, that the ubiquitous Clark was involved even in this first of Daly's Butte transactions. As part owner and superintendent of the Alice, Daly moved permanently to Butte to manage the promising mine atop the hill. The Walkers dismantled their old twenty-stamp mill at Ophir and freighted it to Butte; and Daly had a small force at work by mid-October of 1876.[26]

Under the expert hand of Marcus Daly and the sound fiscal management of the Walkers, the Alice proved to be an outstanding silver mine, famous throughout the West. Its output and profits steadily mounted; and by 1880, when it was incorporated at $10,000,000, it had sixty stamps crushing silver ore. Since both the Alice and the Lexington, as well as other mines like the Moulton and the Allie Brown, lay up the hill well to the north of Butte, the hamlet of Walkerville grew up there to house the workers and their families. The *Miner* accurately described the impact of the Alice's development as "the beginning of the Butte boom. . . . It is the first gun to awaken Eastern capitalists to the extent and permanence of our resources."[27] In fact, the Alice Mine and the men who worked it "proved" the Butte hill and awakened outside investors to its enormous potential.

The enthusiasm generated by the Alice boom reached such heights that A. J. Davis was soon grousing to his Helena partner Sam Hauser about the impossibly high prices for good ground. Davis, Clark, and other local promoters desperately sought the kind of capital support that the Walkers provided Daly, but they faced severe problems.[28] Butte was still a primitive camp, far from the railroad and with much to learn about ore reduction. As everyone knew, rails held the key to the camp's future, for they were essential both to import heavy machinery and to market concentrated and smelted ores.

Two railroads aimed in Butte's direction, but both of them had been halted by the Panic of 1873. The Northern Pacific lay dormant in central Dakota Territory, too far away to reach from southwestern Montana. Butte's main artery into national commerce continued to be the old Corinne–Virginia City Road, Montana's principal freight route, which stretched southward over Monida Pass to the Union Pacific depots in northern Utah. Anxious to hold their hegemony over the Montana mining region, Mormon investors led by Brigham Young's son John had joined with eastern capitalists in 1871 to build the Utah Northern Railroad, a narrow gauge line reaching northward over the Corinne Road. Hard hit by the 1873 Panic, the little railroad ground sadly to a halt at Franklin in southeastern Idaho. Thus Montana miners still had to rely upon cumbersome wagon freight, which meant poor service and high expenses. Led by Sam Hauser, Montana boosters pressed the legislature for subsidies to help renew construction; but they consistently failed to work out a subsidy plan, and Butte remained marooned.[29]

Even without rail service, the Butte promoters managed to attract some outside capital. Naturally, banker–mine investors A. J. Davis and W. A. Clark led in this effort. In 1877–78, Davis and his Helena partners, Sam Hauser and Anton Holter, joined with Connecticut capitalists Franklin Farrel and Achille F. Migron to buy the well-established Parrot Mine. Hauser, who also held major mine holdings in the Helena area, took the lead in this drive to lure in the New England copper-brass interests. The Yankee merchants needed new sources of copper both for tapping the burgeoning market for electrical conductors and especially for producing brass, which is a copper-zinc alloy and was rising in demand for machine parts and other corrosion-resistant uses. Davis, Hauser, and their partners held the Parrot for a time, waiting for the approaching railroad; then they incorporated in 1880 as the Parrot Silver and Copper Company. By 1881 the Parrot had a smelter erected and was turning out high-grade silver-copper matte. It soon became a leader in mining technology and pioneered in the use of the Bessemer process in copper smelting. Meanwhile, Davis continued to develop his own great Lexington group of silver mines and mill. He sold the Lexington to a French syndicate in 1881 for $1,000,000, retaining a one-eighth interest in the extremely valuable property.[30]

William A. Clark played an even more decisive role than Davis and Hauser in bringing Montana into the mainstream of American mining technology. In 1877 Clark sent 150 tons of high-grade cuprous ore from his Original Mine to the Boston and Colorado smelting firm of Black Hawk, Colorado, which was controlled by one of the giants of western mining, Nathaniel P. Hill. A former Brown University chemist and future U.S. Senator, Nathaniel Hill had imported German and English metallurgy and Boston capital to master the reduction of Colorado's complex silver ores, which somewhat resemble those of Montana in their composition. He found Clark's shipment highly intriguing and sent one of his experts, Henry Williams, to look over the Butte situation.[31]

The result was the creation in 1878–79 of the Colorado and Montana Company—later known as the Colorado Smelting and Mining Company—with Hill as president, Clark as vice president, Williams as superintendent, and other associates of Hill as coinvestors. The "Colorado Company," pioneering the application of the invaluable lessons of Colorado smelting to Butte, opened a large smelter below the city on the south side of Silver Bow Creek and began operations in August 1879. In 1881 a fifty-ton concentrator was added. Clark made handsome profits from the Colorado Company, both as a co-owner and as the holder of mines like the Original, Colusa, and Gambetta, which fed ore to its plant. Other miners profited, too, as the firm did custom smelting and as Clark bought their ores to form the proper fluxing mixtures to combine with and smelt his own.[32]

Not all of the outside investors had to rely upon Butte insiders for contacts. The highly successful Lewisohn brothers, Adolph and Leonard, were German-Jewish immigrants who prospered as Hamburg- and New York–based importers and sellers of such rare items as horsehair and ostrich feathers. Before long, they concentrated their efforts at marketing two highly demanded commodities: coffee and copper. In 1878 the intelligent and aspiring brothers dispatched a veteran California and Utah copper man, Charles T. Meader, to Butte to look over the prospects there. "No sooner did I land in Butte in 1878," reminisced Meader, "than I saw that I was in the copper district. There exist unmistakable indications of copper all about these hills." Meader purchased the East and West Colusa claims, which lay astride the big ridge east of town, for the Lewisohns; and in 1879 they formed the Montana Copper Company to manage their embryonic Butte holdings. The company erected a smelter well to the east of Butte in 1880. Around this site grew up the settlement of Meaderville, later to become famous as an Italian enclave and a center of gambling and night life.

As the years went by, the Lewisohns came to wield great power in the American copper industry. In addition to their Butte holdings, they built a large electrolytic refinery at Perth Amboy, New Jersey, and a highly lucrative marketing firm based in New York. They joined forces with the powerful Boston copper men Albert S. Bigelow and Joseph W. Clark to buy the great Osceola and Tamarack mines of northern Michigan and later secured more holdings in Arizona. As for Meader, he soon went his own way, buying the Bell Mine and building for it a smelter which shipped matte all the way to Swansea, Wales, for finishing. A colorful Scot who was famous for his gourmet cooking and for the whistles on his smelter, which each morning would ring out the tunes of "Annie Laurie" and the "Blue Bells of Scotland," Meader merits recognition as one of Butte's primary developers. He soon lost his Bell holdings to the bank and moved on, but by then he had planted his valuable copper knowledge in the community.[33]

Obviously, these big-time developers were all depending upon the prompt arrival of rails, which would tie them into the national economy. One frustration followed another, as the Utah Northern seemed hopelessly stalled and undercapitalized. Finally, in 1877–78, Union Pacific executives Jay Gould and Sidney Dillon led a successful effort to reorganize the road, changing its name to the Utah and Northern Railway Company. At long last, rail building resumed, and the tracks reached the Montana line at Monida Pass in March 1880. Butte folks sipped champagne and listened joyously to a telegrapher describing their arrival. The camp had further cause to cheer as it became increasingly likely that the Utah and Northern would choose Butte rather than Helena, the established hub of Montana commerce, as its terminus. As the *Miner* put it: "The trouble is that Helena thinks she is New York or Boston, whereas she is an unimportant village separated from the natural terminus of the road, which is Butte, by a distance of seventy miles and a range of mountains." The *Miner* generously allowed that, at some future date, a branch line might extend on to Helena, and even to "San Francisco and other insignificant villages on the Pacific coast."[34]

As the road built northward through the new town of Dillon and along the Big Hole River, Butte still had some anxious moments about when and if its precious rails would ever arrive. They finally did on the frigid night of 26 December 1881, when a train carrying fifty passengers pulled into the new Butte depot. Although cold weather dampened the festivities that night, Butte now knew that she had truly "arrived." Before long, however, the railroad euphoria turned sour. Early in 1882 the directors of the Union Pacific, of which the

Utah and Northern was a spur, and those of the westward-building Northern Pacific formed a "pooling" agreement typical of the times. The two carriers agreed to pool passenger and freight traffic, to maintain rates, and to divide the market: the Northern Pacific would stay out of Butte, and the Union Pacific would stop short of Helena. The two roads jointly constructed the inter-connecting Montana Union line from Silver Bow westward to Garrison Junction on the Northern Pacific main route.[35] For the time being, at least, this "gentlemen's agreement" squelched competition and thus meant high freight rates for Butte.

So the year 1881, ending with the arrival of rails, was a big one for Butte. After six years of boom, during which major outside investors came upon the scene and production increased dramatically, the camp's status as a big-time mining center could no longer be disputed. Yet, at this very moment, developments at the Anaconda Mine were about to make all of these previous advances seem pale by comparison.

Located on the rise directly east of Butte City, the Anaconda Mine seemed prior to 1880 nothing more than an unexceptional silver prospect. Its locator was Michael Hickey, a New Yorker who had followed the initial gold rush to Silver Bow Creek. One day in 1866, he had noticed outcroppings of copper carbonate atop this rise, soon to be known as the Anaconda Hill. But Hickey sought gold or silver, not copper, and so he did not locate a claim there until late 1875 or 1876. He named it the Anaconda. That name had remained fixed in his mind ever since, as a soldier in McClellan's Army of the Potomac, he had read a *New York Tribune* column in which Horace Greeley predicted that McClellan's army would wrap up Lee's forces like a giant anaconda. Before long, Michael's brother Edward located the St. Lawrence claim adjacent to the Anaconda.[36]

The Hickey brothers were typical small-time miners. They had many claims, which they held for speculation; but they lacked the means and ability to develop them and could barely demonstrate active ownership each year.[37] The big quartz boom which followed 1876 naturally drove up the value of these random quartz claims, and by 1880 several men showed an interest in the Anaconda. The most prestigious of these was Marcus Daly, who was in the process of selling out his share of the Alice for a rumored $100,000. According to one John Branagan, who witnessed these events, Daly seriously considered taking his small Butte fortune and moving back to California, perhaps to his beloved and beautiful former home, Grass Valley.

Whatever his initial intent, he paused instead to ponder several Butte properties. Convinced that "there is a mine in the Anaconda," he worked out a purchase agreement with Hickey and co-owner Charles X. Larabie in the autumn of 1880.[38]

Daly paid $30,000 for the Anaconda, $20,000 to Larabie for his two-thirds interest in September of 1880, and $10,000 to Michael Hickey for his one-third in the following May.[39] Of course, when buying silver mines, the purchase of ground represented only a first installment. One next had to build, lease, or sell to an expensive stamp mill which crushed the ore and a smelter which reduced it. In short, Daly needed backers. It may be that his senior partners in the Alice, the Walker brothers of Utah, were perturbed with him for leaving them and that they refused an offer to invest with him in the Anaconda. There is also some evidence that they did indeed wish to be included in the Anaconda venture and that Daly froze them out. In any case, the Walkers lost out this time, and they remained permanently embittered toward their former partner. It is now certain that Daly had kept in confidential touch with the men who did become his partners, even while he was with the Walkers.[40]

In turning to the San Francisco–based partnership of George Hearst, James Ben Ali Haggin, and Lloyd Tevis for financial support, Marcus Daly demonstrated once again his shrewdness and his prestige in the world of mining. For these men were without equals in their success at the risky business of mining investment. The father of journalist William Randolph Hearst and the founder of one of America's great fortunes, "Uncle George" or "Honest George" Hearst was the quintessential miner, a man much like Daly himself. W. A. Swanberg describes him well as "untidy of dress, almost illiterate, an assassin of grammar, a lover of poker and good bourbon, and an inveterate tobacco chewer whose long beard and shirtfront were generally stained with juice." Like many other frontier capitalists, Hearst lacked refinement and distrusted college trained "experts." But his crude exterior masked a quick and practical intelligence which, along with a gambler's instinct, a genial personality, and a reputation for reliability, made him a spectacular success in the mining West.

Born and raised on a Missouri farm, Hearst had followed the gold rush to California in 1850. He dabbled at mining and merchandising for nearly a decade without much success until he struck it big with the Ophir Mine on the Comstock Lode in 1859–60. Hearst invested his substantial profits from the Ophir into more mines and real estate; but he was a miner—one of the greatest in American history—not a financier. During the later 1860s, he lost much of his wealth. "Uncle

George" really came into his own only in 1870, when he married his mining expertise to the legal and fiscal abilities of Haggin and Tevis.[41]

James Ben Ali Haggin and Lloyd Tevis were brothers-in-law who came early to California from Kentucky in the gold rush of 1849–50. They established a highly lucrative Sacramento–San Francisco law practice, from which they branched out into a broad field of investments. Seemingly a study in contrasts, the two men actually complemented one another nicely. Blond and reticent by nature, the cautious and tight-fisted Tevis excelled at finance and eventually became president of the banking division of Wells, Fargo and Company. Haggin, whose middle name reflected the Turkish ancestry of his mother, was an awesome personality whose swarthy complexion, piercing eyes, and barrel-chested physique lent him an unforgettable presence. Both men achieved great wealth, and both stood tall in the gaudy high society of San Francisco. Haggin, who never failed in a major business venture, invested heavily in livestock and pioneered in the large-scale irrigation of his vast land holdings in the Kern and San Joaquin valleys. While one usually had to seek out Tevis at his Wells, Fargo offices, Haggin was a familiar figure in San Francisco, always wearing his high silk hat and often driving his beautiful horse teams through the parks.[42]

The partnership between these three strong-willed men arose from credits which Haggin and Tevis advanced to the mine plunger Hearst, loans which evolved naturally into coinvestments. With Haggin serving as the lynchpin, each of the partners came to concentrate upon his own favored role: the lawyer-financiers handled credit and management, while Hearst located and assessed the mines. Following the simple rules of never buying into properties which they couldn't control and never paying more for a mine than the value of the ore in sight, they piled success upon success, first at Mineral Hill, Nevada, and then at the great Ontario silver mine in Utah.

Hearst paid $30,000 for the Ontario on a tip from his old friend of Comstock days, "Mark" Daly. "From that $30,000," Hearst later wrote, "everything else came." Between 1872 and 1883, the Ontario yielded $17,000,000 in precious metals. In 1877 Hearst acquired the second of the syndicate's greatest holdings, the Homestake gold mine in the Black Hills, at Lead, South Dakota. Here, beginning with an eighty-stamp mill in 1878, the partners built a paternalistic company town, comparable to the one they would later found at Anaconda. And here, too, the profits were enormous, especially to Hearst, who owned roughly half of the mine.[43]

The Hearst–Haggin–Tevis syndicate eventually came to control

over 100 mines from Chile to Alaska, including one of America's
greatest silver mines (the Ontario), its greatest gold mine (the Homestake), and its number one copper mine (the Anaconda). All three
partners became fabulously wealthy. George Hearst, in addition to
amassing the fortune which launched his son's incredible journalistic
career, also won a seat in the U.S. Senate, where he served colorfully
from 1886 until his death in 1891. As for J. B. Haggin, who died in
1914 at the ripe old age of ninety-two, he must rank as one of the least
known of America's major capitalists. At various stages of his life, he
won fame as the largest landowner in Kentucky, one of California's
largest sheepmen and irrigation farmers, and as the world's foremost
breeder and racer of thoroughbred horses.[44]

As noted, Marcus Daly had kept in touch with Hearst over the
years, especially through the superintendent of the Ontario Mine,
Robert Chambers. After completing his purchase of the Anaconda
Mine in 1881, Daly went to Utah and, carrying a letter of introduction
from Chambers to Haggin, headed on to San Francisco to lay his
plans before the syndicate. There is some discrepancy in the historical
record about how the Anaconda transaction evolved. According to
Hearst's memoirs, the partners at first delayed in responding to Daly,
who then formed an agreement with W. A. Clark to develop the
Anaconda. Hearst writes that Daly proceeded to break his deal with
Clark when the syndicate belatedly came around. This account,
which might conceivably help explain the later "feud" between Clark
and Daly, is unsubstantiated and seems very unlikely.[45]

More probably, when Daly presented his case to the syndicate at
San Francisco in the spring of 1881, he first won over Hearst, who
readily trusted the Irishman's judgment after the Ontario success.
Haggin, like Hearst, had the instinct of a plunger, and he soon became Daly's close friend. Evidently, he came around after Hearst
journeyed to Butte, appraised the mine, and located the site for the
main shaft. Tevis, ever the cautious banker, agreed only reluctantly.
Since the partners did not need to incorporate in order to secure
financing, formal records of their agreement do not exist, but well-
informed reports about their investment indicate their varying de-
grees of enthusiasm for the venture. According to these, Daly sold
the mine to the syndicate for his purchase price of $30,000, with
Haggin, as usual, serving as trustee. They allotted the percentages of
ownership as follows: Hearst, 39 percent; Haggin, 26 percent; Daly,
25 percent; and Tevis, 10 percent.[46]

The partners provided Superintendent Daly with a generous operating budget; and in early June 1881, workmen began sinking an

eight-by-twenty-foot, three-compartment shaft into the Anaconda. Driving out crosscuts at 100-foot intervals and running 300- to 500-foot east-west drifts, they found ore bodies typical of the Butte district: rich deposits of oxidized silver ore, compounded with copper, and often running thirty ounces of silver per ton. Hearst decided against immediately erecting their own mill. Instead, they arranged to lease the old Dexter Mill from W. A. Clark. A handsome silver producer, the Anaconda amply rewarded its owners.[47]

The great turning point in the development of the Anaconda, and of Butte itself, came slightly less than a year after excavation began. At roughly the 300-foot level, as the millable silver was fast playing out, copper ores became suddenly more prevalent. This was due to the eroding process which concentrated heavy deposits of enriched copper sulphide at this depth. When Daly's men brought word of encountering some "new material," he and his lieutenant Mike Carroll came down to observe the drilling and blasting. As the dust settled from a blast, Daly leaned down and picked up a chunk of glistening copper glance. He said, wondrously: "Mike, we've got it!" Indeed they had. It was the greatest moment of his life, one of the great moments in the history of world mining. Daly had just found the largest deposit of copper sulphide that the world had ever seen.[48] His reputed ability to see farther into the ground than any other man alive seemed suddenly real.

This exhilarating turn of events sent Marcus Daly scurrying to California, for the syndicate now faced some alluring but hard decisions. The partners' nice silver producer had suddenly turned into a mammoth, midgrade copper mine. The potential profits were, of course, enormous; but so were the pitfalls. None of them had much experience with copper, especially with such refractory chalcocite ores as these. Entry into big-time copper mining meant huge outlays for a concentrator, a complex smelter, and large commitments to refineries and marketers. Even though copper markets were fast expanding with the rapid rise in electrical usage, they remained limited and prone to overproduction. And the Michigan copper men, commanding massive stores of high-grade ore, seemed to have a nearly impregnable hold on those markets.

Thus Daly faced a difficult task in arguing to his partners the case for a multi-million-dollar commitment to faraway Butte. According to Daly's friend John Lindsay, the Californians balked at such a risk. They seemed ready to dismiss the idea outright. At one point, Hearst and Tevis reportedly acted as if Daly were not even present and turned rudely to discussing other business. Evidently, forceful James Ben Ali Haggin, who had remained silent, suddenly brought his partners into line with the terse statement: "I'll see Daly through on this deal."[49] His decision meant that an investment of thousands would blossom into an investment of millions, and that Butte would soon rise to the front ranks of world mining centers.

The Anaconda syndicate immediately cancelled its order for a pan-amalgamation silver mill and began to consider the key questions: how to expand and consolidate their mine holdings, how and where to erect their reduction facilities. Daly had surprisingly little difficulty in buying up the properties adjacent to the Anaconda. According to Butte folklore, he hoodwinked the neighboring owners by letting it be known that the Anaconda had played out, signaling a general failure of the locality, and then bought them out at bargain rates. This seems doubtful at best, for other silver mines were booming by 1882. The more reasonable explanation is simply that the overextended, small-time speculators who held ground bordering the Anaconda probably agreed to sell out for what seemed at the time a good profit. From Edward Hickey and Valentine Croppf, Daly purchased the highly valuable St. Lawrence Mine, which adjoined the Anaconda and held the extension of its vein system. He also acquired the Neversweat, which became the third of the three great mines of the Anaconda group. Mainly to obtain surface working space and to protect the Anaconda vein structure on its dip, he added portions of the Rob Roy, Nipper, and other claims.[50]

Meanwhile, Daly continued to deepen the Anaconda and St. Lawrence shafts. The Anaconda reached the 600-foot level in the spring of 1883, and by now the vein varied from 50 to 100 feet in width. It yielded an average 12 percent in copper, and in some enriched zones even 45 to 55 percent. Importantly, the ores from these depths continued also to contain appreciable amounts of silver, $10 to $30 per ton. The incidental production of silver and gold considerably widened the margin of profit. Until the partners had their own smelter in operation, they could only ship the high-grade ore eastward for smelting and stockpile the much vaster amounts of lower-grade material. During 1882–84, they shipped 37,000 tons of high-grade ore to smelters at Swansea, Wales, and at Baltimore. The experienced Welsh smeltermen, unfamiliar with chalcocite ores so rich and extensive, were incredulous. Of course, the frightfully high costs of transportation, whether via the Union Pacific to Omaha or after 1884 via the Northern Pacific to West Coast ports, meant that shipping and reduc-

tion costs consumed almost all the profit. In the meantime, the Anaconda and St. Lawrence dumps grew into huge reserves of lower-
grade ore, a great investment in the future.[51]

The syndicate carefully weighed the question of where to locate its
large, complex, and highly expensive reduction works. Since the
sparse creeks of the Butte area were already largely claimed, they had
to look elsewhere. Discarding the possibility of locating on the large
Madison or Jefferson rivers to the east, they finally decided upon a
natural spot—where Warm Springs Creek flows out of the mountains
into the lovely upper Deer Lodge Valley, twenty-six miles west of
Butte. Here, under the supervision of Haggin's San Francisco expert
William McCaskell, construction of the huge concentration and smelting plants began in the summer of 1883.[52]

Along with his friend Morgan Evans, Daly personally laid out the
townsite of the city that would always be his pride and joy. He would
have given it the tongue-twisting name of Copperopolis, had that title
not already been bestowed upon another, long-forgotten Montana
hamlet near present White Sulphur Springs. Instead he settled for the
name of his prize mine, Anaconda. Within a few months, the town
had 500 residents, and its handsome rows of brick and frame
businesses and homes gave it an ordered and prosperous appearance. Well located in an open and attractive area, Anaconda did not
look like the typically grimy "company town." And in a literal sense,
it was not really a company town at all; for independent merchants
and realtors were numerous there from the start. The site evolved
within one year's time from a wilderness to an established city, where
the company alone employed over 1,200 men.[53]

Through late 1883 and 1884, large construction crews labored at the
site of the reduction works. First the concentrator and then the massive smelter and its surrounding structures quickly took shape. The
costs were enormous. According to reports, the syndicate plowed at
least $4,000,000 into the plant before the fires were even ignited.
Reportedly, cautious and hesitant Lloyd Tevis questioned Daly's
huge outlays of cash, and the short-tempered Irishman angrily responded by insisting that his backers come out and assess his work.
Following the long and difficult trip to Montana, Haggin allegedly
made this rather remarkable statement to Daly:

> The property is bigger than you led me to believe, which I suspected was
> the truth before I left home; you have shown me where all the money has
> gone which I was confident I would find. Indeed, I do not see how you
> could do the work with so little money, and you tell me what is needed,

which is clear enough, but I am no better satisfied than I was before I left home, and so all this work of mine has been useless. Hereafter, please keep in mind what I told you when we first began this enterprise: when you need money draw, and keep drawing.[54]

Money, it seemed, presented no problem, and neither did Day's credibility. Small wonder that Daly named the peak near Anaconda Mount Haggin!

The entire effort climaxed in the autumn of 1884. In August, the Union Pacific–Utah and Northern Railroad's Anaconda branch, a thirty-one-mile spur line linking the Anaconda Mine to its smelter, began carrying traffic.[55] The first smelter furnaces were fired in early September, and by late October the plant was in general operation. From the time of its opening, the Anaconda complex ranked as one of the world's greatest. The *Mining and Scientific Press* termed it a "wonder." Over the next two decades, additions, improvements, and replacements would make it the greatest reduction facility on earth. This original 1884 plant, later known as the "Upper" or "Old Works," consisted of the largest concentrator in America and a mammoth smelter capable of treating 450–500 tons of ore daily. The Washoe Smelter, named after Hearst's old Comstock holding, housed thirty-four reverberatory roasting furnaces, twenty-six matte furnaces, and two seventy-ton blast furnaces. It produced a 64 percent copper matte, which for the time being was sent on to East Coast and British refineries for finishing.[56]

The firing up of the Washoe Smelter marked the culmination of a decade-long boom which had begun with Bill Farlin's return to Butte back in late 1874. The rough-hewn, boisterous camp now found itself amidst a boom of such proportions that it would have astounded even the boosters of 1876. According to the reliable estimate of the *Inter Mountain*, the city's new newspaper, Butte was by mid-1884 pouring forth silver and copper at the rate of $1,250,000 per month. In August of 1885, *The West Shore*, a Pacific coast promotional magazine, reckoned that "the largest, busiest and richest mining camp in the world to-day is Butte, Montana."[57]

In fact, Butte was now edging past Leadville, Colorado, which had earlier surpassed the Comstock, as the premier metal mining center of the United States. A mood of feverish excitement permeated the camp during the mid-1880s, as the frenzied boom lifted the district's population toward 14,000. From the three-square-mile central mining district poured forth a daily production of 1,900 tons of ore. Butte's mines, mills, and smelters employed 2,500 men, with a monthly payroll of $540,000 total for all employees. Indeed, the great industrial mining boom, which was centered at and led by Butte, lifted the entire territory of Montana toward the front ranks among mineral producers. Led only by Colorado and vying with California for second place, Montana's silver, copper, and gold mines easily out-produced both Nevada and Utah and exceeded the combined production of Idaho and New Mexico.[58]

Silver now reigned supreme as Montana's premier metal, having displaced gold and having not yet surrendered her preeminence to copper. Served now by two railroads, the Union Pacific–Utah and Northern from the south and the Northern Pacific from the east and west, Montana silver men could at last import heavy stamping and smelting machinery and export bullion with relative ease. As a result, a number of thriving silver camps sprang up throughout southwestern and central Montana. The heartland of the territory's silver boom lay in a triangle connecting Butte on the south with Helena on the north and Philipsburg on the west. Even the great Helena area mines or those near Philipsburg such as the Granite Mountain and the Bi-Metallic, however, could not match the combined production of those at Butte, Montana's silver capital.[59]

Butte's greatest silver mines were the French-owned Lexington, with its complex fifty-stamp mill; the Walker brothers' Alice, which ran a giant eighty-stamp plant; the British-owned Bluebird; and various others such as W. A. Clark's Moulton, the Belle of Butte, the Grey Rock, the Nettie, and the LaPlata. At the crest of the boom in 1887, 290 stamps were crushing about 440 tons of argentiferous ore daily, yielding an average of $25 in silver per ton. From 1883 through the mid-1890s, Butte led Montana to second place among the silver producers of America, and in 1887 the territory momentarily surged to first place. During the year of statehood, 1889, the "Treasure State" smelted one-fourth of all American silver. For the next four years, its annual silver yield hovered near $20,000,000. Much of this silver came, of course, from mines like the Anaconda and St. Lawrence, which unlike those mentioned above, produced it as a byproduct of the mining of copper.

Thus silver, especially Butte silver, powered the mighty economic surge of Montana during the 1880s. Before long, however, the fragile silver mining industry of the Far West, so reliant upon the monetary policies of the world's governments, would collapse, leaving abandoned camps, crumbling mills and destitute families in its wake. Although few could have foreseen it in the mid-1880's, the state's

mining future lay not with silver and gold but with mundane copper—Butte copper. For what Daly was proving in the Anaconda also
held true for most of the other great Butte mines, like the Parrot, the
Colusa, the Gagnon, and the Bell.[60] Below the "water level," at
roughly 300–400 feet, silver as well as gold faded into a secondary
partnership with copper, the dominant metal. During the sixteen
years following the opening of the Washoe Smelter in 1884, Butte
copper and copper barons would rise to dominate the economic and
political life of Montana.

3. The "Richest Hill on Earth"

Butte's emergence as a major copper producer, signaled by the 1884 opening of the Anaconda smelter, must be viewed in broad perspective. Man's use of copper, the red metal of antiquity, is older by far than his written history. Beginning in the Late Stone Age, about 8000 B.C., our ancestors found that the metal could easily be shaped by pounding into useful instruments. Experience taught prehistoric man that copper could be hardened with arsenic and, more importantly, that it could be alloyed with tin through heating to form the valuable metal bronze.

The Egyptians were using copper extensively by 5000 B.C., and mines in the Sinai peninsula and on the island of Cyprus date from at least 3800–3700 B.C. In fact, the Latin word *cyprium*, from which the English *copper* derives, stems from Cyprus, the site of important Roman mines. By 1100 B.C., the great Roman-Spanish mines at Rio Tinto were pouring forth their riches; these large deposits have been worked into modern times. Copper mining in the Western world faded but did not disappear during the Dark Ages. Germany's famous Mansfeld mines, which employed Martin Luther's father, began producing around A.D. 1200.

With the commercial and industrial revolutions, modern copper mining truly began. Great Britain, the pacesetter of industrialization, produced perhaps 75 percent of the world's still tiny output in 1700. Throughout the eighteenth century, the increasing mastery of steam power, blasting powder, and techniques of ventilation transformed the mining of copper, just as these same factors transformed the mining of coal.[1] The later nineteenth century then witnessed a true revolution in the role of copper in human history. With the invention

34

of Morse's telegraph in the 1840s and Bell's telephone and Edison's incandescent lamp in the 1870s, the demand for copper wiring and conductors mushroomed dramatically. Before this time, copper had been valued chiefly for its resistance to corrosion and as an alloy with zinc to form brass. Now its usage expanded with the new age of electricity.

As the United States surged to world industrial supremacy during the years following the Civil War, it also rose to dominate the world of copper mining. Prior to the mid-1840s, American production, like world production, was spotty. Small deposits in Connecticut, Georgia, Vermont, and elsewhere sufficed to meet the limited demand. The great leap forward came in 1844–46 with the opening of the remarkable ore bodies of the Keweenaw Peninsula of upper Michigan, which protrudes like a hawk's beak into Lake Superior. These fabulously rich Michigan ores are the world's only extensive deposits of "native" or metallic copper. They are of such near-total purity that the Indians of the region had merely to break off pieces of the metal and hammer them into shape for tools and weapons. Highly prized Michigan copper instruments traveled through Indian commerce across the breadth of eastern America.

Yankee investors such as Quincy Adams Shaw, Horatio Bigelow, and Alexander Agassiz who seized control of the Michigan "copper country" made some of the most incredible profits in American history. And they made Boston the capital of world copper finance. During the forty years following 1846, the easily mined Michigan copper completely dominated the national marketplace. In some years, it accounted for as much as 90 percent of United States output. Leadership among the various Michigan mining concerns eventually fell to the Calumet and Hecla companies, which opened in the mid–1860s and merged in 1871. With their mastery of these priceless reserves, their easy access to water transportation, and their expert capitalization, the Michigan copper giants seemed truly unassailable. Between 1871 and 1921, the Calumet and Hecla Mining Company alone yielded dividends totaling $152,250,000—$100 for each dollar invested.[2]

The copper barons of Boston and Michigan first sensed trouble in the later 1870s and early 1880s when isolated western camps like Butte, Montana, and Globe, Jerome, and Bisbee, Arizona, began shipping out small quantities of their ores. But these exotic places produced mainly mid- and lower-grade ores; and in any case, their remoteness from East Coast refineries and markets seemed to place them at an impossible disadvantage. Then came the great challenge of the Anaconda syndicate: the gambit that the precious metals compounded with Butte copper could equalize the purity of Michigan copper, and that the syndicate's efficient, mass-production plant and its access to cheap timber, coal, and water could offset Michigan's advantageous marketing location.

The pressure of western competition began squeezing Michigan's hegemony even before the opening of the Anaconda smelter in 1884. United States copper production more than doubled during the 1870s; and then, with Anaconda becoming a major producer, it nearly quadrupled between 1880 and 1888. The natural effects of this boom in output were, on the one hand, to depress prices, and on the other, to expand markets as cheap copper gained a competitive edge against such metals as iron and zinc.[3] The Lake Superior men reacted sharply as the price of their product sagged and as their traditional hold over American markets began to loosen. Since the 1850s, copper prices had generally held above 20 cents per pound, but they fell to 16 cents in 1883 and then to 14 cents in 1884. The "Lake" producers had averaged an 80 percent share of United States copper production during the years prior to 1880. By 1883 their share totaled only 51.6 percent, while upstart Butte garnered 21.4 percent, and the Arizona camps totaled 20 percent.[4]

Reacting desperately to a desperate situation, the Michigan-Boston copper titans elected to depress the market even further by dumping surplus copper, figuring that their western rivals would succumb to the disastrously low prices. The Lake firms formed a pooling agreement under the flag of Calumet and Hecla as their selling agent. Then, reacting to Anaconda's grand opening late in 1884, they slashed the price to 11½ cents per pound. When Anaconda and its Montana brethren refused to cut production or wages, they drove the price down further, to 10 cents in the early spring of 1886. Naturally, these artificially low prices accelerated America's already booming copper consumption; but the market quickly became saturated, and the copper world trembled with anxiety at the threat of collapse.[5]

The Montanans, who had taken the greatest risks, reacted gamely to the Michigan-instigated "price war." Figuring that even the mighty Calumet and Hecla could not hold out long at 10 cents without facing stock collapses and plant shutdowns, the *Anaconda Weekly Review* remarked: "If we mistake not the great Anaconda will 'bob up serenely' some of these times and administer such a lesson to the Calumet and Hecla that she will not forget soon." But this was whistling in the dark. The three biggest Arizona mines shut down prior to mid-1886, as did the smaller Montana operators. In August and September, even Anaconda closed down its mines, mills, and furnaces, laying off most of its employees. The cold and snowy winter of 1886–87, which wrought such havoc upon the stockmen of the Great Plains, proved equally dismal to the Montana mining towns.[6]

In the final analysis, though, the Lake producers could not withstand such crushingly low prices any better than could their western adversaries. They too faced long-term closures. The Anaconda was demonstrating that, with their efficient, mass production plant and with the secondary profits to be made from the silver and gold imbedded in their copper matte, the Butte producers could indeed compete with and even surmount the Michigan mines. Work resumed at Butte early in 1887; and by year's end, Montana had pushed ahead of Michigan into first place among the copper producing states. Somewhat in awe, the prestigious *Engineering and Mining Journal* found that, in this year of transition, Montana produced 78,900,000 pounds of copper, while Lake Superior tallied only 74,660,000. Anaconda alone turned out 57,000,000 pounds, 11,400,000 more than did Calumet and Hecla.[7]

Winning the price war against the Calumet and Hecla group meant far less to Montana's young copper companies than did the sad and simple fact that they continued to face a glutted and depressed market. The only solution to this problem seemed to be some sort of international scheme which would control production. Knowing full well that the miners would bow to nearly any proposal that promised higher prices, a group of French speculators led by a flamboyant character named Hyacinthe Secretan set out to corner the western world's copper supply, limit production, and then cash in on rising prices. Secretan and his Paris-based Société des Metaux (later retitled the Société Industrielle et Commerciale des Metaux des Paris) attracted the support of some of France's greatest capitalists, banks, and investment houses. The Société raised a war chest of $13,500,000 and began buying. Before long, it dominated Europe's copper trade. Throughout 1888 and early 1889, Secretan worked out contracts with the great mining firms of the world—Anaconda, Calumet and Hecla, Spain's Rio Tinto, and the Arizona companies. The miners agreed to curtail output and to sell their product exclusively to Secretan's syndicate, in the hope that rising prices would reward their sacrifices. Buying at 13.5 cents per pound, the syndicate had contracts with thirty-seven mining companies by mid–1888 and controlled roughly 80 to 85 percent of the world's supply.[8]

Outwardly, Secretan's strategy seemed to be succeeding. The instinctively competitive copper miners seemed willing to submit to his controls. Anaconda signed a three-year-contract, but only with severe misgivings. Haggin supported the idea from a pure profits-and-losses standpoint; but Daly, the eager miner who knew only full-bore production, disliked it. Rapidly rising prices, up to 18 cents per pound in 1888, blessed their efforts at first. But in truth, Secretan's plot had no chance to succeed for long. Even while they might for now control production, something few such pools have been able to do for very long, other market factors lay beyond their control. Artificially high prices of 16 to 18 cents brought junk brass and copper pouring into the market. And as the effect of this abated, consumers reacted by cutting purchases, substituting iron and zinc for copper and brass. Desperate to maintain their high price, the Société's directors went deeper into debt, buying up huge surpluses of the red metal.[9]

The inevitable crash came in March of 1889. The Russian government withdrew its 25 million-franc investment from the Comptoir d'Escompte, France's second largest bank and the Société's main financial backer. As a result, a selling panic set in, and both the Comptoir d'Escompte and the Société faced immediate ruin. Copper prices tumbled from an extreme high of 21 cents to an extreme low of 7½ cents per pound, and amidst the wreckage of his plans, a devastated Hyacinthe Secretan took his own life. The copper world stared into the abyss of catastrophe. If the syndicate should fail, and if its creditors should then dump its huge surpluses onto the market, the entire industry would be hopelessly glutted and would be forced into long-term shutdowns and depression.

This nightmare possibility was only narrowly averted. Meeting in New York, James Ben Ali Haggin of Anaconda and Colonel Thomas Livermore of Calumet and Hecla devised a simple and direct strategy. They informed the Rothschilds, Europe's greatest bankers and one of the syndicate's largest creditors, that if the surpluses were released, they would retaliate by flooding the market with so much cheap copper that everyone would suffer alike. The creditors saw the plausibility of this threat, and following a Paris conference of the American producers and the European bankers, a compromise resulted. Both groups agreed to work for a reasonable 12-cent price. The miners would restrain their output, and the creditors would gradually release their surpluses over a four-year period.

The compromise cut off the threat of wholesale disaster, but Secretan's misguided effort to bring order to the booming, cut-throat copper industry had in truth ended in a shambles. The Frenchmen had succeeded to a surprising degree in gaining control of production. But they could not control consumption, and their effort to set artificially high prices led to their immediate downfall. In the end, several key figures in the syndicate narrowly escaped indictment for their intrigues; and the French banking establishment, faced with a panic that could sweep the continent, rescued the Comptoir d'Escompte with a 120,000,000-franc loan.[10]

In the wake of the near-catastrophe, Haggin, Livermore, and other leaders of the industry tried valiantly to stave off a return to unrestrained, tooth-and-claw competition and to place some kind of control on production. Between 1891 and 1893, they succeeded in establishing trade associations that, in theory, represented 75 percent of world production, and agreed to cap output. But Leonard Lewisohn and other key figures in the business refused to cooperate, and by 1894 the efforts to regularize the industry had clearly failed. Copper mining and marketing once again boomed with the expanding use of electricity and the telephone. From a total U.S. yield of 113,181 short tons in 1888, production climbed to 179,499 in 1892, 230,031 in 1896, and 303,059 in 1900.

This cheap copper, so vital to America's and Europe's booming economies, rapidly rewon the markets it had lost temporarily in 1888–89 and gained even more ground on competing metals. Naturally, though, prices remained depressed, hovering around 9 to 12 cents throughout the 1890s.[11] In short, copper remained one of the world's most competitive and turbulent industries. The red metal promised both great profits and great risks. One day, another group of speculators would try to monopolize the world's lucrative copper industry, to succeed where Secretan had failed, but that effort would not come until the turn of the century.

These years of the Michigan-Montana "price war" and the rise and fall of the Société des Metaux were exciting ones for Butte and for Montana. Riding the crest of an exciting wave of copper-silver-gold mining prosperity, Montana gained statehood after a quarter-century's wait in 1889. It chose to call itself the "Treasure State," and on its official seal it placed the frankly materialistic motto "Oro y Plata"—gold and silver! No one could deny that mining had made Montana; and no one could deny, at least at this moment in time, that Montana led the nation in mining. As the Butte Daily Inter Mountain crowed at the dawn of 1888: "The mines of this territory are now undeniably the richest and most productive in the world." Montana's mighty Anaconda poured forth 50,000,000 pounds of copper in 1887, far more than its nearest rivals, Calumet and Hecla and Rio Tinto. At the same time, Philipsburg's Granite Mountain Mine led all silver producers with regular monthly dividends of $200,000; and Marysville's Drumlummon could lay claim to the crown among gold mines with 1887 dividends totaling $1,500,000.[12]

By the late 1880s, Butte reigned supreme among the mining centers of America. Again, the exuberant *Inter Mountain* put it well: "Butte is not only the Leadville of Montana, but it proposes to be its own Denver."[13] Recent improvements in rail facilities now made possible the full development of the Butte Hill. By the mid-1880s, Butte-Anaconda had access both to the Union Pacific via the Utah and Northern and to the west coast and upper midwest via the Northern Pacific, which had not yet built into the city but co-owned a spur to it: the Montana Union line from Garrison Junction. This cumbersome link to the Northern Pacific symbolized the pooling agreement formed between that railroad and the Union Pacific, an agreement which kept production and marketing costs artificially high.

The pool, of course, invited competition. That competition arrived in 1888 with James J. Hill's Montana Central Railroad, a link in what later became the Great Northern. Hill, the hard driving giant of American rail builders, saw Butte as one of the centerpieces in a rail empire which would encompass the entire Northwest. To Marcus Daly, who became his friend, Hill wrote in 1886: "When our lines are completed through to your place, we hope to be able to furnish you all the transportation you want, at rates as will enable you to largely increase your business. What we want over our low grades is heavy tonnage, and the heavier it is *the lower we can make the rates*" (Hill's italics). Jim Hill thus proposed a happy community of interests with Butte and the Anaconda, and that is precisely what eventuated.

Built under the direction of Helena transportation baron Charles Broadwater, but actually masterminded by Hill, the Montana Central entered Butte from Helena and the north in mid–1888. When this little narrow-gauge spur line became welded into Hill's transcontinental Great Northern system a few years later, Butte gained first-rate connections to both the Great Lakes and Seattle on the Pacific. As a result, the Union Pacific–Northern Pacific pool collapsed, and freight rates fell sharply. The Union Pacific had previously charged $17 per ton to haul matte to Omaha; the Great Northern's initial rate was $10 per ton to Chicago. Similarly, once the Montana Central began importing coal from the Great Falls area, the price at Butte fell by nearly 50 percent.[14]

As transportation costs fell, the inflow of outside capital quickened apace, further accelerating the big Butte boom. The dimensions of that boom now made the city, by any standard, the busiest place in the mining West. By 1890 the hill was producing about $30,000,000 annually in metals. The fast evolving Anaconda operation towered over the other Butte companies as the pacesetter of Montana mining. Anaconda's smelting capacity reached 3,000 tons of ore daily by the early 1890s, and its industrial maw consumed 75,000 tons of coal and 15 million board feet of lumber every year. Three thousand men worked its mines, mills, and smelters, and their numbers were increased yearly.[15]

Under the astute management of Marcus Daly and J. B. Haggin, the Anaconda yearly evolved into a more perfectly integrated business. At the basic level of ore reserves, the owners continued adding to their mine holdings. The heart of their empire remained, of course, the "Anaconda group" of mines—the Anaconda, St. Lawrence, and the Neversweat. In addition, by the mid-1890s the syndicate also controlled three other clusters of mines. The Mountain Consolidated group held thirty-eight claims and counted such profitable mines as the Modoc and the High Ore. The lesser Anglo-Saxon group, centering on the Orphan Girl Mine, and the silver-oriented Union Consolidated group also added their riches to the Anaconda coffers.[16]

The focus of the syndicate's investment and employment lay at the reduction works in the burgeoning "company town" of Anaconda, which had by now developed into a full-scale city in its own right. As the Anaconda vaulted to front rank among world copper companies, the management faced an unending problem of enlarging and perfecting its facilities. Under the direction of Otto Stahlman, the concentrator-smelter complex at the original "Upper Works" was enlarged in a spasmodic fashion until a 1,000 tons-per-day capacity was reached. Such makeshift improvements proved woefully inadequate; so Daly and his partners elected to construct an entirely new complex, the "Lower Works," near the original plant. Delayed by serious fires at both the Anaconda Mine and at the plant itself in 1889–90, the new Lower Works came into full operation in the early 1890s. When they did, the two combined facilities gave the Anaconda a 3,000, then 4,000 tons-per-day smelting capacity. Hauling these vast tonnages of ore from mine to smelter proved increasingly expensive, and Daly argued frequently with the Montana Union Railroad about rates and service. He finally chose to build his own ore carrier, the ambitiously named Butte, Anaconda, and Pacific Railroad, to link his smelter complex with its sources of copper.[17]

Moving hesitatingly into the lucrative "downstream" end of copper processing, the syndicate erected a refinery at Anaconda in 1891, greatly enlarging and expanding it in 1893–95. Receiving blister copper at 98 percent purity from the smelter convertors, the Anaconda electrolytic refinery removed the final traces of impurities and precious metals and by 1896 was turning out 100 to 120 tons of marketable copper every day. During these years, the company still shipped roughly half of its smelted, blister copper to East Coast refineries, where labor costs were drastically lower, and refined the rest at Anaconda.

With mine production still mounting, Daly made his final major move toward expansion in 1900 when he and his capable plant manager, Frank Klepetko, designed an entirely new reduction works, highly automated with electricity, capable in itself of handling 5,000 tons of ore daily. This mighty complex, separately incorporated as the Washoe Copper Company and capitalized at $20,000,000, was the wonder of its day in the world of copper. Opening in 1902, two years after Daly's death, it sprawled across 300 acres and boasted the world's largest smelter. Soon, the tallest smokestack on earth would rise above it, carrying the troublesome, noxious gases high into the skies above the Deer Lodge Valley.[18]

As the syndicate moved downstream toward the marketing of refined copper, it simultaneously integrated its operation on the upstream end by acquiring vast holdings of critically important raw materials. Fresh water flowed abundantly from the mountains towering west of Anaconda; and at Butte, Daly and his partners bought up existing water works and in 1891 formed them into the Butte City Water Company. Coal and lumber were equally crucial. By the turn of the century, the Anaconda was consuming over 400 tons of coal every day. At first, the company contracted for its coal, primarily with the Wyoming mines of the Union Pacific Railroad. Before long, Daly began purchasing and mining his own coal, at Diamondville, Wyoming, at Storrs and Cokedale near Bozeman Pass, at Sand Coulee and Belt near Great Falls, and intensively at Washoe and Carbonado near Red Lodge, Montana.[19]

Lumber presented much thornier problems than either coal or water. The Anaconda, like its smaller neighbors, devoured wood on a colossal scale—for fuel, for construction, and for miles of deep shaft timbering. By 1888 the firm used 40,000 board feet per day in its mines alone, especially for the big square-set braces which filled its deep stopes. In order to meet this demand, Daly entered a partnership in 1882 with the newly constructed Northern Pacific Railroad, whose land grant held vast tracts of woodland, and with Missoula lumber barons Andrew B. Hammond, R. A. Eddy, and E. L. Bonner. They capitalized their firm, the Montana Improvement Company, at

$2,000,000, with the railroad holding just over one-half of the stock. Tough-minded A. B. Hammond, who ruled over much of western Montana in the grand manner, dominated the organization. By mid-1883 the Montana Improvement Company had seven sawmills working double shifts in the Missoula region.[20]

Cheap and abundant supplies of timber offered Daly and other Montana mining barons an invaluable competitive edge, but their heavy-handed logging operations also got them into serious trouble. In 1878 Congress had enacted the Timber and Stone Act, which forbade commercial timber cutting on the public lands. Such booming western territories as Montana howled in protest that Washington was mindlessly stifling their progress. Prior to 1885, the law had little effect. Much of the public domain remained unsurveyed, and federal conservation statutes were enforced laxly or not at all. So the Montana Improvement Company, along with W. A. Clark and other mining-lumber operators, went blissfully on, logging both their own land and the unpoliced federal lands surrounding them. Even during the 1890s, when the creation of federal forest reserves and the revision of homestead laws tightened federal regulation, the mining-lumber interests still held access to these lands. They purchased large tracts of timberland, frequently using "dummy entrymen"—bogus homesteaders—to acquire them under the provisions of the homestead laws for as little as $2.50 per acre. And they continued logging on public land, sometimes with legal permits, sometimes without them.[21]

The Montanans' problems really began in 1885, when the environmentally conscious Democratic administration of Grover Cleveland took office. Unlike his predecessors, Cleveland's Land Commissioner William Andrew Jackson Sparks took the matter of trespassing on federal woodlands seriously and filed numerous suits against the culprits. Backed by public sentiment, the Montana lumberman argued in return that the lack of federal surveys forced them to cut freely, that such cutting was essential to the local economy, that such practices had become commonplace with federal approval, even that it was their God-given right.[22]

But rhetoric alone could not save them. The timber trespass suits became incredibly entangled, hanging for years in the federal courts like swords of Damocles over the heads of the mining barons. Federal prosecution of the suits ebbed and flowed for years due to shifts of policy and personnel. In the meantime, as we shall see, they served to stir up political trouble in Montana. Two of the three major cases were finally resolved in 1906. In the case of *U.S. v. W. A. Clark*, which featured federal charges of large-scale fraudulent purchases, the U.S. Supreme Court finally found in Clark's favor. Giving Mr. Clark a benefit of doubt which he undoubtedly did not deserve, Justice Oliver Wendell Holmes reasoned incredibly in his majority opinion that Clark had not been aware of the tricks his subordinates played upon Uncle Sam through fraudulently acquired homesteads.[23]

The considerably more tangled case of *U.S.* v. *Bitter Root Development Co. et al.* involved federal charges that Marcus Daly along with several of his associates, including Dan J. Hennessy, William Wirt Dixon, John R. and William Toole, had willfully denuded federal lands of $2,000,000 worth of standing timber. Daly had formed the Bitter Root Development Company in 1890 to handle his growing timber acreages in far western Montana, and in 1894 he had deeded it over to the Anaconda for over $1,442,000. Following Daly's death in 1900, a grand jury returned 102 indictments in the case; and by 1906 it, too, lay before the U.S. Supreme Court. But by now Daly's company had passed into the hands of the lords of Standard Oil, and the attorneys of his estate and codefendants pleaded that his widow and innocent stockholders were being unfairly maligned. Lamely, the U.S. Department of Justice agreed to a settlement of $156,000—Attorney General Charles Bonaparte shamefully applauding it as "perhaps the largest sum recovered in any one instance for trespass upon the public land."[24]

The last of the major lumber cases, *U.S.* v. *A. B. Hammond*, lingered on in the courts until 1917. In this perennial litigation, the government charged that Hammond, as manager of the Montana Improvement Company and its corporate successors, had between 1885 and 1894 illegally cut 21,185,410 board feet of lumber from the public domain. Remarkably, the tough and crusty old lumberman finally managed to quash the charges by paying a paltry settlement of only $7,000.[25] Thus after years of expensive litigation, and after years of looting the public domain, the big-time offenders got off easily. The mining-lumber interests acquired millions of dollars' worth of public timber, paying a mere pittance in return. Viewed in perspective, the whole, ugly episode seems a monumental miscarriage of justice, a disgrace to American jurisprudence.

As the litigation continued, so did the Anaconda's direct involvement in the lumber business. It made less and less sense as the years went by for Daly to rely upon the Big Blackfoot Milling Company, heir to the old Montana Improvement Company, especially after his political falling out with Hammond and his Missoula allies in 1888–89 (see pp. 85–86). So he struck out on his own with an initial purchase of 6,000,000 feet of standing timber in western Montana and with more purchases soon afterward. Daly built mills at Hamilton and St. Regis in western Montana and at Hope, Idaho, and he formed the Blackfoot Land and Development Company to promote the cutover timberland for agriculture. Still lacking sufficient production, Daly took the final great step in August of 1898 by paying Hammond and his partners nearly $1,500,000 for their huge timber holdings and their extensive millworks, dam, and power plant at the company town of Bonner, east of Missoula.[26] With these acquisitions, and with others that followed, the Anaconda achieved self-sufficiency in the vitally important resource of lumber; and the company's presence extended even farther into far western Montana.

Thus by the mid-1890s the Anaconda operation had evolved into a giant, highly integrated organization, owning huge reserves of ore, coal, and lumber, the world's greatest reduction works, and a new refining arm. It also owned urban real estate, farmland, hotels, rails, water and electrical works, and various commercial holdings.[27] The Anaconda loomed over Butte, and over Montana itself, like a monstrous leviathan whose every twist and lurch became a life and death concern.

In 1891, the Anaconda entered a period of highly significant reorganization. For more than a decade, it had remained a closed operation, completely owned and controlled by the Hearst-Haggin-Tevis-Daly syndicate, with J. B. Haggin acting as sole trustee. The tremendous growth of their operation and its capitalization, however, inevitably forced the syndicate to incorporate. On 19 January 1891, they formally incorporated as the Anaconda Mining Company, with a capital stock of $12,500,000. Only a few weeks later, genial old Senator George Hearst died at age seventy-one. Hearst owned seven-sixteenths of the Anaconda at the time of his death; and this holding formed a major part of the estate, conservatively valued at $18,000,000, which he left to his wife Phoebe and his son William Randolph.[28]

Incorporation, of course, allowed outsiders to invest in the Anaconda Mining Company, and the desire of Phoebe Hearst and her son to sell their shares guaranteed that this would happen. During the aftermath of the Secretan fiasco, the powerful European banking house of Rothschild had extended loans to Anaconda and had acquired an option to bloc-purchase its newly issued stock, an option that now seemed highly lucrative in light of the firm's $2.3 million annual rate of profit. Through their London-based investment house, the Exploration Company, Limited, the Rothschilds next acquired a second option and had a full analysis and audit performed by the prestigious mine consultant Hamilton Smith and two of his associates. "Take it for all and all," reported Smith, "it can be considered the most extensive mining property in the world." With this assurance, the Exploration Company in 1895 purchased $7,500,000 of Anaconda stock, which had since been expanded to a total of $25,000,000 at $25 per share. Almost the entirety of the Rothschild purchase came from the Hearst shares. Phoebe Hearst turned these bountiful earnings over to her beloved son Willie—whom father George had not trusted with money—allowing him to branch out from San Francisco into New York newspaper publishing.[29] Thus did Butte wealth underwrite the most notorious career in the history of American journalism.

The Rothschilds' buying up of over one-fourth of the Anaconda Mining Company's stock forced a reorganization of the firm. On 15 June 1895, it was reincorporated as the Anaconda Copper Mining Company, a title which it would keep until 1955 when it renamed itself simply the Anaconda Company. In the 1895 reorganization, the expansion of the company was reflected in an enlargement of the capitalization to $30,000,000—1,200,000 share at $25 each. In mid-1895, the Exploration Company exercised its further option and purchased another 270,000 shares, thereby delivering to the Rothschilds almost one-half of the stock of the corporation.[30]

James Ben Ali Haggin continued to serve as president of Anaconda, and Marcus Daly as superintendent. But with the Hearsts no longer involved, and with European investors holding roughly half the stock, which began appearing on the London Exchange late in 1896, the management future seemed highly uncertain. The European speculators, however, felt uncomfortable in the uncertain world of American mining. The *Economist* of London described "coppers" as "dangerous things" and warned its readers: "Leave the Americans in undisputed possession of their own copper mines. They know more about them than we do."[31]

Before long, the Rothschilds and other European speculators unloaded their Anaconda stocks, which gravitated heavily back toward Boston and New York. Control of the corporate giant thus remained firmly in the traditional hands of Haggin and Daly. Profits, meanwhile, continued to soar. In the three years following the 1895 reorganization, Anaconda yielded a total net profit of $12,945,969, about half of which went out as dividends and half of which was reinvested.[32] So the mighty Anaconda stood at century's end as one of the great American corporations—independent, beautifully integrated, conservatively capitalized, and astutely managed. Indeed, as events would soon prove, its wondrous earning powers were so tempting that some of the world's most powerful capitalists began to conspire for its outright takeover.

So great was Anaconda's sway over the region that many people simply assumed that Butte and the Anaconda Copper Mining Company were synonymous. They were badly mistaken. In fact, a number of large and profitable firms, some older and some newer, vied for the riches of the Butte Hill. The older, established operators, such as W.. A. Clark, the Walker brothers, and the Parrot and Lexington companies, focused as much on silver and gold as they did upon booming copper. And prior to the 1893 depression, they did very well at it.

In Walkerville, lying north of Butte and up the main slope of the hill, the great Lexington and Alice mines continued, along with the Anaconda group, to lead in Butte silver production. Joseph Walker and his Utah brethren maintained their control of the Alice Gold and Silver Mining Company; and William E. Hall, the popular mayor of Walkerville, managed it locally following Marcus Daly's breach with them. With two large mills and with such fine properties as the Alice itself, the Magna Charta, and the Blue Wing, the firm prospered. So did Walkerville's other great silver king, the Lexington, which A. J. Davis had developed and then sold to a French syndicate in 1882. Davis died in 1890, and control of the Lexington remained lodged in the hands of a group of Paris and London speculators. Many of Butte's bonanza silver-gold mines were dwindling in output by now, but they were nonetheless still big producers in the early 1890s.[33]

Like the Anaconda group, the Parrot and Clark mines typified Butte itself, yielding primarily copper but also sizable quantities of silver and lesser amounts of gold. Employing 500 to 600 men, the Parrot Silver and Copper Company owned nineteen claims, including the famous Parrot itself, and developed one of the camp's best reduction facilities southeast of town. Both W. A. Clark and Helena silver king Samuel T. Hauser held sizable blocs of Parrot stock, but control of this closed corporation rested in New England. The Bridgeport Copper Company of Connecticut refined most of its product and marketed it as brass and as copper sheets and wire.[34]

Even by the mid-1880s, William A. Clark's many Butte holdings had made him a fabulously wealthy man. His well-established operations, like the Moulton Mining and Reduction Works and the Colorado Smelting and Mining Company, the partnership which he had formed a decade earlier with Nathaniel P. Hill, consistently served him well. The Colorado company held four of Butte's best mines: the

Gagnon, the Fredonia, the Burlington, and the Nettie. Clark owned many other mines as well, large and small, such as the Odin, Stewart, Oro Butte, Acquisition, Black Rock, and Clear Grit properties. Under his managerial genius, they all seemed to blossom. With so much ore pouring from so many mines, he eventually needed still larger concentration and smelting facilities. So in 1886, W. A. Clark and his brother Joseph bought the Butte Reduction Works and enlarged its plant so that it could handle 300 tons of ore daily. The Butte Reduction Works, which did much custom work for smaller operators, rose to become a major factor in the Butte economy.[35]

Naturally, Butte's rise to copper domination during the later 1880s acted as a powerful magnet in attracting further investment. Among the newer firms created, none loomed larger than the two founded in 1887–88 by powerful Boston and New York copper men: the Boston and Montana Consolidated Copper and Silver Mining Company, and the Butte and Boston Consolidated Mining Company. The key figures in these two well-endowed corporations were Albert S. Bigelow, scion of a wealthy Boston copper family, and especially the ubiquitous Lewisohn brothers of New York, who had entered into Butte mining a decade earlier by forming the Montana Copper Company in partnership with Charles Meader. Three of the five Lewisohn brothers—Leonard, Adolph, and Philip—involved themselves directly in these companies. Leonard, a cultivated, domineering, exceptionally shrewd and tough individual, came in time to dominate both corporations.[36]

Of the two companies, the Boston and Montana loomed much the larger. Bigelow and the Lewisohns created it in close collaboration with "Captain" Thomas Couch, who served as its superintendent for years. In every sense the epitome of the expert Cornish miner, Couch was capable, imperious, conservative, and opinionated. He supervised every detail of the "B. & M." operation meticulously and prided himself as a Protestant and Republican pillar of the community. Wellmanaged and well-financed, the Boston and Montana came to rank among the world's greatest copper companies. The authoritative *Copper Handbook* described it glowingly in 1902: ". . . its profits, per pound of copper made, are the greatest of any of the world's big mines, and it is not too much to say that the mine is the best in Montana, despite the greater development and production of Anaconda."[37]

The Boston and Montana was built upon the base of the Lewisohn's established Montana Copper Company, which operated the Leonard and Colusa mines and a smelter at Meaderville, east of Butte.

To these properties were added some highly valuable new mines: the Mountain View, West Colusa, Pennsylvania, Liquidator, Comanche, Wandering Jew, and Badger State, among others. The company now needed, of course, greatly increased plant facilities. Leonard Lewisohn debated between locating the new Boston and Montana works along the broad Missouri River near Helena or downriver at Great Falls. His choice boiled down to which railroad, the Northern Pacific at Helena or the Great Northern at Great Falls, would offer the best rates. In the end, Jim Hill helped Lewisohn decide upon Great Falls, where Hill owned much real estate, by coolly giving him 1,500 shares of the Great Falls Townsite Company. Drawing upon ample hydroelectric power from generating plants at the falls of the Missouri, the company extended the copper industry northward to Great Falls in a big way, with a large smelting and refining complex in full operation there by 1893.[38] The great "B and M" plant at Great Falls, eventually capped by a monumental smokestack, evolved into a main fixture of the Montana mining economy.

The Butte and Boston Company also owned a handsome cluster of mines, including several acquired from A. J. Davis. Among the best were the Mountain Chief, Silver Bow, Grey Cliff, LaPlata, Blue Jay, and the Belle of Butte. But this firm never measured up to its Siamese twin, the Boston and Montana. The Lewisohns gained increased control of the Butte and Boston and then fed its ores into the Boston and Montana's Great Falls reduction works, which meant that most of the profits went to the latter company. It thus evolved into a satellite of the larger firm, and the two would eventually merge. Together, the two Boston companies represented one of the strongest and most profitable mining operations in the United States.[39]

At about the same time that the Boston companies were taking shape, young F. Augustus Heinze came to Butte, beginning perhaps the most sensational of all the careers and companies associated with that city. Young Heinze was a physically impressive fellow, "standing five feet ten inches in height, weighing 200 pounds, with the torso of a Yale halfback, muscles of steel, and a face of ivory whiteness, lighted up with a pair of large blue eyes." Butte folks took to him immediately, as people always did, judging him at first to be an amiable and rather lazy chap who was mainly interested in pursuing the good life. They were half right. Heinze became a favorite of the denizens of Butte's saloons and gambling dens with his hard-drinking, fun-loving antics; and women loved his shy demeanor and his polished manners. Before long, his parties and escapades would be the talk of the town. But there was much more to the man than that. Heinze's quick intelligence, excellent education, and incredible audacity would rapidly carry him to the top in western mining circles and would one day rank him alongside Daly and Clark as the big three "copper kings" of Butte.[40]

Unlike Clark and Daly, Heinze came from a wealthy and cultured family. His German immigrant father, Otto, made a modest fortune as a New York-based importer; and his mother, Eliza Marsh Lacey, was born into a long distinguished Irish-Episcopal family which had transplanted to Connecticut. Despite persistent Butte political rumors to the contrary, the Heinze family had no Jewish blood. The Heinzes raised five children, and they brought them up in a refined and learned atmosphere of close family ties. Fritz Augustus was born on 5 December 1869. As a boy, he came to dislike the German name Fritz and preferred to be called F. Augustus or Frederick Augustus. Disliking such formality, the Butte faithful dubbed him Fritz whether he liked it or not.[41]

Young Heinze received the best education his world had to offer, first at Brooklyn and then in Germany, where his proud father enrolled him in gymnasia at Leipzig and Hildesheim. Like his brothers, Fritz learned the classics in an atmosphere of discipline and cultural pride. He also acquired, as a boy, a consuming interest in geology which would shape his entire future. Heinze's European education, reinforced by family conversations at the supper table in German and French, left a permanent imprint upon the man. He grew up to embody the Victorian ideal of manhood: the muscular he-man with the suave and confident air of the cosmopolitan aristocrat. Following his return from Germany, the boy completed his education with study first at the Brooklyn Polytechnic Institute and then at the School of Mines at Columbia University, from which he graduated in 1889.[42]

Following his graduation, the headstrong youth bitterly disappointed his father, who wished to fund him for two years of advanced study at the University of Freiburg in Germany. He chose instead to head west on his own, first to look over the booming quartz towns of Colorado, then on to Salt Lake City. In September of 1889, approaching his twentieth birthday, the cocky New Yorker detrained at Butte, the city of his destiny. Heinze's excellent credentials quickly won him a good job as a mining engineer with the Boston and Montana Company. He rented a simple shack in Meaderville, worked hard by day and played hard by night. By carefully plotting vein structures below ground, by poring over charts at night and by talking to the right people, he thoroughly acquainted himself with Butte's complex geology. He came to the sound conclusion that a custom smelting operation which applied the latest in technology and offered low rates to small-scale miners offered a fine potential for profit.[43]

A year after his arrival, Heinze quit his job and returned to New York in order to raise capital for his venture. His cautious father disappointed him by refusing to put up the required $100,000; and at any rate, market conditions were unfavorable. So he spent the winter of 1890–91 working for the prestigious *Engineering and Mining Journal*, which later remembered him as "the only man who habitually came to the office wearing a top hat and frock coat. . . . A handsome young fellow, genial in manner, popular among his associates, but exhibiting no great liking for hard work." During this New York interlude, Heinze struck up an acquaintance with the Lewisohns, an acquaintance that would sour one day and lead to tremendous legal complications.[44]

Restless and frustrated, Fritz Heinze returned to his old job at Butte in the spring of 1891. His father died later that year, however, and again he returned to New York, this time convincing brothers Otto Charles and Arthur to join him in investing much of the family fortune in Butte. He spent a large part of 1892 in Europe, lining up creditors and sandwiching in a cram course in geology and mining at the University of Freiburg. In March of 1893, the Heinze brothers incorporated their firm, the Montana Ore Purchasing Company, with F. Augustus holding 51 percent of the stock and his brothers owning most of the remainder. Capitalized at $2,500,000, the "MOP Company" opened its highly sophisticated Meaderville smelter in the first week of 1894. Its low prices for custom work made Heinze a hero of the small operators, and its modern technology made it a pacesetter in the camp's evolving industrial order.[45]

At first, the financially strapped Heinze brothers had to rely upon leased mines, along with ores from independent miners, to keep their smelter running at an efficient capacity. But very soon, F. Augustus demonstrated an amazing ability to locate rich ore bodies in hitherto lackluster mines. Folks about town whispered that Fritz wielded a "magic pick," that he had a genius to rival that of Marcus Daly. It was true. Under his leasehold, both the Glengarry and the Estella mines blossomed into fine producers. In the case of the Estella, Heinze also proved his ability to wheel and deal. He leased it from the flamboyant millionaire mineowner James Murray, who was known as one of Butte's cagiest investors, with the agreement that Heinze, as the operator, would retain the lion's share of the profits so long as the ore mined was low-grade. Heinze made sure the ore was low grade by mixing waste rock into it as it emerged from the mine. Profits accumulated so rapidly that in 1895 the Heinzes were able to lay out $300,000 for direct purchase of the Rarus Mine, which Fritz correctly figured must hold the eastward extension of the great Anaconda-St. Lawrence lode. The Rarus turned into one of Butte's premier mines. For $100,000, they also purchased a one-half interest in the Snohomish claim and soon added fractional shares of the Glengarry and Johnstown properties.[46]

The Montana Ore Purchasing Company prospered beyond anyone's expectations. Its highly efficient reduction plant and amazingly productive mines yielded the brothers a quick and fast growing fortune. Within four years of its founding, the company employed 700 men, turned out 20-25,000,000 pounds of copper per year, and issued its stockholders' dividends of 32 percent annually. As one awestricken observer noted: " . . . in two years he had developed properties which cost him a million and a half dollars into properties that were worth from twenty to thirty millions."[47]

In the midst of his Butte empire building, Heinze made a curious but highly profitable move northward into the Kootenay mining district of British Columbia. He came audaciously to the remote Canadian Mountain town of Rossland in mid-1895. Securing a local newspaper, he proceeded to set himself up as the champion of the neglected district against those whom he depicted as its oppressors: the unpopular Canadian Pacific Railroad, the provincial government in Victoria, and his rival developer, Daniel C. Corbin of Spokane. Heinze built a small smelter at nearby Trail Creek and dazzled the local populace with his grandiose plan to develop a regional mining industry and outfox the Canadian Pacific by constructing a railroad of his own to the sea at Vancouver. The government actually awarded the Heinzes land grants to build their railroad, and in 1897 they mortgaged the Montana Ore Purchasing Company in order to raise funds. Soon, however, the bubble burst. Badly overextended, F. A. Heinze abruptly pulled out of the Kootenay in February 1898, selling his smelter and embryonic railroad to the Canadian Pacific for a tidy $900,000 and retaining the lucrative land grants.[48]

This curious Canadian maneuver raises some interesting questions about F. A. Heinze. Did he seriously intend to develop the Rossland district? Or was he simply posing as the champion of the area in order to shake down the Canadian Pacific and to extract profitable land grants from the provincial and national parliaments? The latter explanation seems more convincing. In any case, the Canadian incursion proved to be prophetic. What Heinze did there closely parallels what he would later do on a grander scale at Butte, posing as the hometown champion and eventually forcing a high price for selling out to the opposition. By the late 1890s, observers on both sides of the border well knew that this was a man to watch.

As a result of all these developments—the remarkable growth of Anaconda and of its older and newer sister corporations—Montana surged dramatically ahead in its leadership of the world copper industry during the 1890s. By 1890 the Treasure State was mining 50 percent of all U.S. copper. Among individual producers, Anaconda led the pack in 1897 with a yield of 131,471,127 pounds of copper marketed. Michigan's Calumet and Hecla ran a distant second with 88,378,986 pounds; the Boston and Montana ranked third with 60,000,000; and Arizona's rising United Verde and Copper Queen enterprises trailed considerably in the fourth and fifth positions. In fact, the 1890s marked the zenith of Butte's ascendancy over the horizon of American and world copper production. Having vanquished the high-grade mines of Michigan, Montana still outpaced the upcoming desert mines of Arizona and of Utah, where the great Bingham Canyon Mine was just opening in the mid-1890s.[49]

The 1890s marked a period of transition in copper, not only in terms of rising western domination of the industry, but also in terms of technological innovation. In the wake of the Montana-Michigan price war and the failure of the Secretan syndicate to control production, unrestrained output flooded the world market with cheap copper. Even the exploding demand for electrical wiring and brass machine parts could not absorb such rampant production, and as a result, prices remained depressed. The major companies tried to form trade associations to limit production, but they could not achieve adequate cooperation and all their efforts failed. In the short run, at least, their best hope for heightened margins of profit lay in technology, in lowering the costs of production.

The application of the Bessemer process to copper had the same dynamic impact upon the red metal that it had upon steel. This system, pioneered by Butte's Parrot Silver and Copper Company and adopted by Anaconda in 1890, fired currents of air into molten copper in convertors and efficiently yielded blister copper of high purity. By the mid-1890s, a second major innovation, the use of electrolysis to refine copper of its last traces of impurity, was also serving to increase efficiency and lower the costs of production. The United States led in both of these technological breakthroughs, with the result that it by now far surpassed England and Germany as the world's integrated leader in copper mining, reduction, refining and marketing. By 1895 the United States produced more than half of the world's supply. Thus America reigned supreme in the world of copper, and Butte reigned supreme in America.[50]

It must be remembered, though, that Montana's mining economy relied heavily upon the production of precious metals, as well as upon copper. In the early 1890s, the Treasure State ranked second in the nation in silver output and fourth in its production of gold. But the good times turned suddenly bad in the terrible depression which struck the region in 1893. Silver mining, so vital to the economy of the Intermountain West, collapsed spectacularly; and its collapse wrought havoc upon dozens of towns and thousands of people.[51]

Prompted by a sharp drop in the nation's gold reserve and a stock market break in May and June, the United States economy fell into the most severe depression in its history up to that time, the Panic of 1893. The business community and the conservative Democratic administration of Grover Cleveland both reasoned that the root cause of the problem lay in the Sherman Silver Purchase Act of 1890, which provided for large-scale purchases of silver as a basis for issuance of paper currency redeemable in either silver or gold. This silver purchase program served to expand a badly deflated currency, but it also amounted to a hefty subsidy of the western silver mining industry. Furthermore, it caused a run on the gold reserve as holders of paper preferred to redeem it with the more valuable and stable metal. In October of 1893, Congress followed President Cleveland's advice and voted to repeal the 1890 law.[52]

Even before the autumn repeal of the Sherman Silver Purchase Act, plummeting silver prices and the clear approach of disaster paralyzed the industry in Montana and other silver states of the region. Castle, Montana became a near ghost town almost overnight. When the great Granite-Bi-Metallic Consolidated Mining Company, located near Philipsburg, closed down on 1 August, the mine engineer issued notice by tying down the plant's steam whistle. The eerie, dying wail told the plant's employees the news they had feared, and 3,000 of them left Granite in twenty-four hours. By summer's end, Butte's biggest non-copper yielding silver mines, the Alice, Lexington, Gagnon, and Moulton companies, had all locked their gates.[53]

As the year of calamity 1893 came to a close, one-third of Montana's workforce, 20,000 men, was unemployed. Butte and Helena teemed with idle men. Many single workers lived off free lunches in the saloons, and the companies tried to carry as many family men as they could with credits and with leases to veins and equipment. But as things worsened, such stopgap measures inevitably played out. Businesses failed as the hard times persisted, and droves of workers fled the state. During the first year of panic, 130 businesses failed in the lightly populated state of Montana. Many of them were banks. Even Sam Hauser's once mighty First National Bank of Helena failed in 1893. Then, after reopening, it closed its doors for keeps in 1896, leaving the once all-powerful Hauser a rather pathetic character. Six-thousand Treasure State workers remained unemployed in 1895; and by then, an estimated 8,000 had already moved on to greener pastures.[54]

A mood of fear and panic gripped the state. "Butte is looking very savage," Marcus Daly wrote to J. B. Haggin. "There are over 3,000 idle men on the streets. They are discontented and dissatisfied." As usual, Daly sided strongly with his men. He firmly opposed the prevailing talk of wage cuts, arguing that cuts would destroy workers' families and that, in a purely practical sense, they might prove counter-productive by causing bloodshed and property destruction. This intelligent and benevolent attitude kept labor turbulance to a minimum. Workers and capitalists at Butte seemed quite united in the belief that their real problems lay not at home but in the East, where evil "goldbug" banker-industrialists and their political allies had ruthlessly destroyed silver. This perception, as we shall see, found its fullest expression in the newborn Populist Party.[55]

Thus the unrest fostered in Montana by the Panic of 1893 focused outward, not inward, as rich men and poor men joined hands in a common cause, the fight to restore silver purchases. When a motley group of Montana workers led by "General" William Hogan seized a train at Butte in order to join Jacob Coxey's celebrated 1894 silver-protest march on Washington, local mining magnates actually offered them sympathy and help. It did the protesters little good, for "Hogan's Army" was soon detrained by federal troops at Forsyth. Labor and farmers' groups returned the favor by joining with miners and businessmen to protest their plight. At a well-publicized Helena convention in July of 1893, a broadly based group of prestigious citizens formed the Montana Free Coinage Association, with Marcus Daly elected as president, to carry the banner of reaffirming "free silver."[56]

The Panic of 1893 lingered on through 1896. Eventually, silver production revived at many of the larger mines. But silver as a vital, driving force in the Montana economy was dead, never really to rise again. Copper, on the other hand, came through the panic in reasonably good shape. Despite low prices, expanding markets meant continued high production. Seen in broad perspective, therefore, the Panic of 1893 marks a major turning point in Montana's mining history. The collapse of silver meant that copper now dominated Treasure State mining, with silver and gold dwindling in importance to the point that at Butte they became mere byproducts of copper mining. Some once great mines remained closed. Others operated for several years only on a limited scale. And yet others, which like the Anaconda yielded both copper and precious metals, continued to mine intensively through the panic but suffered severe losses in earnings.[57]

Copper was truly king in Montana, and so indeed was Butte itself. The fall of silver dealt lethal and near-lethal blows to once-great quartz mining towns like Philipsburg, Kendall, Maiden, Castle, and Neihart. Some of them, it is true, would live on into the twentieth century, and some would even prosper on occasion. Their days of glory and prosperity, however, lay clearly in the past. At Butte, in sharp contrast, the future seemed rosy and bountiful. The "copper camp's" massive deposits of ore seemed truly beyond limit, and the flow of capital and people into the city continued unabated. In a state which had once boasted hundreds of gold camps, and then dozens of bustling silver towns, only this one great copper city would live on, the uncontested center of Montana mining, population, and political power.

4. Boom Town

Since its earliest days, Butte has impressed people as a rough, squalid, unique, and fascinating place. For roughly seventy-five years, it dominated the economic and political life of the rural state of Montana. Butte was a peculiar urban oasis which seemed strangely incongruous in a thinly populated commonwealth mainly devoted to agriculture. Joseph Kinsey Howard summed up the attitude of many Montanans when he referred to the city as "the black heart of Montana." One encounters this same theme, of Butte as a sinister Baghdad in the midst of rural innocence, in such childhood reminiscences as those of John K. Hutchens and Chet Huntley.[1] As a modern-day wisecrack puts it, Butte is the world's only island completely surrounded by land! Even though our purpose here is to focus upon the economic-political struggles of the time, a glimpse into Butte society is both revealing and fascinating.

During its heyday, the late nineteenth and early twentieth centuries, Butte was indeed the quintessential mining town. An air of transience, fatalism, and ribaldry, so typical of western mining camps, pervaded the place. Long after impressive business blocks rose up to symbolize its urbanity, Butte continued to call itself a "camp," like a suddenly rich wastrel who could not fathom her riches. Butte was self-conscious of its ugliness, of its cultural isolation, of its wild side. Above all, Butte was frenetic. As one shift endlessly followed another, milling through its "uptown" streets at all hours of the clock, the city seemed never to sleep, or even to rest. Edwards Roberts reported in *Harper's*, following an 1888 visit, that "the very activity of Butte is sometimes wearisome. It never ceases." Ray Stannard Baker, the prominent journalist-historian, found it in 1903 to be

57

"the most Western of American cities. . . . It gives one the impression of an overgrown mining-camp awakening suddenly to the consciousness that it is a city, putting on the airs and proprieties of the city, and yet often relapsing into the old, fascinating, reckless life of the frontier camp. . . . A nearer view gives one an impression of tremendous disorder, of colossal energies in play."[2]

Butte City grew up in fits and lurches during the boom which set in during 1875–80. In 1875–76, when the big silver excitement began, only a scattering of wretched buildings stood forlornly along the furrowed slope of the russet hill. Simon and John Hauswirth's elegantly named "Hotel de Mineral," located at the future corner of Main and Broadway, was the center of activity. Nearby stood W. A. Clark's bank, still housed in a log structure, and the typical gambling house, featuring "tanglefoot" whiskey, faro, and poker. A random scattering of businesses, cabins, and outbuildings made up the rest of the settlement.[3]

Naturally, the spectacular boom spearheaded first by the Alice and then by the Anaconda caused the city to surge in growth. Butte City was incorporated in 1879, occupying a 183-acre, 45-block area enclosed by the future Mercury, Quartz, Arizona, and Washington streets. The census of 1880 registered 3,363 residents in the city; and in the spring of 1881, it became the seat of Silver Bow County, which was carved out of Deer Lodge County. By the mid-1880s, the Anaconda excitement had dramatically intensified the boom and pushed Butte dramatically ahead as a rival to Helena as Montana's leading city. The copper metropolis boasted 10,723 inhabitants in 1890, 30,470 in 1900, and 39,165 in 1910. Since Butte and its "suburbs" made up almost the entirety of Silver Bow County's population, the county's growth rate more accurately reflects the camp's demographic profile. The county claimed 23,744 people in 1890, 47,635 in 1900, and 56,848 in 1910. We must also keep in mind that these statistics do not include the city of Anaconda, twenty-six miles away, which remained in Deer Lodge County. Anaconda had about 9,500 residents by 1900.[4]

In contrast to the shiftless, overwhelmingly male populace of earlier days, the great population surge following 1880 brought a more settled, family-based society to the mining city. But it remained, after all, a mining town, and it always had more than its share of the wilder element. An eastern newspaper calmly described the town during the early years of the boom as "simply an outpost of hell . . . the few women and children there looked with indifference upon crime of every kind." Another shocked East Coast paper reported that: "Every business man in Butte and every miner is a walking arsenal. He carries a brace or two of pistols in his belt and a bowie knife in his right boot. Bronchos [sic] are ridden into public and private houses, as it suits their drunken riders. Men, women, negroes, Chinese and Indians daily and nightly congregate in one common assemblage around the gaming tables with which the dissolute, hilarious camp abounds."[5]

This, of course, was the wildest and silliest sort of exaggeration, but the camp undeniably did have its troubles growing up. A bad fire ravaged the city in 1879, and the destruction served to quicken the pace of the stone and brick construction which followed. Alarmed by the growing numbers of "undesirables" in town, the "better element" formed a vigilance committee in 1881 with A. J. Davis as president. The Butte vigilantes patterned themselves after the earlier Montana heroes of Bannack and Virginia City, even borrowing their warning numbers "3–7–77." They refrained, however, from executing anyone and generally confined themselves to issuing warnings, for instance "to opium smokers and vagrants to vamoose the ranch."[6]

By the later 1880s, these days seemed far behind. Admittedly, Butte still seemed in many ways raw and untamed. Plank sidewalks still wound shabbily down the hill, and mud was a horrendous problem for weeks on end. "It was the muddiest place I ever saw," recalled showman Eddie Foy, who entertained in the camp for a stint of several months. By now, however, the city's impressive central business blocks, concentrated at the corners of Park and Main streets, heralded Butte's maturation into a leading commercial city of the Pacific Northwest. The leader among the city's business establishments came to be Hennessy's, the so-called company store managed by Marcus Daly's henchman Dan J. Hennessy. Opening in 1898, the $600,000, six-story department store housed on its fabled "sixth floor" the head offices of the Anaconda Company. The superb, brick and stone Victorian architecture of old uptown Butte is still impressive today, even after the ravages of time, repeated fires, and the abandonment of many buildings.[7]

To the west of the centrally located business district towered the pyramidal "Big Butte" which had given the city its name; and running southward along the east slope of this rise was Missoula Gulch, which at this time marked the city's western extremity. Butte's best residential areas of the 1890s lay on the west side. To the south and southwest, closely knit blocks of brick and framed workmen's homes reached down toward the "flats" at the foot of the hill, where a motley array of mills, breweries, and dumps fronted on Silver Bow Creek and the railroad tracks. The notorious "Cabbage Patch" cov-

D. J. Hennessy, from *Just for Fun: Cartoons and Caricatures of Men in Montana* (1907) (courtesy of Eric Myhre)

ered a six-block swath on the city's southeast flank. The patch was one of America's most picaresque slums, a congestion of cabins, lean-to's, hovels, saloons, and whorehouses squatting amongst waste dumps and rubbish. Here one could find some of Butte's legendary derelicts, like "Blasphemous Brown," the foulest mouth in town; the hermaphrodite "Liz the Lady," who walked and talked like a woman but seemed otherwise to be a man; "Nigger Riley," a baritone singer and drug addict; "Chicken Lee," a giant Negro hophead famed for raiding chicken houses and fighting with straight razors; or "Fay the Lady Barber," who reportedly murdered at least three of her hapless boyfriends.[8]

To the north and east of the city lay the central mining districts. Atop the hill, out of sight and usually out of mind, was the tiny but smartly named settlement of "Seldom Seen." Walkerville, lying well to the north of Butte and housing such substantial mines as the Lexington and the Alice, counted a considerable population by now, roughly 2,500 people. Another community, Centerville, slowly took form, lapping into Walkerville on the north and Butte on the south. Directly east of uptown Butte loomed the mighty Anaconda Hill, accentuated by the famous seven smokestacks of the Neversweat Mine. Novelist Gertrude Atherton aptly described the Anaconda Hill as a "tangled mass of smokestacks, gallow-frames, shabby grey buildings, trestles . . . [looking] like a gigantic shipwreck."

The Anaconda Hill and its environs have been consumed by the yawning, shovel-mined cavity of the Berkeley Pit, but in the old days this area was the main focus of Butte mining. The ugly sprawl of Dublin Gulch, with its colorful Irish and later Slavic multitudes, wound down from the hill into the city. Across the hill to the east lay Meaderville, the site of the Boston companies' and the Heinze brothers' smelters, and the McQueen Addition. At first, Welsh and Cornish smeltermen and their families made up most of the population in this area. By the 1890s, however, Italians and Slavs were taking over, and Meaderville eventually became known as "Little Italy." A colorful little "suburb" of 2,000, Meaderville gained widespread fame for its restaurants, night spots, and gambling.[9]

All in all, the great hill presented a colorful panorama, a vast American mosaic of bustling men and machinery. So large was the mining district that an unfathomable labyrinth of interconnected tunnels reached all the way from Walkerville, well over two miles to Meaderville. In contrast to many other districts, Butte's mines produced few gases; and since the tunnels were interlocked, hoisting and exit from them was relatively easy. One could literally move underground from one end of the camp to the other. By 1900, most of the bigger mines had electric lighting and power, and many had three-compartment shafts reaching to depths of 2,000 or more feet. Above ground, the steel gallows frames rose over 100 feet above the shafts. With their top-mounted, clanging cable wheels eternally raising and lowering cages of men and material into the depths of the mines, the gallows frames came to symbolize the city itself. It seemed anomalous to see the gallows, flanked by lumber piles, ore bins, and waste dumps, standing along main traveled streets, backstreets, and amidst shoddy neighborhoods. Railroad tracks criss-crossed the hill, carrying busy little steam- and electric-powered ore trains at all hours to the smelters and to the Butte, Anaconda, and Pacific Railroad. Butte's own electric trolley system used many of these same tracks.[10]

Most visitors to Butte were astounded by the stark desolation and ugliness of the place, and by the incredible air pollution caused by open roasting and unregulated smelting of its ores. Novelist Dashiell Hammett depicted Butte as "an ugly city of 40,000 people, set in an ugly notch between two ugly mountains that had been all dirtied up by mining." Laborite "Big Bill" Haywood recalled that: "In approaching Butte I marvelled at the desolation of the country. There was no verdure of any kind; it had all been killed by the fumes and smoke of the piles of burning ore." Admitting that, ". . . if Butte is the ugliest city in the United States, she knows how to make amends," Gertrude Atherton wrote: "They [smelters] ate up the vegetation, and the melting snows and heavy June rains washed the weakened earth from the bones of the valley and mountain, leaving both as stark as they must have been when the earth ceased to rock and began to cool. Since the smelters have gone to Anaconda, patches of green, of a sad and timid tenderness, like the smile of a child too long neglected, have appeared between the sickly grey boulders of the foothills, and, in Butte, lawns as large as a tablecloth have been cultivated."[11]

The smoke, heavily laden with sulfur and arsenic, arose not only from the smelter furnaces, but even more so from the open roasting of ores. Local mining companies would dump the sulfide ores either in giant stalls or in pits of up to a block in size, pile in logs for fuel, and then burn them for days upon end to eliminate as much of the sulfur as possible. Mining engineer J. B. Steiger described the result: "The ore treated in Butte every twenty-four hours gives off from 260 to 300 tons of sulphur." When the usual westerly breezes prevailed, the smoke blew away with minimal problems. But during inversions and easterly air flows, it created an appalling situation. Ominous clouds hung low over the hill, so dense that darkness enveloped the city in midday and lamps had to be lit. One could barely see across the street uptown, and on the flats below, the settling smoke made life itself nearly impossible. In the words of the *Engineering and Mining Journal*: ". . . the unfortunate traveler from South Butte traces his way not by landmarks, for these are utterly invisible, but by the hacking cough of his forerunner, who though a few feet away is completely veiled in smoke."[12]

The smoke caused some deaths, many illnesses, vomitings, and nosebleeds, and it killed off most of the city's fragile vegetation. According to the *Anaconda Standard*, only four trees remained alive in 1890; and local wags reported, perhaps with tongues in cheek, that cats died of licking arsenic from their whiskers. Public opinion, backed by the press, finally launched a "smoke war" in the early 1890s which led to an antiroasting ordinance and the installation of abatement devices on most smelters. The smoke problem did not really subside, however, until the early years of this century, when the consolidation of the hill led to the transfer of almost all smelting to Anaconda and Great Falls. Even then, until a giant smokestack was erected over the Anaconda smelter to lift the acrid smoke high into the windy sky, smoke damage in the upper Deer Lodge Valley led to livestock deaths and severe legal troubles.[13] At long last, trees and shrubs began forlornly to reappear in the mining city.

Despite its dismal appearance, anyone who spent much time in the "Copper Camp" knew that it was a remarkably engaging and fascinating place—wide open, tough and unabashed, fun-loving and convivial. Above all else, what gave Butte its unique personality was its richly cosmopolitan population, for Butte was one of America's most striking "melting pots" of immigrant nationalities. Mary MacLane, the city's notoriously prurient but brilliant young writer, graphically described a colorful street scene at the turn of the century:

There are Irishmen—Kelleys, Caseys, Calahans, staggering under the weight of much whiskey, shouting out their green-isle maxims; there is the festive Cornishman, ogling and leering, greeting his fellow-countrymen with alcoholic heartiness, and gazing after every feminine creature with lustful eyes; there are Irish women swearing genially at each other in shrill peasantry, and five or six loudly vociferous children for each; there are round-faced Cornish women likewise, each with her train of children; there are suave, sleek sporting men just out of the bath-tub; insignificant lawyers, dentists, messengerboys; "plungers" without number; greasy Italians from Meaderville; greasier French people from the Boulevarde

Addition; ancient miners—each of whom was the first to stake a claim in Butte; starved-looking Chinamen here and there; a contingent of Finns and Swedes and Germans; musty, stuffy old Jew pawnbrokers who have crawled out of their holes for a brief recreation; dirt-encrusted Indians and squaws in dirty, gay blankets, from their flea-haunted camp below the town; "box rustlers"—who are as common in Butte as bar-maids in Ireland; swell, flashy-looking Africans; respectable women with white aprons tied around their waists and sailor-hats on their heads, who have left the children at home and stepped out to see what was going on; innumerable stray youngsters from their dark haunts of Dublin Gulch; heavy restaurant-keepers with toothpicks in their mouths; a vast army of dry-goods clerks—the "paper-collared" gentry; miners of every description; representatives from Dog Town, Chicken Flats, Busterville, Butchertown, and Seldom Seen—suburbs of Butte; pale, thin individuals who sing and dance in beer halls; smart society people in high traps and tally-hos; impossible women—so-called (though in Butte no one is more possible), in vast hats and extremely plaid stockings; persons who take things seriously and play the races for a living; "beer-jerkers"; "bisquit-shooters"; soft voiced Mexicans and Arabians;—the dregs, the elite, the humbly respectable, the off-scouring—all thrown together and shaken up, and mixed well.[14]

Census statistics reveal the strikingly large extent to which Butte was a city of immigrant proletarian families. In 1890, the foreign-born made up 10,659 of Silver Bow County's total population of 23,744—45 percent. By 1910, when the county's total population stood at 56,848, the foreign-born numbered 20,075; thus they still constituted well over one-third of the populace.[15] Actually, the immigrant presence was much larger than these figures indicate, since many of the "native-born" were actually the children of close-knit immigrant families. The shifting composition of this immigrant population closely reflected national patterns. Prior to the last years of the nineteenth century, most of them came from northern and western Europe, especially from Ireland and Great Britain. After that time, a rising tide of unfamiliar newcomers arrived from southern and eastern Europe, most notably from Italy and from present-day Yugoslavia.

Two immigrant groups which came early and in large numbers to Butte, and which together exerted the greatest influence over its character, were the Irish and the Cornish. In Butte as in so many western mining towns, Irish refugees from the 1850s potato famine and from the crises which followed it formed a large and boisterous part of the population. Marcus Daly, who never lost his sentimental attachment to the old sod, sought out his countrymen for employment and even encouraged immigration directly from Ireland itself. Over 2,300 Irish-born immigrants lived in Silver Bow County by 1890, nearly 4,600 by

1900.[16] Because they were so numerous, so clannish, so strongly politicized, and because of Daly's leadership, whom they idolized, the Irish took control of Butte. They took control of its culture and of its politics, and that control remains surprisingly intact even today.

As in Boston or San Francisco, the Butte Irish clung to their ancestral ways with a remarkable persistence. With few traditions of industrial living to guide them, they had to cling to the old ways in order to survive. As recently as the 1930s, an Irish newspaper commented that one heard more Gaelic spoken in Butte than in Dublin. Irish Catholicism pervaded the city, and much of its social and cultural life revolved around the parish churches and schools. Similarly, Irish loyalty to the Democratic Party became a sort of secular religion. Even the notorious Cabbage Patch, with its black and Mexican minions, had an Irish boss—one McNamara, whose reign ended spectacularly when a distillery he was working on exploded, killing him instantly. A tight little group of Ulster-Protestant Irish also lived in Butte. The majority Catholics called them "Far-Downs," and perhaps in consciously contrived behavior, the Ulstermen always blessed themselves with their left hands.

As more radically anti-British newcomers joined the earlier arrivals after 1900, the big Irish bloc came to look more like a salad bowl than a melting pot. P. J. Brophy observed in 1912: "We have Home Rulers, Sinn Feiners, physical forces fanatics, Ulstermen and Coronians—all pulling in different directions." Still, the Irish prevailed at Butte, and everybody knew it. The "Shamrock City's" favorite holiday was St. Patrick's Day, celebrated both on 17 March and on Easter Monday; its favorite name was Sullivan; and its favorite drink was a boilermaker, known locally as a "Shawn O'Farrell."[17]

The Cornishmen, or "Cousin Jacks," never approached the Irish in numbers or political power, but they too had their influence. They came from Cornwall in southwestern England, an area of long-established mines, and in America their highly valued skills made them the aristocrats of metal mining, the "hard-rock men." After 1885, as Butte rose to copper preeminence, and as the Comstock Lode played out, the Cousin Jacks poured into the camp. Stocky and round-faced, they differed from the Irish in many ways, tending to be taciturn and conservative, Republican in politics, and Methodist in religious persuasion. Their fondness for mackerel and pilchards, saffron cakes, and especially the delicious meat pies they called "pasties," which are still today a Butte delicacy, made them seem peculiar to the other miners. Even their names seemed peculiar. Although many bore typical Anglo-Saxon names, such as Wilcox or Woodward, others could easily be identified by certain prefixes and suffixes. School children often recited this familiar rhyme:

> By Tre–, Pol–, Pen–, and –o
> The Cornishmen you come to know.

They came in such numbers to the camp that historian A. L. Rowse recalls of his Cornish hometown, Tregonissey: ". . . the goings-on in Butte, Montana, were more familiar to us than those in London."[18]

The English Cousin Jacks and Cousin Ginnies typically held the "shanty Irish" in contempt, both as miners and as human beings. At the Mountain View Mine, whose work force was so Cornish that it was called the "Saffron Bun," the foreman airily dismissed Irish job seekers with the famous line: "Thee are in the wrong line, my boy!" Each group had its own churches, its own bars, and its own sports. The Irish preferred Celtic football and boxing, while the Cornish loved greyhound racing and their own special brand of wrestling, in which the opponents wore heavy vests with straps on them by which each tried to throw the other. Each had its own brotherhoods: the Irish Ancient Order of Hibernians, and the Cornish Sons of Saint George. Admittedly, the two groups eventually learned to get along. They finally came to intermarry freely. On occasion, they even exchanged celebration of their favorite holidays, St. Patrick's Day and St. George's Day.[19]

Especially in the early days, however, they more often collided. Mineowners took frequent advantage of English-Irish animosities by mixing their work forces in order to break up laboring class solidarity, and the unions often resounded with their quarrels.[20] Since both groups loved to drink, barroom brawls broke out frequently. None ever quite matched the infamous "A.P.A. Riot" of 1894. The American Protective Association, a nationwide nativist, anti-immigrant and anti-Catholic organization, took quick root among Butte's English populace. It had about 2,000 local members by 1894. On the fourth of July that year, two West Broadway saloons proudly displayed shields in their windows lettered "A.P.A." Predictably, a riot resulted, complete with hailstorms of paving stones, dynamite blasts, and the death of a policeman. When the fire department arrived to hose down the rioters, the Irish crews gleefully turned their hoses upon the offending saloons, blasting out their insides. The militia finally restored order, and Mayor Dugan solemnly deplored the damage to the Protestant saloons![21]

Thus the Irish and the English set the style at Butte, but other nationalities had their influences as well. Over 800 Germans inhabited Butte by 1890, many of them brewery workers who lived in the suburb of Williamsburg southwest of the city. They formed a "Lieder-kranz" singing society as early as 1881 and an athletic turnverein in 1888 with 165 members. A comparable number of French Canadians lived in and around the camp, attracted in large part by its demand for lumber workers. Similarly, the camp's need for stout woodmen drew in many Scandinavians. By the turn of the century, Butte claimed 754 Swedes, 355 Norwegians, and nearly 600 Finns. The powerfully built, athletic Finns won great favor with Marcus Daly and other superintendents due to their ability at timbering underground. By 1910, their number had swollen to over 1,300. A "Finn-Town" grew up along East Broadway, a street which became known as "the Fish"—because it had "fins" on both sides, of course! As in other camps, the Finns of Butte were famed for their rough-and-tumble games, their radical politics, their beloved bathhouses, and their big boarding houses, like the landmark "Big Ship," a huge establishment which housed and fed 500 workers on endlessly rotating, eight-hour shifts.[22]

There were many others: by 1910, nearly 2,000 British Canadians, who of course blended easily with the native Americans; 260 blacks, most all of whom moved on, leaving little behind; 367 Welshmen, mostly smelter workers; and 358 Scots. Interestingly, the cosmopolitan copper camp also attracted significant numbers of Jewish and Lebanese peddlers. Oldtimers, in fact, often claimed that A. B. Cohen was the first child born at Butte. Coming mainly from eastern Europe, the Jews numbered at least 500 by 1900. Nearly as numerous, for a time, were the Christian Lebanese, who gathered in a "Little Lebanon" along East Galena and Mercury streets. Although established businesses finally drove most of the door-to-door peddlers out of work, a number of Jewish and Lebanese families still remain in Butte today. Several of them are leading businessmen.[23]

The mining city's two most picturesque minority groups were the Chinese and the Indians. Like most mining areas, the Silver Bow diggings drew in many Chinese miners, veterans of California and Nevada who could subsist on worked-over claims which the whites had abandoned. In fact, when the majority of white miners abandoned the town of Rocker for Butte, about 100 Chinese took it over and renamed it Foochow. From the 1880s through World War I, Butte's Chinese population hovered between 400 and 600. They worked mainly in their "washey-washey" houses and their exotic restaurants, and at gardening, peddling, and house-cleaning—menial tasks which the whites allowed them. Most of them dwelt in the inevitable "Chinatown," complete with its noodle parlors, opium dens, pungent smelling shops, and an elaborate, pagoda-topped joss house.[24]

As elsewhere, the Chinese suffered from white prejudice and persecution. A local newspaper characteristically denounced Orientals as "opium-eating, leperous, lying, thieving, yellow heathens," and concluded that Chinese could no more serve as citizens than could a coyote. Mayoral candidate William Owsley triumphed with the slogan: "Down with the Chinese cheap labor." In the area's first hanging, two whites strung up an unoffending Chinese, just "for the hell of it." Year after year, Butte's "better element" wrung its hands over the opium dens, the gambling, and the alleged white slave trade in Chinatown. Montana's attorney general received a steady stream of complaints from Butte about the "state of horror" in Chinatown, about "scarlet scenes" in Chinese watering holes, about the pursuit of gamblers-drug pushers like "this fellow Wong . . . alias Hum Yum, Hum Yen Wong, Wing and Clas. Wong." Unrest among the Chinese of faraway San Francisco sometimes spread to Butte. As recently as 1927, a Chinese died in a tong war between the Bing Kong and Hip Sing tongs. In the end, most of Butte's Chinese became Americanized, and many became Christians. Jimmy July, one of the city's best-known Chinese, became a Christian and a naturalized U.S. citizen before American law made the latter impossible. Almost all of the Chinese left: only a handful remained in Chinatown by the 1940s.[25]

Beyond a doubt, Butte's most colorful "ghetto" was the encampment of Cree, Chippewa, and Meti Indians down by the city dump near the foot of Timber Butte, south of town. These impoverished, "landless" Indians, mostly refugees from Canada, entered Montana in scattered bands after 1880 and ended up in forlorn camps like the ones at Butte and at "Hill 57" in Great Falls. During the warm season they lived mostly off the dump, but during the long winter, they had to rely upon the county for assistance. To repay Butte's generosity, the Indians staged each year a gala, two-day celebration for Indians and whites alike, complete with horse races, war dances, and such delicacies as the roasted meats of horse, dog, ground squirrel, and rodents from the dump. Eventually they, too, moved on, many of them to the Rocky Boy's Reservation near Havre.[26]

By the mid-1890s, as noted previously, the general trend of rising immigration to America from southern and eastern Europe found an accurate reflection at Butte. From overpopulated Italy and from the turbulent south-Slavic regions of the Austro-Hungarian Empire came hordes of desperately poor, often illiterate peoples. The corporations welcomed them and sometimes even brought them in on contracts because of their willingness to work for lesser pay scales. By 1910 Silver Bow County numbered nearly 1,000 Italians, many of them concentrated at Meaderville, with its colorful neighborhoods and "strange smelling, exotic little restaurants."[27]

Predictably, the established, Anglo-Irish families of Butte reacted angrily to the Italian newcomers, especially when the "Wops" competed for their jobs. They reacted even more angrily toward the "Bohunks," as they called the Slavs who came mostly from Serbia and Croatia. Most of the "Bohunks" were destitute young men, often hired by consignment and then herded into shacks along Dublin Gulch, or in Cork-Town or the Boulevard or McQueen additions. Nearly 2,000 had arrived by 1910, and local resentment against them soon boiled over. Everything about them seemed strange, from their Greek Orthodox Catholicism to their indecipherable speech to their paganlike pre-Lenten festival of the Mesopust, when an effigy named Slarko Veljacic was tried and executed amidst much dancing and drinking. Gertrude Atherton referred to them as "'dark men,' an inferior class of southern Europeans, who live like pigs and send their wages home."

Laborite Peter Breen drew cheers in a St. Patrick's Day speech when he said that, had Marcus Daly lived, he would never have allowed their importation. Under a sensational 1910 headline: "The Story of the Butte Bo-hunk—The Dark Skinned Invader," The *Butte Evening News* predicted that they would soon take over the camp.[28] The "Rustler's Song" of this era summarized Butte's resentment:

> Molly dear, and did ya hear
> The news that's goin' round?
> They're cannin' all the shovelers
> A-workin' underground.
>
> I've rustled at the Diamond,
> And I rustled at the Con,
> The dagoes are the only ones
> That they are putting on.[29]

In the end, however, the prophets of doom proved to be wrong. Although tension surrounded the relations between the Slavic and Italian newcomers and their fairer-skinned neighbors for years to come, the great melting pot that was Butte eventually assimilated them all. The last mayor of Butte, before it consolidated with Silver Bow County, was the long-term chief executive Mario Micone, who was popularly known, interestingly, as "Mike." Justifiably, the city still prides itself as a domicile of many nationalities, one of America's most fascinating centers of international commingling.[30]

Like most mining towns, Butte had more than its share of squalor, violence, and tragedy. Respectable middle-class citizens frequently voiced their despair over the city's dismal appearance and its filthy neighborhoods with their abject poverty. One civic-minded gentleman put it well in a letter to the city council, lamenting the "hundreds of yards and many of the alleys [which] are foul and dirty, and covered with decayed and decaying matter," and the owners and occupants who ignored the city's orders to clean up and often simply ran in hogs to police their grounds. Others forlornly decried the armies of bums and prisoners who were marched through the streets in chains to work the rock pile, the "chronic drunks, and habitual users of morphine, opium, and cocaine," and "the professional hobos, rounders and pimps (especially the latter class), of which our community is infested."[31]

Violence was open, unflinching, usually casually disregarded. In 1899, for instance, Jack Gallagher and G. H. "Parson" Ward decided to settle a quarrel in the ring, before a sizable crowd. Gallagher suffered a broken arm in the sixtieth round, but he killed Ward with a blow to the temple in the one-hundred-and-fifth round. Since the sheriff would make no arrest unless someone swore a warrant, Gallagher went free. Then there was the notorious case of Niccolo Salvanti, who was tried for murdering his lady friend, "Dutch Rose" Hartz. Salvanti won acquittal by calmly explaining that Rose had shot at him, and had died when the bullet ricocheted off the wall and struck her instead. Sometimes the violence drew in large numbers of participants, as in the "A.P.A. Riot" of 1894 or the famous slug-fest which occurred at Gregson Hot Springs near Anaconda in 1912. The latter scrap erupted when the Butte Miners' Union and the Anaconda Smeltermen happened to schedule their picnics at the same park on the same day. The beer flowed freely, and a battle of epic proportions ensued. "The afternoon sun," wrote an imaginative reporter from the *Butte Miner*, "was hidden from sight by the clouds of flying bottles." Special trains hauled the wounded back to Butte and Anaconda hospitals that night.[32]

Butte, like all deep mining towns, lived fatalistically under the constant fear of disasters. And disasters occurred with frightening regularity. The worst of them were the "big explosion" of 1895 and the Speculator Mine fire of 1917. In January of 1895, a serious fire broke out at a cluster of warehouses east of Arizona Street. The gathering crowds and firemen did not know that one of the structures contained huge stores of dynamite, which exploded in several eruptions, scattering debris and dismembered bodies and killing fifty-eight people, including all but three members of the city fire department. The terrible catastrophe at the Speculator Mine occurred in June of 1917 when some frayed insulation caught fire and, fanned by an updraft, ignited a roaring volcano of flame. Fire and the gases it caused killed over 160 men in this, the worst of Butte's mining disasters.[33]

Desolation, fatalism, and despair: these were aspects of Butte which immediately caught the eye. But Butte also had another side, for it housed one of the most incredible social orders to be found anywhere. The key to understanding Butte was simply to keep in mind that it was, after all, a giant mining camp, where a characteristic get-rich-quick attitude, an unassuming democracy, and an unquestioning tolerance of one's fellow man prevailed. Millionaires, bums, working stiffs, well-groomed ladies, and whores all bumped elbows on common terms, and Butte seldom bothered to make any pretenses. Describing a typical gaming house, Lemuel Eli Quigg of the *New York Tribune* wrote:

> I doubt if anything happens in Butte that doesn't happen contemporaneously in Boston. The only difference is that they are more candid in Butte than in Boston. . . . Enter such a place and you see everybody: Mr. Jones, lawyer; Mr. Smith, banker; Mr. Brown, miner; a street fakir 'dropping' on black and white the proceeds of his night's wrestle . . . two or three women, likely to be French or African; a heathen or two, silent, patient, but usually lucky, huddled in a lump watching the mechanical movements of the long-bearded elderly chap as he slides this card that way and that card this way.[34]

Mining-camp democracy meant, in other words, social commonality, wide-open tolerance of drinking, whoring, and gaming, and a peculiarly unrestrained kind of individualism. Journalist-poet Berton Braley caught this mood precisely when he wrote that, at first, Butte "seemed a gawd forsaken hole. . . . But, once acclimated, I became as staunch and true a lover of Butte as the oldest inhabitant. . . . Butte was a town of personalities. Don't tell me democracy doesn't make for the development of the individual! That camp was the most democratic place I've ever lived in, and had more individualities to the block than Madison had to the square mile.[35]

Braley was right, for democratic Butte seemed to abound, indeed to revel in the most outlandish characters. Take, for instance, "Diamond

Tooth" Baker, the oversized pimp who filled his cavitied teeth with diamond fillings, lived in sumptuous splendor, and boasted that he always had at least twelve girls supporting him. Or "Dublin Dan," who ran a giant "Hobo Retreat" saloon, with sawdust floors and bubbling vats of free stew for bums. Dan once had his cronies waiting outside a revival with signs announcing in all seriousness: "For a good cold scoop of lager after the services or a shot to warm your innards go to Dublin Dan's just around the corner." Then there was the famous hack driver "Fat Jack" Jones, tall, thin, and cadaverous, always decked out with a top hat, who drove such celebrities as Teddy Roosevelt, William Jennings Bryan, and Mark Twain careening through the streets of the city. Wandering the streets of Butte, one might encounter Mary MacLane, the comely lass who made a national sensation in 1902 when she published *The Story of Mary MacLane*, her prurient musings. Or Rabbi Jacob Ehrlich, better known as "Cockelevitch," who attracted crowds of kids to watch him slaughtering Sabbath chickens in front of his Main Street shop. Or "Colonel" James Rutledge of Virginia, "Colonel Buckets" as he was called, a pretentious "aristocrat" and racetrack hanger-on who became such a sentimental favorite that he was breveted a colonel in the Montana militia so that he might have a title.[36]

This affable and fun-loving kind of individualism expressed itself in other ways as well. Partly because so many names here were unpronounceable, but mainly because monickers made all men equal, Butte was a city of nicknames. Titles such as "Nubbins," "Red Neck," "Bohunk," "Busted-ass," and "Hammerhead" abounded. As Neil Lynch recalls, a typical gathering of the Butte faithful might include "Oogie" Popovich, "Droopy Drawers" Donovan, "Boozer" Boyle, "Jew" Mose, "Termite" Rossland, and "Greasy" Tomich. Nicknames were so commonly accepted that they sometimes gained immortality by being inscribed on gravestones, as in the case of John "Lunk" Lowney—not to be confused with all the other John Lowneys of Butte![37]

Indeed, the camp's sentimental attachment to the individual even found reflection in its devotion to animals, especially the Cornish racing greyhounds and other dogs and the horses and mules in the mines. For example, "Old Jim," a fire department horse that survived the explosions of 1895, had free run of the city. So did "Dynamite," an intelligent collie who dined in grandeur at local restaurants, turned up unfailingly at fires, and often took the trolleys to evening baseball games. "Kelly the Ghost," a great white cat with shining eyes, wandered at will through the labyrinths of the deep mines, where he frequently terrified workers with his sudden, ghoulish appearance. Perhaps Butte's most bizarre pet was the "Centerville Bull," which roamed the upper hill, sometimes making a pest of himself by leading cows astray and chewing clothing from the lines. Sadly, the bull met a tragic end when an angry housewife shot him in the gonads, leading him to jump in anguish down a mineshaft. Or so the story goes! Butte's fondness for animals found its best expression in the following favorite old miners' song.

> My sweetheart's a mule in the mine.
> I drive her with only one line.
> On the dashboard I sit
> And tobacco I spit,
> All over my sweetheart's behind.[38]

The miner in question was spitting at the Anaconda brand on the mule's flank, a gesture of contempt. Despite all its eccentricities, Butte had its share of civility and refinement. Its school system, with 200 teachers and nearly 8,000 grade-school and high-school students, measured up to those of other cities of comparable size. Every Sunday, its dozens of churches filled to capacity. Its handsome west side homes, like the lavish mansions erected by W. A. Clark and his son Charley, represented wealth and social aspiration. So did the pretentious Silver Bow Club, where Butte's captains of industry entertained such magnates as J. P. Morgan, Jim Hill, and H. H. Rogers. Beginning in the 1880s and 1890s, impresarios like John Maguire and the renowned "Uncle Dick" Sutton brought in nationally noted "road companies." Eddie Foy played the camp for an extended period in 1882, and was followed over the years by such favorites as Sarah Bernhardt, Lotta Crabtree, Billie Burke, Charlie Chaplin, W. C. Fields, and Harry Lauder, who once interrupted his performance to hear a Scottish miner in the audience sing "Loch Lomond."[39] After the turn of the century, vaudeville troupes arrived regularly. Fascinated by the place, they often parodied and publicized it on their tours, frequently by transposing the words "butt" and "Butte."

What set Butte apart, though, was not its upper crust, but rather its wild side. Drinking, carousing, whoring, and gaming seemed to be the favorite avocations of the city's sizable working class. Butte had always been a hard drinking camp, ever since Dennis Leary set up its first wretched bar, complete with two lean-to's outside with Indian prostitutes, one of whom won notoriety as "the ugliest whore on either side of the divide." Like all mining towns, Butte drowned its fear of tragedy, its dread of such omnipresent diseases as tuberculosis and miners' consumption, its loathing of isolation and long winters, in drink. By 1893, the city directory could boast of 212 "drinking establishments." These ranged in status from the huge Atlantic Bar, which claimed that its block-long counter, employing fifteen bartenders at a time, was the world's largest, to such notorious dives as the infamous Clipper Shades, the Alley Cat, and the Bucket of Blood.

Many of the saloons never closed, a fact which they proudly demonstrated by either removing the locks from their doors or by dropping the key down the toilet on opening day. Twenty-five four-horse brewery wagons worked the streets to service the bars. "One thing I have noticed," a liquor dealer told Julian Ralph, "is that if a man quits drinking here, he will be dead within a month." Hardly a miner, it seemed, missed hitting his favorite pub at shift time, whether for a "one-bit" shot of whiskey, a "growler" (a bucket of beer to go), a nickel beer with all the free food you wanted, or a dime "Shawn O'Farrell"—an ounce of whiskey to cut the dust from the lungs and a beer chase to slake the thirst of an eight-hour shift.[40]

Night and day, the fun never ceased. At the city's sixteen "licensed gambling hells," mobs of men, many of them still in working clothes, worked intensely at their games of faro, craps, stud poker, and roulette. The fact that gambling was illegal troubled some, but in fact it made little real difference.[41] Prostitution came to rank as one of Butte's major livelihoods. Along Galena Street, and later the infamous "Venus Alley," there grew up a seedy red-light district that in its prime rivaled the Barbary Coast of San Francisco and the Corduroy Road of New Orleans and closely resembled Leadville's "Stillborn Alley" and "Coon Row." Up on Mercury Street, meanwhile, appeared the higher-class "parlor houses," with their refined and wealthy madames and lovely girls for wealthier clients. Along the sin center of Galena Street, hundreds of whores plied their trade. Some worked out of big, multipurpose places like the Casino, which ran a hundred girls. World middleweight boxing champ Stanley Ketchell started out there as a bouncer. Many other girls leased tiny little "cribs," equipped with call-boxes to order drinks from the parent saloons.

The discriminating customer could find prostitutes of all shapes, sizes, and nationalities, often working under such "noms de crib" as "Nigger Liz," "Jew Jess," or "Mexican Maria." Elegant pimps, known as "John McGuimps," "P.I.'s," or "McGoofers," oversaw the operations like proud barons. Everyone loved to hate them. During the district's heyday, roughly 1903–17, it presented an incredible spectacle. On a given Saturday night, as many as 4,000 men and women could be found milling around the area. Charlie Chaplin remembered it vividly fifty years later:

> The red-light district of Butte, Montana, consisted of a long street and several side streets containing a hundred cribs, in which young girls were installed ranging in age from sixteen up—for one dollar. Butte boasted of having the prettiest women of any red-light district in the West, and it was true. If one saw a pretty girl smartly dressed, one could rest assured she was from the red-light quarter, doing her shopping. Off duty, they looked neither right nor left and were most acceptable.[42]

Such was the copper camp in its prime. Butte seemed not to take itself, or anything else, very seriously. When Billy Sunday reprimanded it as the hardest drinking town he had ever seen, Butte paid little attention. When Carrie Nation went on a 1910 crusade through the red-light district, she met large crowds of laughing disbelievers and was rudely ejected from a parlor house by matronly madame May Maloy.[43] Butte was tough, yet Butte was tender. Stark and ugly, warm and unpretentious, fatalistic yet fun-loving and convivial, the city left visitors aghast, but it struck an enduring affection and loyalty in the hearts of its people. Once known, Butte was never forgotten.

Butte seemed on the surface to be a remarkably turbulent and disjointed place, torn asunder by ethnic, political, religious, and economic forces. In truth, however, a number of powerful bonds served to unite the residents of the city. Chief among these ties were the Catholic faith and the Democratic party allegiance of the Irish and of many others as well. An even stronger centrifugal force was the awesome strength of organized labor. During the 1880s, Butte became the mightiest bastion of unionism in the Intermountain West. Everyone, it seemed, even capitalists, paid homage to the unions.

The deep miners of Butte increased steadily in numbers over the years: there were 9,000 by 1905. As excellent recent studies by Richard Lingenfelter, Mark Wyman, and Ronald Brown reveal, the hard-rock miners of Butte closely resembled their compatriots throughout the region. In addition to the highly skilled miners who drilled and blasted, there were legions of timbermen, "muckers" (shovelers), "trammers" (ore haulers), and others who labored beneath the surface. The hard-rock men lived a hard, frenetic life. They were in constant fear of accident and illness, and Butte knew plenty of both. During the period from 1894 to 1908, Montana miners suffered a fatality rate of 3.53 per 1,000 men employed annually—a higher rate than Colorado's, Idaho's or South Dakota's, and a much higher percentage than the 1.14 of Great Britain or the 1.07 of Germany. Men died, here as elsewhere, in fires, cave-ins, gassings, and falls. In 1891, nineteen men fell to their deaths when a cable broke, dropping their hoisting cage down a shaft in the Anaconda Mine. Even more dangerous was the threat of miners' consumption ("miners' con"), which was really phthisis or silicosis. In a study of Butte miners made during 1916–19, two experts discovered that 42 percent of those tested suffered from this terrible, coughing and gasping affliction, which was caused by inhaling dust from drilling. Miners' con killed thousands, often by bringing on tuberculosis and pneumonia.[44]

Working under such conditions, it is hardly surprising that hard-rock miners usually lost little time in organizing. The first stirrings of labor agitation at Butte came amidst the boom of the later 1870s. In June of 1878, the Walker brothers at the Alice Mine and A. J. Davis at the Lexington arbitrarily cut wages for unskilled underground workers from $3.50 to $3.00 per day. The skilled miners, even though not directly affected, stood by their fellows. Led by an able young Indiana miner named Aaron Witter, they peaceably protested the cuts; and, generally supported by public opinion, they won reinstatement of the prevailing $3.50 wage scale. In the process of winning this first strike in Montana's history, the workers formed the Butte Workingmen's Union, with Witter as president, on 13 June 1878. All workers, regardless of craft, were welcome, and in two weeks' time the union boasted 300 paid-up members.[45]

The great boom touched off by the rise of Anaconda coincided with a decline of the Comstock and other Nevada mines in the early 1880s. As a result, thousands of veteran, skilled miners, many of them Cornish, swelled the ranks of Butte's work force. Most of these Nevada-California miners were union veterans who had taken part in the "4.00 Fight" for higher wages in Nevada's silver mines. The union registered 810 members by 1882; and by 1885, when its fine new, multipurpose union hall was completed, the organization surged ahead of the Comstock unions with 1,800 dues-paying workers. In March of 1885, the union reorganized itself, changing its name to the Butte Miners' Union and disaffiliating all members who were not actual miners. These workers who no longer belonged to the Butte Miners' Union formed their own smaller craft organizations. Under the auspices of the B.M.U., some of them joined the all-inclusive Knights of Labor; and in 1886 they all gathered under the banner of the parent B.M.U. to form the powerful Silver Bow Trades and Labor Assembly.[46]

The 1890s thus dawned upon a fully unionized work force in the

Butte district. In 1887 the laborers demonstrated just how strong they were when, after threatening to lynch the recalcitrant superintendent of the Bluebird Mine, they won full recognition of the closed shop. Joined under the umbrella of the Silver Bow Trades and Labor Assembly, thirty-four separate unions now represented nearly all of the camp's 6,000 workers. Here, clearly, was a force to reckon with: "the greatest single social force of the working class in the western part of America," as laborite "Big Bill" Haywood put it. Haywood, who was well qualified to make such judgement, further concluded that Butte labor might have won control of the entire Montana political structure if it could have avoided internal dissension.[47]

It seldom could. In the early years, the main source of labor discord sprang not from clashes with management, but rather from the ethnic-religious friction between Irishmen and Cornish-Englishmen. Led by two vigorous spokesmen, Patrick Boland and Peter Breen, the Irish element usually held sway, steering the labor bloc toward the Democratic Party and the whims of Marcus Daly. The smaller Cornish bloc, in contrast, prided itself upon representing the aristocracy of the working class and sometimes inclined more toward a management viewpoint than toward labor solidarity. This Anglo-Protestant exclusiveness struck sparks and occasionally caused the pot to boil over. After openly opposing an eight-hour workday law in the 1891 Legislature, the caustic Cornish labor leader W. J. Penrose was shot to death one night on a dark uptown street corner. Penrose's murderers escaped conviction, even though the national Sons of St. George invested thousands in trying to track down the guilty parties. The Sons suspected that a Montana version of Pennsylvania's violent Irish underground, the "Molly Maguires," may have been responsible.[48] They were probably right.

Such troubles are easily exaggerated, though, for the Butte Miners' Union usually closed ranks when vital issues were at stake. No one could dispute its social, political, and economic power. It not only sponsored smaller craft unions at Butte but also set up "branch" unions at other Montana mining towns, like Granite, where the local had 1,000 members by 1888, and Castle, Neihart, Barker, and Champion. The B.M.U. was a citadel of labor strength, extending support to camps hundreds of miles away. When violence and federal repression struck the Coeur d' Alene district of northern Idaho, the Butte Miners' Union sent in thousands of dollars in support and then mortgaged its buildings to send more.[49]

The basis of the union's strength lay not only in numbers but also in its friendly relationship with management. As Richard Peterson notes in his comparative study, *The Bonanza Kings*, mineowners and managers who worked their way up through the ranks and who harbored political ambitions tended to treat their workers far more benevolently than did those who came from the ranks of business or from the "outside." This was true of James Fair and John Mackay of the Comstock, of Dennis Sheedy and Thomas Walsh of Colorado; and it was certainly true of George Hearst, Marcus Daly, W. A. Clark, and F. A. Heinze of Butte. In many industries, rags-to-riches owner-managers tended to lose empathy with their "men"; but in the egalitarian metal mining industry, they tended to keep it.[50]

Both Daly and Hearst were veteran miners who looked and acted the part. Both enjoyed bumming around with "the men." At both the Homestake Mine in the Black Hills and at Butte-Anaconda, the Hearst-Haggin-Tevis syndicate ungrudgingly paid the prevailing $3.50 daily wage and pioneered in such benign concepts as company hospitals, health plans, free kindergartens, and public libraries. Even after the Hearst Estate's divestiture of Anaconda, George Hearst's wife Phoebe built a "free library" at Anaconda, eventually turning it over to the city in 1904. Butte's major resident managers—Daly, Clark, Heinze, Thomas Couch of the Boston and Montana, and William Hall of the Alice—all enjoyed a peculiar, dual sort of status. In a seemingly contradictory way, their employees easily identified with them as fellow workers who had "made it," and yet also deferred to them as a privileged managerial and wealthy class. The managers relished this role, showering such benefits on their fiefs as choice vein leases for loyal workers, free turkeys at Christmas; college educations for promising children of the poor, small brick homes for the families of workers killed in accidents. This kind of industrial feudalism translated naturally into political feudalism as well. Yet, until "outsiders" gained control of the big Butte firms at the turn of the century, it kept the peace surprisingly well.[51]

The prosperous and fast-growing Butte Miners' Union demonstrated its sway in 1893 by taking the lead in creation of a new region-wide brotherhood of unions, the Western Federation of Miners. On 15 May 1893, forty delegates from fifteen regional unions, representing most of the mining states of the West, met at Butte to hammer out a larger organization which would represent their interests. Worried especially by the turmoil in Idaho, they adopted a rather sober platform, calling for an eight-hour workday, extolling labor-management harmony, and denouncing such oppressive tactics as company stores and the uses of child and convict labor and Pinkerton detectives to pry into union affairs. Most vigorously, the resolutions demanded that Congress resume the "unlimited" coinage of silver dollars and denounced the "damnable action of the gold bugs of Wall Street . . . in reducing silver to a commodity thereby destroying the chief industries of our silver states and robbing the people of their lawful money."[52]

The Butte Miners' Union became Local Number One of the newborn Western Federation of Miners. John Gilligan of Butte served as its first president, and the Butte local dominated the W.F.M. during its first, troubled years. Before long, however, the Butte moderates lost control of the union to more radically inclined leaders like Ed Boyce and "Big Bill" Haywood. The Western Federation of Miners soon earned a reputation for radicalism and violence, especially in Idaho and Colorado. It would one day participate in the founding of America's most renowned radical union, the Industrial Workers of the World.

But in the state of its birth, the W.F.M. and its main local, the Butte Miners' Union, continued to live in general harmony with management. By 1895, the B.M.U. and its affiliates had succeeded in forming a statewide labor assembly, the State Trades and Labor Council, to represent their interests. This outfit, like its main sponsor, the B.M.U., consistently joined the mineowners and the general business community in rallying support for Montana's sagging silver industry and for other mutual concerns.[53] Butte's peculiar labor-management harmony thus persisted through the 1890s. As we shall see, though, it would not long survive the great industrial consolidations which would come with the turn of the century.

5. Politics: The Clark-Daly Feud

As big-time mining and the city of Butte began to dominate Montana's economy, one of the most blatant and bizarre political struggles in United States history ensued. The Clark-Daly feud was a bitterly personal affair, fought crassly and ruthlessly. In essence, it was a baronial contest. Both Clark and Daly unquestioningly assumed that their economic powers conferred upon them political powers to match. For a dozen years from 1888 until the turn of the century, their onslaughts, conniving, and bribing both unsettled and debauched the political life of the newborn state of Montana. In the end their feud turned up, like a crying orphan, on the doorstep of the United States Senate, where it drew national bewilderment and revulsion. Remote and little-known Montana gained in all of this an unenviable reputation as a political and economic pawn—bought, sold, and sullied by mining wealth.

The barons of Butte relished their hard-won wealth and prestige. Each, having risen from poverty to vast riches, could boast of being a truly self-made man. And each loved to flaunt his wealth in the grand manner of gilded age millionaires. Aside from being hard-nosed mining millionaires, however, the two men were a study in contrasts. Approaching fifty by the late 1880s, Marcus Daly still bore the clear imprint of his Irish peasant and mining frontier background. Wealth and success seemingly changed him little, if at all. Unassuming, awkward in speech and expression, quick to love and to hate, he remained a man of the earth, a man of simple tastes and emotions. Daly loved the flourishes which great wealth brought to him: showering money upon the Democratic Party and upon Irish causes, consorting with such statesmen from the Emerald Isle as Michael Davitt and

Charles Parnell and millionaires like Jim Hill and J. B. Haggin. His private rail car, the "Hattie," was rumored to be the finest in the land; and Mark Daly beamed when his fellow "industrial statesmen," such as Hill, pulled their cars off the mainline to visit his "place." Yet, despite all that, what he liked best was his simple friendship-lordship status at Butte-Anaconda. He could often be found perched on a curbstone, swapping yarns with his Irish cronies, eating in a mess hall with his men, or sharing a bare hotel room with the lowliest mucker from his mines. To the end, he remained a devout Roman Catholic and a devoted husband and father to his wife and four children.[1]

Daly doted on the bustling little city of Anaconda, his fiefdom and his pride and joy. Early each morning, after breakfasting on coffee and beefsteak, he would ride to work behind a team of handsome black horses from his tree-lined Sixth Avenue estate to the plant, waving to friends and casting a proud eye upon the fruits of his labor. His impressive Montana Hotel, completed at Anaconda in 1888, formed the nucleus of the city's social and business life. Daly often dined there in regal isolation, in a room that could seat 500. He regularly held court in the hotel's magnificent Victorian bar, with its beautiful inlaid head of the racehorse Tammany on the floor. Anyone who stepped on this head had to buy drinks for the house.[2]

During his later years, Marcus Daly spent more and more time at his impressive Bitter Root Stock Farm in far western Montana. The 20,000-acre farm with its handsome mansion was a real showplace; Daly showered much of his attention upon it and upon the nearby town of Hamilton. Like his partners Haggin and Hearst, Daly loved horses. With elaborate stables at his Bitter Root ranch and large race-tracks at Butte and Anaconda, he ran one of the world's greatest racing enterprises. His favorite horse, Tammany, won the Eclipse stakes at 60–1 odds in its first race; and in fourteen starts the great horse finished first eight times. Other famous Daly horses included Ogden, which scored a sensation by winning the 1896 Futurity at Sheepshead Bay, and Hamburg, which won $75,000 in 1898. Butte and Anaconda folks loved Marcus Daly and his horses, especially when he gave his men a day off for the races, and they loved to tell stories of his prodigality. On one occasion, he casually shrugged off the loss of $40,000 when he carelessly left a winning ticket in a work suit which burned up in a fire. Following Daly's death, his estate sold 369 horses for $728,755 in a series of auctions in 1901, the greatest racing stock sales America had ever seen.[3]

One of the striking oddities of the feud was the marriage of Clark's brother J. Ross to the sister of Daly's wife. Beyond this, they had little else in common. Unlike Daly, William Andrews Clark strived to place his commonplace background far behind him. He openly pined for status, dressed and behaved like a refined gentleman, and plotted incessantly for high political office. Always, he strove to show the world that he had truly arrived, that he was in fact one of America's wealthiest, most cultured, and most respected statesmen. In this longing for political prominence, Clark resembled such other successful mining kings as George Hearst of California, James Fair of the Comstock, and Nathaniel Hill of Colorado.

Fifty years old in 1889, Clark ranked by now as one of America's most astute and wealthy businessmen. The Clark empire was growing at a mighty pace. In addition to mines, mills, and smelters at Butte, it comprised banks, retail stores, newspapers, coal mines, water, electrical and street railway utilities, and large lumber holdings in the Big Blackfoot and Missoula valleys. Clark made the greatest of all his acquisitions during these years when, after noticing samples from Arizona's remote United Verde Mine at the 1884 New Orleans Exposition, he shrewdly saw that these complex base ores held lucrative and retrievable quantities of gold, silver, and copper. Quickly, he purchased 70 percent of the United Verde, and eventually he acquired almost total ownership. Clark poured millions into the mining town of Jerome, Arizona, into his nearby smelter town of Clarkdale, and into a winding, twenty-six-mile railroad linking the complex to the Santa Fe Railroad. United Verde, a difficult, water-starved and costly operation, grew into a major mining center which employed nearly 1,500 workers. Clark devoted much of his attention to it, and in return the "Verde" yielded him untold riches. At its peak, the great mine produced annual profits of $10,000,000, and its owner reportedly once refused a purchase offer of $100,000,000 for it.[4]

Unlike Daly, W. A. Clark seemingly devoted little of his time and attention to family matters. As millions piled upon millions, he took to shipping wife Kate and the children off to Europe, where he joined them for long visits during the winters. Usually, when they returned to America he would locate them in New York or California. He seemed, in his private as in his public life, a cold and distant man, little given to warm, personal relationships. As the years progressed, his cultural interests grew, and he immersed himself in art collecting. Clark was much caught up in the *fin de siècle* mood of French cultural "depravity," and according at least to reports, he grew increasingly fond of sumptuous living and the attentions of the opposite sex.[5]

But his real love was public adulation, which he earned through his genius and hard work as a businessman, and which he lusted for as an aspiring politician. Cultural and civic distinction would symbolize his triumph over adversity, would show polite eastern society that he was more than a crass and ill-mannered mining magnate. In 1876, Clark served as Montana Territory's featured orator at the Philadelphia Centennial Exposition. His presentation is still valuable today for its close insights into the state of the commonwealth. When the Nez Perce Indians fled through southwestern Montana on their epic retreat of 1877, he won acclaim for his hard-riding and well-publicized campaign to raise militia forces in the Butte–Deer Lodge area. Fortunately for all concerned, Clark and his troops never saw action against the Indians. Increasing wealth and prestige brought more laurels his way. By the time he reached age forty-five in 1884, he had served as Grand Master of the Montana Masonic Lodge, territorial commissioner to the 1884 New Orleans Exposition, and in the same year, president of Montana's second constitutional convention, which failed like its predecessor to achieve statehood.[6]

It was William A. Clark's pursuit of high political office that stirred his feud with Marcus Daly into an open conflagration. Just how, why, and when their enmity really began will remain forever shrouded in legend. Perhaps, given the willfulness of two such big figures in such a small arena, it was simply inevitable. Some of the old accounts of the feud's inception can easily be dismissed, for instance George Hearst's recollection that Daly had initially invited Clark to join him in the Anaconda venture and that he had then turned him aside in favor of Hearst and his California partners. This account is unsupported by other evidence, and in fact, Clark later stated categorically: "I was never directly or indirectly interested in any business deal with him. I always mistrusted him, as I do now."[7]

One story, that of Ben E. Stack, traces the feud back to Daly's arrival at Butte in 1876–77. According to Stack, a friend of Daly who had a cabin near the Alice Mine, W. A. Clark attempted to cross Daly in his purchase of the Alice for the Walker brothers, since he wished to acquire it himself. The wily little man allegedly advised the mine's owner, Rolla Butcher, that Daly was an imposter and even refused to honor his draft at the bank, forcing Daly to issue an order for the funds via Wells Fargo to Salt Lake City. Stack's account has two major weaknesses. On the one hand, it is vintage "oral history," subject to fabrication and unsupported by hard evidence. On the other, it fails to dovetail with the fact that Daly made part of the original purchase of the Alice lode from the Clark and Larabie Bank directly, which hardly indicates an obstructionist attitude on the part of Clark.[8]

Probably the most widely believed tale of the battle's origin involves Daly's purchase of land and water rights along Warm Springs Creek for the site of his smelter complex in the early 1880s. Legend has it that, when banker Clark learned of the syndicate's plans, he bought up the properties there for $80,000—nearly three times what Daly had offered the owners—and then forced the syndicate to pay a cool $150,000 for them. Admittedly, such a ploy seems consistent with the Clark style; and Marcus Daly's daughter, among others, believed it to be accurate. It may be, but a search by K. Ross Toole among the records for claims belonging to Clark in this vicinity failed to turn up any evidence to that effect. John Branagan, who knew Daly and his business well, flatly denied the whole story.[9]

A lesser known but somewhat plausible explanation for the feud's beginning traces it to a disparaging remark about Daly's favorite partner, the Turkish-American James Ben Ali Haggin. Supposedly, when Clark was invited only belatedly, as an afterthought, to a miners' meeting at which Haggin presided, he tartly declined with the remark that he had "no wish to meet with a member of the Ethiopian race." Another version simply has Clark disparaging the swarthy Haggin as a "nigger." According to M. G. O'Malley, who knew Daly and collected Butte lore for years, the Irishman once told him how he owed Haggin everything for his support when the other California partners doubted him. Daly reportedly said: "It was a Clark-Haggin feud. I couldn't go back on Haggin. He was too loyal to me." Years later, Montana Senator T. C. Power once commented to Haggin about Clark's election to the U.S. Senate: "He got there." Haggin pointedly replied: "Not while I was interested in Montana."[10] It may thus be that Marcus Daly inherited the feud from his friend Haggin. If so, he lost little time in making it his own.

Regardless of how the Clark-Daly hatred began, one thing is certain: the feud flared into an open and public battle in the election of 1888. In this election campaign, Montana's last as a territory, the animosity between the two mining barons first appeared as a visible pollutant in the political mainstream. During its long gestation period as a territory (1864–89), Montana had evolved in a fashion rather typical of the territories of the Intermountain West. Created during the Civil War, Montana was wracked in its early years by partisan turbulence—"chaotic factionalism," as historian Kenneth Owens has aptly phrased it. The passing years, however, brought a measure of economic and political maturity. By the prosperous 1880s, the territory stood on the threshold of statehood, a fast-growing commonwealth whose economy rested solidly on booming livestock and industrial mining industries.[11]

The mining cities of Butte-Anaconda and Helena clearly dominated the economic and political life of Montana Territory. In 1890 Butte housed 31.2 percent of Montana's population; Anaconda held 9.5 percent, and the capital city of Helena had another 33 percent. The mining cities' thousands of miners and skilled workmen, heavily unionized and heavily comprised of Irish Catholics, formed the largest, most cohesive, and most potent voting bloc in the territory. Here as elsewhere, this Irish labor element leaned heavily toward the Democratic Party, the party which had held sway over Montana Territory since the year of its creation. The territory's major capitalists also gravitated toward the majority Democratic faith. Montana's quartet of leading businessmen—the "Big Four" as they were popularly known—proudly stood at the helm of the party: Clark and Daly of Butte, and silver king Samuel T. Hauser and transportation magnate C. A. Broadwater, both of Helena. Everyone knew that the "Big Four" called the shots in faraway Montana.[12]

Thus in 1888, when the Democratic convention nominated W. A. Clark for the highest elective office in the territory, delegate to Congress, few doubted that he would coast to an easy victory. Clark evidently had little desire for the office at first, preferring to wait for one of the coveted seats in the U.S. Senate that statehood would soon bring. He reportedly accepted the unanimous nomination only after the two prestigious former Democratic delegates, Martin Maginnis and Joseph K. Toole, had declined to accept it.[13] Certainly, few took seriously the challenge of his little-known Republican opponent, Helena lawyer Thomas H. Carter. Spindly and rather awkward looking with his bizarre chin whiskers, Tom Carter seemingly had only one asset—Irish immigrant parents. That lone advantage would surely do him little good against Clark and the Democrats.[14]

The 1888 campaign in Montana mirrored national themes quite accurately. Clark followed the lead of Democratic President Grover Cleveland in calling for a lower tariff. Like GOP presidential aspirant Benjamin Harrison, whose son ranched near Helena, Carter voiced the Republican high-tariff position, a strategy that won him plaudits among protection-minded stockmen. Otherwise, Clark seemed quite secure. Thousands of laborites turned out for his rallies and cheered Democratic Chinese-baiting promises to "keep the Mongolian race from our shores" and to "give the poor, struggling white woman the washing and daily housework which will enable her to earn an honest livelihood."[15]

Right up to the end of the campaign, Democratic victory seemed assured. Behind the scenes, however, Marcus Daly and his allies secretly plotted Clark's defeat. Why? Because Daly's source of cheap lumber, the Montana Improvement Company, faced severe difficulties with the Democratic administration of Grover Cleveland. As noted earlier, the Montana Improvement Company, like numerous other freewheeling lumber outfits of the West, brazenly logged the often unsurveyed public timberlands. Cleveland's Interior Secretary, Lucius Q. C. Lamar, and Land Commissioner William A. J. Sparks, in contrast to their predecessors, took strong exception to such practices and instituted federal suits against the culprits. These suits loomed in the courts by 1888; and Daly's Missoula lumbermen partners, Andrew Hammond and E. L. Bonner, pressured him to take political action. It seemed likely that Republican Benjamin Harrison would win the national election. Since Cleveland's administration had proven to be impossible, and since the Republicans seemed more permissive with the public lands, it appeared logical to dump Clark and elect Carter as the Republican emissary to a Republican administration.[16]

Marcus Daly quietly agreed, late in the campaign, to join his cohorts in the dump-Clark maneuver. Even as 1,000 of his Anaconda smeltermen traveled to Butte to join in a Clark rally, the Irishman put the finishing touches on his clandestine campaign. On election day, 6 November 1888, his shift bosses and political operatives glibly pulled off their coup. Employees of the Anaconda and of the Montana Improvement Company turned in their thousands of ballots with Carter's name pasted over Clark's. The Australian secret ballot had not yet been adopted in Montana, and this allowed shift bosses to inspect the ballots and check their compliance. Even in Clark's home precinct, gangs of Daly men hit the polls as repeaters. The final vote count showed the result, with Carter beating Clark by a margin of 22,486 to 17,360 and carrying fourteen of the territory's sixteen counties. Amazingly, the Anaconda-Democratic bastions of Silver Bow and Deer Lodge counties, along with Missoula, joined Republican eastern Montana in achieving this result.[17]

The Republicans and Daly Democrats disingenuously crowed that, as the GOP *Butte Daily Inter Mountain* put it, "The Issues Settled It." In other words, they maintained that Clark's ties to sagging Grover Cleveland and his low-tariff policy had dragged him down to defeat. This was partially true, for the rural-agricultural areas overwhelmingly favored the protectionist stand of the Republicans. Still, Daly's subterfuge undoubtedly figured largely in Clark's loss. Daly himself always denied coercing his men. They usually followed his lead without being coerced. He did admit telling them how he felt and allowed that he "took a negative part in it." Most observers had no doubts.

The Clark-owned *Butte Miner* attributed his loss to "the deepest kind of treachery among the supposed friends of Mr. Clark," and the sympathetic *Helena Independent* agreed that he was "wounded in the house of his friends." Even the Democratic *Great Falls Tribune* clucked at Daly and his allies: "The perfidy of these men will not soon be forgotten."[18]

Hardly a naive soul, William Andrews Clark clearly understood what had happened. "The conspiracy was a gigantic one," he wrote to Martin Maginnis, "well planned, and well carried out, even though it did involve the violation of some of the most sacred confidences. . . . However as you suggest the day of retribution may come when treason may be considered odious." Indeed, the vain and intense mining baron would never forgive or forget this affront. A dozen years later, he railed before the United States Senate about "the treason of Mr. Daly" and the "envious and diabolical desire on his part to forever destroy my political influence in the Territory."[19] The "War of the Copper Kings" had begun.

Clark's 1888 defeat had many ramifications. For the victor, Congressman-elect Thomas Carter, the election marked the beginning of a prominent public career. A stout Republican and a staunch, pro-corporate conservative, Carter rose rapidly in state and national circles. He held the favor of Daly and his associates by attempting, without complete success, to use his influence to quash the timber suits. At the national level, he benefitted from a close and enduring friendship with President Benjamin Harrison. When Carter lost his House seat in the 1890 Democratic landslide, Harrison appointed him Commissioner of the U.S. Land Office, where his loose controls made him a favorite out West. In 1892, Harrison made Carter his campaign manager—a tribute to his trust—and appointed him chairman of the GOP National Committee. Eventually, Carter went on to serve two terms in the U.S. Senate, 1895–1901 and 1905–11. He played a major role in the formation of the postal savings system, in the creation of Glacier National Park, and in advocating tariff protectionism and opposing the creation of national forests. "Corkscrew Tom" Carter was a shrewd, tough, and conniving politician who survived many a battle by adept maneuvering and by consistently allying himself with wealth and power.[20]

As for Daly and Clark, politics would never again be tranquil after 1888. The "Big Four" now headed their separate ways, and from here on the dominant theme in Montana politics would be the Clark-Daly rivalry. Early in 1889, Daly shared his frustration with Sam Hauser, lamenting that "to tell you the truth I am so disappointed and so disgusted that I have now quit politics for good."[21] This, of course, was sheer poppycock. The baron of Anaconda actually moved deeper into political involvement. He soon agreed to take over the chairmanship of the Montana Democratic Party and to try putting back together the pieces he had scrambled only months earlier.

Marcus Daly's first big problem lay in trying to bring his Missoula lumber associates back into the Democratic fold. Andrew Hammond and his minions, C. H. McLeod, E. L. Bonner, and R. A. Eddy, now felt with astute logic that their interests led instead into the Republican Party, which controlled federal land policy and the fate of the lumber suits. When they rebuffed Daly's Democratic overtures, he lost his legendary temper and showed them the mailed fist. The "White Czar," as the Missoulians called him, angrily canceled Anaconda's contracts with Hammond's Big Blackfoot Milling Company, heir to the old Montana Improvement Company, and reportedly vowed that he would "make the grass grow on the streets of Missoula."

Daly proceeded to declare war on several fronts. He financed his crony D. J. Hennessy to open a large commercial store challenging the Hammond crowd's Missoula Mercantile chain, announced plans to form a major bank in Missoula, and threatened to extend his Butte, Anaconda, and Pacific Railroad to Hamilton, which might then compete with Missoula for hegemony over the Bitterroot country. The Hammond organization managed, however, to protect its turf. In the local elections of October 1889, it swept Missoula County for the GOP, and soon Daly prudently abandoned his war plans. Eventually, the Anaconda and Missoula's lumber interests patched up their quarrel; and as earlier described, Daly finally bought out the Big Blackfoot Milling Company in 1898.[22]

The "White Czar's" main political attention focused, not on the Missoulians, but on W. A. Clark, who made no secret of his burning lust for revenge. Since Clark owned a major newspaper, the *Butte Miner*, Daly set out to build a better one to serve as his mouthpiece. Early in 1889 he chanced to meet John H. Durston, former owner-editor of one of New York's oldest papers, the *Syracuse Standard*. Durston, a courtly and dignified man, held a doctorate in philology from Heidelberg University and had been chairman of the Modern Languages Department at Syracuse University. When Daly first approached him about managing a local daily paper, Durston demurred, fearing that Anaconda lacked a sufficient population base to support it. But the Irishman's enthusiastic talk of a $100,000 investment and tapping the larger Butte–western Montana market finally won him over.

Durston bought an elaborate plant and brought in excellent journalists like C. H. Eggleston and Arthur L. Stone; and on 4 September 1889, the first issue of the *Anaconda Standard* rolled off the presses, announcing itself to be a Democratic daily, "the vigorous child of a wide-awake town."[23] The *Standard* served as a highly effective voice for Daly and Anaconda, and it grew up to become one of the Northwest's better-known newspapers. On the negative side, though, the appearance of the *Standard* signaled an ominous fact that few recognized at the time: mining money was seeping into and beginning to contaminate the workings of the free press.

While Daly expanded his political operations, William A. Clark continued to plot his quest for public office. Clark had presided at the unsuccessful Montana Constitutional Convention of 1884. In mid-1889 he, along with Daly, served as delegate to yet another convention, which this time wrote the constitution whose ratification and acceptance by Congress brought statehood in November. Clark once again won election as president of the convention, and once again he won praise for his leadership. Applauding "those brave pioneers who have come out here and have made the wilderness blossom as the rose," he led a coalition of mineowners and their lawyer-associates who wrote a highly favorable "net proceeds" form of mine taxation into the heart of the new state's organic law. This provision, which paralleled the laws of other western mining states, offered mineowners a bonanza by taxing only those ores actually removed, thus exempting those remaining as real property in the ground. Contrary to some charges, the mineowners apparently did not really have to conspire or coerce the convention in order to gain this tax advantage. Rather, most delegates seemed willing to accept it as a necessary incentive to building the state's key industry.[24]

In a lighter moment, Clark demonstrated a rarely seen sense of humor while boosting Butte for the state capital and poking fun at those who decried its smoke problem:

> . . . I must say that the ladies are very fond of this smoky city, as it is sometimes called, because there is just enough arsenic there to give them a beautiful complexion, and that is the reason the ladies of Butte are renowned wherever they go for their beautiful complexions. (Laughter) . . . . I say it would be a great deal better for other cities in the territory if they had more smoke and less diptheria [sic] and other diseases. It has been believed by all the physicians of Butte that the smoke that sometimes prevails there is a disinfectant, and destroys the microbes that constitute the germs of disease.[25]

With statehood in November 1889, of course, came representation for Montana in the U.S. Senate. After his galling defeat in the congressional race of 1888, Clark was now more than ever determined to secure one of these two Senate seats. By joining the Senate "Millionaire's Club," as it was then popularly known, the Iowa farm boy–Montana mining king could take his rightful place on the national stage alongside such millionaire senators as Nelson Aldrich of Rhode Island and George Hearst of California. Prior to 1913, when the seventeenth amendment to the Constitution took effect and provided for popular election, the state legislatures chose U.S. Senators. Clark thus had to deal with the Montana legislature to reach his goal. Seldom, if ever, has anyone dealt with a legislature in quite the manner that W. A. Clark did with this one.

In a special election of 1 October 1889, Montana not only ratified its state constitution; it also chose its first state legislature and an entire slate of state officials. An air of excitement surrounded the campaign. Rumor had it that the "Big Four" were pouring $300,000 into the contest in an effort to gain control of the state government and of the two Senate seats. Admittedly, this seems a gross exaggeration, but investments did run high. Both the Republican and the Democratic national committees poured money into local legislative races, for the new senators from Montana and the other newborn Northwest states could vitally affect the narrow partisan balance in the U.S. Senate. (The four Northwestern "Omnibus States" admitted to the Union in 1889 were Montana, Washington, North Dakota, and South Dakota.) In the end, a strong Republican trend nearly swept Democratic Montana from its traditional moorings. Republican Thomas Carter held onto his hard-won seat in the House of Representatives as Montana's lone member, and Democrat Joseph K. Toole only narrowly won the governor's chair. More to the point, the legislature deadlocked. The state senate paired eight Democrats against eight Republicans, with the GOP lieutenant governor holding the tie-breaking vote. Membership in the state house of representatives stood at twenty-five from each party, with a critical five seats disputed.[26]

Montana was not the only state to experience legislative deadlock during these politically unsettled and closely competitive times. A spate of deadlocks occurred during the late 1880s and early 1890s. Colorado boasted two assemblies, each with its own speaker, in 1891; and the New Jersey Supreme Court had to resolve a similar episode in 1894.[27] The Montana impasse of 1889–90 loomed especially large, however, for it hamstrung the state's very first legislature and tied up its first two senatorial appointments, thus launching the state erratically upon the path of self-government.

The real problem lay in five disputed house seats from Silver Bow

County, which each party claimed as its own. Whichever party could gain these five seats would control not only the house of representatives, but also the majority in the joint balloting to elect the U.S. senators. According to the Republicans, the large Democratic majority posted at Precinct 34 east of Butte, the voting site for laborers working on the Northern Pacific's Homestake Tunnel, had been garnered by improper campaigning and recording methods and thus must be rejected. If the ballots of Precinct 34 were discarded, the five contested seats would go Republican. If not, they would go Democratic. In the absence of a firm law stating precisely how legislators should be certified, each party showed up in Helena certifying and protecting its five contested representatives from Silver Bow County.[28]

An incredible farce ensued. The house of representatives split in half, with each party meeting separately and sheltering its five disputed members. Meanwhile in the senate, the Democrats refused at first to attend or to vote, their purpose being to keep the Republicans from forming a quorum and then meeting with the house to elect the U.S. senators. When the majority Republicans secured arrest warrants to force the Democrats to attend, several of them fled the state to avoid capture. One of the errant lawmakers, William Becker, was caught at Glendive on Montana's eastern border and brought back to Helena. Released on the promise that he would stay put, he promptly fled to Idaho, where the law could not reach him. From 23 November 1889 until 20 February 1890, the legislature remained deadlocked. Each separate house enacted laws, but the senate failed to pass any of them. So Montana's first legislature ended as it had begun, in deadlock, and passed no laws at all.

One should not conclude that such silliness was confined solely to Montana. U.S. senators of each party in Washington were carefully advising their brethren in the Montana legislature what to do, for they desperately needed the two Senate votes that were at stake. Finally the legislators of each party met separately in joint session, and each party chose its own two U.S. senators. The Democrats chose two of their most prominent men: W. A. Clark and Martin Maginnis. The Republicans did the same, selecting the aging vigilante hero and party stalwart Wilbur Fisk Sanders and the wealthy Fort Benton-Helena tycoon T. C. Power. Of course, this charade simply removed the contest from Montana's ruptured legislature and transferred it to the U.S. Senate, where the narrow majority of Republicans seated their fellows from the Treasure State and sent the Democrats home.[29] For Clark, who sat watching in the gallery as the Senate rejected him, it represented a second bitter blow, coming so soon after the 1888 loss. Even Clark admitted that Daly had had nothing especially to do with this Senate defeat, but it nevertheless served to rub salt in the wound of his damaged pride.

For the newly created state of Montana, and for much of the Mountain and Plains West, the 1890s would prove to be a time of economic troubles, frenzied politics, and scrambled party lines. Free-wheeling mining barons openly manipulated state government and boasted of their dominance over the Montana political economy. At the same time the most powerful third-party movement in modern United States history, Populism, swept into the region, leavening and vastly complicating its politics. The combined forces of mining manipulation and Populism made this the most turbulent period in Montana's political history, a decade of party irregularity and radical ideology which would cast a long shadow into the future.

The People's or Populist party sprang up in the early 1890s, primarily in response to agricultural unrest. Its roots reached back to the inflationist ideas of the old Greenback party, and more directly to the Farmers' Alliances which had flourished in the South and Midwest as agrarian cooperative movements during the 1880s. The party itself took shape beginning with a Cincinnati organizational meeting in 1891 and then with a full-fledged nominating convention at Omaha in July 1892. In its famous Omaha Platform of 1892, the Populist party aimed at a farmer-labor alliance with a remarkably forward-looking, even radical, agenda of reform. It called for an immediate inflation of the currency to counter the deadening deflationary trend which was afflicting farmers; a government takeover of rails, telephone, and telegraph facilities; a national subtreasury system through which farmers could secure credit upon their stored crops; and such dramatic proposals as a graduated income tax and the direct election of U.S. senators.[30]

With a respectable showing in the 1892 elections, the Populist party grew rapidly throughout the South, the Midwest, and the Far West in a wave of reaction against economic exploitation by the eastern financial centers. The main centers of Populist strength lay in the agrarian heartland of the nation, but the movement also had great appeal to the mining-labor interests of the Intermountain region because of its call for the free coinage of silver dollars as a means of inflating the currency. Thus as the late historian Thomas Clinch so aptly demonstrated, Populism took immediate hold in Montana, not so much among the state's small scattering of farmers as among its armies of mining investors and workers. Populist demands for the "free and unlimited" coinage of silver dollars at a ratio of 16 to 1 with gold dollars and its cry for the revocation of the Northern Pacific's huge and unpopular land grant rallied together a large and seemingly incongruous following of unionists, capitalists, reformers, and farmers.[31]

In short, Populism and "free silver," which really meant government subsidies for the state's key industry, quickly loomed up like a political hurricane, blowing down both class and party barriers and creating a regional political movement which seemingly nothing could withstand. The Montana Populist party was formed at a January 1892 convention in Anaconda which 230 delegates attended. By the following June, when the party held its nominating convention at its Butte headquarters, the unions and the burning issue of silver held sway. Avoiding a policy of "fusion"—joining forces with the majority Democrats—the Montana party maintained its independence during the 1892 campaign.

Then came the hard times and mass unemployment of the 1893 Panic, which brought thousands of recruits to the Populist cause. The Cleveland administration's demonetization of silver in 1893 struck the region like a thunderbolt, wreaking havoc upon the centers of silver mining (see pp. 54–56). This "criminal" demonetization of silver became the central issue of the Mountain West, raising the fortunes of the pro-silver Populist party, bending the Democratic party toward an alliance with the Populists, and splitting the GOP into a conservative gold faction and a more liberal, pro-Populist silver faction. Party regularity crumbled away and unrest mounted.[32]

The twin forces of Populism and the Clark-Daly feud commingled in the 1892 campaign to scramble political lines in Montana. Clark sought to secure control of the Democratic party in 1892 in order to insure his election by the legislature to the U.S. Senate. Meanwhile, Marcus Daly focused upon the one goal which truly touched his heart: making his pet town of Anaconda the state capital. The Constitutional Convention of 1889 had ducked this hot issue of locating the permanent state capital, leaving it for the people to decide in a later election. Democratic party complications had actually surfaced a year earlier, in 1891, when Clark had scored a coup against Daly by denying him control of the Butte water franchise. Daly badly needed this concession in order to insure his water supply; and when Clark checked him by maneuvering the city council, Daly declared war on the Democratic councilmen who had betrayed him. This issue came to a head in the mayoral contest of 1892. When the pro-Clark, pro-city council element gained control of the Democratic slate, Marcus Daly quietly deserted the party—as he had back in 1888—and joined forces with Lee Mantle and the Republicans.[33]

Lee Mantle was a man to take seriously. Approaching age forty in 1892, the short, stocky and handsome English immigrant was a successful businessman-politician and a spell-binding orator. A veteran of Butte's city government and of the territorial legislature, he played a key role in the Montana Republican party. His paper, the *Butte Daily Inter Mountain*, provided him a major voice in public affairs. His alliance with Daly in the "Dirty Water Campaign" of 1892, which leveled charges of dereliction against the city government and its water franchise, paved the way for Lee Mantle to become mayor of Montana's largest city. Daly's backstage alliance with the Republicans staggered the Democratic party, which thereby lost a number of important offices, including some Silver Bow County seats in the legislature. The "White Czar" was not particularly happy about having to make medicine with the Republicans. Reportedly, when Mantle crowed publicly about his mayoral victory, Daly dampened his enthusiasm by remarking that he "would have elected a yellow dog had the Republicans named one that year."[34]

Marcus Daly's intrigues with the Republicans, which would resurface in the 1893 legislature, seriously complicated an already tangled election outcome in November 1892. With the Daly faction voting Republican, and with the Populists stealing their thunder on the silver issue, the majority Democrats took a beating in Montana. The Treasure State voted against the winning Democratic presidential candidate, Grover Cleveland, and the Democrats lost their grip on the governor's chair and on the state's lone congressional seat. Barely holding control of the state senate through holdovers, the Democrats fell into a 26–26 deadlock in the house of representatives, which left the three Populist members holding the balance in that body. Clark Democrats could point to Daly as the spoiler, but he too suffered disappointment. Daly's bid to make Anaconda the capital fell short of victory, with Helena finishing in the lead and Anaconda leading the pack of contenders, which also included Boulder, Bozeman, Butte, Deer Lodge, and Great Falls. Since no city won a majority of the popular vote, a runoff election was scheduled for 1894.[35]

With Daly attempting to drum up support for Anaconda in the next election, and with Clark feverishly trying to put together a coalition behind his U.S. Senate candidacy, the 1893 legislature took on the appearance of a bazaar. Mining money and intrigue now began to appear openly in the lawmaking arenas. In order to win command of

Lee Mantle, from *Just for Fun: Cartoons and Caricatures of Men in Montana* (1907)
(courtesy of Eric Myhre)

the house of representatives, the Democrats had to coalesce with the three Populist members, and this meant granting them strong concessions. Two Populists from Butte, Thomas Matthews and Absalom Bray, were conceded the offices of house speaker and speaker pro tem. As the lawmakers debated the location of state colleges and other new public institutions, the mining kings and their agents worked behind the scenes to win support for their goals. Advocates of Helena and Great Falls, led by the statesmanlike future U.S. Senator Paris Gibson, generally pleaded responsibly for one central campus to serve the entire, sparsely populated state. But the Anaconda crowd, according to widely believed reports, pressed for a fragmented system in order to trade their support of other cities as college sites in return for reciprocal support of Anaconda for capital. Some Helena supporters probably played the same game. Not surprisingly, the logrollers won this high-stakes contest, for the lawmakers prodigally scattered the new state's public institutions. They conferred campuses upon Missoula, Butte, Bozeman, and Dillon; an orphanage upon Boulder; a reform school upon Miles City; and a planned second state prison upon Billings.[36] Future generations would pay dearly for this shortsighted dispersal of state institutions.

The key issue of the 1893 session was once again, as in the first state legislature of 1889–90, the election of a U.S. Senator. Senator Wilbur Fisk Sanders, the Republican incumbent, had drawn the short, three-year term in 1890 and now stood for reelection. At first, Sanders had the support of the GOP caucus. Unflinchingly tough, unbending, and conservative, Wilbur Sanders was a legend in his own time—the vigilante hero of the 1860s, the "Mephistopheles of Montana Politics," the grand old man of the Grand Old Party. The Democrats, who with Populist support commanded a majority in the joint session, should have been able to unseat Sanders. Once again, the problem hinged on the Clark-Daly feud. When the Democratic caucus endorsed W. A. Clark for Senator, the eight Daly Democrats jumped the traces and supported instead ex-Congressman William Wirt Dixon, Daly's chief attorney.[37]

Federal law required that state legislatures ballot every day until a senator was chosen. As the session dragged on, an endless, daily series of ballots for senator ensued. Republican Sanders at first led Democrat Clark by a narrow margin, while Dixon and other marginal candidates kept either of the major contenders from winning a majority of the legislative vote. This went on from 11 January until 10 February, when the Republican caucus saw the futility of running Sanders any longer and dumped him in favor of Lee Mantle, who seemingly had the ability to woo Daly Democratic votes. But the Daly Democrats continued to support Dixon, and the stalemated balloting ground on. Probably with tongues in cheek, the Daly leaders offered to settle for a compromise Democrat if Clark would step aside, but the Clark supporters angrily refused to budge. Clearly, if Clark were to win, he must reach out for Republican votes.[38]

Behind the ballots, a frenzied battle unfolded as the Clark and Daly organizations vied for the loyalties of wavering legislators. There can be little doubt of the truth of rumors that Clark agents beat the bushes with bribe money for the support of Republican legislators, or that Daly's men just as avidly sought to buy them back. Beyond a doubt, Daly used Pinkerton detectives to dig up dirt and evidence. Some of the lawmakers behaved like "disorderly school boys," wrote one of Sanders' relatives: "It is said some of the legislators will go home ten thousand dollars richer than when they came to Helena this winter." No one ever proved these charges of bribery, but few ever doubted them. Ballot followed ballot, and the rumored price of a vote mounted apace. Excitement climbed to a fever pitch, and yet no break appeared in the deadlock.[39]

In the end, neither side flinched. The Clark Democrats refused to give way to a compromise choice, and the Daly forces held on to Dixon. On the final ballot of 2 March 1893, the vote stood at Clark 32, Mantle 25, Dixon 11, and Thomas Carter 1. W. A. Clark thus fell three votes short of the 35 which would have brought him victory. In so doing, he won the cross-over votes of six Republicans and two previously anti-Clark Democrats. One has difficulty disagreeing with the sentiment of the time: that these men accepted bribes to vote for him. The grim-visaged millionaire suffered insult upon injury as he once again felt the pangs of defeat. As 2,000 excited spectators milled around the capitol, Clark sat with an acceptance speech in his hand and watched the collapse of his nefarious campaign. Daly ally Senator E. D. Matts of Missoula County, the "Bald Eagle," stood before the assembly and pointed accusingly at the "traitors" who had switched to Clark at the last minute. Matts emotionally predicted that someday Clark's tombstone would bear the epitaph: "Here lies the man who thought he could buy up the legislature of sovereign Montana and got fooled." "THEY FELL DOWN," crowed Daly's *Anaconda Standard*: "The grandest fight that was ever fought in Montana."[40]

So ended the third Montana legislature, a body sadly tainted by mining money and later described by Lee Mantle as a "band of bribe takers and bribe givers . . . a stench in the nostrils of all honest men, and a by-word and jeer throughout the Union." Yet even now, the scheming for the still-vacant Senate seat continued unabated. After the final, inconclusive ballot, the Daly Democrats adroitly joined the Republicans in voting for adjournment. This left Republican Governor John Rickards with the choice of either calling the legislature into special session to continue the balloting or exercising his authority to appoint a senator to the now-vacant position formerly held by Sanders. On 4 March, soon after the adjournment of the legislature, Rickards indicated his decision by appointing none other than Lee Mantle to the U.S. Senate. Clark's *Butte Miner* asked the obvious question: "Was Rickards Influenced?" Indeed, it seems probable that the Daly strategy had all along been to deadlock the Senate balloting until adjournment and then to convince the governor to appoint his Republican friend to the seat so coveted by his enemy Clark.[41]

The Mantle appointment ran into stiff opposition in the U.S. Senate, where feelings ran high against allowing gubernatorial appointments in cases where the state legislatures simply failed to act. On 28 August 1893, the Senate voted 31–28 to deny the Butte publisher a seat in that body. Washington rumor had it that both Clark and his friend Sam Hauser had lobbied for this result, hoping that it would force Governor Rickards to call a special session which might yet send one or the other of them to the Senate. Rickards came under intense pressure from silver interests in both parties to call the session. They argued that he must send another silver senator to defend the cause in the national arena. Knowing that a special session would most likely choose a Democrat, Republican Rickards steadfastly refused, with the result that, for over a year, Montana had only one U.S. Senator.[42] Thus the Clark-Daly imbroglio had not only debauched and hamstrung the 1893 legislature: it also ended up costing the Treasure State representation in the U.S. Senate itself.

Montana had little time to recover from the political carnival of 1892–93, for the approach of the 1894 campaign brought even bigger issues. In this election the voters would choose between the two top contenders of 1892, Helena and Anaconda, for the permanent state capital. They would also elect a legislature which would fill not one, but two Senate seats in 1895: the one held by T. C. Power since 1890 and the one vacated in 1893 by the unseating of Lee Mantle. The stakes were very high in 1894, and so was the pitch of emotions. Democrats and Populists flirted with the idea of "fusion," or presenting a united front against the pro-gold Republicans like some other western state parties were doing; and the anti-Catholic American Protective Association was stirring up xenophobia in Butte, Philipsburg, and other mining centers.[43]

The capital fight stole the show in 1894. In this case, for the first time, Marcus Daly's ego was on the line, and W. A. Clark enjoyed the luxury of taking revenge. Never longing for high office himself, Daly wanted simply to immortalize his pride and joy—his barony of Anaconda as the capital of a sovereign state. Clark undoubtedly swung to Helena's defense not just to spite his enemy, but also because he saw the chance to gain the favor and support of that community and its powerful political order. As the campaign season approached, the "White Czar" of Anaconda found himself outgunned. Clark and Helena's well-connected mining-banking mogul Samuel T. Hauser were busily welding together a powerful coalition to oppose him. Both sides reached out to all corners of the state for support. And the contaminating flow of mining money, which had hitherto funneled mainly into the legislature, now spread out into the corpus of the body politic itself. Nobody will ever really know how much money the copper kings spent in this contest; but if journalist Christopher Connolly's guess of $2,500,000 by Daly and $400,000 by Clark is correct, then they spent over $50 for each vote cast! Actually, Connolly no doubt exaggerated. Daly later testified that his side spent "only" $450,000, and Clark placed the total expenditure at roughly $1,000,000. In any case, the money flowed freely, and its effects proved to be both intoxicating and debilitating.[44]

Each side garnered strong allies. The Northern Pacific Railroad backed Helena, which lay on its main line, while Jim Hill and the Great Northern supported their great customer at Butte-Anaconda. Most of Butte and its politicians, like Lee Mantle, backed nearby Anaconda. But the other large Butte mining companies, resentful of the Anaconda colossus, threw their support to Helena. Thomas Couch and A. S. Bigelow of the Boston and Montana–Butte and Boston companies campaigned hard for Helena. Couch boasted loudly that he would carry "his" smelter city of Great Falls for the cause. Arbitrarily, the Walker brothers sacked their capable Walkerville superintendent W. E. Hall when he persisted in campaigning for Anaconda. Old alliances snapped under the strain. For instance, Daly's ally Tom Carter of Helena broke with him and joined other Helena politicos such as Wilbur Sanders in stumping for their home town.[45]

Each contestant city blistered its opponent with classical frontier bombast. Clark's *Butte Miner* characterized Daly as the "employee" of an "alien, soulless corporation" and asked rhetorically: "Should the capital of the great state of Montana be located in a town owned and controlled by one corporation?" With considerable logic, a Helena pamphlet questioned the wisdom of "the removal of the seat of government to a town that is located about fifty miles from the southwestern boundary of the state and owned by a rapacious and despotic corporation." Reacting good-naturedly to accusations that their city was hoglike in its political appetites, Helena newspaper cartoonists delighted in depicting the "Helena Hog" mesmerizing the Anaconda snake or strutting around James Ben Ali Haggin of the Anaconda, always parodied as a Turkish merchant wearing a fez. In fact, the Helena crowd focused less upon the popular Daly than upon the swarthy Haggin: "Mr. Haggin, of New York, San Francisco, Deadwood and Constantinople."[46]

As a company town located off the beaten track, Anaconda had the worst of it, but she nonetheless fought tooth and nail. Responding to Helena's charges of corporate domination, the Anaconda-Butte boomers aimed their attack at the adversary's patron, the Northern Pacific Railroad, which was currently bankrupted by the 1893 Panic and highly unpopular due to its effort to seize mineral claims with its huge land grant. The *Anaconda Standard* and its supporting papers portrayed Helena as being "wholly in the power of the Northern Pacific—the land-thieving octopus." They also hammered away at the pretentiousness of "the cultured temporary capital," with its ostentatious millionaires and their imposing Victorian mansions. Pulling all stops, the Anaconda crowd found Helena to be an anti-labor, "scab-loving" town, marred by the presence of far too many Chinese, blacks, and "lawless and criminal classes." By late October, John Durston's staff at the *Anaconda Standard* was pouring sixty inches of editorials per day into the contest.[47]

The Clark and Daly forces and their allies reached out into every community in the state, brandishing money, threats, and promises in a frantic search for votes. At Billings, for instance, the *Gazette* figured that the Anaconda element spent $10–15,000 in its campaign; but the paper still found it in the interest of agricultural eastern Montana to keep the capital at Helena, rather than "enthroned amid the smelter chimneys of Anaconda." The *Great Falls Tribune*, on the other hand, reacted angrily to the Boston and Montana Company's campaign for Helena and came out instead for Anaconda and Daly, who, the editor reminded his readers, had led the effort to maintain wages during the Panic of 1893. Bozeman reacted similarly. Its newspaper pointed to Butte-Anaconda as the main market for the farm produce of the fertile Gallatin Valley and lashed out at Helena for its indifference when Bozeman had lost its federal fort, and for its perceived designs upon the town's newborn state agricultural college. "For years," concluded the *Bozeman Weekly Chronicle*, "Gallatin County has been subject to the beck and call of dictatorial Helena."[48]

Address to the Voters.

CITIZENS OF MONTANA:

On next Tuesday, we are by our votes to locate permanently the Capital of our beloved State, which is to grow into a Commonwealth as great in population, wealth and political importance as it is vast in territory.   The convenience, prosperity and liberty of untold thousands are centered in our ballots.   These ballots are ours upon condition that we cast them in the spirit of independence for the good of all, both present and future.   Let us reflect seriously upon the magnitude of the interests now in our hands.   With neither passion nor prejudice, but with charity for all, let us obey the dictates of reason and conscience.   In sincerity of purpose and soberness of mind, let us put a patriotic conviction into our vote, and make it tell, to-day and forever, for the protection of labor and the purity of the franchise.

It is within our power to rebuke corruption and rescue our State from impending disgrace.   It is our high privilege to strike down the enemies of political freedom and break the chains in readiness for the Goddess of Liberty.   It is our solemn duty to light the fires of patriotism upon the mountain tops and proclaim to all the world that this is a land of freedom.   Send out the cheering declaration that no monopoly can rule here.   Make it clear that a million dollars cannot buy the vote or control the election of Montana.   By the heroic patriotism of your action publish everywhere the fact that this is the Switzerland of America, the home of an exalted spirit of liberty.   Then the young will seek our towns and pour their energies into our common life.   Then the laborer, oppressed by eastern corporations, will make a home on our free soil, where he may raise his children free from the blight of trusts and the tyranny of the Boss.

As American citizens, proud of our blood-bought institution of freedom, let us so vote that our children will be proud of our action.   Let us so vote that the Stars and Stripes will be raised a little higher rather than trailed in the dust.   Let us keep the American eagle free from the copper cage cunningly prepared for it.   We may well awake to the danger which will befall us, if our legislature becomes the vassal of this gigantic corporation; a tenant upon its ground and a boarder at its table. We shall do well to realize before-hand the disgrace which will cover us throughout the Nation if we allow these methods of corruption to succeed and the dictation of a mammoth monopoly to go unrebuked.   Let us also remember that the larger the majority against this dark design, the safer will be our common laborers and the larger the prosperity of the region.   With these great facts in mind, let us make next Tuesday the red letter day in our State calendar, which our children will celebrate as the anniversary of the independence of our commonwealth from the hateful despotism of money in politics.   The people have made the fight their own, and a careful canvass of the State just completed by the Committee, demonstrates the hopelessness of the Anaconda cause in opposition to the voice of the unpurchased and unpurchasable voters of Montana.   Onr canvass shows that Anaconda will certainly be defeated by a substantial majority, and we confidently appeal to every patriotic citizen of the State to join in an earnest, honest and determined effort to enlarge the majority and to preserve the State for the people by relieving it from threatened corporation rule.

Helena Capital Committee.

Helena, November 1, 1894.

Courtesy of the Montana Historical Society, Helena

HELENA MONTANA

WONDERFUL AGGREGATION!

THIRTY-ONE SHOWS IN ONE!!

LOOK! LOOK!

Last and Final Appearance in Montana
of the World Famous Tragedian

BEN ALI HAGGIN

In the Soul Harrowing Drama

ANACONDA

OR THE

WIZARD OF LAST CHANCE

Under the Obsequies of the

HELENA HOG.

Superb and Magnificent Cast of Stars !!

The Anaconda, Third of its Kind,	Ben Ali Haggin
Old Man [Friend of Labor]	Marcus Daly
Lord of the Treasury,	John R. Toole
Head Eunuch,	J. Eggleston
Chief Crier to Ben Ali,	J. H. Durston
Chief Counsellor to Ben Ali,	J. J. Hill
The "Voice" [Silent Now]	E. D. Matts
"Thumbs Up"	Lee Mantle
Lightning Change Artist,	Nelson Story
Snake Charmer,	W. A. Clark
Machievello, a Diplomat,	L. H. Hershfield
Helena's Leading Printers,	STATE PUBLISHING CO.

Courtiers, Knaves, Dudes, Tin Pails, Hitch Kickers, Chinese, Cyclones,
Typhools, and five miles of social supremacy in the play.

The Bewildering Tableaux.

WATCH US WIN! THE BRILLIANT FINISH! WHO IS ALLEN?
STRIKE ON THE BUTTE, ANACONDA FOR THE
CAPITAL AND PACIFIC R. R.

A Gin Phiz Reel by the Silk Night Shirt Club of 146.

—IN THE—

QUADRUPLEX CIRCUS TENT

Will be found a choice assortment of Swing Pythons
Anacondas, Boa Constrictors, Copper Heads and
Tails, Rattlesnakes, Vipers, Cobras, Slow Worms,
Copper and Blue Bellies, Side Winders and Wonders
Galore.

1,250 Batrachians from Ravalli! A Car Load
of Horned Toads from Flathead.

THE ANACONDA!!

Will be specially exhibited at the close of the play. We Guarantee it has three
forks to its tongue, three lids to each eye which are capable of very great dilation. It
is warranted to have 700 ribs in pairs of two attached by ball and socket joints to the
vertebræ throughout its whole length. There is no backbone, but by special arrangement the gall is attached to the posterior lobe of the liver by a mucilagenous process
which prevents any motion from side to side or any vertical undulations which might
endanger its own safety.

Small Boys and Children and Non-Voters will not
be permitted to handle the Anaconda or approach
within 100 feet of the Circus Tent

Handbill lampooning Amalgamated, November 1894 (courtesy
of the Montana Historical Society,
Helena)

The populous Missoula area, with its prosperous farms and bustling lumber mills, was a key target of both sides. Missoula stayed out of the bidding for capital in order to assure its acquisition of the state university, but it now found itself in the center of the fray. A. B. Hammond, the baron of Missoula, reported that Daly was "prepared to sacrifice everybody and everything for the capital": ". . . if we choose to support Anaconda for the capital we can get anything we want from him. . . . But if we should elect to do otherwise we will have war such as we have had in the past." Nevertheless, the Hammond group went along with Clark and Hauser against its old adversary, the "White Czar." Hammond's lieutenant C. H. McLeod traveled the Bitterroot Valley and its environs, spending thousands of Hauser and Hammond dollars on booze and publicity for the Helena cause. Daly's hint that he might route his Butte, Anaconda, and Pacific Railroad westward into the Bitterroot and to Missoula backfired badly by arousing that city's fear of its rival, Daly's town of Hamilton. The *Missoulian* growled: "What has Anaconda ever done for Missoula anyway? If Christ came to Anaconda he would be compelled to eat, sleep, drink and pray with Mr. Marcus Daly."[49] In the end, though, Daly far outspent the combined Clark-Hauser-Hammond interests and narrowly carried Missoula County, which lay nearer Anaconda than Helena.

The battle centered, of course, upon Butte, the center of the state's population and mining influence. Although the camp leaned naturally toward its mining sister Anaconda, the Clark, Boston, and Alice forces struggled mightily to swing its allegiance toward Helena. The Clark people struck off thousands of little copper collars, with the obvious message of what a vote for the opposition would mean: being yoked to the despotic Anaconda Company. Daly workers handed out thousands of Anaconda-for-Capital cigars, which Helena partisans branded as products of scab labor. Both sides plastered the city with broadsides, handed out trinkets and favors on the streets, and staged parades, band concerts, and fireworks displays. Agents of the two copper kings outdid one another in buying drinks for the house and sometimes even in handing out greenbacks to passersby.

So the money and the booze flowed freely, and Butte had a grand old time. Frank Linderman, one day to become a noted writer, once saw to his surprise a fellow Butte and Boston Company employee marching in an Anaconda parade at Butte. When later asked about this odd behavior, the man replied that he, like many others, had received a five-dollar gold piece for his effort. Linderman later heard an illiterate Irishman tell an election judge: "I don't give a damn how I votes, so long as I votes for Pat Sullivan for Treasurer, and Anaconda for the capital." But the Judge later told Linderman: "That Mick voted for Helena for the capital, and Johnson for Assessor." One day at Helena, an exuberant chap was mobbed and jailed when he strolled down Last Chance Gulch shouting "Hurrah for Anaconda." When Daly heard of this, he sent two lawyers to spring the fellow. He then provided the man with a lease on a vein which made him rich, but withdrew it in disgust because his ward was blowing his money on drunken debauchery.[50]

In the election of 6 November 1894, the Republicans won a sweeping victory in Montana, mainly because of the sagging fortunes of President Cleveland's depression-ridden Democratic party, and because, as in 1892, the Populists and Democrats failed to unite. This meant that Democrat W. A. Clark would face no prospect of election to the Senate in the 1895 legislature, whose Republican majority would instead send Lee Mantle and Thomas Carter to Washington. In the balloting for location of the capital, Helena won a narrow victory: 27,024 to 25,118 for Anaconda. "Three Cheers!" shouted Clark's *Butte Miner*, "The People are supreme! Tyranny has reached its Waterloo!"[51] A study of voting patterns indicates that several factors led to Anaconda's downfall. Except for Cascade County, where Great Falls backed Marcus Daly, the thinly populated, agricultural counties of east-central Montana voted for Helena and against locating the capital in the clutches of corporate mining. As political scientist Ellis Waldron notes, most counties ended up voting for the capital site nearest to them. This favored centrally located Helena and hurt out-of-the-way Anaconda.[52] The issue of corporate domination no doubt damaged Anaconda severely, but beyond a doubt, it was only the free spending campaign of Clark and Hauser that saved Helena from Daly's onslaught. In the final analysis, the real importance of the capital fight lay less in geopolitics than in the fact that mining money and manipulation was now spreading like a cancer through the body politic.

At last, William Andrews Clark knew the thrill of victory. When his train arrived in Helena on election night, a mob of grateful townsmen unhitched the horses and pulled his carriage through the streets by hand. Following his victory oration, Clark sported the city to an evening of drinking and hilarity, with all drinks on his tab. Harried bartenders finally resorted simply to casting the bottles into the outstretched hands of the thirsty. Clark's bar bill for the night reportedly totaled $30,000. For once in his life, Clark was loved, and Helena would never forget him for what he had done. Marcus Daly, on the other hand, fell into a deep despondency. Friends reported that he never forgot or forgave the defeat of his beloved Anaconda. During his last years, he spent less and less time there, as if his broken dream made the place unbearable. Instead, he devoted most of his time and money to his Bitterroot stock farm.[53]

Thus the wild "capital fight" of 1894 capped six years of partisan warfare in Montana, six years during which the ambitions of Clark and Daly shattered the lines of party regularity. In fact, Daly's ill-advised attempt to make Anaconda the capital brought this partisan turmoil to a new height of confusion. Party loyalties, even past personal loyalties, meant little in 1894. What counted most were geography and economic and civic attachments. The Anaconda found itself at cross purposes with Butte's other corporate powers, and Daly saw former allies like Tom Carter abandon him. In the wake of this epic fight, no one could foretell how the Treasure State's scrambled political kaleidoscope might realign.

Surprisingly, an interlude of political calm and consensus followed the capital fight. With the capital issue finally settled, and with no senate contest due until 1898–99, Montana's economic and political interests found it expedient to close ranks on the most pressing issue of the time—silver. As previously discussed, the Cleveland administration's demonetization of silver and its end of the federal silver purchase program prostrated this locally vital industry. The crusade for "free silver"—the resumption of federal purchases and coinage of silver dollars at a content ratio of 16 to 1 with gold dollars—became a grand rallying cry which promised to join businessmen and laborers, Democrats and Republicans, Clarkites and Dalyites into one great and united army.

With the national Democratic Party of Grover Cleveland seemingly as wedded to a solid gold currency as were the Republicans, Montanans turned increasingly toward the Populists, who made "free silver" one of their key tenets. Seventeen Populists won election to the legislature in 1894, and 1896 loomed as the possible year of triumph. Unlike the farm states of the Midwest and South, where the Populist party focused upon radical solutions to the farmers' plight, the mining states of the Rockies and the Great Basin produced a brand of populism which emphasized "free silver" as its dominant, cure-all issue. Nevada's Populists, for example, simply referred to themselves as the "Silver Party."

Montana's great mining kings had nearly as large a stake in silver as they did in copper. Famed copper mines like the Anaconda still produced appreciable amounts of silver which, if the price rose, could double net profits. Like their counterparts in Colorado, Idaho, and other silver states, the Montana mining barons looked with favor toward the Populists and began to pull at their old Democratic party moorings. For instance, W. A. Clark squelched ill-founded rumors that he might consider a vice-presidential race alongside Grover Cleveland with the simple retort: "I am for free silver first and for democracy afterward."[54]

As the Panic of 1893 deepened, the mining kings increasingly trumpeted the idea of "fusion" between Populists and pro-silver Democrats, both at the state and at the national levels. They also invested heavily in pro-silver promotional outfits, like the nationwide American Bimetallic League and the statewide Montana Free Coinage Association. Marcus Daly served as president of the latter organization, and Sam Hauser chaired its executive committee. The Montana Free Coinage Association, like its counterparts throughout the region, tied into the national network of the American Bimetallic League; and 100 of its members attended the league's great Chicago convention on 1 August 1893. Daly poured so much money into the league that, according to one questionable authority, he "largely subsidized it."[55]

By mid–1896, what Lawrence Goodwyn calls "one-issue Populism" had come to push all other questions aside in western Montana and other mining regions. "Free silver," writes Goodwyn, "meant full employment in the Western mining centers. Unlimited coinage meant the opening of marginal mines. It meant Western business expansion. It meant prosperity."[56] In Montana, the silver issue captured not only the Populist party but also the majority factions of the two older parties as well. The strategy of fusion, or welding the silver factions of all parties together, seemed sure of success locally and maybe even possible nationally. Prior to 1896, the Montana Populists, silver Democrats, and silver Republicans had shunned fusion as a violation of their party principles. Now, with the mining men priming the fiscal pumps, they came to see the logic of the situation.

Montana nicely mirrored national trends in the 1896 campaign, and Montana personalities appeared frequently on the national stage. The silver interests faced their roughest sledding in the conservatively inclined Republican party. In Montana, most of the Republican leadership, especially Senator Lee Mantle and congressional candidate Charles Hartman of Bozeman, joined enthusiastically in the silver crusade. The more conservative and partisan element followed old Wilbur Fisk Sanders in standing by the gold standard. Middle-of-theroaders like Senator Thomas Carter waffled awkwardly on the issue. Senator Carter, as retiring national party chairman, presided over the convening of the GOP convention at St. Louis in June of 1896. In the battle-royal over the gold plank in the Republican national platform, the Montana delegates joined other westerners led by Senator Henry Teller of Colorado in battling for a silver standard. Only Sanders and a hesitant Tom Carter—both of them strongly wedded to the national party leadership—failed to join in this fight to the death. After the Republicans adopted a solid gold platform and nominated gold candidate William McKinley for president, Lee Mantle and his fellow silverites angrily abandoned the GOP and announced their affiliation with Teller's silver Republican party.[57]

The Democrats staged their national convention at Chicago in July. Rebelling against the conservative, pro-gold stance of Grover Cleveland, the party instead nominated the silverite Nebraskan William Jennings Bryan, who had electrified the gathering with his spellbinding "Cross of Gold" speech in the keynote address. The Montana delegates, led by Sam Hauser, knew Bryan well, admired his silver stand, and happily backed his candidacy. Meeting at St. Louis later in July, the Populists faced a cruel dilemma. They had to choose between fusion with the Democrats by co-nominating Bryan, which promised a real hope of success for free silver, or nominating their own candidate. The latter choice would preserve the integrity of their party but would probably assure a Republican victory by splitting the silver vote. In the end, they chose the practical option of fusion, which meant that their other, more far-reaching principles must be submerged in the interests of the silver-inflation crusade.[58]

Fusion at the national level led naturally to fusion at the state level. Following the lead of the silver barons, the Montana Populists now hastily abandoned their opposition to alliance with the Democrats. Meeting at Helena on 2 September, the Populists chose a conference committee to travel to Missoula, where the Democrats convened the following day. The Populist emissaries then met with a Democratic conference committee and hammered out a fusion ticket which both party conventions promptly ratified. Granting the Democrats two presidential electors and the Populists one, the committees gave nominations for lesser state offices mostly to the Democrats and allowed the three choicest slots to the Populists: Robert B. Smith for governor, A. E. Spriggs for lieutenant governor, and T. S. Hogan for secretary of state. The Democrats also received the congressional berth but failed to nominate anyone, thus tacitly accepting popular silver Republican nominee Charles Hartman.[59] A spirit of togetherness pervaded the Missoula convention, nicely captured by the actions of sixteen little girls and one boy. Representing the ratio of silver to gold, they handed out flowers to the cheers of the crowd.

This awesome Democratic-Populist fusion ticket left the Montana Republicans in a tough predicament. At their Helena convention on 9 September the Republicans were clearly and hopelessly divided into silver and gold factions, with the former holding most of the votes. Following a tirade by defiant old Wilbur Sanders against the silver heresy, the delegates divided into two groups according to a prearranged scheme. The gold and silver factions agreed, in effect, to disagree. Each chose its own congressional nominee, presidential electors, and central committee; and both agreed to support the rest of the party ticket.[60] It was a strange arrangement, and it doomed the GOP to certain defeat. Mantle, Hartman, and the Silver Republicans could avidly support Bryan and silver, but they had little fondness for the liberalism of many of the fusionists otherwise. Sanders and the "gold bugs" enjoyed attacking the silver heresy, but they had no hope of victory. Compromising moderates like "Corkscrew Tom" Carter tried desperately to straddle both stools—free silver and McKinley conservatism—and were pilloried by each side without mercy.

With the fusionists certain to win, the 1896 campaign generated little anticipation in Montana. The gold Republicans offered only lighthearted resistance, and the "Popocrats" were so sure of victory that they mounted only a lightly orchestrated statewide effort. Instead, the Montana silverites spent most of their time carrying the gospel beyond the state's borders. Hartman and Mantle campaigned heavily in the Midwest, and Robert Smith worked extensively in California. With the local press nearly unanimous in its praises of Bryan and free silver, the politicians had little to add.[61]

Montana contributed much more than mere speakers to the Bryan campaign. When the Democratic national chairman, Senator James K. Jones, called urgently for campaign funds, the various Bryan organizations of the state merged their efforts into the Montana Bimetallic League. Through this and other outfits, a great deal of Montana mining money poured into the Bryan coffers. Precisely how much will never be known. Marcus Daly's son-in-law, James Gerard, later estimated that Daly contributed $300,000 to the 1896 campaign. Undoubtedly, the Anaconda tycoon was Bryan's greatest benefactor. The eastern press buzzed with reports of enormous contributions from Montana and the mining West. On 16 October, the *New York World* reported that a $300,000 war chest had already been raised in

Montana, including $50,000 from Clark, $100,000 from Daly, and $60,000 from Anaconda employees, with much more to follow. The magnates from Butte, said the *World*, "care nothing for parties or candidates, except as both serve their ends. They are working for the free silver issue purely for private profit. It means wealth beyond the dreams of avarice for them. The politicians who serve them are either their agents or their dupes."[62]

"Infamous Lies," cried Lee Mantle's *Daily Inter Mountain*. Actually, the *World* was probably quite accurate in assessing the Butte barons' motives, but like other eastern Republican spokesmen, it exaggerated the hold of the western silver interests upon the Bryan campaign. The eastern press no doubt tended to maximize silver contributions in order to offset the mounting criticism of the much larger war chest that Republican king-maker Mark Hanna was accumulating from America's greatest capitalists for the McKinley campaign. Overblown estimates of the silver kings' expenditures sometimes found their way into later histories. Matthew Josephson, for example, maintains that Daly, F. A. Heinze, and the Hearst estate donated a total of $289,000 to lining up pro-silver delegates to the 1896 Democratic convention and that Daly then contributed at least $50,000 more to the general campaign. He is probably right about the $50,000; but it is doubtful that Daly, Phoebe Hearst, and Heinze ever collaborated on anything, or that they raised such a large war chest as $289,000 to influence the national convention. Admittedly, however, Daly still put forth a great deal of money. Combined with lesser amounts from Clark and others, it made Montana a key source of Democratic-Populist funding.[63]

In the November 1896 election, the Democratic-Populist fusion swept to a near total victory in Montana, carrying every major state office and the house of representatives and leaving the Republicans with only a fragile hold on the state senate due to holdovers. Bryan carried all of Montana's counties except for two—Dawson and Custer on the eastern border—and buried McKinley by a staggering margin of 42,537 to 10,494. This contrasted sharply, of course, to McKinley's nationwide victory, which was a source of great anguish to the mining West.[64] Despite the defeat of Bryan and silver in 1896, the Montana fusionists remained hopeful and loyal to the cause. When Bryan visited Butte in August 1897, he received an incredible reception. A score of mine and smelter whistles welcomed him to town, and cheering throngs lined his triumphal route as "Fat Jack" Jones drove his hack up the hill from South Butte to Walkerville. Bryan breakfasted at Clark's home before addressing a huge crowd at the Butte racetrack and then traveled to Anaconda, the first city in the country to name a school for him. There, he breakfasted with Daly before addressing another large audience.[65]

The hopes of the fusionists and of William Jennings Bryan for a bimetallic currency faded rapidly after 1896 as returning prosperity restored widespread confidence in the gold standard. Nevertheless, Populism and free silver would remain potent forces in Montana for several more years. Increasingly, both would become pawns of the warring copper kings. As for the remarkable unity of 1896—the solidarity for silver which welded together the warring elements of Montana politics—it soon evaporated. The terrible tension between Clark and Daly, which had cooled momentarily after 1894, quickly reappeared as Clark once more fixed his aim upon the United States Senate.

6. Mr. Clark Goes to Washington

The Clark-Daly feud reached its climax in the incredible legislative session of 1899, and in the equally incredible events which followed it. Having been defeated for Congress once and for the Senate twice, William Andrews Clark apparently decided that it was now or never. Now approaching sixty, the dapper multimillionaire was at the height of his powers and influence. He evidently determined that this time, regardless of the monetary or moral costs, he would be elected to the U.S. Senate, where the world must finally take account of his merits. Thus began one of the most remarkable, most sordid political spectacles in the history of the United States.

There had been no Senate contest in 1897, but the 1899 legislature would choose a successor to the incumbent Republican senator, Lee Mantle. According to his own and to others' accounts, W. A. Clark did not at first intend to make the race this time. Rather, he intended, as he should have, to devote his energies to his far flung business empire. Then, only weeks before the beginning of the 1898 election campaigns, which would select the members of the 1899 assembly, several of Clark's close political associates prevailed upon him to run. This group included John B. Wellcome, Cark's capable and likable attorney; Samuel T. Hauser, his wily old Helena ally and veteran of Montana political intrigues; John S. M. Neill, the fiery and outspoken owner-manager of the *Helena Independent*, a major state newspaper which Clark himself subsidized; and Walter Cooper, the powerful Bozeman lumberman-entrepreneur.[1]

This group of business and political leaders persuaded the old man with an argument he was bound to find convincing. Clark must throw his financial resources and his political organization fully into the fray at once, they reasoned. Otherwise the "Boss Irishman," as Hauser called Marcus Daly, would take complete control of the state's entire political structure. The Anaconda was rapidly expanding at this time, with new plant facilities and mounting employment. In this very year, the company was buying control of A. B. Hammond's great Missoula-based lumber operations. The independent business-men of western Montana feared, with considerable logic, that the Anaconda titan would come to dominate them all. As the pro-Clark people viewed it, Daly's political power rested not only in his control of the big blocs of Democratic votes in Silver Bow (Butte) and Deer Lodge (Anaconda) counties. It lay even more threateningly in the fusion of Democrats, Populists, and silver Republicans which he and his allies had orchestrated so successfully in 1896. Now in 1898, Daly's subsidies and his alliances with such key figures as Populist Governor Robert B. Smith and silver Republican Senator Lee Mantle still held the broad but fragile silver alliance together. Clark and his friends had to win back control of the majority Democratic party from the Daly fusionists.[2]

At first, Clark resisted the overtures of his friends to run again, agreeing only to put up $100,000 for the campaign. Their blandish-ments finally took effect, however, and the old warrior promised them that he would lead the "fight for the integrity of the democratic party." By now, August 1898, the hour was already late, and they would have to move fast. Aided by restive anti-fusion regulars in the Democratic, Republican, and Populist conventions of September, the well-disciplined Clark forces proceeded to beat back the fusionists with surprising ease. At the all-important Democratic convention in Anaconda, Clark Democrats won majority control of the party. But their victory was far from complete, for Daly still maintained his customary command of the big Butte-Anaconda bloc.[3]

Everything now hinged upon the legislative contests in the general election campaign. Once more, as in 1893 and 1894, the Clark and Daly machines vied with one another in attempting to woo the vot-ers. Following a conversation with Clark in early October, John Neill reported to Hauser: ". . . he is disposed this time to be absolutely unlimited in the amount of money that he will put up for the election of democratic members of the Legislature in this State." Perhaps a measure of the Clark forces' desperation may be seen in the bizarre occurrence at Butte Precinct 8 in the early hours of 9 November, the morning following the election. While the election judges were tal-lying the votes in this Irish-Daly stronghold of Dublin Gulch, two armed men burst in and held them up. A scramble developed, and one of the judges was shot and killed. The intruders got away, and no one ever learned whether they were after money or ballots. Since the votes in this precinct were overwhelmingly anti-Clark, people suspected the worst.[4]

The 8 November 1898 election resulted in a dramatic Democratic victory. With the collapse of fusion many disenchanted Populists, like Governor Smith, wandered back into the Democratic fold. Yet even though the Democrats would hold a sizable majority in the joint state house-senate balloting for a U.S. senator, Clark could take little comfort. Daly's Butte-Anaconda candidates won. This meant that Clark could count on only forty-three firm Democratic votes, well short of the necessary majority. Lee Mantle's *Butte Daily Inter Mountain* applauded "the retirement of Mr. Clark from the senatorial prize ring," and Marcus Daly headed off to New york on business, confident that Clark had shot his bolt. Nevertheless, the Clark forces pressed grimly ahead. From one end of the state to the other, as later revelations would shockingly prove, they began executing a ploy of remarkable audacity—buying up some newspapers and offering favors to others, offering lucrative business deals to legislators, throwing money wherever it promised to return political gain. Only later would the magnitude of their efforts appear to the public.[5]

Montana's big spectacle began with the dawn of the new year, 1899. When the legislature convened early in January, W. A. Clark already had his headquarters set up in a suite of rooms at the Helena Hotel. Adjacent to his were the rooms of two men who would serve as his key agents in gathering legislative votes for the Senate: his handsome head lawyer John Wellcome and his spindly and pale twenty-six-year-old son, Charlie Clark. Two memorable quotes would later be attributed to the Clarks as a result of what was about to happen. According to Charlie: "We'll send the old man to the Senate or to the poor house"; and Charlie's father: "I never bought a man who wasn't for sale." To these quotes might be added another, which was attributed at this time to Marcus Daly: "I want to say, too, that if Clark shows his head in the senatorial race, even if he is nominated, for the senate, you fellows will hear something drop that will drive Clark and his friends out of politics and send some of them to the penitentiary."[6]

Helena echoed with rumors of Clark bribery, even before the session opened. The most persistent rumors had it that the old man would lay out $1,000,000, if necessary, to get himself elected, and that lawmakers could make a cool $10,000 by coming to terms with him.

That was a tidy sum in those pre-income-tax days of deflated dollars. The city of Helena, eternally loyal to the man who had saved her in the capital fight, seemed to condone and even to defend what was happening. In the words of Christopher Connolly, a bright young Dalyite lawyer who later gained national fame as a "muckraking" writer:

> The women of the capital—the best of them—carried on their crusade for Clark in their drawing-rooms and at their dinner-tables. They lobbied and entertained. They thronged the galleries of the State House.
>
> The business men of Helena became almost a unit in declaring that bribery was a necessity, and in defending it. Hundreds of school children might be seen wearing Clark badges. The man who stood out against bribes found that his old friends stood aloof from him. He became conscious of a lack of sympathy, of a curious isolation on the streets and at his club. He found himself marooned on the cold eminence of moral rectitude.
>
> The purchase of votes was talked about almost as freely as the weather, almost as familiarly as the markets. The morning salutation of everyone was: "What's the price of votes today?" [7]

With such rumors in the air, and with papers like the *Anaconda Standard* flaunting them, the two houses of the legislature were forced to establish a joint committee to investigate them. On the evening of 9 January 1899, the night before legislative balloting for selection of a U.S. senator was to begin, the committee received the testimony of four men: Democratic Congressman A. J. Campbell, a hard-boiled Daly man; and three state senators—Henry L. Myers of Ravalli County, William A. Clark of Madison County (no relation to William A. Clark of Butte), and Fred Whiteside of Flathead County.

Senator Whiteside proved to be the key witness. A handsome and forceful man of engaging personality, he had come to Montana two decades earlier as a young buffalo hunter still in his teens. He stayed to become a successful architect-contractor, and he erected some of Montana's most prominent buildings. As a member of the legislature several years earlier, Whiteside had figured largely in an exposure of bribery in the construction of the state capitol building. During the political struggles of the 1890s, Whiteside usually sided with Clark against the Daly faction. Now, however, even though he remained on good terms with the Clark crowd, some of them suspected him of treason. To complicate matters even further, as the session opened, Whiteside's credentials as a state senator were under investigation. A senate committee was sitting on charges by his Republican opponent, John Geiger, that Whiteside had been improperly seated since a number of improperly marked ballots should have been discarded. [8]

Panorama of Butte, 1875, before the boom (courtesy of Montana Historical Society, Helena)

Marcus Daly, portrait by W. H. Hoover (courtesy of Montana Historical Society, Helena)

William Andrews Clark, 1898 (courtesy of Montana Historical Society, Helena)

Territorial Governor S. T. Hauser, photograph by R. H. Beckwith (courtesy of Montana Historical Society, Helena)

(*Left*) Senator George Hearst; (*right*) James Ben Ali Haggin (both photos courtesy of the Bancroft Library, University of California, Berkeley)

(*Above*) Walkerville, showing the Moulton and the Alice mills and hoisting works, from the *Holiday Miner*, 1887; (*below*) the Colorado Smelter (both photos courtesy of Montana Historical Society, Helena)

Anaconda Hill and Dublin Gulch, ca. 1905 (courtesy of Montana Historical Society, Helena)

Anaconda, 1887, photograph by Hazeltine (courtesy of Montana Historical Society, Helena)

Train load of ore for the Washoe Smelter (courtesy of Montana Historical Society, Helena)

Old works of the Anaconda Company, Anaconda, from the *Holiday Miner*, 1888 (courtesy of Montana Historical Society, Helena)

(*Above*) The Anaconda Mine, (*below*) Anaconda smelters, from the *West Shore*, 1885 (courtesy of Photo Collection, University

F. Augustus Heinze (courtesy of Montana Historical Society, Helena)

Copper smelters and mines (courtesy of Montana Historical Society, Helena)

The Montana Hotel, Anaconda (courtesy of Montana Historical Society, Helena)

The W. A. Clark mansion, Butte, 1890 (Haynes Collection, courtesy of Montana Historical Society, Helena)

Thomas H. Carter, 1900 (courtesy of
Montana Historical Society, Helena)

Panorama of Butte, 1890, view from the west, with the Anaconda Hill in the distance
(Haynes Collection, courtesy of Montana Historical Society, Helena)

Looking down Main Street from Granite Street, from *Northwest Magazine*, 1890 (courtesy of Photo Collection, University of Washington Library)

Looking up Main Street from Granite Street, from *Northwest Magazine*, 1890 (courtesy of Photo Collection, University of Washington Library)

The Lizzie Block, the Court House, and the Caplice Building, from the *West Shore*, 1885 (courtesy of Photo Collection, University of Washington Library)

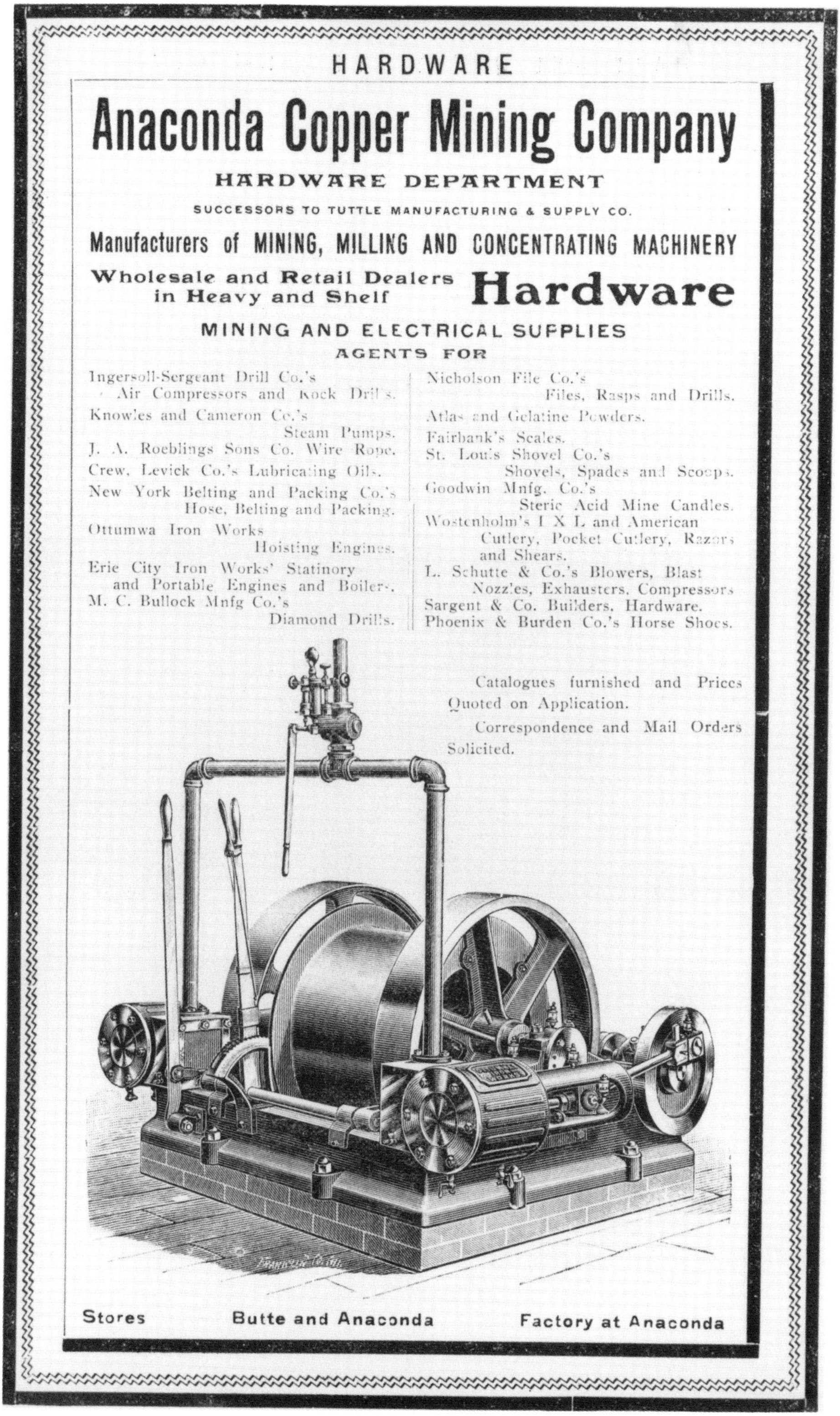

Advertisement from *Butte City Directory*, 1895

Perspective map of Butte, 1890 (courtesy of Montana Historical Society, Helena)

Steel gallows frame, 125 feet high, from Freeman, *Butte, Above and Below Ground* (1900) (courtesy of Photo Collection, University of Washington Library)

(*Above*) Crew of the Neversweat Mine, ca. 1902; (*below*) drillers at work 1,900 feet under Butte, photo by N. A. Forsyth (both photos courtesy of Montana Historical Society, Helena)

(*Above*) Miners' Union Day, Butte, photo by N. A. Forsyth; (*below*) miners' drilling contest, Columbia Gardens (both photos courtesy of Montana Historical Society, Helena)

Money offered as bribe to members of the Sixth Legislature, 1899 (courtesy of Montana Historical Society, Helena)

Claims at the center of mining litigation, from *Mining Claims, Butte City*, 1893 (courtesy of Montana Historical Society, Helena)

Henry H. Rogers

John D. Ryan (courtesy of Montana Historical Society, Helena)

A. Clark and daughters, at
lumbia Gardens (courtesy of
ntana Historical Society,
lena)

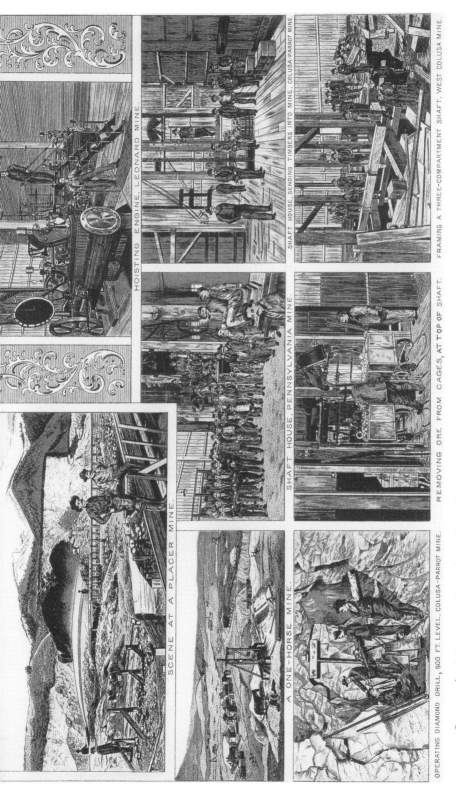

HOISTING ENGINE, LEONARD MINE.

SHAFT HOUSE, SENDING TIMBERS INTO MINE, COLUSA-PARROT MINE.

FRAMING A THREE-COMPARTMENT SHAFT, WEST COLUSA MINE.

SCENE AT A PLACER MINE.

SHAFT HOUSE, PENNSYLVANIA MINE.

REMOVING ORE FROM CAGES, AT TOP OF SHAFT.

A ONE-HORSE MINE.

OPERATING DIAMOND DRILL, 900 FT. LEVEL, COLUSA-PARROT MINE.

Scenes of mining operations, from *Butte Illustrated*, 1897 (courtesy of Photo Collection, University of Washington Library)

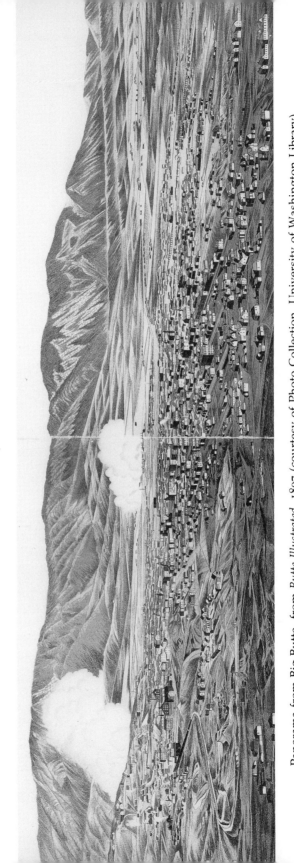

Panorama from Big Butte, from *Butte Illustrated*, 1897 (courtesy of Photo Collection, University of Washington Library)

The story which Whiteside told the committee, and which Senators Myers and Clark affirmed, was a gripping one. He produced $30,000 in crisp bills, which he alleged was bribe money given to him by John Wellcome to purchase the votes of himself, Myers, and Clark. If Whiteside told the truth, he had acted bravely. After receiving the money, he said that he acquired a gun, for word had it that anyone who betrayed the Clark cause would die for it. He then hid the money, first in a safe deposit box at the bank and then in his hotel room. Just a few hours before going to the joint committee with his story, Whiteside was allegedly cornered by Wellcome, Charlie Clark, and a group of the W. A. Clark faithful. Suspicious of his intentions, they first threatened him and then attempted to dissuade him with an offer of $300,000. Whiteside coolly protested his innocence and his loyalty to Clark, and winning them over, managed to get away.

Far into the night, Whiteside and his allies then met with the committee members and poured out their testimony. On the next day, the legislature met in joint session to hear the report of the investigating committee. An atmosphere of unbearable tension and shifting eyes gripped the proceeding as the testimony of the witnesses was read. At the close of the reading, the clerk displayed the $30,000. Whiteside then addressed the assembly in bold language:

> I know there is a sentiment in this community which favors the election of W. A. Clark to the United States Senate by fair means or foul. I know that the course I have pursued will not be popular, but so long as I live, I propose to fight the men who have placed the withering curse of bribery upon this state. I had rather go back to the carpenter's bench where I learned my trade, and spend the rest of my days in toil and obscurity, and be able to hold my head erect and look the world in the face, than to be a silent party to the knowledge of this crime. The man who is weak will come out of this contest infamous, while he who is strong will emerge from it sublime. What has become of the men who were bribed in the legislature of 1893? They are shunned by their fellow-citizens, and even spurned by the very scoundrels who caused their downfall. This contest between two men has already culminated in murder in Silver Bow County, and the life of the man who dares to oppose the element that committed that crime is not safe. My own life has been threatened, but I defy the men who have made the threat; for, when weighed against honesty and honor, life has no value; and if this be the last act of my life, it is worth its price to the people of this state.[9]

The Whiteside accusations produced an immediate sensation. "Clark Bribers Caught At It Red Handed," crowed Daly's *Anaconda*

Standard. "A Damnable Conspiracy," replied clark's *Butte Miner,* charging a frame-up: "Daly Crowd Spring Their Promised Sensation, Bungling Work at the Outset." The pro-Daly *Great Falls Tribune* saw Whiteside as "an honest man of unspotted reputation," while the pro-Clark *Helena Independent* depicted him as "a Self-Confessed Criminal." During the months prior to the opening of the legislative session, the Clark people had carefully groomed the state press, subsidizing and investing in some papers and even treating editors to free "informational" trips to Helena. This ploy now payed off as the large majority of Montana papers defended Clark and disparaged his accusers. Even Whiteside's hometown sheet, the *Kalispell Inter Lake,* joined in the attack: ". . . it is a noteworthy fact that here in his own county, where people are supposed to know him better than anywhere else, it is next to impossible to find a single person who will say that he believes Whiteside is honest in the matter, or that he is telling the truth in making the charges." [10]

In truth even today, eighty years later, one cannot be sure about these charges. Fred Whiteside seems to have been a man of character and veracity, and his charges have the ring of truth. Later testimony before a U.S. Senate committee seemed to prove beyond any doubt that agents of W. A. Clark indulged in wholesale bribery. But we must also keep in mind that all four of Clark's initial accusers— Whiteside, Clark, Myers, and Campbell—had direct political or economic ties to Marcus Daly. Congressman Campbell was a close political ally of Daly, and Myers hailed from the Irishman's western Montana bailiwick of Ravalli County. Whiteside had building contracts with the Anaconda, and Clark enjoyed legal and investment ties to Daly in Madison County. [11]

Whiteside's sensational exposure momentarily disrupted the Clark strategy. The Clarkites had boasted the day before that they had fifty-four votes in hand; but with the first ballot on 10 January, only seven legislators dared cast their votes for him. Compounding Clark's troubles, the joint session called upon the Lewis and Clark County district court to impanel a grand jury to investigate the charges. During the two-week period beginning on 11 January, the grand jury called in forty-four witnesses, and the public waited with baited breath for the verdict. The Clark people, meanwhile, struck back. Republican John Geiger's challenge to Senator Whiteside's seat from Flathead County still lay dormant in the state Senate Committee on Privileges and Elections. Holding a majority on that committee, the Clark forces now pressed forward with the investigation of election improprieties. [12]

For three weeks following the incredible exposures of 10 January 1899, the Helena scene resembled a three-ring circus. The grand jury and Whiteside–Geiger probes went on in the shadows while the balloting for U.S. senator ground on in the full glare of center stage. Despite his pathetic showing of only a handful of ballots on the first vote, Clark's fortunes slowly improved as his more timid legislative supporters began drifting back to support him. By 13 January, he had picked up fourteen more votes. Even then, Clark stood far behind his main challenger, W. G. Conrad, who tallied thirty-five votes to his twenty-one, with the other votes scattered.[13]

Clark's problem remained unchanged: Marcus Daly held the loyalty of enough Democrats to deny him a majority vote from his own party. In order to win, he had to get Republican votes. This would be hard to do in the glare of publicity aroused by Whiteside's accusations. Republican stalwarts warned their legislators to stand firm. Party spokesmen like the *Billings Gazette*, probably whistling in the dark, bravely announced that the GOP lawmakers were "solid as a rock," "still standing as firm as a stone wall." Publicly, candidate Clark wooed the Republicans by announcing his warm feelings these days for tariff protectionism, but the real campaign went on behind the scenes. As a later investigation would reveal, Clark's lieutenants were now offering bribes which reached as high as $20,000, and at least once even $50,000 per vote. As Clark agents such as John Wellcome, Walter Bickford, and Ben Hill worked one side of the street, Daly men such as John Toole and A. J. Campbell worked the other. Daly himself remained on the East Coast during the legislature, nursing his ailing heart and negotiating the future of his business, but he kept a close watch on Helena. The capital seemed, in the words of Christopher Connolly, "a city hysterical with guilt and greed":

> Since the vote was not sufficient to elect a Senator, the balloting went on for eighteen days after that—eighteen days in which open bribery and attempts at bribery were infinitely more common subjects of conversation in Helena than was the weather. If a legislator had a weakness in his nature or in his circumstances, Clark's lieutenants found it. His debts, his indiscretions in conduct, his best sentiments even, were turned into weapons against him. His business was threatened; his friendships were menaced; his wife, his sister, even his mother were often made intercessors for his vote. His old associates, his creditors, his family doctor were put upon his trail.[14]

Nothing, not even the potent Daly organization, could stop the big Clark money machine. From a high of thirty-eight votes on the second ballot, Conrad's total shrank to thirty-three on 21 January, when Clark tied him for the first time. Still, with other contestants scattering the vote, it seemed that the assembly might again deadlock short of a majority as it had back in 1893, thus electing no senator at all. Then on 26 January came two developments which clearly portended Clark's victory: a grand jury "vindication" of Clark, and a remarkable defeat of Whiteside. The Helena grand jury undoubtedly reflected the pro-Clark bias of the community. According to the rumor mill, the jurors were also being treated to the same bribe offers as were the legislators. In any case, the grand jury ruled inconclusive evidence. The jurors held that, despite the clear existence of $30,000 in tainted money, the available evidence would not warrant conviction. This ludicrous decision, which pro-Daly Attorney General C. B. Nolan violently denounced, seemed to end the immediate threat of legal action against Clark or his men. "Conspirators Foiled," headlined Clark's *Butte Miner*. "They Simply Fell Down Flat!," gloomily replied the *Anaconda Standard*.[15]

The incredible unseating of Senator Fred Whiteside resulted when the senate investigating committee eliminated his majority vote by choosing to reject certain ballots which had been marked with an "x" *after* rather than before his name. Clark's *Butte Miner* heralded this bit of chicanery as "vindication," referring to Whiteside as a "moral leper," "a perjured and conscienceless villain," "a masculine strumpet, a political bawd, a well-paid harlot." The resolute Whiteside, however, had the last word as usual. On the day of his unseating, he stood before the joint assembly and delivered what must rank as the most remarkable speech in the history of the Montana legislature. Whiteside gave them a tongue-lashing which they well deserved and which they would never forget. At one point, he directly accused Representative H. H. Garr, also from Flathead County, of taking bribes. Garr, looking ashen, rose in his seat and denounced Whiteside as a liar and perjurer; but later in the session he wept openly in his chair. Regardless of his motives, whether they be completely pure or not, Whiteside's valedictory remarks should be remembered:

> I understand that the fiat has gone forth that this is the last day I am to be a member of this body. If I failed to express myself at this time, I feel that I would be false to myself, false to my home, and false to the friends that have stood so manfully by me.
> Let us clink glasses and drink to crime. The crime of bribery, as shown by the evidence here introduced, stands out in all its naked hideousness. There are forty members seated here who today are ready to embrace it. And what is the motive? Answer me that question, you who sit with bloodless lips and shifting eyes—answer if you dare!

There are some features of this senatorial contest which would be ridiculous if it were not for its serious import to the people of this state. It has reminded me of a horde of hungry, skinny, long-tailed rats around a big cheese. Something falls in the room. There is a panic and stampede, and only seven have the courage to remain. As time goes on, the courage of those who fled gradually returns; they smell the cheese; and one by one they timidly come out of their holes until the vanishing cheese is again surrounded and we can hear the chorus of "Who's afraid?"

I am not surprised that the gentlemen who have changed their votes to Clark recently should make speeches of explanation, but I would suggest that their explanations would be much more clear and to the point if they would just get up and tell us the price and sit down.[16]

Now, clearly, the end was near. Both sides were emotionally drained, and Clark himself visibly showed the signs of his anguish and anxiety. The day of judgment dawned crystal clear and lovely on Saturday, 28 January 1899. Clark now had forty-one of the forty-seven votes he needed, and rumor had it that he would garner the others on this day. When the minority Republicans met that morning in secret caucus, eleven of them, led by Simeon S. Hobson of Fergus County, stood up and left the room when challenged as to how they would vote. Incredible as it seems, this meant that only four regular Republicans—J. R. McKay of Custer County, Tyler Worden of Missoula County, W. A. Hedges of Fergus County, and William Lindsay of Dawson County—had held out against the siren calls of the Clark "boodlers." The names of these men deserve to be remembered.[17]

On the first roll call that Saturday morning, the tally surprisingly remained identical to that of the day before; but then the Clark forces called for and won a second balloting. This time, the pliant Republicans crossed over to join the Clark team. When John Geiger, the Republican who had replaced Whiteside, cast his vote for Clark, he ludicrously tried to clear himself: "I say to you gentlemen that I am doing this with hands clean, pockets empty [he turned his pockets inside out], and conscience clear. . . ." As the lawmakers announced their votes, the galleries echoed with cat calls, hisses, and applause. Hecklers shouted charges of bribery and even yelled out the amounts of the individual bribes. Daly's lieutenants lashed out in frustration at the crossovers to Clark. Representative E. D. Matts lectured his fellows: "I am sorry to see this man go to the Senate of the United States, like Richard III, over the bodies of disgraced men. I am sorry it is necessary for the manhood of Montana to be dishonored in order that any man may attain his end." House Speaker Henry Stiff of Missoula announced that he had turned down the Clark bribers and declared Clark's election to be invalid because tainted by fraud. On this eighteenth and final ballot, Clark won with 54 of the 93 votes: 38 Democrats, 11 Republicans, 4 silver Republicans, and 1 Populist.[18]

Pandemonium gripped the capitol as wildly cheering Clark partisans pushed past the despondent Daly men and surged into the streets. As in 1894, Helena geared up for another debauch at Clark's expense. "It was a glorious victory," the senator-elect wired, thanking Sam Hauser: ". . . there will be 'a hot time in the old town tonight!'" Indeed, there was. All afternoon and night, Helena's pubs handed out free champagne, and on that raucous night an unruly procession wound through Last Chance Gulch, celebrating the great man's triumph while fireworks and bonfires lit the sky. Clark's champagne bill for that night supposedly totaled $30,000. His other expenses, of course, dwarfed the bar bill. According to the Dalyites, who were probably close to the truth, Clark had bought forty-seven votes for $431,000, not including the $30,000 that Whiteside had turned over to the legislature. He had allegedly offered another $200,000 to thirteen other lawmakers who refused to take it.[19]

The pro-Clark press of Montana applauded his "vindication." "Voice of the People Heard," heralded his *Butte Miner*, ". . . the crime of '93 Avenged." "The Members Rise Above Party Lines," agreed the *Helena Independent*, undoubtedly with tongue in cheek. More objective papers denounced the obvious corruption of the legislature. The *Great Falls Tribune* saw it as the "Triumph of Corruption"; the *Billings Gazette*, as the "prostitution" of the Republican Party; the *Fergus County Argus* as a win "on a Foul." Old Wilbur Sanders, the Diogenes of the GOP, spoke for all party purists in castigating the eleven Republicans who went over to Clark: "The word ingrate is a harsh word, but they will be thankful before they die if they can compromise by having it only written over their sepulcher [sic]." At Big Timber an effigy of W. W. Beasley, one of the turncoat Republicans, was burned by his neighbors on Main Street. Beasley launched a $20,000 libel suit against them but failed.[20]

The regional press watched all of this with fascination and revulsion. The *Salt Lake Tribune*, estimating W. A. Clark to be "possibly the richest man in the world," admitted it had been "one of the most remarkable legislative sessions ever held in the United States," but still felt that he "will make a valuable Senator." Few observers concurred. The *Rocky Mountain News* of Denver appropriately likened the Clark boodlery to the earlier case of Alexander Caldwell of Kansas, who had similarly bought up legislators like "a drove of cattle" and had been rejected by the Senate back in 1871. The *Denver Post* was equally appalled: "The spectacle presented in the Montana senatorial contest furnishes another object lesson of the sad degeneracy of state legislatures." In a humorous vein, the *St. Paul Dispatch* carried a front page cartoon depicting a sheaf of $1,000 bills, with the caption: "The kind of bill most often introduced in the legislature of Montana."[21]

It might have ended there, with William Andrews Clark quietly assuming his long-coveted Senate seat, and with his defeated enemies accepting their fate. But Clark's embitterment knew no bounds; and he now rubbed salt in the wounds, gloating over his victory and reiterating his earlier charges that the $30,000 had been a Daly set-up. At a gala Butte celebration of his triumph on 4 February, complete with the famed Boston and Montana Band and a fireworks display, Clark delivered a fighting speech. He argued once again that his victory meant "vindication" against his wicked foes, who had resorted to "treachery, falsehood, deceit, diabolical conspiracy and almost every crime within the calendar of crime." The eleven Republicans, he said, had stood with him as a matter of principle: "The people have risen in their majesty and power and have forever set the seal of their condemnation on a merciless combination which sought to subjugate the people of this state."[22] The *Miner* continued to hammer away at this theme.

Even before Clark's address, both Fred Whiteside and E. D. Matts had stated that the Daly organization would press the fight against his seating in the U.S. Senate itself, which has the right to refuse acceptance of any member. Marcus Daly had remained in New York until now, and his personal feelings remained unstated. At this point, he returned to Butte and gathered together his henchmen under the leadership of Congressman Campbell to carry on the battle. He promised to bankroll the effort and voiced his outrage: "The crime of bribery, gentlemen, was bad enough, but to try to fix that on some innocent people was still worse, and I think we should satisfy Mr. Clark with an investigation. . . ." Early in March, the Anaconda baron hosted a banquet for his friends, who included several key members of the state Democratic central committee, and reiterated his plans to unseat Clark. The *Butte Miner* acidly noted that Daly had neglected to explain "what I done to purify politics."[23]

Preliminary to the big battle in Washington, the Daly people launched two flanking attacks: libel suits by Whiteside against the *Miner* and the *Helena Independent*, which were aimed primarily at gathering evidence, and disbarment proceedings against Clark lawyer John B. Wellcome. Whiteside filed the motion to disbar Wellcome before the Montana Supreme Court in May of 1899, charging him with the bribery of eight legislators. The court refused at first to hear the case, but then reversed itself and appointed pro-Daly Attorney General C. B. Nolan to assist as a friend of the court in the prosecution. Nolan convinced the justices to hear the case, instead of returning it for criminal trial in the lower courts, by arguing that Wellcome was not subject to criminal prosecution since he had already been forced to testify before the Helena grand jury. The disbarment case turned into another battle-royal, and agents of both sides fought desperately. Defeat for Wellcome would bode ill for Clark in the Senate hearings.[24]

According to their own later testimony before the U.S. Senate committee, the justices of the Supreme Court were now approached by the Clark minions. Helena physician William Treacy twice seduced Judge William Hunt, offering $100,000 if he would vote to reject the case. Judge Hunt recalled how the doctor came over to see him, and while standing in his lawn discussing the judge's frail health, "he said that if the Wellcome disbarment matter could be dismissed by the Supreme Court, friends of Wellcome would give me one-hundred thousand dollars with which I could go abroad, free of worry, and regain my health and perhaps save my life." Although desperately needing the money, Hunt refused. Clark attorney Frank Corbett discussed the case with Judge William Pigott in a manner that seemed suspect. Chief Justice Theodore Brantly received a visit from the Reverend A. B. Martin, president of a small college at Deer Lodge and a Clark ally, in which he was strongly lobbied although not actually offered money. The ubiquitous Dr. Treacy also came to Attorney General Nolan with blandishments, but Nolan dismissed him with the abrupt words: ". . . if his [Clark's] body were skinned and the skin filled with gold, it wouldn't be any inducement to me." Finally, the Clarkites had run into strong and honest men whom they could not swerve. The court, in the end, elected to disbar Wellcome. Maintaining his silence to the end and never implicating Clark, the popular lawyer took his medicine stoically.[25] Hard hit by this defeat, the senator-elect now faced a much greater challenge in Washington.

William Andrews Clark took his seat in the United States Senate on 4 December 1899. On that same day, Senator Thomas Carter, who had patched up his earlier quarrel with Daly, presented to the Senate two memorials from Montana which called upon that body to reject him. One of the petitions came from anti-Clark members of the legislature, the other from Governor R. B. Smith and other prominent Montana citizens. Both were emphatic in their charges and accusations. The citizens' memorial named individual legislators who had allegedly taken bribes and included evidence gathered in the grand jury and Wellcome disbarment hearings, as well as in Whiteside's suit against the *Miner*. On 7 December, the Senate referred the matter to the Committee on Privileges and Elections, chaired by willful Republican Senator William Eaton Chandler of New Hampshire.[26]

The Chandler committee hearings unfolded during the first three months of the first year of the new century. Each side drew upon the country's foremost legal talents. Clark's chief attorneys were Roger Foster of New York and former Congressman Charles Faulkner of West Virginia. The Daly forces relied upon ex-Senator George Edmunds of Vermont, former U.S. Attorney for the District of Columbia A. A. Birney, and the ever-present Congressman A. J. Campbell of Montana. A flow of subpoenas soon descended upon Montana legislators and other figures in the case; and ninety-six witnesses—many of them clearly terrified—eventually appeared before the committee. Washington's Raleigh and Arlington hotels teemed with nervous, tragicomic Montanans, many of whom were seeing the big city for the first time. The Montana witnesses, even though carefully prepared by the opposing counsel, faced a tough grilling from Senators Chandler and George Hoar of Massachusetts.[27]

The hearings of the Committee on Privileges and Elections revealed to all the world the ugly political culture which had germinated in Montana. Clark, Daly, and Sam Hauser all admitted and defended their use of large amounts of money to secure their political ends. Asked if his political expenditures were "legitimate," Hauser replied: "It would depend upon what you would call legitimate expenses. I presume East some of those expenses would hardly be called legitimate, but there was none of it for the purpose of actually buying votes. . . ."[28]

Clark and Daly provided the committee with a study in contrasts as witnesses. In one sense, Daly had the better of it, for he opened his books to the committee. Clark, on the contrary, testified that he had destroyed his checks for the period in question, as was his custom, several months earlier. In general, though, Clark was cool and composed, a far more articulate defender of his cause than was Daly. He argued, as he had before, that his expenditures had gone only for proper methods of political organization, never knowingly for bribery, and that he had incurred the wrath of the Anaconda merely by defending the independence of his state. Desperately ill by now and confined to bed most of the time, Marcus Daly was barely able to make an appearance, and the committee had to accommodate him with brief sessions and hesitations for rest. Embarrassed by his almost pathetic clumsiness of language, Daly denied that he had coerced his employees to vote his way ("I never thought of it. I never had to."), or that he had forced them to buy at the company stores. With less candor, he denied ever using Pinkerton detectives, denied having any great political power, even denied any major involvement in the war against Clark.[29]

The committee unearthed ample evidence of wrongdoing by both sides. Deservedly, Clark took much the worst of it. It seemed abundantly clear that his agents, like son Charlie, Walter Bickford, and John Wellcome, had thrown his money around in a way that he could hardly have disapproved. Even though he had allegedly destroyed his canceled checks, the committee was able to subpoena and examine his bank statements, which revealed heavy expenditures. But Daly took his lumps, too. The committee learned that his batman, Congressman Campbell, had used such shoddy tactics as surreptitious entry into the quarters of Walter Bickford and the illegal opening of his mail. The senators found that both sides, first Clark's and then Daly's, were pouring money into the purchase of Montana newspapers in a grim battle to muster public opinion. For instance, the *Bozeman Chronicle* had backed Daly until Clark gave $2,500 to its owners, which prompted them to change positions. Daly countered by simply buying the paper for $11,000. Faced with a statewide press lined up on Clark's side, Daly went on a buying spree. He had by now acquired papers in Madison, Ravalli, Carbon, and Park counties to follow the lead of his *Anaconda Standard*. Freedom of the press in Montana seemed in dire peril.[30]

Ultimately, the Clark cause foundered because of the disgrace of those legislators who appeared before the committee to explain, with downcast eyes, how they had acquired such sudden wealth. Take the case, for example, of John Geiger, the Republican who had replaced Fred Whiteside in the state senate. By his own testimony, Geiger had come down to Helena with "no regular occupation." Yet he returned home with $3,600. Geiger claimed that he had gotten some of the money playing faro and betting on the horses, and that he had found the rest in his hotel room. Stories like this led to the silly legend that the Clarkites had handed out bribe money by simply throwing it through open hotel transoms. H. H. Garr, the man whom Whiteside accused openly from the floor of the assembly, had had to borrow $25 to get to Helena for the session. When he returned home, he coolly paid out $3,500 for a ranch. W. W. Beasley, the legislator who was burned in effigy by his neighbors, had come to Helena owing money.

He departed after the session's close for St. Paul with $5,000. Beasley claimed that he had brought the money to town with him, keeping it in his vest pocket throughout the session instead of depositing it in a bank.[31]

The stories seemed to vary only in detail and in imaginative flourishes. Although previously a Daly man, Democratic Representative E. P. Woods of Ravalli County ended up voting for Clark. After the session, he paid off the $6,500 he owed on the title to his ranch. State Senator D. G. Warner of Jefferson County sold some town lots at Boulder to Charlie Clark at remarkably inflated prices. A week later, he deposited $8,000 in the bank. Through Walter Bickford's maneuvering, Missoula lumberman-lawmaker H. W. McLaughlin became a business associate of none other than W. A. Clark, to whom he sold in the process $24,684 worth of woodlots and sawmills at a drastically inflated rate of exchange. B. F. Fine, a down-on-his-luck mine operator, sported $5,000 after the adjournment of the legislature. He claimed to have rendered "services" for the money, but he could not explain what the services were. Democrat Stephen Bywater, a railroad conducter by trade, first voted for Clark on the fateful eighteenth ballot. On 3 March 1899, he banked $15,000. Republican S. S. Hobson, who had chaired the GOP caucus and had played a pivotal role in rounding up Republican votes, turned up with $25,000 deposited in the Continental Bank of Chicago, a firm with which the banking house of W. A Clark and Brother maintained a business affiliation.[32]

Generally, the most impressive witnesses were those who supported the Daly cause: the three state supreme court justices and the cool and impressive Fred Whiteside. Many of the others severely embarrassed themselves and their home state as well. Some of them clearly forfeited any right to credibility. Z. T. Cason of Butte testified before the Montana Supreme Court that he had offered bribes for Clark, then took money to retract this admission, then went into hiding, then was discovered and brought to Washington, where he told his forlorn tale under subpoena. Or Ben Hill, a tough customer who served the Clark cause at first, then admitted that he had taken money from Campbell to work and testify for the other side. Before the committee, he remarkably contradicted his own earlier affidavit as a "pack of damn lies." This prompted Senator Hoar to remark: ". . . this witness cannot be treated by any human being, after his own statements, as a source of testimony. Nobody would say that anything he would say has the slightest title to be believed by any human being because he says it." Responding to this and to other incidents of the hearings, the *Yellowstone Journal* of Miles City voiced a common sentiment: "THEY ARE ALL LIARS." [33]

Following the closing arguments by opposing counsel, the Committee on Privileges and Elections held its final deliberations on 10 April 1900. By unanimous agreement, the members determined "that the election to the Senate of William A. Clark, of Montana, is null and void on account of briberies, attempted briberies, and corrupt practices" and "*Resolved*, That William A. Clark was not duly and legally elected to a seat in the Senate of the United States by the legislature of the State of Montana." Two members of the committee, Senators E. W. Pettus of Alabama and W. A. Harris of Kansas, agreed with the majority that Clark should be denied his seat; but they filed a minority statement criticizing Chairman Chandler's arbitrariness, the admission of so much hearsay evidence and failure to follow strict court procedures, and the equally dubious methods practiced by Campbell and the Daly faction.[34]

Senator Chandler, who was openly and bitterly critical of Clark, presented the committee's findings to the full Senate on 23 April 1900, with the recommendation to his fellows that the Montanan's election be declared void due to bribery. This left Clark in a difficult position. He had initially declared that he would resign if the committee found against him. But now he waffled when it did so, and in late April he even announced that he would indeed not resign. Nonetheless, he almost had to, for the full Senate would clearly vote to adopt its committee's recommendation. Thus on 15 May 1900, Senator W. A. Clark rose before his colleagues on a point of "personal privilege" and announced his resignation. In so doing, he lashed out at his "manifestly unfair treatment" at the hands of Chandler and the committee, retold the tale of his long and bitter persecution by Daly, and defended his conduct as the champion of his state against the Anaconda behemoth. Tearfully and with breaking voice, he concluded: "I was never in all my life, except by such characters as are now pursuing me, charged with a dishonorable act, and I propose to leave to my children a legacy, worth more than gold, that of an unblemished name." Several senators strode up to him as he finished, expressing their sympathy and even support.[35]

Clark's emotional resignation seemed to close the book forever on his ill-fated political career, and to leave the pro-Daly, Populist-returned-Democratic Governor Robert B. Smith with the authority to appoint his successor. Not quite, however. Even before his resignation speech, Clark and his henchmen had begun plotting a bizarre move that, for sheer audacity, would outrank any of his previous ploys. For the past month, the Butte millionaire and his minions had been weighing various schemes, all of which revolved around the idea of removing Smith temporarily from the scene and placing Lieutenant Governor A. E. Spriggs, a friend of Clark, in the position of acting governor.

One option, which they discarded as unworkable, was to have Spriggs then call a special session of the legislature which could legally return the old man to Washington. They chose, instead, an even more outrageous strategy: to have Spriggs simply reappoint Clark to the Senate seat he had just vacated. In a strictly legal sense, this was not implausible. If Clark had not resigned, and if the Senate had then gone on to vote him out, there would have been no legal "vacancy" in his Senate position, because the original election would have been voided as improper. But he had in fact resigned, and his resignation clearly created a vacancy which the state's chief executive must fill by temporary appointment.[36]

The Clark forces removed Governor Smith from Helena by a clever bit of scheming. They had one Thomas Hinds, a seasoned Butte politico with ties to both the Clark and Daly camps, conduct Smith to California in order to assess a mineral property there for mineowner Miles Finlen. A lawyer, Smith owed Finlen $2,000, and he could easily discharge the debt through this service. The California property, near Grass Valley, lay sixty-five miles from the nearest railroad, which meant that Smith would be safely incommunicado. Meanwhile, Lieutenant Governor Spriggs was attending a Populist convention at Sioux Falls, South Dakota. Immediately after Smith's departure, the Clarkites sent Spriggs a cryptic telegram: "Weather fine, cattle doing well"—his signal to hurry home. Charlie Clark had been holding his father's letter of resignation for days. Now, at almost the precise moment when the old man was standing before the Senate and resigning, Charlie inserted the correct date and handed the letter to Acting Governor Spriggs. Within a few hours, arguing that the people's choice for senator must be allowed to stand, Spriggs appointed William A. Clark to the Senate position that he had just resigned.[37]

Clark's enemies reacted swiftly. "Clark Executes a Little Cat-Hop," sneered the *Anaconda Standard*. "I reckon the trick won't work," commented Senator Chandler. Severely embarrassed, Governor Smith rushed back to Montana, protesting his innocence of any scheme and denouncing both Spriggs and Clark. Stopping at Ogden, Utah, Smith told the press: "This is only another one of the many dirty tricks, perjuries and crimes resorted to by Clark and his minions to fasten him on the state as a senator, and no just or fair minded man can look upon this whole proceeding with anything but contempt and a sense of shame. . . ." Ex-Senator Sanders saw the whole episode as "an unparalleled atrocity. . . . This bedraggled barter and bribery is a stench in the nostrils of every honorable man and decent woman in Montana."[38]

Back in Helena, Governor Smith revoked Spriggs's appointment of Clark and announced his own appointment to the Senate, long-time Democratic stalwart and former Congressman Martin Maginnis. But since Spriggs had actually held the legal power of appointment, both appointees' credentials now rested in the Senate, which faced the task of choosing the proper one. A number of silverite senators, including George Vest of Missouri and John P. Jones of Nevada, urged Clark to fight once again for his Senate seat. Senator Chandler, on the other hand, continued to argue that Clark had no claim because his initial election had been voided by fraud. Since a major fight loomed again over the question, and since the Senate was about to adjourn anyway, both the friends and the foes of Clark chose to let the issue lie.[39] So once again, as in 1893–94, Clark was beaten, and the Clark-Daly feud had again left Montana with a vacant seat in the United States Senate.

It seems nearly impossible to explain Clark's motives in this last, ridiculous maneuver. The desperate act of a desperate man, it may have begun as a ploy which he thought could succeed and have ended as a thumbing of his nose at the world which had once more rejected him. His anger knew no bounds. In a hot-tempered address at Butte in June, he decried "the most devilish persecution that any man has ever been subjected to in the history of any civilized country." He struck out again at Senator Chandler, who, he claimed, "had bulldozed the committee into reporting against me." Still managing the case against Clark in the Senate, Chandler responded:

> No rogue e'er felt the halter draw
> With good opinions of the law.

According to reports, Clark threatened to settle scores with Chandler by going into New Hampshire to defeat him when he next faced reelection. For whatever combination of reasons, Chandler faced a well-funded opponent in his next contest, and he went down to defeat in 1901.[40]

The whole, sordid episode brought down a storm of well-deserved opprobrium both upon W. A. Clark and upon his adopted state.

Within Montana, Clark's nurturing of a friendly press still continued to yield him undue sympathy, although more and more independent papers began to wince. The *Billings Gazette* characterized the attitude of agrarian eastern Montana in denouncing both sides and concluding that Daly "and his crowd are just as corrupt as Clark and we will never have any decent politics in Montana until both are shorn of power."[41] The national media, in contrast, watched the revelations before the Committee on Privileges and Elections in early 1900 and then the Spriggs caper of May with unqualified revulsion. The question of unseating U.S. senators was all the more pressing at this time because Matthew Quay of Pennsylvania had been ejected just before Clark resigned. Like Montana's Lee Mantle in 1893, Quay had been appointed by the governor after the legislature had failed to act.

Only a few Democratic papers, like the *Washington Times,* felt that Clark deserved to keep his seat. Most believed that the evidence against him was conclusive. The *Nation* agreed with those members of the Committee on Privileges and Elections who "describe the affair as the most intricate case of corrupt politics ever known." Only the earlier and similar case of Alexander Caldwell in Kansas and the unsuccessful, marathon attempt of promoter John "Gas" Addicks to win election in the legislature of Delaware could compare to the Clark fiasco. The *New York Press* saw the whole business as "a nasty reproach to Montana and the United States senate," and the *Chicago Evening Post* viewed it as a reflection of "the seamy and corrupt side of Montana politics." Said the Washington reporter of the *Boston Transcript,* it "shows what a war between two not overly scrupulous multimillionaires can accomplish for the political degradation of a commonwealth." Most observers felt, with the *Boston Post,* that the integrity of the Senate itself was on the line: "The purchase of seats in that body with the money of millionaires can not be tolerated." The proposed constitutional amendment which would allow popular election of U.S. senators, meanwhile, lay buried in Senate committee after having been passed by the House of Representatives. Despite the scandals of Clark, Addicks, and others, it would not become a part of the Constitution (the Seventeenth Amendment) until 1913.[42]

Thus, after a year-and-a-half of contention and acrimony, the political career of William A. Clark seemed destroyed and disgraced beyond redemption. So, too, did the reputations of the state of Montana and of those public and private citizens who had disgraced themselves by taking his money and serving his ends. Like sharks in a feeding frenzy, men of ordinary demeanor seemed suddenly transformed from their usual torpor by the scent of immediate riches. One must agree with Fred Whiteside's appraisal, and one would like to accept his self-assessment:

> Almost without exception they were men of small means who had tasted the bitter waters of defeat in the struggle of life, and public opinion was inclined to condone the acceptance of such money.
>
> As for myself, I had lived in the era of easy opportunity that engendered a contempt for money. . . . My own self-respect was worth more to me than all the money in the world. There is a lot of satisfaction in knowing that one is beyond the reach of a man with millions.[43]

7. "Consolidation": The Amalgamated and the Independents

In a true sense, the epic struggle between Clark and Daly was merely a noisy diversion from the really significant contest, the battle over ownership of the massive ore deposits beneath the Butte Hill. "Consolidation," the grouping together of the various Butte properties under common management and ownership, was inevitable. Scattered ownership guaranteed only waste, contention, and endless litigation. Marathon legal hassles often erupted in the efforts to "rationalize" and centralize control of the great mining areas of the West. During the years prior to 1866, more than 250 cases and $10,000,000 in legal costs resulted from the struggle to dominate Nevada's Comstock Lode. Simeon Reed faced monumental problems of litigation over his Bunker Hill and Sullivan properties in north Idaho's Coeur d'Alene district. The wily George Hearst spent hundreds of thousands buying up adjacent ground bordering his fabulously productive Homestake Mine in the Black Hills. Only by so doing could he be certain of secure title. With its hundreds of rich claims and its many well-established mineowners, the sprawling Butte district staged the greatest of all legal-political battles in the history of western mining. The final result, though hard won, was preordained: consolidation under one central management.

As the nineteenth century drew to a close, the trend of the time made it almost a certainty that efforts would again be made to corner the world copper industry. The booming industry was nicely concentrated: a handful of large firms—at Butte, Montana, and in Michigan, Arizona, and at Rio Tinto in Spain—dominated world production. By cornering Butte and by securing some accord with the others, a shrewd monopolist could corner the market. This very moment in history, the turn of the twentieth century, marked a major movement toward consolidation throughout American industry. During the four years following 1898, more than 2,600 mergers occurred among businesses in the United States, involving properties valued at over $6,300,000,000. Giant new super-corporations, or "trusts" as they were often called in those days, sprang up to dominate the major industries of the nation. Modeled after John D. Rockefeller's monopolistic Standard Oil Company, the new trusts wielded awesome power. Among the greatest of them were International Harvester, American Tobacco, International Steamship, and J. P. Morgan's $1,400,000,000 United States Steel Corporation.[1] In nearly every sector, the trend seemed to be toward monopoly.

The movement toward consolidation found ready reflection in the turbulent, high risk-high gain mining industry of the West. In 1899 for instance, a group of capitalists which included H. H. Rogers and Leonard Lewisohn, both of whom would play a large role in the Butte consolidation, merged together $65,000,000 worth of western silver-lead smelters, plants, and properties to form the American Smelting and Refining Company. ASARCO, whose holdings included smelters at Great Falls and at East Helena in Montana, acquired the valuable properties of Meyer Guggenheim and Sons in 1901, and the Guggenheims soon gained control of the entire organization.[2]

The formation of ASARCO closely paralleled what was happening in coppers. A five year period of boom and high prices set in during 1896 as the economy recovered from the 1893 Panic, as the electrical industry continued its rapid expansion, and as American exports flooded European markets. The price climbed to 19.25 cents per pound on a wave of buying in 1899. Financially, the center of world investment remained in Boston, whose staid State Street capitalists maintained their mastery over the old Lake Superior district, as well as over mines at Butte, and in Arizona and elsewhere in the West. In terms of production, Butte continued to dominate the industry, as it had for the past decade. The Calumet and Hecla group still figured largely in coppers, but it trailed the cluster of Butte firms led by Anaconda. The booming copper towns of Arizona were on the rise, but Arizona still trailed Montana, and so, by a much wider margin, did the less developed mines of Utah and Alaska.[3] In short, Boston and Butte ruled the world of copper at the close of the nineteenth century.

Had they been more aggressive and daring, the Bostonians might have tried to corner the markets themselves, but they seemed content to sit back and gather in their ample dividends. Cecil Rhodes, the British-South African empire builder and developer of gold and diamond mines, actually formed a scheme to corner copper by gaining control of Anaconda. He was in the process of dispatching the great mining engineer John Hays Hammond to America for this purpose when the eruption of the Boer War forced him to abandon the effort. Instead of Rhodes, who died soon after, it was speculator Thomas W. Larson who hatched the big copper scheme. A bundle of contradictions, the bluff, hearty, and overbearing Lawson seemed a born promoter if ever there was one. He thrived on controversy and self-advertisement. Born and bred in New England, he had garnered $60,000 in stock speculation by age sixteen. Lawson went on to gain, lose, and regain several fortunes. Polite Boston folks found him disreputable and tried to keep him off the stock exchange, but he gave better than he got and always kept them entertained. Lawson once wrote a tome entitled *Why Priests Should Wed*, on another occasion paid $30,000 to have a variety of carnation named for his wife, and was one of the first promoters of those baseball cards which generations of kids have loved to buy and trade.[4]

Lawson, a shrewd and impetuous stock market plunger, first got interested in Butte by speculating successfully in the depreciated stock of the Butte and Boston Company. He correctly figured that the firm was being drained of its profits by insiders who managed it in favor of its companion Boston and Montana Company. Lawson bought up nearly one-fourth of the stock in Butte and Boston and elbowed his way into the halls of its management. From this vantage, he gazed wondrously upon the vast earning potential of coppers. He came in 1896 to envision a corner on world production, a corner based on initial control of the two Boston firms of Butte. From this base he would expand to dominance of the rest of Butte, and then to hegemony over the other copper mining centers.[5] Thus did the dream of Hyacinthe Secretan and of Cecil Rhodes reappear in the fertile mind of Thomas Lawson.

With a mere 46,000 shares of Butte and Boston, Lawson had a long way to go. He needed big-time capital, and he found it in the persons of Henry Huttleston Rogers and William Rockefeller, two key figures of the mighty Standard Oil trust. William Rockefeller, younger brother and business associate of the legendary John D. Rockefeller, was approaching sixty at this time, a kindly and retiring fellow who played second fiddle to his brother and to Henry Rogers. In entering the world of copper, William Rockefeller followed the lead of Rogers. Sixty years of age in 1900, handsome Henry Rogers looked the part of a captain of industry with his full head of greying hair, out-thrust jaw, penetrating gaze, and haughty manner. One of the forgotten giants of the "Robber Baron" era, he provides a near perfect example of the schizoid nature of the business titans of his generation. Allan Nevins described him well: "Virile, arrogant, and ruthless in business, magnetic and witty in society, Rogers still had a lunar dualism—dark on one side, bright on the other."[6]

In his private life, Henry Rogers seemed the perfect Victorian gentleman. "Genial and gentle in his personal and domestic relations," he lavished millions on churches and public buildings for his hometown, Fairhaven, Massachusetts. He magnanimously befriended Mark Twain when the great author's personal finances collapsed, and he selflessly devoted his own time and expertise to putting Twain back on his feet again. Twain, in turn, idolized him. He referred to Rogers as "my closest and most valuable friend," "the best-bred gentleman I have met on either side of the ocean in any rank of life from the Kaiser down to the bootblack." In the world of business, however, H. H. Rogers seemed a totally different man, a brutal, tooth-and-claw infighter. "Hen" Rogers had joined the Standard Oil team in 1874 and had risen rapidly to its front ranks through his traits of quick intelligence and ruthlessness. By the late 1890s, as John D. Rockefeller moved toward retirement, Rogers occupied the key position at Standard Oil. With a grudging respect, Wall Street insiders referred to him as the "Hell Hound" because of his piratical tactics.[7]

H. H. Rogers and William Rockefeller, along with A. C. Burrage and James Stillman, the president of New York's First National City Bank whose two daughters had married William Rockefeller's sons, formed part of a group popularly known as the "Standard Oil Gang." These and other Standard Oil magnates, such as Henry Flagler and John Archbold, had made fantastic profits during the 1880s and 1890s, profits which drastically increased as they came through the deflationary Panic of 1893 relatively unscathed. Between 1893 and 1901, Standard Oil had yielded $250,000,000 in dividends. Now, as mighty John D. Rockefeller retired to enjoy and give away his millions, the Rockefeller lieutenants were heading out on their own, seeking new worlds to conquer.

They poured their money into many enterprises. Rogers, for instance, put his money into Staten Island and Virginia railroads and into the Union Pacific. Along with William Rockefeller, he went into New England gas utilities and fought a wild series of battles there with the notorious John "Gas" Addicks. In 1901 he became a director of U.S. Steel. The gang's most spectacular move was into copper, where they envisaged another empire to rival the one they had built in petroleum. It is important to note that John D. Rockefeller did not join his minions in their copper caper. In fact, he strongly disapproved of it and later censured the boys when they got in trouble. The public, understandably distrustful of the old man, often failed to grasp this fact and blamed him for the sins of his proteges. In fact, the emerging copper trust would often be referred to as simply an arm of Standard Oil, when in reality it had no corporate connection to that firm at all, only to its executives.[8]

Rogers and friends first encountered Thomas Lawson in their New England gas wars, and they listened now with interest to his copper schemes. Once their meticulous research convinced them that Lawson was more than a visionary, they decided to join up with him. They began buying heavily into Lake copper, into the emerging Utah Consolidated Copper Company, and especially into Butte. State Street buzzed with commotion as the Boston crowd perceived that New York money was at last invading its domain. Since Calumet and Hecla was so tightly and conservatively controlled, the Rogers-Rockefeller-Lawson team focused its energies upon the twin Boston companies of Butte. In 1897 they joined forces with the Lewisohn brothers and A. S. Bigelow, the established powers of these two firms, to consolidate the companies in a formal marriage.[9]

Thomas Lawson had intended all along to base the first stock issue in his gestating copper trust upon the Boston and Montana–Butte and Boston. But complications now disrupted his plans. For one thing, as we shall soon see, these firms became hopelessly mired in litigation by 1898. For another, Lawson found to his dismay that his Standard Oil pals had crossed him. Rogers and Rockefeller had been buying heavily into Anaconda and had gained a growing voice in its management. With both George Hearst and Lloyd Tevis dead by 1899, James Ben Ali Haggin and Marcus Daly firmly held the reins of company control between them. Both men were aging, and both were coming to see the logic of a copper consolidation. Daly, the unschooled frontier miner, found himself increasingly out of touch with the college-trained experts of the new generation, whom he failed to trust or understand, and was willing to move up into the exclusive realms of management. He would join in the consolidation while Haggin, ever the tough independent, would sell out.

Just how Anaconda came into the great copper combine is unclear. According to Lawson, Rogers told him that Marcus Daly had been hoodwinking his partners for years by secretly saving rich veins for later development. Rogers reportedly boasted that: " . . . it took me only a short time to get under his waist coat and find just what he had out there." In short, Rogers believed he had found a real bargain in Anaconda. Wall Street confidante Clarence Barron, on the other hand, reported years later that Daly "buncoed Rogers into paying a bigger price than he had asked before [since the Boston companies were tied up in court] and the temptation to Rogers was that he could get a still bigger price from the public." Lawson's report seems doubtful. Daly would probably never have crossed his beloved friend Haggin. And as mining engineer Alexander Leggat reasoned, it would have been nearly impossible to conceal such rich veins. Barron, on the contrary, may well be right. The truth is probably quite simple. Daly and Haggin both realized the dangers of endless litigation and were willing to sell out for the right price. Unable to secure free control of the Boston companies, Rogers had to have the Anaconda, and so he agreed to the high price. When he announced this to Lawson, the Boston speculator protested angrily, holding out for the favored Boston twins which he had been promoting to his clients. Rogers had the upper hand, though, and Lawson finally went along.[10] The Anaconda would be taken first, the Boston firms later.

By early 1899, distant Montana clearly foresaw the approaching shadows of copper consolidation. First of all, a phalanx of corporate lobbyists, led by Anaconda's E. D. Matts, pressed the all important House Bill 132 through the legislature, the same compromised assembly that sold out to Clark. H.B. 132 stipulated that corporate transfers might be accomplished by a vote of a two-thirds majority of the stockholders. The bill was essential to the consolidation, since otherwise a tiny minority of stockholders in any company might frustrate it, and the mining companies joined hands to support it. Governor R. B. Smith, an anti-corporate Populist-Democrat despite his ties to Daly, vetoed the measure with the garbled but portentous warning that: "If you do not assert your independence now and defeat this measure, it will be too late when the tentacles of this octopus have fastened their fangs on the strong limbs of this fair commonwealth." The lawmakers ignored the warning and overrode his veto.[11]

Meanwhile, Wall Street rumbled with rumors of a forthcoming copper combination. The *Wall Street Journal* quoted widespread reports that Rothschild, Morgan and Rockefeller money was pouring into the embryonic trust. When it became clear that the Standard Oil Gang was involved, the *Engineering and Mining Journal* reported that: "Boston has gone wild, and takes no account of the reaction which will follow." Buyers of coppers, scenting the wind, raced to board the bandwagon before it was too late, and stock values surged upward.

But Rogers and Rockefeller had beat them to the punch by investing millions into Anaconda and its sister companies before the public realized what was happening.[12]

The great copper excitement crested on 27 April 1899, with the incorporation at Trenton, New Jersey, of the Amalgamated Copper Company. Capitalized at $75,000,000, with 750,000 shares at $100 each, the Amalgamated was designed as a "holding company" typical of the times. Such holding companies as Amalgamated Copper were designed to own and control the actual operating companies. Through their use, capitalists could effectively monopolize an industry while their lawyers convinced sympathetic courts that no illegal monopoly corporation had been formed since the holding companies were only investing in various operating firms. The Butte-based companies included in the "first section" issue of Amalgamated stock were the Anaconda Copper Mining Company and its reduction arm, the Washoe Copper Company, also the Parrot Silver and Copper Company and the Colorado Smelting and Mining Company. The merging of these companies would, of course, permit a cost-saving consolidation and centralization of reduction facilities. As Daly wrote later in 1899: "The Amalgamated Copper Company wants to increase the capacity of its smelting works in Montana to handle the Butte product. We want to condense those works so that one great organization will handle it and our railroad facilities and everything will be the most economical. We want to locate at Anaconda unless there are greater advantages at Great Falls. . . ." As noted previously, the Amalgamated vastly enlarged the smelting-concentration works at Anaconda to handle the consolidated mines at Butte, while also continuing to employ the Boston and Montana facilities at Great Falls.[13]

After participating in the formation of Amalgamated, James Ben Ali Haggin liquidated his Anaconda holdings for $15,000,000, pocketing 50 percent greater earnings on his stocks than the Hearst estate had gained a few years earlier. The rugged and shrewd old man promptly created a syndicate to plunge his earnings into the Cerro de Pasco silver mines of Peru. He continued adding to his great fortune until his death, at age eighty-seven, in 1914. Unlike Haggin, Marcus Daly elected to gamble on the Amalgamated. He took stock in the trust in return for his Anaconda shares and agreed to come aboard as president of the Amalgamated. While Daly's symbolic presence at the helm served to reassure the copper world of expert management, the real locus of power could be seen in the fact that Henry Rogers served as vice president and William G. Rockefeller (William's son) as secretary-treasurer. The directors of the trust included Rogers, William

Rockefeller, Daly, James Stillman, A. C. Burrage, and other Wall Street luminaries.[14] Clearly, control of Butte and its destiny now rested in Wall Street hands.

"The Amalgamated Copper Company is the biggest financial deal of the age," trumpeted the *New York Times*, reckoning that Standard Oil brains and fiscal muscle seemed destined to control world copper. Lawson's carefully orchestrated bally-hoo immediately set off a pandemonium of excitement as investors fell over themselves to buy shares in the trust before they ran out. Four uniformed guards had difficulty fending off the crowds and closing the great doors of the National City Bank on the first day of sales. Even after the rejecting of many millions of improperly submitted and late purchase orders, the subscription of Amalgamated stock ran to $130,000,000—the largest stock subscription Wall Street had ever seen.[15] The buying public obviously figured that anything the Standard Oil touched must surely turn to gold.

Even hard-nosed Henry Rogers gasped at the near hysterical eagerness of the investment world to join in his copper venture. The public would soon regret it, for the Amalgamated was a pawn which was being cynically manipulated by insiders. The Rogers-Rockefeller team had acquired their "first section" of Butte holdings for a total of $39,000,000, the purchase price of Anaconda and its sister corporations. They covered this purchase with a credit from the National City Bank. The "Crime of Amalgamated," as Thomas Lawson later called it, came when they flagrantly overcapitalized their holding company at $75,000,000, or nearly twice its proven assets. In what can only be termed a callous fleecing of the public, Rogers and friends now coolly issued the subscribers one share for each five shares solicited in the oversubscription. This brought in $26,000,000. Measured against the $39,000,000 purchase price, this meant that the investing public was paying for two-thirds of the real cost of Amalgamated's properties. But the investors thereby acquired with their $26,000,000 only slightly more than one-third of the heavily watered shares of Amalgamated stock. All of which meant, of course, that the Standard Oil gang, having really invested only $13,000,000 of their own dollars, now held nearly 500,000 shares of Amalgamated worth roughly $50,000,000![16]

The "Crime of Amalgamated" did not end here. In a typical Standard Oil maneuver, Rogers brought the powerful Lewisohn Brothers into the Amalgamated, not only because of their Boston and Montana–Butte and Boston involvement but also because with their giant new refinery at Raritan, New Jersey, and with their well-established metals brokerage, they were selling well over half of all the copper mined in the United States. Rogers smoothly cornered the crafty and tough Leonard Lewisohn. Now that Amalgamated was absorbing his client mines, Lewisohn had either to come aboard or see his sources of the red metal cut off. Left with no choice, Lewisohn agreed to incorporating his family concern as the United Metals Selling Company. United Metals, in which the Lewisohns shared control with the Rogers crowd, would serve as the lucrative sales arm of Amalgamated. It soon became clear that the Lewisohns were being shouldered aside. According to Lawson, this defeat deeply embittered the once proud Leonard Lewisohn, who had dreamed of keeping the business in the family. He died soon afterward, in 1902.[17]

Rogers and associates continued, during the months that followed, to prey upon the Amalgamated shareholders. After their initial harvest of profits, they began cashing in by unloading their inflated stocks. The stock fell to $75 on a wave of selling as many marginal holders sold out at a loss; the insiders then resumed buying and adding to their ill-gotten gains. In 1901, amidst a blare of publicity similar to that of 1899, the clique brought forth their "second section" of Amalgamated, based this time upon the long-awaited absorption of the Boston and Montana–Butte and Boston Consolidated Mining Companies. With little regard for the true value of these firms, they casually increased the capitalization of the trust from $75 million to $155 million and raised the value of each share from $100 to $130. Of course, this once again meant that gullible investors more than paid for the properties with water while the insiders took the real profits. Then, the gang mercilessly slashed the dividend and unloaded vast quantities of stock, driving its market value down to an incredible 33! Thousands of small stockholders lost their shirts while the insiders bought back at bargain rates for yet another round of profits.[18]

Such was the Wall Street morality of 1899–1901. The big Amalgamated shakedown prompted howls of outrage and warnings that the Standard Oil gang aimed to merge the world's oil, lead, and copper industries into one great supertrust. Even the sedate *Engineering and Mining Journal* offered its readers "a very distinct warning to outsiders to let it [Amalgamated] alone." As one angry citizen complained to the U.S. Bureau of Corporations: "Rogers has taken more millions from the Amalgamated minority stock holders than all the thieves in the 46 state prisons." Yet, even with the advent of the alleged "trust-buster" Theodore Roosevelt to the Presidency, who openly disparaged Standard Oil and the Rockefellers, the Amalgamated group went its own way behind a wall of secrecy.[19]

That wall of secrecy was breached dramatically in 1904–5 when insider Thomas Lawson published a spectacular series of expose articles in *Everybody's* magazine entitled "The Story of Amalgamated." Lawson's articles touched off a sensation and pushed *Everybody's* momentarily to the top rank in circulation among American magazines. The series did much to stimulate a "muckraking" trend in journalism, and it was published in 1905 as a best-selling book entitled *Frenzied Finance*.[20] Writing floridly and with verve, Lawson depicted himself as the unwitting dupe of the villainous H. H. Rogers. Admittedly, his sincerity is open to question, for the book is full of self-serving explanations of his own conduct; but his indictment of Standard Oil executives convinced the public at the time. Indeed, it is still quite convincing today. Typically, the gang remained silent in the face of Lawson's accusations. They filed no libel charges, even though their ex-cohort described their bilking of the public in graphic detail. The great Amalgamated rip-off, as Lawson demonstrated, left thousands of ruined investors in its wake. At the same time, it wrought momentous changes upon the Butte mining district.

Even as Rogers and his friends plotted their copper consolidation, events at Butte served to demonstrate why such a unification of ownership and management was necessary. As noted, litigation usually frequented the great American mining centers, usually eroding profits and sometimes paralyzing operations. What happened at Butte, though, seemed to be in a class by itself. Before the carnival of litigation had run its course from 1896 to 1906, tens of millions of dollars worth of mining properties would shut down; thousands of employees would lose their income; the camp would stare into the abyss of outright warfare; and the Amalgamated trust itself would face imminent disaster.

Much of the problem lay in the vagaries of federal mining law. In the big rushes of the 1850s and 1860s to California and Nevada, the frontier miners worked out their own local codes for defining mining claims. Based upon these local customs, California law evolved away from the English and Spanish traditions of establishing the ownership of mineral deposits by simply extending surface boundary lines downward. It came instead to embrace the "apex" theory: that whoever owned the surface ground where the vein "apexed" or came nearest the surface owned the entirety of the vein, even when it faulted or meandered downward laterally beyond the sidelines of the surface claim and beneath the ground owned by its neighbors. Championed by the legal wizard of the Comstock Lode, Senator William Stewart of Nevada, the Apex Law was written into the federal code in 1866 and was revised and strengthened in 1872.[21] Time and again, it would prove to be a mighty source of mischief, nowhere more so than at Butte.

Legal hassling began at Butte almost as early as did mining itself, but the grim showdown battle set in during the mid-1890s. The contestants were the well-heeled Boston and Montana–Butte and Boston companies and the Heinze brothers' fast rising Montana Ore Purchasing Company. Brash, bold, and ingenious, the *wunderkind* of Montana mining, F. Augustus Heinze would prove himself in this marathon contest to be not only an exceptional miner and developer, but more than that—a tough and ruthless capitalist and political manipulator capable of facing off even the lords of mighty Standard Oil.

Young "Fritz" Heinze first demonstrated his gall and cunning in a hot contest with the shrewd mining millionaire Jim Murray over the Estella Mine during 1893–95. Murray was a likable and big-spending chap, whose prodigal displays of money back East helped form the popular image of garish western mining kings. But he more than met his match in Heinze. Fritz negotiated a lease on the Estella which stipulated that he must pay Murray 50 percent on all high-grade (over 15 percent) ores, but nothing at all on lower grades. He then simply had his men mix waste rock into the ores, so that none of them approached 15 percent in richness. Thus he paid Murray nothing. Although Murray brought suit, Heinze emerged relatively unscathed from a jury trial. Butte enjoyed his antics; and even Jim Murray commented with good-humored, mining camp wryness: "If I'd known that young fellow ten years ago I'd have owned all of Butte."[22]

Just how and why the legal battles between the Heinzes and the Boston companies began is a matter of question. One bit of Butte lore, recorded by M. G. O'Malley, credited Marcus Daly with inciting "that Irish Jew"—as he mistakenly dubbed Heinze—against the Bostonians. Daly, the working miner, hated litigation; but Anaconda claims abutted those of the Boston companies and disagreements ensued. Furthermore, the Irishman never forgave Thomas Couch and the Boston and Montana management for opposing him in the capital fight. It may even be that he aimed to keep the Boston companies tied up in court so that he could sell his Anaconda at a higher price. In any case, O'Malley's story has it that Daly talked the impetuous Fritz Heinze into settling some scores for him.[23] This is dubious at best, but there may be some truth in it.

Heinze himself often told his version of how the war began. According to him, the trouble started when his chief engineer, C. H. Batterman, deserted the Montana Ore Purchasing Company and, taking valuable mine maps with him, went over to the Boston companies with the argument that Heinze's great Rarus Mine actually apexed on the Butte and Boston Company's adjacent Michael Davitt property. When Heinze tried to settle with A. S. Bigelow of Boston for $250,000, Bigelow supposedly refused with the haughty remark that he had been abused in Montana and that he would make an example of this young upstart. Heinze claims that he replied: "Mr. Bigelow, you have a great deal more property which is subject to the same kind of litigation as that in which you are about to thrust me. If it is your determination that we shall fight, why I will give you a fight that will be heard from one side of this continent to the other." [24]

Heinze's account seems a bit boastful and self-serving. A more plausible explanation of the origins of the litigation is that offered by copper management expert Thomas R. Navin: since Heinze was beginning to market copper through his brother Otto's New York dry goods importing and merchandising business, he posed a direct threat to the great marketing firm of the Lewisohn Brothers, who also dominated the Boston companies of Butte. On the other hand, when the Rogers group began building toward consolidation in 1897, they severely threatened the Montana Ore Purchasing Company of the Heinzes, which relied upon the ores of independent mines. These independent mines seemed destined for inclusion in the trust. [25]

However and for whatever reasons it began, the battle between the Heinzes and the Boston companies flared rapidly into a full-scale war, with fights on many fronts. Since the Standard Oil group had targeted them for inclusion in the trust, the Boston firms had the muscle not only of the Lewisohn-Bigelow team behind them, but the support of the Rogers-Rockefeller crowd as well. Heinze, in contrast, had to rely heavily on his own pluck, and he would frequently find himself a mere step away from bankruptcy. He did enjoy one asset that most observers overlooked at the time: the capital and credit backing of Otto Heinze's flourishing New York business. Fritz Heinze proved himself a remarkably daring and resourceful antagonist, who won many a fight on sheer audacity. At the height of the war, for example, he employed thirty-seven attorneys, led by his able lawyer-brother Arthur. Many of them were involved strictly in ferreting out new lawsuits to pursue. [26] Butte folks dubbed him a "court-house miner."

The most difficult of all the cases was *E. Rollins Morse* v. *Montana*

Ore Purchasing Company. Morse, a Boston banker-broker, was deeply involved in managing the Boston companies. In the Ninth Circuit Federal District Court of Judge Hiram Knowles at Butte, the consolidated Boston companies argued early in 1898 that major ore bodies of Heinze's Rarus actually apexed in the Butte and Boston's Michael Davitt Mine. Judge Knowles, who had allegedly once served as counsel for the Boston companies, directed the jury to find for the Boston and Montana–Butte and Boston. But the jury balked amidst rumors of a 10–2 sentiment in favor of the popular Heinze and reached no verdict at all. Ordering a retrial at Helena, Judge Knowles issued an injunction closing down all operations in the area bordering the two valuable mines.[27]

Even as the Morse case lay stalled in federal court, the odds mounted steadily for both sides. Each company, especially Heinze's, needed access to the ores to keep its reduction works running at peak efficiency. Back in Boston, meanwhile, A. S. Bigelow and his entourage were being pushed aside by Rogers and his cohorts. Such was Bigelow's fall from power that, according to well-informed Clarence Barron: "When he went west to the Pacific coast to meet his boy, he notified Rogers that he was going and Rogers told him not to go near Butte, and he did not." So, when the case came to retrial at Helena in 1900, Heinze now faced the Rogers gang, who were at this very moment preparing the Boston twins for entry into Amalgamated.

During the six-week-long trial, Heinze demonstrated his political savvy, as he would again and again, by having his lieutenants and the friendly *Helena Independent* hammer away at the hated Standard Oil-Amalgamated as an alien trust attempting to colonize the state. On one occasion, the *Independent* depicted Rogers and friends as "a crew of political cut-throats . . . employing all the tactics of sea pirates to throttle and destroy the liberties and the property of all who do not bow the knee in abject servility to them and give tribute to their rapacity." As a result, the Helena jury found for Heinze. The Amalgamated forces, however, easily won yet another retrial on the basis of unfavorable publicity; and so the case went off to the distant San Francisco circuit for one more hearing. Thus the contested veins remained inaccessible to both sides for months to come, and attention turned to other, more pressing cases.[28]

An especially tangled mass of litigation arose with the so-called Pennsylvania cases. Like most of the cases here considered, these went to one of the two benches of the Second Montana District Court at Butte (a third judge was added to the Second District in 1900). By what one lawyer termed at the time "some clerical jugglery," it seemed that most of the cases vital to Heinze ended up in the court of one of history's most bizarre judges, William Clancy. Paunchy, unkempt, with a flowing beard stained by tobacco juice and sometimes caked with food, Judge Clancy was a political accident who had slipped into office as a Populist in the 1896 fusionist landslide. He seldom demonstrated much expertise at law, casually dozing or spitting impressive streams of tobacco juice during hearings, even interrupting arguments of counsel to set forth his own political views. But he did demonstrate an unflinching loyalty to Fritz Heinze, who became his political patron and who people assumed had bribed him. In truth, the key to Heinze's political power lay in his control over one, and eventually two of the Butte judges. Marcus Daly, who may have set Heinze off on this course, supposedly once boasted: "He [Heinze] will come creeping to me on his belly in thirty days. I elect the judges. Heinze, without me, is only wind and water." That, surely, was one of the old man's worst appraisals.[29]

The Pennsylvania ruckus started in early 1898 as a suit between the Montana Ore Purchasing Company and the Boston and Montana, with the former arguing that the latter's northernmost Pennsylvania veins apexed on its Johnstown and Rarus properties. Late in 1899, Judge Clancy found for the "MOP" Company on every point, but the Boston and Montana promptly filed another suit for $600,000 in damages. The contestants unleashed a barrage of cross-cutting suits which dragged on for years. At one point, the Montana Supreme Court nearly jailed officers of the Montana Ore Purchasing Company for ignoring its injunctions and continuing to mine the disputed veins. Often, however, Heinze fared quite well with the Supreme Court in his arguments against the hated eastern corporations, for Montana opinion often flowed in Heinze's direction. The court eventually allowed him to mine along the contested peripheries of the Pennsylvania under a bond to cover losses to his adversaries in future decisions. Seeing that Heinze was boring out the veins as fast as possible, the Boston and Montana–Amalgamated then successfully convinced the court to raise the bond, figuring that they could destroy him by breaking his credit. Heinze outfoxed them by having brother Otto set up an East Coast dummy corporation, directed by himself and his employees, called the Delaware Surety Company. The Supreme Court of Montana accepted the bond of this hollow outfit, and Heinze went on mining. As for the Pennsylvania litigation, it would go on until the final stages of the Butte legal war.[30]

Faced with disaster in the hostile courts of Montana, the Boston–Standard Oil men attempted in the spring of 1898 to transfer

Judge William Clancy, from *Just for Fun: Cartoons and Caricatures of Men in Montana* (1907) (courtesy of Eric Myhre)

their corporate charter from the Treasure State to New York. This would allow them, through a plea of "diversity of residence," to route their cases into the friendlier federal courts. Unfortunately for themselves, the Boston and Montana management decided upon this ploy without first taking up the matter at a stockholders' meeting. When they brought up the issue at the next meeting, they learned that two Heinze men—John MacGinniss, vice president of the MOP Company, and James Forrester, one of the Heinze brothers' New York attorneys—had each purchased 100 shares of Boston and Montana stock. Forrester and MacGinniss immediately brought suit, arguing that their rights as minority stockholders were being violated by the transfer. They demanded that a receiver be authorized by the court to manage the corporation.[31]

Judge Clancy accepted the Forrester-MacGinniss argument and issued an injunction forbidding the transfer. House Bill 132, authorizing stock transfers with only a two-thirds majority of stockholders' consent, would not become law until well into 1899; so the Montana Supreme Court upheld Clancy's ruling on appeal. Always accommodating, the good judge then appointed crafty Tom Hinds, the ubiquitous Butte businessman-politician, as receiver of the Boston and Montana's Butte–Great Falls operations under a bond fixed at $100,000. Panic swept the Boston brokerages, and Boston and Montana stock plunged twenty-eight points in one day. Hearing rumors from the East that Heinze was stonewalling peace overtures from Rogers and Lawson, Butte geared up for a fight.

The Boston companies' officers shut down their mines and smelters, barricaded their properties, and even fled in order to avoid having court orders served on them by the sheriff. Word around town had it that they would flood the mines before turning them over to Hinds. But this would have amounted to suicide, and on 8 April 1899, the Boston men gave in and submitted to the receiver. Five days later, the Supreme Court ordered Hinds to turn back the property to the company's management under a $250,000 bond posted by the Boston and Montana Company. Even after that, Clancy issued contempt citations against the Boston and Montana officers and behaved in such a partisan manner that the higher court reprimanded him for conduct "unworthy of emulation." As a parting shot, the judge awarded Hinds a highly profitable settlement for his modest efforts. It was not until the spring of 1900 that the case was finally settled and the receivership completely lifted.[32]

The Boston and Montana receivership case had far-reaching impact. It served to cripple the once highly profitable firm as a payer of dividends and severely depressed its stock. More importantly, however, it tied up the consolidated Boston and Montana–Butte and Boston companies so tightly in litigation that Rogers and crew could not work out the stock transfers necessary to bring them into Amalgamated. This delay, as seen earlier, allowed Marcus Daly to fetch a high price for his Anaconda holdings from the Standard Oil gang, since they now had to base their holding company upon it. One can thus understand the persistent rumors that Daly had taken a hand in what Heinze and Hinds had done.[33] In any case, Heinze had twisted the Standard Oil lion's tail with dexterity; and before long, he would use his minority stockholders trick to advantage again.

In other, lesser cases, Fritz Heinze demonstrated again and again his ingenuity as a "courthouse miner." For instance, the celebrated Jim Larkin case. This humorous episode arose in March 1898 as a struggle between the Heinzes and the Butte and Boston over control of two valuable mines, the Snohomish and the Tramway. The Butte and Boston Company had acquired one-half ownership of the former and two-thirds of the latter from a nondescript miner named Jim Larkin, who died later in an insane asylum. Devilishly, Heinze hired detectives who tracked down Larkin's daughter Clara in the remote back country of Oregon. He then got himself named her guardian and the executor of the Larkin estate and went to court arguing that old Jim had been mentally incapable of transferring his properties to the Butte and Boston. Butte got a hearty laugh out of this one, and it dragged on in district court, the Montana Supreme Court, and eventually the federal courts for years.[34] It remained unsettled when the legal wars ended in 1906.

For sheer audacity, the best of Heinze's maneuvers was the much discussed Copper Trust case. In the spring of 1899, Arthur Heinze and engineer J. H. Trerise located two tiny, triangular slivers of land which remained unclaimed among the interstices of the adjoining claims at the heart of the great cluster of Anaconda mines. The two triangles together amounted to merely 0.009 of an acre—in other words, about the equivalent of a small room. Nevertheless, the Montana Ore Purchasing Company at once filed patent upon them. Heinze revealed his sense of humor by naming his claim the Copper Trust, as if it held the riches of a mighty corporation. His henchman Burdette O'Connor then went before Judge Clancy with the mind-boggling argument that the Copper Trust held the apex of a major portion of the great Anaconda-St. Lawrence lode. In all history, no case ever so well demonstrated the silliness of the Apex Law. "An astounding piece of audacity," gasped Daly's *Anaconda Standard*. Unflinchingly, however, the judge issued a temporary restraining order to show cause why he should not grant an injunction closing down operations in portions of the Amalgamated's great Anaconda, St. Lawrence, and Neversweat mines until ownership could be determined. Clancy allowed O'Connor free access to inspect the said mines, and the Amalgamated immediately closed down the affected workings, putting over 500 men out of work. At once, howls of outrage fell upon the judge from the armies of the unemployed. Facing reelection and reacting to threats of personal injury, he rescinded the restraining order. The case died quietly two years later in the Montana Supreme Court.[35]

The ill-conceived Copper Trust fiasco brought Heinze into direct conflict with Marcus Daly and the Anaconda. Reacting angrily, the ailing Irishman ordered editor John Durston to show the world "that he is a blackmailer, a thief and a most dangerous and harmfull [sic] man to the business and property interests of Butte." Indeed, Daly and his friends had much to fear from Heinze. By 1900, the snowballing mass of Heinze-inspired litigation threatened hopelessly to ensnarl the giant Amalgamated Copper Company which Daly and H. H. Rogers had just created. This could mean only one thing. As Daly phrased it in January 1900: "The long fight has reached the decisive battle and this is the crisis."[36]

The opening barrages of this "decisive battle" sounded in the political campaign of 1900, the most turbulent and complex election in Montana's history. Three factors combined to make it such:the emergence of Amalgamated Copper, the rise of F. Augustus Heinze, and the burning desire of William Andrews Clark to vindicate his reputation by recapturing his lost seat in the U.S. Senate. In light of Clark's humiliating, forced resignation in May 1900, it would seem incredible that he could cherish any real hope of a political comeback. But two factors now worked in his favor. On the one hand, the Daly organization, which had so often blocked him in the past, was now being absorbed into the Amalgamated, a distrusted "alien" corporation which seemed synonymous with the notrious Standard Oil Company. On the other, Clark had a natural ally in the person of Heinze, who had his own fight going with the Amalgamated. A natural alliance thus formed between the two main independents, Clark and Heinze, who had been left out of the orbit of Amalgamated. Each had something to gain in the 1900 campaign. For Clark it was a friendly legislature which would not have to be bribed as in 1899. For Heinze it was a further control over the government, and especially the judgeships, of Silver Bow County. They faced a common foe and foil in Amalgamated, and they turned the nationally popular theme of antitrust crusading to their own peculiar advantage.

The lords of Standard Oil were, of course, no strangers to intrigue and brass-knuckle politics. An adage of the time, made famous by Henry Demarest Lloyd in *Wealth Against Commonwealth,* said that: "The Standard had done everything to the Pennsylvania legislature except refine it." At first glance, it might have seemed that Amalgamated had such mighty resources that nothing in Montana could stop it. No other economic force in the sparsely settled state could resist the wishes of the mining interests in those days before the great homestead rush of 1909–18 brought in a sizable agricultural population. And within the mining industry, Amalgamated now clearly held sway. Counting the Boston companies, which it was in the process of absorbing, the Amalgamated employed 6,060 men in Montana by 1900: 3,657 in the Anaconda, 1,085 in the Boston and Montana, 628 in the Butte and Boston, 282 in the Parrot, 215 in the Colorado, and 193 in the Washoe. Clark, by comparison, employed only 428 in his Butte operations; and the Montana Ore Purchasing Company a mere 453.[37]

In short, Butte ran Montana, and Amalgamated seemed sure to run Butte. Even with its huge employment edge and its unlimited political war chest, however, the Amalgamated faced some severe problems. Its own employees, fearful of their new corporate masters, were far from loyal. And the political machine of Marcus Daly, which now became the Montana nerve center of Amalgamated, was in disarray due to its leader's illness and absence. Most significantly, the Standard Oil gang now found themselves confronting a pair of Montana barons who were just as tough and unprincipled as they were, and who had the great advantage of fighting on their own turf.

Clark and Heinze formed an unlikely team: the former graying, trim, and reserved; the latter stocky, young, and brash. But each brought strengths to the alliance. As a consequence of his 1899 harvest of legislators, W. A. Clark now commanded a complex and efficient organization whose political and business ties reached into every county in the state. The old man could bankroll about as big a campaign as he chose to, and his *Butte Miner* set the tone for a number of papers that he either subsidized or cajoled. Young Heinze, unlike Clark, concentrated his efforts at Butte. He also had a newspaper by now, the *Reveille,* or as Butte folks called it, "The Reviler." As editor, Heinze employed the capable and caustic Pat O'Farrell, a genial Irish hatchet man whom he had picked up on his Canadian caper.

Fritz Heinze was fast proving himself to be a superior political boss to either Daly or Clark. He gathered in a sure-footed group of henchmen, sometimes called the "Heinze Cabinet" or the "Liberty Hall Cabinet." Among Heinze's lieutenants were such old-time Butte politicos as "General" Charles Warren, Edward Hickey, ex-Sheriff Jack Quinn, Tom Hinds, and laborite Peter Breen, as well as younger devotees like John MacGinniss, his right-hand man, and Pat Mullins, the unlettered chap whom he made mayor of the city. Mullins once convulsed Teddy Roosevelt on a Butte visit by introducing him as the "hero of San Diego Hill" (evidently confusing San Juan Hill with Santiago, Cuba, with San Diego) and by ordering the shutters opened at a formal breakfast, "so the boys outside can watch the president eat." One of the many street orators hired by Heinze was young Ole Hanson, who would gain fame and notoriety two decades later as the Communist-baiting mayor of Seattle in the Red Scare of 1919.[38]

Heinze had a captain for each of Butte's ethnic groups and for each of its unions, and he kept a vigilant lieutenant in each of the Silver Bow County voting precincts. Like the Daly and Clark machines, Heinze's organization maintained an elaborate list of deceased voters, so that it could rush in strangers to vote for them even a decade after their deaths. The trick, naturally, was to get to the polls ahead of the opposition. Fritz seldom missed a bet. Since Clark gave his men free turkeys at Christmas, he gave turkeys to his employees on both Thanksgiving and Christmas, also free candy with grocery orders from friendly stores, a monthly bottle of wine, and a bottle of bourbon on payday for the old man. Ingeniously, he boosted the circulation of his papers, the *Reveille* and the later and more sedate *Evening News*, by lowering the rates to newsboys, who thereby increased their profit margins by pushing his papers harder on the streets.[39]

By late spring of 1900, the Clark and Heinze papers and orators were pounding away at the theme of Standard Oil domination and the warning that Hennessy's was being turned into a feudal company store like those in the coal and oil towns of Pennsylvania. Strictly speaking, the system of Hennessy's stores headquartered at Butte were not "company stores," at least not in the sense that employees were forced to buy from them. But the threat that they could become such seemed real enough. Their strategy aimed at winning over labor, seizing control of the majority Democratic party, and then putting together a fusion ticket with the Populists and other fragmentary groups. The first real battle took place at the Democratic convention of 20 June at Butte, the purpose of which was to choose delegates to the national convention. When the Daly faction won control, the

Clarkites bolted and held their own convention. Each group wrote a platform denouncing the other, and each sent a slate of delegates to the Kansas City national convention in July. Ironically, the opposing delegations were headed by the two men whose appointments to the U.S. Senate were still lying in the committee: Clark and Martin Maginnis. According to rumors, the Democrats at Kansas City maneuvered desperately to get onto the Credentials Committee, where they might become the beneficiaries of the fabled Clark political payoffs. For whatever reason, the Clark delegation won and was seated. Clark saw this as a "glorious victory," for back in Montana, he could bill it as national recognition of his leadership of the state's Democratic party.[40]

On the home front, Clark and Heinze concentrated their efforts upon winning over the critically important labor vote. This would not be difficult now; for the workers, traditionally loyal to Daly, viewed Amalgamated's Standard Oil connections with increasing unease. The *Miners' Magazine,* Denver-based spokesman for the Western Federation of Miners, editorialized in July 1900 that the Amalgamated "holds the people of the state in its grip as firmly as a slimy reptile holds an innocent lamb in its coils before devouring it." On 13 June 1900, Miners' Union Day, the allied barons played their trump card. They had letters read to a huge Butte gathering which announced that they would immediately grant their men the eight-hour workday while maintaining the prevailing $3.50 daily wage. The miners' unions of the Mountain West had campaigned hard for the eight-hour day for more than a decade and had scored their first victory in Utah in 1896. Clark and Heinze's announcement now opened the door to victory in Montana. Although Amalgamated at first refused to go along, thereby wounding itself in the 1900 campaign, it soon had to relent. The 1901 Montana legislature would enact an eight-hour day law, and in 1904 the voters approved an amendment which riveted the law into the state constitution. Other western mining states rapidly followed the Utah-Montana trend. In the gala Miners' Union Day parade, Clark and Heinze rode together in a flower-draped carriage, basking in their glory as thousands saluted and cheered them.[41]

Politics then quieted down, as usual, during the halcyon days of Rocky Mountain summer. Clark headed off for a two-month respite in Europe, leaving behind a $100,000 donation to the Democratic national campaign fund. In Montana his lieutenants, led by son Charlie and publisher John Neill, joined the Heinze cabinet in plotting strategy for the fall campaign. The key to that strategy lay in a "fusion" of Democratic-Populist and splinter parties of such complexity that it made Daly's maneuvers of 1896 seem like mere child's play. Everything depended upon holding firm control of the Democratic party, and in keeping the restive labor element united behind them.[42]

In their next foray, the Clark-Heinze forces suffered a not unexpected defeat. The Montana Republican party held its convention at Helena on 5 September, and agents of the competing mining interests were everywhere in evidence. Bitter memories of the 1899 legislature found quick expression at the gathering as the Republicans condemned their eleven legislators who had gone over to Clark while inviting the four who had stood firm to take places of honor on the platform. On this and on other issues, the Grand Old Party showed signs of serious strain and division. The gold-silver split of 1896 still caused tension, and so did the extreme bitterness between Senator Tom Carter and ex-Senator Wilbur Fisk Sanders. Sanders caustically accused Carter of aiding the Clark cause in 1899, and Carter responded by attacking Sanders for his close ties to Daly. The one point that the two men could agree upon was their enmity toward the Clark-Heinze fusion, and it was soon clear that the Republican majority would line up against the fusionists and tacitly in favor of the Amalgamated.[43]

The allies found better hunting on 19 September, when the Democratic, the Populist, and the newly formed Union-Labor parties all held their conventions at Helena. From the outset, the Clark men controlled the Democratic assembly, just as they had in 1898. They wrote a platform denouncing the Amalgamated and company stores, and John R. Toole sullenly led the Daly faction in a walkout. The Democrats and the dwindling Populists then worked out a fusion ticket led by Clark's choice, popular Democrat "Honest Joe" Toole for governor, and by Populist Caldwell Edwards for Congress. Once reunited, the "Popocrats" adopted a stirring platform which attacked the Amalgamated and played to labor with calls for free silver, the eight-hour day, the exclusion of Oriental labor, and a stepped-up federal antitrust policy. At first, the Union-Labor group balked, holding out for their own gubernatorial candidate; but they, too, later joined the fusionist alliance. The eight-hour day issue left them little real choice. Returning to New York from Europe, Clark boasted that he was now the demonstrable choice of the people in Montana. In an unguarded moment, he also offered his feeling about his old foe: "Marcus Daly is now dying the victim of his own spleen. He is the most violent tempered man I have ever known."[44]

The Clark-Heinze fusion presented the Daly-Amalgamated leaders with a nearly unbeatable combination. Clearly, the Democratic-

Populist alliance, joined by laborites and a scattering of antitrust and pro-silver Republicans, had a large edge with the voters. In an effort to salvage as much Democratic support as possible to merge with their Republican following, the Daly men formed the so-called Independent Democratic party at Butte on 2 October. Like the majority Clark faction, the Independent Democrats happily championed William Jennings Bryan, the national party's nominee for president. Otherwise, it was strictly a Daly show, chaired by Governor Smith and running ex-Populist Thomas Hogan in a labor-splitting bid for governor and fast rising Amalgamated attorney Cornelius Kelley for congressman.[45]

Things looked grim indeed for the Amalgamated. If the Clark-Heinze fusion should win, the trust would face a hostile legislature and state government. It would also face a pro-Heinze city government at Butte and two pro-Heinze district judges in the persons of William Clancy and Edward Harney. With Heinze so popular at Butte, their only hope seemed to be in building their vote-getting power throughout the rest of the state. According to widespread reports, Rogers and company set up a $1,500,000 war chest especially aimed at getting newspapers. This meant a vast intensification of the Clark-Daly buying campaign of the year before. In addition to Daly's *Anaconda Standard* and to the *Bozeman Chronicle*, the *Livingston Enterprise*, and the *Virginia City Madisonian*—all of which Daly had already secured—the Amalgamated now bought or started new papers, such as the *Hamilton Democrat*, the *Kalispell Bee*, the *Philipsburg Democrat*, and the *Red Lodge Democrat*. Some of these, like the *Bozeman Chronicle*, the trust would soon sell or liquidate; others, like the *Livingston Enterprise*, it would keep. The trust forced a number of formerly independent publishers, such as Lee Mantle, to join them by threatening to start up competing papers against them. Meanwhile W. A. Clark, who had long ago started all of this, also continued to build his press support. For example in 1900, he bought the *Great Falls Tribune* from its owner, O. S. Warden, only to sell it back to him after the election.[46] The two sides, in short, wheeled newspapers into position much like opposing armies would mount artillery.

For all its vast financial resources, the Amalgamated could not react quickly enough to counter its well-established Montana foes. With Clark's money to draw upon, Heinze orchestrated the importing of talent, the likes of which the Treasure State had never before seen: vaudeville songsters who parodied Standard Oil to the tune of "The Wearing of the Green" ("We must down the kerosene, boys, We must down the kerosene!"), also clowns from New York, and black,

Fed in Montana, Milked in the East.

From the *Butte Miner*, November 1900 (courtesy of the Montana Historical
Society, Helena)

banjo-strumming minstrels in smart red jackets. He brought in expert
cartoonists who graphically lampooned the trust—for instance as a
rapacious gorilla stalking up a mountainside carrying the fainted
maiden Montana in its arms. Heinze brought W. A. Thompson, the
former director of the Boston Lyric Opera, to Butte to direct his
vaudeville shows and hired America's current heart-throb, Cissy Lof-
tus, to entertain the crowds.[47]

Above all else, the Clark-Heinze forces enjoyed the marvelous
advantage of targeting upon Standard Oil, the despotic wrecker of
small business and corrupter of government. Clark's *Butte Miner*,
John Neill's *Helena Independent*, and Heinze's *Reveille* had a field day
blasting "Standard Oil despotism" and "the grasping, avaricious
hand of corporate greed." They slashed away at Henry Rogers ("a
thoroughly able villain"); "Oily Tom" Carter, who had allied himself
firmly with Rogers; Amalgamated's resident manager G. M. Hyams,
with his semitic nose distorted in cartoons; and Daly's alter-ego John
"Kerosene" Toole, who the *Reveille* claimed was so two-faced that
barbers charged him double rates for a shave! "Wages shall be cut,"
warned the *Reveille*, "and the company store will take all those wages.
Conditions similar to those in the Pennsylvania coal fields or in the
Russian Ukraine will be established in Montana."[48]

The allies' most potent weapon turned out to be Fritz Heinze himself. He had never tried political oratory before, but now he suddenly
blossomed as a spellbinder of considerable talents. Cleverly, Heinze

aimed his barbs at John D. Rockefeller and Henry Rogers of Standard Oil, carefully avoiding attacks upon the still popular Daly. "I know not by what soft blandishments Mr. Rogers persuaded Mr. Daly to join this unholy alliance," he commented. "I know it was totally and absolutely opposed to the traditions which seemed in the past to have guided Mr. Daly. . . ." He would then invariably picture himself as the workers' ally against the soulless trust: "My fight against the Standard Oil is your fight. In this glorious battle to save the State from the minions of the Rockefellers and the piracy of Standard Oil you and I are partners. . . . If you stand by me I shall stand by you. No man or woman has ever heard that Heinze ever played a friend or associate false . . . together we shall curb and crush and pulverize the machinations of the Rockefellers and the Standard Oil Trust."[49]

While Heinze concentrated upon the mining communities, Clark and the smooth and popular gubernatorial candidate Joseph Toole, who had held this office previously, back in 1889–93, toured the broad expanses of rural Montana. Everywhere, their message was the same: the giant copper trust threatened to crush the economic and political freedom of the state. Standard Oil, they charged, already controlled the opposition Republican party, causing the antitrust and pro-labor elements of that party to defect. And then, they claimed, the same corporate manipulators had created their own rump Independent Democratic party because they could not master the main organization. As for his Senate aspirations, Clark dismissed the "villifiers and scandal mongers" who charged him with bribery and shrewdly responded that the people themselves would render the final judgment in this election.[50]

The Amalgamated-Republican side fought back bitterly but ineffectively. Old Wilbur Sanders assailed the Democrats with his usual bombast as vote buyers, and his GOP rival Tom Carter joined him in the attack. However, both men suffered from counter-charges that they were on legal retainers from firms now held by Amalgamated. Amalgamated spokesmen could and did make convincing arguments: that they had poured $90,000,000 in investments into Montana, far more than their opportunistic opponents; and that consolidation would benefit capital and labor alike in assuring increased and steadier profits and employment. But usually the agents of the trust fought just as meanly as did the opposition. According to the *Anaconda Standard*, W. A. Clark—the "Paris Millionaire," the "disreputable man-buyer," the "man who never personally bribed anyone"— actually payed "shinplaster currency" in *his* company town, "dirty Jerome," Arizona. "Shall We," asked the *Standard* rhetorically, "Insult the Senate?" On election eve, Butte and Anaconda were blanketed with copies of a telegram from the absent Marcus Daly, imploring his men and his friends to stand by the company, as they had so often in the past.[51]

In the Montana election of 6 November 1900, the Clark-Heinze-Democratic fusion ticket swept to victory. Bryan for president, Toole for governor, and Edwards for congress all won by lopsided margins. More to the point, the Democratic-Populist-Labor candidates won firm control of both houses of the legislature, assuring Clark an easy election to the U.S. Senate. And Heinze's two judicial candidates, along with his entire slate of Silver Bow County officials, coasted into office. Three-thousand cheering fans massed at the Butte Hotel on election night to hear victory statements from their champions. Heinze told them that they had "given the death-blow to tyranny and despotism, to coercion and blackmail, the like of which has never been accomplished in any other part of the union." Clark was even more euphoric: "Tomorrow's sun will rise from the horizon upon the emancipated people of Silver Bow county. . . . The voice of the people is the voice of God." Watching from Salt Lake City, Joseph Walker, like most independent businessmen, applauded this blow to "the domination of the Amalgamated Copper Co. and the Daly outfit. After this, no doubt, they will hang their heads, as they ought to, like a whipped cur. . . . It will not help Daly much in his sickness in New York, when he hears of it. It must have a bad effect on him indeed."[52]

It must have, indeed. Marcus Daly's later years had been rich and fulfilling ones. He relished the happy days at his baronial estate in the Bitterroot, the celebrated victories of his horses, the renown which his millions and his company brought him. And in contrast to Clark, he treasured the warmth of a happy home, the affection and adulation which his wife, his three daughters, and his son bestowed upon him. The creation of Amalgamated in 1899 brought new laurels by placing him in the presidency of one of the world's greatest corporations, where the lords of Wall Street listened to his opinions with respect. Then suddenly, in the summer of 1899 amidst the frenzied launching of Amalgamated and the gearing up for his challenge to Clark's Senate seating, the rugged Irishman's robust health began to fail.

The problem stemmed from Bright's disease and from the dilation of an overworked heart. At first, Daly attempted to stay at work on a more relaxed schedule. He blacked out and nearly died in October

1899, then partially recovered. As his health continued to decline, he traveled to Bermuda and then to the German spas at Carlsbad and Nauheim. Nothing seemed to help, however; and when he returned to New York in September 1900, he was a desperately sick man. His physicians ordered him immediately to bed in his suite at the Netherlands Hotel. During these final weeks, it was clear that death was imminent. Yet he followed the campaign in Montana with great care and alarm. When his friend and protégé William Scallon arrived at Daly's bedside on 11 November, he was cautioned not to tell the old man of Clark's triumph for fear of upsetting him. Scallon felt, nevertheless, that Daly knew of it, simply because of the heavy silence about matters political. For several more hours, Marcus Daly drifted slowly toward death, lapsing in and out of consciousness. And then on the morning of 12 November 1900, he regained his awareness and said to his family: "Only a little while more, a little bit more, and all will be over." Soon he was dead. Nearly 3,000 people attended his funeral at St. Patrick's Cathedral in New York. At Butte, Anaconda, and Hamilton, the towns which idolized him, thousands more joined tearfully in mourning his departure.[53]

Perhaps the 1900 campaign, which brought triumph to Clark and a smashing defeat to Anaconda and Amalgamated, hurried the end for Marcus Daly. Perhaps not. In any case, there is stunning irony in the fact that the man who had built Anaconda into a mighty corporation should die amidst the aftershocks of his company's absorption into the maw of a holding company. The death of Marcus Daly seemed, in fact, to symbolize the passing of the great captains of frontier industry and to herald the emergence of the giant and impersonal new supercorporations.

Marcus Daly was a man to remember, a Horatio Alger hero who had fought his way from dire poverty to fabulous riches, a true empire builder. He was a man of polar extremes in his character: as Clark's *Butte Miner* put it, "a friend to his friends, to his enemies bitter, remorseless and unforgiving."[54] Seen at his best, Daly the father-figure watched over his family, his friends, and employees with a genuine, heartfelt benevolence; and history must note that, so long as he ran the Anaconda, it treated its employees better than most corporations of the time. At his worst, he was ruthless, vindictive, and tyrannical. Like the mining frontier that molded him, he was rough-hewn and unlettered, yet also sentimental, decent, and generous. His legacy seems as polarized as his character. More than any other man, he built the mining industry of Montana. As much as any man, he defiled the political life of Montana. Perhaps the greatness of

Marcus Daly finds its truest reflection in the common sentiment of many Butte folks following his death: if the old man had lived, he would have guarded his people from the evils which now immediately befell them. One would like to believe that, even if it seems highly unlikely.

8. The Battle for Butte: 1901–6

The campaign of 1900, and the period which immediately followed, marked a critical turning point in the struggle for mastery of the Butte district. Up to this point, the Clark-Daly feud had dominated the political sphere in Montana. Now, both of these older mining barons faded from view. Marcus Daly died soon after the election. As for William Andrews Clark, he would quickly make his peace with the expanding Amalgamated Copper Company; and, as his ripening political and economic concerns led him farther afield, he would devote less and less time and attention to his home state. During the final phase of the battle for Butte, 1901–6, the contest evolved into a bitter struggle between the two newly arisen adversaries of 1900: F. Augustus Heinze and the Amalgamated trust.

It seems remarkable, in hindsight, that the Heinze brothers and their allies could have held out for as long as they did against such odds. Consolidation was clearly inevitable, and the Amalgamated held the upper hand in resources, employment, and political muscle. In truth, the Heinzes held out through a combination of pluck, resourcefulness, and foul play. And in the end, they would win what was probably their primary objective all along, a high price for their holdings. But inevitably, they would lose the bigger battle, the battle of the independents against absorption into the trust. While it lasted, the contest raged as an epic struggle, one of the roughest in the roguish history of western mining.

The Clark-Heinze team, which had won in the 1900 campaign by blasting the trust as a threat to Montana's independence, basked in the glow of the victory with the dawn of 1901. F. Augustus Heinze now held a firmer grip than ever upon the government of Silver Bow County. His two candidates for the judgeships of the Second Montana District, incumbent William Clancy and newcomer Edward Harney, took their seats early in 1901. These two judges could easily outvote the newly installed third judge, independent John B. McClernan, and thereby assign the major cases to themselves. Like Heinze, W. A. Clark also had what he had so long wanted, a compliant legislature which would send him to the Senate, this time without the "need" for bribes.

The seventh Montana legislature convened early in January of 1901. From the outset, it was clear that Clark commanded enough Democratic and fusionist Populist-Labor votes to win. On 16 January the joint assembly of the legislature, in quiet contrast to the rancor of 1893 and 1899, elected the aging mining king to the U.S. Senate. Clark won 57 of the 93 votes cast, easily downing his veteran Republican rival Thomas Carter, who tallied only 31. Later in the session, the lawmakers would elect Great Falls promoter Paris Gibson to fill the shortened Senate term (1901–5) vacated by Clark with his 1900 resignation. Looking happy and relaxed, the old man accepted the plaudits of Heinze and other supporters who rushed to his side when the vote was announced. Then he delivered the customary speech of acceptance, departing from his text to chortle about the defeat for Senate reelection in New Hampshire of his bitter enemy William Chandler. Few in the audience doubted that Clark dollars had contributed to the political demise of the sharp-tongued Senator Chandler.[1]

It must have been a golden moment for William A. Clark, after so many humiliating defeats at the hands of Marcus Daly. One more time, Helena enjoyed a party hosted by its godfather. "Mr. Clark bought all the wine in Helena," reported the *New York Times*, "and it is being served free, together with cigars and lunch, over two bars to all comers." The festivities lasted all day and long into the night. A special train arrived from Butte in the morning, bringing an army of the Clark faithful and also the superb Boston and Montana Band; and an "impromptu" parade soon began wending its way up the twists and turns of Last Chance Gulch. That night, Clark hosted an open house at the plush Montana Club, where he and Heinze once again regaled the Helena set with a retelling of their glorious victory.[2]

Thus, after the expenditure of hundreds of thousands of dollars, the soiling of dozens of lives, and the debilitation of an entire state's body politic, W. A. Clark won his cherished Senate seat. He took office on 4 March 1901. Clark still lived in fear, however, that a renewed challenge to his credentials, based on the briberies of 1899, might lead again to his unseating. This fear no doubt serves to explain Clark's sudden about-face: for he now unceremoniously broke with Heinze and the antitrusters of 1900 and made peace with the Amalgamated. The reasons for this turn-around are not difficult to fathom. A conservative at heart, Clark had no real ideological quarrel with the trust and no personal quarrel with its masters, now that Daly was dead. Nor, being an unprincipled and unsentimental man, did he seem to flinch at breaking with Heinze and the others who had supported him in the recent campaign. The jerry-built fusion of 1900 could not, in any case, have lasted for long. Most likely, Heinze's *Reveille* hit upon Clark's real reason for changing sides—rumors that Henry Rogers and Thomas Lawson had threatened to turn the vast resources of Standard Oil toward challenging his seating in the Senate unless he abandoned his opposition to them.[3]

Whatever his motives, Clark's dramatic truce with Amalgamated reflected miserably on his sincerity, for it made a mockery of his stand in the 1900 campaign. Heinze's *Reveille* hotly denounced the Senator-elect as "The Traitor of Montana": "The man who threw down his best friends will yet repent his dirty actions." Many of Clark's allies, like grizzled old Sam Hauser, followed him into his new alliance with the lords of Standard Oil; but others rebelled on principle. John S. M. Neill, for instance, had backed Clark through thick and thin in his earlier battles, but he now broke with the Clark-financed *Helena Independent* and formed his own paper, the *Press*, in opposition. Bitterly, Neill concluded that Clark "no longer sees danger to the state from control of the state by the Standard Oil Amalgamated Copper combination." "William A. Clark has betrayed his friends and his party," wrote the Helena editor, concluding that Daly, at least, had always stood by those who stood by him.[4] Meanwhile, strange to behold, the Amalgamated papers suddenly found new, hitherto unseen virtues in Daly's old adversary.

The full implications of Clark's defection surfaced only in time. In the 1901 legislature, the Clark Democrats honored their campaign commitment and supported the eight-hour workday bill, which Governor Toole signed into law on 2 February. They also backed the bill which forbade payment of wages in scrip redeemable only in company stores, a measure aimed at curbing potential abuses by the trust. In the long run, though, the Clark–Amalgamated accord could mean only one thing: the isolation and defeat of Heinze, and the triumph of the trust. Clark evidently demanded certain hard concessions from Amalgamated, one of which was the purging of certain Daly men, like the vitriolic attorney Christopher Connolly, whom he despised.

The Rogers-Daly group was willing to accommodate him, for alliance with the senator and his organization promised them almost certain control of the Democratic party. And this, of course, meant a sure control of Montana politics in general, since ex-Senator Carter and the Republicans were already in Amalgamated's camp.[5]

F. Augustus Heinze seemed anything but intimidated by Clark's desertion of his cause. Quite the contrary, he made it crystal clear that he intended to carry on his crusade against the trust to the finish. As a result of his phenomenal showing in the 1900 campaign, Heinze now stood at the apex of his career. Barely past thirty years of age, this man whom Joseph Kinsey Howard once described as a "gay, handsome, industrial desperado and demagogue" and "the most adept pirate in the history of American capitalist privateering," had come to command national attention as a captain of industry and a key figure in American mining.[6]

Butte idolized him, for Heinze always put on a fine show. He was a workingman's man who spent considerable time underground examining his workings and who kept his muscular physique well toned through road work. And he was a ladies' man who charmed the opposite sex with his boyish good looks, his seemingly shy reserve, and his impeccably cultured manners. Equally at ease among millionaires and among whores, he frequently hobnobbed with the city's polite set early in the evening and then joined up with the more tawdry element later. His extravagantly hosted parties, complete with multicourse meals, fine attire, and chaperones for the young ladies, were the talk of the town. Yet so were his hard-drinking, wild-gaming antics, which made him a legend in a hard-drinking and fun-loving town. Thomas Lawson, who appreciated a good showman, described him admiringly: "Seven nights in the week he could drink under the table every man among the licentious company that frequented these gilded establishments, and then sit in a faro game whose proprietor had never been known to put on a limit and make him 'quit.' Actresses of a certain color adored him, and to the ladies of the red-light district of Butte Fritz Heinze was the beau ideal of manly beauty and heroism."[7]

Fritz burned his candle at both ends, and for this he would pay the ultimate price of broken health and early death. For now, however, the world seemed to be his oyster. His nightly carousing did not seem to detract from his attention to business, and Heinze pressed steadily ahead in building his operations and battling the trust. To complement his well-established Rarus Mine and Montana Ore Purchasing

Company, Heinze consolidated and incorporated newer properties like the Cora-Rock Island, the Nipper, the Belmont, the Minnie Healy, and the Johnstown Mining Company. In 1902, consciously imitating and challenging the Amalgamated, Heinze and his New York brothers formed the United Copper Company. Chartered in South Dakota and capitalized at $80 million, United Copper was designed as an Amalgamated-style holding company which would control and manage the various Heinze operating firms. While doubtlessly overcapitalized, the company did in fact hold assets of great value. The question on most minds was: what would Heinze do with it? John Neill observed at the time: "There can be no question but what Heinze is preparing for a big fight. . . ."[8] Whether he was fighting as a heroic David against the Standard Oil Goliath on pride and principal, or whether he was simply extorting the highest possible sell-out price from the trust, that was—and still is—a tougher question.

On the political front Heinze demonstrated that, even without Clark at his side, he could continue to hold the Amalgamated beast at bay. Looking toward the 1902 campaign, Henry Rogers had initially professed "no disposition to mix up in Montana politics." He probably meant this, for the 1900 canvass had graphically revealed the trust's unpopularity, its ineptitude, and its vulnerability to attacks by home-state antitrusters. Besides, with Clark on his side, Rogers could no doubt count on a friendly Democratic party this time. At the Democratic convention at Bozeman late in September 1902, the party faithful witnessed a peculiar sight: Senator W. A. Clark fraternizing happily with Daly captains John Toole, A. J. Campbell, and Dan Hennessy. The Clark-Amalgamated people effortlessly took control of the party apparatus, wrote up a platform praising the senator and muting the anticorporate stand of 1900, and pushed the Heinze crowd out into the cold.[9]

Rogers and Clark seriously underestimated the ingenuity of Fritz Heinze. Defeated at the Democratic convention, Heinze led his faction of the party off the reservation and set about assembling yet another crazy-quilt fusion of antitrust elements like the one he and Clark had put together in 1900. Laborites, antitrust Republicans, the lingering hard core of the fading Populist party—all joined the Heinze Democrats in swarming once more to the Pied Piper's antitrust tune. Deftly, Fritz shattered party lines and worked up a fusion so complex that the *Anaconda Standard* jokingly referred to it as the "Heinzeantitrustboltingdemocraticlaborpopulist ticket." Facing the enmity of the majority factions of both the Republican and Democratic parties,

Heinze carefully limited his aims this time. He focused his efforts upon Silver Bow County and upon supporting GOP Supreme Court candidate William Holloway, whom he found acceptable to his cause.[10]

Heinze and his lieutenants threw their support to any candidate of any party who would hint at opposing the trust, which quickly found itself once more in serious trouble. As in 1900, Fritz put on a circus campaign complete with touring trains, fireworks displays, gleeclubs, minstrels, free champagne, and lots of antitrust oratory. His singers usually lyricized Clark as "Buster Bill," a popular cartoon character of the time, lampooning both the Senator's lengthening hair and his retreat from his earlier antitrust stance:

> Montana sent to Washington
> A man named Buster Bill,
> For Buster was a likely chap.
> We trusted him until
> He worked a sneaking game on us,
> For six more years you see,
> And now we've got the biggest dunce
> In Washington, D.C.[11]

The political regulars and pro-Amalgamated forces fought back desperately. They accused "Chinese Heinze" of favoring oriental labor and spread rumors that he was Jewish. When Heinze countered by playing up his mother's Irish ancestry, their papers renamed him "O'Heinze" or "McHeinze." Each side maneuvered openly to gain the votes of labor and even of the rapidly growing Socialist party, offering subsidies, secret contributions, even outright bribes. But this was Heinze's game, and in the end he demonstrated anew that public opinion agreed with him about the vices of Amalgamated. In the November 1902 election, the young copper king won most of what he wanted, particularly the elevation of Holloway to the Supreme Court and the retention of his control over Butte's city government.[12]

Heinze's control of Butte, however, remained tenuous and tense, as was demonstrated in May of 1903 when President Theodore Roosevelt visited the mining city. A Butte delegation headed by Heinze's mayor, Pat Mullins, journeyed to Billings to meet the president's train; but Mullins muffed his lines when he arose to greet the guests. "Mr. President, I-I-I-oh hell, I never could make a speech," he stammered, collapsing in his chair. Convulsed with laughter, Roosevelt responded: "Bully, Pat, I never could either." When he hit Butte, the president was treated to a wild and careening ride through the city at the hands of legendary hack driver "Fat Jack" Jones. Knowing of the deep divisions within the city's political order, Roosevelt arranged for equal numbers of Heinze and Amalgamated people to be seated facing one another at the banquet in his honor that night. The police frisked the guests as they arrived and relieved them of a number of concealed weapons.[13]

In accounting for Heinze's continuing victories against the mighty trust, it must be noted that the executives of Amalgamated, both the Rogers group at New York and their subordinates at Butte, faced distractions and reversals which kept them constantly off-balance. The builders of Amalgamated faced inevitable troubles of their own making. Their holding company was heavily overcapitalized, and they were disadvantaged in trying to control an industry in which several large producers remained outside their combine. Through 1901, as the directors absorbed the Boston companies and raised their capitalization to $155,000,000, the company paid solid 1.5 percent quarterly dividends and maintained a high world price by controlling Butte production and by stockpiling. This policy delighted the independent Michigan and Arizona producers, who massproduced under the umbrella of the trust's fixed price for handsome profits. But by the close of 1901 this artificially contrived price-fixing had saddled Amalgamated with a colossal copper stockpile approaching 200 million pounds in size. Responding to the inevitable, the directors slashed the dividend and began unloading their reserves to the tune of falling prices. Of course, this led to an uproar in the copper industry and fanned dissension among the independent producers, who had hitherto accepted the leadership of the trust. More than that, it signaled a major failure for the Amalgamated group, which seemed to be going the way of the earlier Secretan syndicate in its inability to control the world of copper.[14]

Obsessed with these problems, Henry Rogers and his cohorts had to rely upon their gang on the sixth floor of the Hennesy building at Butte to cope with Heinze. This group, too, was in transition and in trouble. The Amalgamated leadership at Butte numbered some old and some new faces. Lawyers W. W. Dixon, John Toole, and A. J. Campbell, who had served as Daly's political spear carriers as well as they did as his counsel, continued in the same roles for Amalgamated. Similarly, Daly cronies like Dan Hennessy, Miles Finlen, and Lee Mantle simply transferred their Anaconda loyalties to the new holding company. In the Amalgamated's legal department a cluster of younger men gathered together to fight the courtroom wars against Heinze. They were a capable, and reputedly a hard-nosed lot, including A. J. Shores, L. O. Evans, and the ramrod-straight and tough D'Gay Stivers—an ex-Texas Ranger who had led the Montana contingent in the Spanish-American War and who later headed up the company's "goon squad." The fastest-rising star of the group was young Cornelius F. Kelley, the son of Daly's pal Jeremiah Kelley. Young, red-headed and gregarious, "Con" Kelley combined the marvelous gifts of intelligence, cunning, wit, and charm. He would climb the corporate ladder rapidly and would one day preside over the corporate empire built by Marcus Daly.[15]

The two men who stood at the helm of Amalgamated's Montana operation during this transitional time were William Scallon and John D. Ryan. Scallon, a Canadian by birth and a lawyer by profession, came to Butte from the Lake Superior district in 1884. Beginning with the 1891 incorporation of Anaconda, he came to handle much of Daly's legal work; and with the emergence of Amalgamated, he became deeply immersed in the Heinze litigation. Following Daly's death, the directors of the trust made him president of Anaconda and their manager of Montana operations. He did not, however, take well to this new role. According to the outspokenly progressive Montana journalist Jerre Murphy, William Scallon, a soft-spoken, gentlemanly, and reserved man, flinched at the heavy-handedness of the war against Heinze. In early 1904 he would resign to resume his law practice, later becoming a partner of Senator Thomas J. Walsh in Helena.[16]

John D. Ryan, handsome, suave, and charming, also cold, ruthless, and calculating, seemed perfectly to embody the shift from the old, baronial management to the new, corporate world of mining. Thirty-seven years of age in 1901, when he moved to Butte, Ryan came from the copper country of upper Michigan, where his father was a highly respected mine manager. A youthful rebellion against his father's plans to send him to college had brought the quiet and willful young man to Denver, and there he found employment as a traveling salesman for Continental Oil. Ryan's trade brought him to the copper city and to a fast friendship with Marcus Daly, who was taken both with his abilities and his demure Irish wit and personality. Following Daly's death, his estate appointed Ryan president of the Daly Bank and Trust Company. This post won him the attention and acclaim of Henry Rogers, who quickly brought Ryan into the Amalgamated organization. Climbing the corporate ladder with spectacular haste, he became a director of Anaconda in 1904, and in the following year he assumed the presidency of that company. In 1908, failing in health, Rogers brought his young protégé to New York to assist him; and in

1909, following Rogers' death, Ryan rose to the presidency of Amalgamated.[17]

To admiring businessmen like Daly and Rogers, John Ryan seemed to represent the best that the younger generation had to offer. In his private life, Ryan seemed beyond reproach, a devout Catholic and devoted family man. And in his professional career, he combined a remarkable ability with a total dedication to his company. To the critics of corporate exploitation, on the other hand, Ryan personified the worst traits of soulless capitalism. Jerre Murphy commented of him: "Organized greed could teach him nothing in selfishness and no awakening conscience disturbed the dreams of his avarice." On a less personalized note, it is interesting to note that, although literal control of Amalgamated's Butte operations now rested in faraway New York, the Irish-Catholic protégés of Marcus Daly actually held onto a dominant position within the trust. First Scallon and then Ryan and Con Kelley, who became secretary of Anaconda in 1905 and general counsel of Amalgamated in 1908, maintained the Montana coloration of Anaconda-Amalgamated.[18]

The managers of Amalgamated, both at 26 West Broadway and at the sixth floor of the Hennessy Building, faced a myriad of tangled problems. Heinze's onslaughts were clearly striking a responsive chord with the public, and the trust obviously had to make some concessions. When it became apparent that the legislature would enact an eight-hour workday law, Amalgamated voluntarily implemented the system without wage cuts in February 1901, well before the law went into effect. Scallon assured the unions that the eight-hour day would remain in effect, even if the courts should strike down the law. Wisely, the company announced early in 1904 that it had no interest in the mercantile business and sold out its holdings in the chain of Hennessy's stores to D. J. Hennessy, attempting to deprive Heinze of the emotional issue of company stores exploiting the workers.[19]

In general, however, the men of Amalgamated reacted defensively, heavy handedly, and often foolishly to Heinze's baiting of them. To counter Fritz's popularity, the trust continued to pour money into buying up newspapers and running them at reportedly heavy losses. According to Clarence Barron, who knew the world of American "coppers" as well as any observer, the Amalgamated squandered vast amounts of capital upon trying to secure its political base in Montana. Barron's informants told him that the company carried numerous hangers-on and "grafters" on its payroll and that it handed out $500,000 worth of lucrative vein leases each year to influence important people. The richly productive Boston and Montana Company paid most of these "political" expenses, which robbed it of its vast potential profits. Without the sympathetic Marcus Daly at the helm, the company rapidly lost its old rapport with labor. As we shall see, the managers of Amalgamated came increasingly to treat their workers as mere pawns in the accounting of profits and losses, and to manipulate and undermine their unions with predictable results. All of this would soon lead to severe troubles for all concerned.[20]

Amalgamated's biggest headache of all continued to be the Heinze litigation. By 1901 the suits between the Heinze companies and the various firms which were now gathered into the Amalgamated had mounted in both the number and value of properties involved to bewildering proportions. Even with a third judge added to the Second Judicial District, the Butte courts were swamped. The district court calendar for the February term of 1901 registered twenty-three separate suits. "Evidently," commented the *Engineering and Mining Journal*, "the law is a profitable pursuit in Butte." Each side marshalled high-priced legal, geological, and engineering talent to press its cases. Experts devised elaborate scale models, some of them costing up to $25,000 apiece, to demonstrate their arguments as to the meanderings and faults of vein structures. They dug highly expensive "litigation drifts" to prove what the models theorized.[21] If the expenses were high, the stakes were higher still. The fate of mines and plants worth tens of millions rested upon the judgments of unkempt Judge William Clancy and of Judge Edward Harney, a former Nebraska cowboy, and of the three justices of the state supreme court sitting in Helena.

Amidst numerous lesser cases, several larger ones merit special attention. Along the boundary of Heinze's Johnstown claim and the Boston and Montana–Amalgamated's Pennsylvania, a staccato of apex suits and countersuits continued to break forth, as it had since 1898. These "Pennsylvania cases," involving heavily complex arguments as to the dipping planes and faults of real and imagined veins, ground on for month after month, year after year. They would never abate until ownership of the veins was secured in one single corporate entity.[22] Similarly, the "Jim Larkin Case," Heinze's imaginative attempt to seize total control of the valuable Snohomish and Tramway properties, wound its way endlessly through the labyrinth of state and then federal courts.[23]

Another marathon apex battle erupted in 1899–1900 over possession of the veins running between Heinze's Nipper Consolidated

Mine and the Little Mina, a property of the Amalgamated's Parrot Silver and Copper Company. Typically, the ever-obliging Judge Clancy found for Heinze and placed the disputed Little Mina ground in receivership. The Montana Supreme Court reversed Clancy, but Heinze simply countered with new suits that dragged on into mid–1903 with neither side winning a clear victory.[24] In these cases as in so many others, both sides lost heavily in legal fees, and each succeeded only in harassing the other.

Three monumental battles outshone all the others in significance: the struggle to secure ownership of the Minnie Healy Mine, the long-standing Apex fight between Heinze's Rarus and the Amalgamated's Michael Davitt mines, and Heinze's attempt once again to bring down the trust through minority stock owners' suits. The fight for the Minnie Healy fathomed the depths of political corruption. The Rarus-Davitt contest led to war within the bowels of the earth. And Heinze's manipulation of minority stock holdings brought on the climax of the battle for Butte, the great Amalgamated shutdown of 1903.

The Minnie Healy was an inconspicuous mine in the Meaderville district, a mere 350 by 700 feet in size, lying alongside the Boston and Montana Company's rich Piccolo and Gambetta claims. The Heinzes held a half-ownership in the mine. Half of the remaining half belonged to Miles Finlen, the familiar Butte investor and hotel owner whom Pat O'Farrell once described as a wild Irishman from County Wexford who "loves Marcus Daly as the savage loves the sun." As for the remaining one-quarter, it was tied up in litigation amongst the heirs of John Allport. Adding to the complexity of the situation, Finlen held a lease to mine the entire claim. He had no luck in doing so, however; and in November of 1898 he allegedly had made an oral agreement to sell his rights and leasehold for $54,000 to Heinze, who was busily trying to consolidate his hold on the mine. Fritz had an idea that the Healy contained undiscovered riches, and with his legendary prowess, he quickly proved this to be the case. Of equal importance, Heinze also believed, or purported to believe, that the claim held the apexes of the rich Piccolo and Gambetta vein structures of the Boston and Montana Company. Thus the Minnie Healy threatened to become the base for another series of Apex raids against the Amalgamated. When Daly heard of Finlen's mistake, he flew into a rage and ordered him to get the property back, but it was too late. The only hope now was to go to court and attempt to nullify the oral agreement. Finlen signed over his rights to the mine to the Boston and Montana; this, in turn, brought the Amalgamated into the fray with its takeover of the Boston and Montana in 1901.[25]

In 1901, the Minnie Healy case, *Finlen* v. *Heinze*, went to trial in the court of newly seated Judge Edward Harney. Elected through the support of the Heinze machine, Harney had the reputation of being a skilled lawyer, but also of being a hard drinker who had fallen into a life of dissolution. Following a two-month trial, Judge Harney found in favor of Heinze; but on appeal, the Montana Supreme Court reversed the judge on the ground that he "was completely lost to all sense of decency and propriety, and that he made of the occasion, while off the bench, a carnival of drunkenness and debauchery." Behind this ruling was the airing of a remarkably sordid story.[26]

Evidence revealed before the supreme court, as well as in the partisan press, showed clearly that some bizarre things happened during the 1901 trial in Judge Harney's court. According to this evidence, the judge, although a married man, had entered into liaison with one Ada Brackett, a Butte stenographer who had her own shop but also worked for Heinze's Montana Ore Purchasing Company. Two agents of the trust testified before the supreme court that they had befriended Harney and Brackett one evening and ended up with them in a room at Butte's Thornton Hotel. The judge came into the room, they claimed, "very much under the influence of liquor and after a fit of vomiting ordered and drank a bottle of champagne." Ms. Brackett allegedly told them of having "intimate" relations with Harney, and he boasted of having fathered her daughter.[27]

Especially damaging to Judge Harney were the so-called dearie letters, which he and Ada had sent to one another via a courier with the unlikely name of H. M. Heimendinger, and which supposedly fell into the hands of Amalgamated agents. The letters, which Harney admitted were at least in part authentic, did not definitely prove that he took bribes from Heinze; but they clearly implied it. Assuring the judge that "I love you," Brackett wrote "that all they [the Heinze faction] want you to do is to be honest in every decision, whether it is for or against them. . . . As for your future, after you leave the bench, if you will allow me, I am empowered to promise you certain things which will assure that most generously." Her final admonition was widely quoted: "Be very careful of this letter, dearie."[28]

All of this proved highly embarrassing to the judge, of course, but the revelations in the case of *Finlen* v. *Heinze* also embarrassed the Amalgamated. For Judge Harney counterattacked with his own account, substantiated by others, of how the trust tried to blackmail and bribe him with threats of exposure and impeachment to admit having been bought by the other side. Late on the night of 5–6 August 1901, according to these accounts, Amalgamated agents A. J. Shores,

D'Gay Stivers, and Charlie Clark corraled Judge Harney, his attorney Jesse Root, and later also Ada Brackett at a room in the Thornton Hotel. They offered the judge, in return for his resignation and a signed admission of having taken bribes, a cool payment of $150,000. Brackett was offered $20,000. Even after Clark raised the offer to $250,000, Harney steadfastly refused any such admission. The participants were drinking, and the scene became intensely emotional. At one point, Clark remarked: ". . . for a tenth of what I have offered you, you might be put out of the way when you start for home some night, and nobody would ever hear of you again." The judge replied: "I have five brothers; and, if they do that, while my wife is crying, some other woman's eyes will not be dry." Nothing could bring the judge to admit taking bribes. Either he was innocent, or he was irrevocably wedded to Heinze. He and Ada Brackett finally left for her home at 6:00 A.M. When they got there, Harney blurted out to Heinze's awaiting lieutenants with breaking voice: "I have had a hell of a night."[29]

The story eventually reached the public. First, the trust leveled its accusations against Judge Harney in carrying its case to the state supreme court. Later, it attempted to have him impeached by the legislature in 1903. This maneuver failed, largely because Heinze still had considerable strength in that body, and also because the Standard Oil-tainted corporation remained highly unpopular in Montana. The judge, in his turn, fought back with requests for disbarment of Shores and Stivers and bribery charges against Charlie Clark, who rushed to California to avoid summons. On the rather pathetic argument that the $250,000 was not really meant to be a bribe, but rather a compensation for the judge's self-embarrassment, Shores was acquitted and the case against Stivers was dismissed. As for the case of *Finlen* v. *Heinze*, the supreme court remanded it to the lower court for retrial. This meant that, in his own sweet time, Judge William Clancy would now decide the fate of the Minnie Healy![30]

The sensations of the Healy case kept Butte agog, but even more important battles were shaping up by 1903 in the controversies surrounding the Davitt-Rarus dispute and the ownership by Heinze men of stocks in Amalgamated subsidiaries. Following an earlier series of cases in 1898–1900, it will be recalled, the Apex litigation involving ownership of the valuable ore bodies commingling between Heinze's Rarus and the Butte and Boston–Boston and Montana's Michael Davitt Mine remained pending in federal court. An injunction forbade mining in the contested zone until legal title could be determined. By mid-1903, the Heinzes desperately needed access to these ores. Many of their best high-grade veins were tailing out; others were now also under injunction. Thus they must have these lodes— especially the rich Enargite and Windlass veins—to keep their mills and smelters running at full capacity and efficiency. So on 24 August 1903, the Heinze brothers made a truly audacious move. They trans- ferred ownership of the Rarus from their Montana Ore Purchasing Company to another of their corporations, the Johnstown Mining Company. Mustering the far-fetched argument that the Johnstown Company was not subject to the injunction, Heinze sent his crews down to drive crosscuts into the forbidden ground of the Davitt. His foremen stealthily sealed off the underground approaches from the Amalgamated's adjoining Pennsylvania Mine and poured hundreds of men into the stopes, blasting around the clock to remove the ores and seal the cavities with waste rock before they could be stopped.[31]

This meant outright war with the Amalgamated, and war with the United States courts as well. But before Heinze's outlandish raid into the Michael Davitt was discovered, an even greater crisis erupted in Judge Clancy's court. At issue was Arthur Heinze's ploy of buying stocks in the companies belonging to the trust, the same maneuver that the Heinzes had used earlier to drive the Boston and Montana Company into receivership (see pp. 144–47). Back in 1901, Fritz and his brothers had launched another series of minority-stockholder suits against Amalgamated, the most notable being *Forrester and MacGin- niss* v. *Boston and Montana Consolidated Copper and Silver Mining Co.*, *MacGinniss* v. *Boston and Montana Consolidated Copper and Silver Mining Co.*, and *Lamm et al.* v. *Parrot Silver and Copper Co. et al.* In these cases, Vice President John MacGinniss and attorneys James Forrester and Daniel Lamm of the Montana Ore Purchasing Company posed arguments similar to the ones they had used in the stock-transfer cases of 1898. They argued that their rights as minority stockholders were being prejudiced by the absorption of these companies into the trust, that the trust itself was an attempt to create an illegal monopo- ly. Most directly to the pont, they maintained that the transfer of ownership of these companies to Amalgamated without their consent was illegal, since the companies in question had been chartered prior to the passage in 1899 of the law requiring the consent of only two- thirds of all stockholders for such decisions. Thus, even though the plaintiffs owned only a few dozen shares of the Boston and Montana and the Parrot, they asked the court to restrain the holding company from issuing dividends drawn from these subsidiaries. In effect, they were asking for the dissolution of Amalgamated.[32]

Judge Clancy took some testimony on the cases and then pro-

ceeded to sit on them for the next two years. They hung like a guillo-
tine blade over the head of Amalgamated, and that is probably just
what Heinze meant for them to do. William Scallon, Henry Rogers,
and their cohorts worried incessantly about when and how the blade
might fall. They thought seriously of filing impeachment charges
against Clancy but gave up on this idea for fear that neither a jury nor
the legislature would ever rule against him. The judge enjoyed
watching them squirm and behaved with increasing arrogance. In
August of 1903, he reprimanded Cornelius Kelley for even raising the
subject of the cases in court: "I don't want to accuse you lawyers of
trying to pester me, but I've got too much of this business, and I
won't hear you."[33]

Suddenly, on 22 October 1903, Judge Clancy delivered two far-
reaching decisions which led instantaneously to the culmination of
the great Montana mining war. He awarded the Johnstown Mining
Company full legal title to the Minnie Healy Mine, a decision which
not only afforded the Heinzes roughly $10 million in proven ore
reserves but also provided them new opportunities for Apex suits
against the surrounding mines. More importantly, the judge found
for MacGinnis, Forrester, and Lamm and issued injunctions prohibit-
ing the Amalgamated from possessing the stocks of or drawing dividends from its Parrot and Boston and Montana subsidiaries. By
implication, this ruling meant that the holding company could not
operate any of its Montana firms at all. If these rulings should stand,
the trust was illegal and finished in the state. As if to lighten the
occasion, the judge announced that he intended to sign the injunctions and then "break away to the woods tomorrow," to hunt for elk
and jackrabbits.[34]

The Amalgamated responded suddenly and dramatically to Judge
Clancy's decisions. Upon orders from Henry Rogers in New York,
Scallon ordered a complete shutdown in regional operations. All
signs pointed to a long-term closure. At Butte, the mines were immediately shut down, with only pumping and guard crews left on
duty. Nearly 6,500 men picked up their checks. Even the horses and
mules were hauled up to the surface, where they blinked in wonder
at the sun and ran and rolled over frolicking in the grass. At Anaconda and Great Falls, the smelters and refineries locked their gates and
even extinguished their fires, a sure sign of a lengthy closure. In the
lumber camps of the Missoula area, in the coal towns of Cascade,
Gallatin, and Carbon counties, in the railroad yards of Butte, Anaconda, Great Falls, and Havre, sullen workers milled nervously in the

streets and pubs. Fifteen-thousand workers, the bulk of Montana's labor force, were soon out of work, with more following every day.[35]

At last, the mighty trust had bared its fangs. Once more, as in the Clark bribery scandals of four years earlier, the big shutdown of 1903 called national attention to the prostitution of the commonwealth of Montana by mining interests. The motives of Amalgamated were clearly suspect. Its directors announced that, since they could not issue dividends, they must close down operations at once in fairness to the stockholders. Any informed observer could see, however, that this was only a pretext. The company's legal department was busy preparing appeals to the state supreme court, and it could readily gain a stay of proceedings pending the appeal. At once, F. Augustus Heinze charged that the Amalgamated had really closed down in order to reduce its 150,000,000-pound surplus of copper and to maintain the seventeen-cent price. His charge rang true, for the copper giant was staggering under the weight of its futile purchasing effort to sustain the price. The trust, he claimed, aimed to intimidate and break the recalcitrant state of Montana, to turn it into an abject colony.[36]

Heinze had a point, and many Americans agreed with him. In measured tones, the *Engineering and Mining Journal* doubted the honesty of either side and saw it as merely "the latest outcome of that bewildering tangle of litigation which has emphasized the defects of the United States mining law and debauched the politics and corrupted the judiciary of a state." The sudden shutdown made front-page headlines across the country and fueled the rising fires of popular anger at corporate malfeasance which President Theodore Roosevelt was beginning to denounce in his theatrical antitrust campaign. William Randolph Hearst's *San Francisco Examiner* agreed with Heinze that the Standard Oil gang was up to its old tricks of fleecing the public and figured that "War in Butte is Surely Coming." The *Portland Oregonian* predicted a grave Montana winter unless things changed, and the *Denver Post* issued a florid moral pronouncement about the whole nasty business: "It has been the battle of the whale of capital and the thresher shark of capital. . . . O ye workers for clean, pure politics, O ye believers in the inherent honesty of citizenship, go to Montana and learn that when kegs of gold are broached like barrels of tar heaped upon flames, that the political purist has as much chance as a snowball in hell."[37]

A mood of fear, anger, and mounting anxiety gripped the cities of Butte, Anaconda, and Great Falls. When and upon what terms would the trust reopen operations? Facing a Montana winter without income meant disaster for the workers and their families, and many of them pulled up roots and left. Socialist orators harangued Heinze and the Amalgamated on street corners, pointing to the evils of corporate exploitation. Not surprisingly, the workers' anger focused less upon the trust than upon the hitherto popular Heinze, who along with his "kept" judges was viewed as the root cause of the problem. Battered by a storm of public anger, Judge Clancy chose to cancel his hunting trip and remained in town, protected by police guards. One possibility of breaking the impasse seemed to arise when a mass meeting of thousands of miners offered to buy up the troublesome Parrot and Boston and Montana stocks and then dismiss the suits. Bankers W. A. Clark, John D. Ryan, and A. J. Davis II offered to furnish them the funds to do so. This proposal put Fritz Heinze squarely on the spot. When he received the offer at the Butte Hotel, he promised the miners that he would respond publicly at 4:00 P.M. on the following day, 26 October, on the steps of the Silver Bow County courthouse.[38]

When Heinze climbed the courthouse steps that afternoon, he faced an incredibly tense situation. The largest single crowd that Montana had ever seen, estimated at 10,000 in number, spread down the steps and far out into the streets. Most of these men, of course, worked for Amalgamated. Most of them were hostile, and many were reportedly armed. Outwardly calm and composed, Heinze stood solemnly before them while one of his men, an armed marksman, stood alertly behind him. Brazenly, he told the assembled crowd that he had chosen to meet openly with them, insinuating that their leaders, some of whom were standing beside him, had been influenced by corporate payoffs and hence could not be trusted. President Ed Long of the Butte Miners' Union angrily tried to stop Heinze. When he failed, Long and his committee stalked angrily from the scene. Heinze then launched into a bitter and brilliant excoriation of Standard Oil and Amalgamated, much of it drawn from his campaign speeches of 1900 and 1902:

> The statement has been made that I am hounding the Amalgamated Copper Company in the courts of this county and state. Six or seven years ago, these gentlemen came to me and said: 'You must leave the state. If you don't get out, we will drive you out.' They have been trying to do that ever since. They have injunctions against me at this time which, if removed, would make it possible for me to give employment to two thousand extra men. They have fought me in every possible way. They have beaten me a dozen times in one way or another, and I have taken my defeats like a man. I fought my own battles, explaining them to the public when I had the opportunity, and asking their support at the polls. I will stake my life on

the statement that there are within the sound of my voice a hundred men, now in my employ, who have been offered bribes ranging all the way from a thousand to ten thousand dollars to commit perjury for the purpose of defeating me in my lawsuits.

My friends, the Amalgamated Copper Company, in its influence and functions, and the control it has over the commercial and economic affairs of this state, is the greatest menace that any community could possibly have within its boundaries. That stock of Mr. MacGinniss' is a bulwark to protect you and others here in Butte, miners and merchants, from the aggressions of the most unscrupulous of corporations, the Standard Oil Company. Rockefeller and Rogers have filched the oil wells of America, and in doing so they have trampled on every law, human and divine. They ruthlessly crushed every obstacle in their path. They wrecked railroad trains and put the torch to oil refineries owned by their competitors. They entered into a conspiracy with railroads, by which competitors were ruined and bankrupted. Sometimes they were caught in the act, but they bought the judges [!] and saved themselves from prison stripes and punishment. The same Rockefeller and the same Rogers are seeking to control the executive, the judiciary, and the legislature of Montana. . . .

It is true that I am deeply interested in the outcome of this struggle. My name, my fortune, and my honor are at stake. All have been assailed. You have known me these many years. You are my friends, my associates, and I defy any man among you to point to a single instance where I did one of you a wrong. These people are my enemies, fierce, bitter, implacable; but they are your enemies, too. If they crush me today, they will crush you tomorrow. They will cut your wages and raise the tariff in the company stores on every bite you eat and every rag you wear. They will force you to dwell in Standard Oil houses while you live, and they will bury you in Standard Oil coffins when you die. Their tools and minions are here now, striving to build up another trust whose record is already infamous. Let them win, and they will inaugurate conditions in Montana that will blast its fairest prospect and make its name hateful to those who love liberty. They have crushed the miners of Colorado because those miners had no one to stand for their rights.

In this battle to save the state from the minions of the Rockefellers and the piracy of the Standard Oil, you and I are partners and allies. We stand or fall together.

He had them with him now, and the youthful copper king proceeded to lay out his terms for a settlement. MacGinniss and Lamm would sell their stocks to the union at cost if, in return, the Amalgamated would turn over to him its litigious five thirty-sixths share in his Nipper claim. An arbitration committee jointly selected by both sides, he proposed, could then negotiate all remaining disputes. Pandering to the crowd, he demanded that Rogers and Scallon promise to maintain the prevailing $3.50 daily wage for at least three more years and that they agree to no further shutdowns for at least one year.[39]

A masterful performance, Heinze's brilliantly articulated speech demonstrated anew not only his oratorical skills but also his courage and demagogic cleverness. The crowd marched away loyal to him once more, hateful toward the trust once more. Yet, his momentary rallying of the Butte faithful quickly fell flat. Heinze's bromides lost their sparkle overnight, and reality dawned once again on the bleak city. Within a few days, Rogers and Scallon flatly turned down his proposals and counter-proposed the scheme they had been preparing all along. They demanded that the governor call a special session of the legislature at once to enact their pet "Fair Trials" law. This measure, which has often been referred to mistakenly as a change of venue law, would provide for the simple disqualification of a district judge upon charge of bias by a litigant and would allow for bringing in another judge to replace him. The legislature had enacted a similar law earlier in the year, but the Montana Supreme Court had voided it. Unlike a change of venue law, this unprecedented proposal would allow the speedy and uncomplicated removal of troublesome judges.

This, of course, was blackmail; for only after the legislature pulled the fangs of Heinze's judges would Amalgamated put Montana back to work. Governor Joseph Toole, elected in 1900 as a Clark-Heinze man, had vetoed the law when the legislature initially passed it, and now he balked at company pressure once again. Desperate to break the logjam, area unions and businessmen's groups put together a distinguished arbitration committee made up of Governor Toole, Senators Clark and Gibson, Congressman Joseph Dixon, and James J. Hill of the ore-hauling Great Northern Railroad. The committee failed even to get the two sides together and dissolved in a few days.[40]

As the freezing days of early November signaled winter's approach, the two sides continued to cannonade one another, and Montanans anxiously weighed the Amalgamated demands. Heinze and Thomas Lawson of Amalgamated, two well-matched performers, leveled a barrage of charges and counter-charges back and forth. Lawson repeatedly issued press statements—probably accurate, in the main—that he and Heinze had been meeting to negotiate a sellout to Amalgamated. Heinze just as repeatedly denied that any such meetings had taken place.[41] The man in the hot seat now, though, was not Heinze but Governor Toole, who silently pondered the trust's insistence upon a special legislative session. For days, the governor remained so reticent that the *Anaconda Standard* began portraying him in cartoons as the "Montana Sphinx." Meanwhile, labor unions and other groups flooded his office with resolutions and petitions demanding the special session and a speedy return to work. Most Montana newspapers called for the special session, but spokesmen for the eastern plains region, who were less directly affected, had some reservations. The *Miles City Independent* dismissed the papers advocating the session as "nothing but the mouthpieces of an unscrupulous corporation," and the *Glendive Independent* urged Toole to "soak both companies with their own oil and apply the torch." On 10 November, the governor gave in and announced that he would convene the legislature in early December. The Amalgamated responded at once by beginning to reopen its plants.[42]

Even though he had precious little choice, Toole's decision led inevitably to charges that he had sold out to the trust, or at least that he had bowed unmanfully to naked coercion. These charges would gain credence when the company supported him for reelection in 1904. Toole's submission to the will of the trust convinced those who still needed convincing among nationwide observers that Montana ranked lowest among the forty-five states in its subservience to corporate domination. Like some other industry watchers, the *Mining and Scientific Press* saw the affair mainly as "a bull movement in the copper market," in other words as an effort to cut production costs while liquidating surpluses. More pertinently, the *Outlook* viewed the Montana spectacle as a "king's war": ". . . to permit a rich corporation to call for and get an extra session of the Legislature is to establish a precedent that is both preposterous and dangerous." The *American Labor Union Journal* bemoaned Toole's genuflection to "the iron fist of despotic power," and the *New York Journal of Commerce* concluded: "It looks as tho [sic] the real governing power in Montana was the Amalgamated Copper Company, or likely to become so."[43]

Indeed, the cornered copper trust had lashed out like a wounded beast, grasping a supposedly "sovereign" state in its bite. Toole had done what he had to; for without his order, the wage earners of the state could not have survived the winter. But in doing so, he served to demonstrate the extent to which this remote, thinly populated, much-abused mountain commonwealth had become a pawn in the world of capitalist intrigue and manipulation. The image of the dramatic shutdown of 1903, burned into the consciousness of a generation, would live long into the future.

Montana's legislators, so often humiliated over the past five years, gathered in Helena to hear the governor's somber, noncommittal message on 1 December 1903. Even as they met, nearly 500 of the Heinze faithful, many of them employees of his firms, gathered in a gala convention at the capital and launched an antitrust party to carry on the fight. Despite the tough talk of "Down the Kerosene," and despite the presence of such prominent folks as ex-Governor Smith and Billings Mayor W. B. George, the vaunted new party represented little more than a regrouping of the established Heinze political forces.[44]

The lawmakers paid little heed to the goings-on at the political gathering across town. After a minimum of debate, they passed the mandated two laws on 10 December. The first of these clarified when a case might qualify for change of venue and, in effect, paved the way for the second, the judge disqualification law. This "Fair Trials" or "Clancy Law" dealt a staggering blow to the Heinze camp, for it neutralized Fritz's hammerlock on the Butte courts. Henceforth, his friendly judges could simply be challenged for bias and replaced. Such a law had no precedent in 1903, but other states have since adopted similar procedures.[45] It was not the law itself that was offensive, of course; it was the means taken to force its adoption. After so many losses, the trust had squeezed the state into submission and won the biggest battle of all.

While the shutdown and reopening of the mines and smelters were taking place aboveground, a bizarre and extremely dangerous "underground war" erupted below. Heinze's brazen decision to mine the rich Enargite and Windlass veins along the Rarus-Davitt border, under the specious argument that his Johnstown Mining Company was not enjoined by the federal court injunction, was sure to cause grave trouble. His men blasted around the clock, desperate to remove the high-grade ores as rapidly as possible, and before long Amalgamated men began to hear the distant rumbles from the adjacent Pennsylvania Mine. In a risky maneuver, a party of Amalgamated men led by Anaconda geologist Reno Sales and Butte and Boston superintendent George McGee removed a bulkhead and sneaked into the Rarus at the 600-foot level on the night of 10 October 1903. Moving into the forbidden zone, they witnessed a strange spectacle: armies of men swarming like ants through the stopes, hauling the prized ores out into the Rarus drifts.[46]

Since the Davitt claim had no shaft, and since the entries from adjoining company mines were blocked, Amalgamated lawyers led by veteran John Forbis petitioned U.S. Judge Hiram Knowles, who had been handling this litigation since 1898, for a right of inspection through the Rarus. Desperately and flagrantly defying the court, Heinze actually stepped up the pace of illegal mining and went into hiding to avoid service of the court order. On one occasion, he barely escaped the marshal by fleeing through a rear window and down a fire escape. Finally, sixteen days after their initial discovery of the Heinze raid into the Davitt, geologists Sales and H. V. Winchell gained access to the workings. What they found was a bewildering mass of crosscuts and stopes, filled with waste rock from excavations which had been cut in the past few days. The court ordered further assessments, particularly measurements of the cavities which would allow fines for damages. But once again, Heinze and his lieutenants flouted the court by obstructing entry.[47]

One stands in awe of Heinze's gall. Quite clearly, he meant to intimidate the federal judge, for his press spokesmen pounded away at Knowles as being biased in favor of the trust. By now, the Heinzes' appeal of the case of *Heinze* v. *Butte and Boston Company* had reached the U.S. Court of Appeals in San Francisco, and that court dispatched Judge James H. Beatty of Idaho to Butte to take jurisdiction. Beatty had little more luck than Knowles in establishing his authority, though, even after threatening contempt citations. When the Amalgamated geologists finally regained entry in December, they once more found the MOP–Johnstown crews mining at full speed, this time without any effort to conceal their activities. No one could any longer doubt Heinze's intent: to disembowel the veins before the courts could stop him and before his credit expired, regardless of risks. The Amalgamated geologists found huge cavities where high-grade ore had been removed; but before they could return to measure them, Heinze's men caved them in with dynamite blasts.[48]

As the rule of law failed aboveground, the law of the jungle broke out below. Foremen for both sides dispatched their crews to mine disputed veins and to checkmate the advancing crews of the opposition. In both the Michael Davitt and the Minnie Healy, which the Amalgamated was desperately trying to retain on appeal of Clancy's October ruling to the Montana Supreme Court, guerilla warfare broke out. Each side worked to drive out the crews of the other. They fouled the opposition drifts by burning trash and rubber and pouring slaked lime through vents. They fired back and forth with high-pressure hoses, tossed homemade grenades, even dynamited tunnels and electrified the metal turn plates on which ore cars moved around corners. Wild fistfights ensued when crews came suddenly upon each other. Full-scale underground war seemed imminent.

Late in December two Amalgamated miners, Sam Olson and Fred Divel, died in an accident when Heinze men blasted a bulkhead from the opposite side.[49] Amalgamated crews attempted to drive crosscuts into the Enargite vein from the Pennsylvania Mine, but MOP forces drove them out with smoke and lime. Squads from both companies poured into Vein 7 of the Pennsylvania and disemboweled it, even though it was under an injunction of the court. Miners from the Rarus blasted their way into the Amalgamated's Mountain View Mine and fought hand-to-hand with opposing crews until driven back with homemade smoke grenades. From the Minnie Healy, Heinze's men secretly entered the neighboring Leonard Mine of the Boston and Montana Company and began hauling its ore out through their own tunnels.

More than once, disaster was only narrowly averted. MOP men once tried and failed to blast out the main shaft of the Pennsylvania Mine, a very dangerous maneuver. A key battleground was the famous "firing line" sector lying along the border between the Healy and adjacent Amalgamated claims, which Clancy had enjoined from operation by the trust. When Heinze forces penetrated this rich zone, the Amalgamated reacted hysterically and sent in sappers who demolished the veins with 100 blasts. Ironically, the courts later conceded this ground to the trust. At one point, Heinze's men attempted to force the opposition out of the firing line by tapping water mains and diverting the flow into their workings. Company miners allowed the water to accumulate in the Leonard and then planned to blast out the walls and flood it back into the Healy, blowing their steam whistles to warn the workers inside. A large crowd of wives and relatives rushed to the mine, and MOP agitators incited them by shouting that their loved ones were drowning below. At the last minute, the foremen of both sides reached a truce by calling off the flood plan and assuring the crowd that the men were alive.[50]

Two factors finally curbed this dangerous lawlessness in the spring of 1904. Thoroughly alarmed, the two sides regained their senses and pulled back from the prospect of real warfare, which would surely mean the wholesale loss of lives and investments. At the same time, the courts finally managed to assert their authority. Late in March of 1904, Judge Beatty hailed F. Augustus Heinze and his foremen Al Frank and J. H. Trerise into court and found them in contempt. The judge angrily denounced Heinze's fraudulent ploy of mining through his Johnstown Company and condemned his flagrant defiance of one court order after another. "I have been involved in mining litigation and mining operations for the last 32 years," he commented, "and in all of my experience I have never known an order of the court violated as this has been. It is simply beyond all reason." Nonetheless, bowing to the "unusual conditions" prevailing at Butte, Beatty flinched from really punishing Heinze, whose newspapers accused anyone crossing him of being a corporate stooge. He held prison sentences in abeyance and issued the ridiculously light fines of $20,000 to Heinze and $1,000 apiece to his lieutenants. The $20,000, groaned the *Anaconda Standard*, represented about what the Heinze crowd could make on six months' interest from the stolen ore. In truth, Fritz had made a killing from his raid into the Michael Davitt. He found rich deposits amidst the faults of the Enargite-Windlass veins that the more conservative Amalgamated geologists had missed. In all, he probably took $500,000 to $1,000,000 worth of high-grade ore from the forbidden ground.[51]

The Davitt case, like those involving the Tramway and the Nipper, remained in litigation until the Butte mining war came to an end. Others were settled along the way. Early in February 1904, the Montana Supreme Court predictably overruled Judge Clancy in the MacGinniss and Lamm minority stock cases and freed the trust to hold and profit from the stocks of its subsidiaries. In April 1905, on the other hand, the court upheld Clancy's awarding of the Minnie Healy to Heinze, a major victory for the besieged mining king.[52] It is interesting to note that the supreme court, perhaps reflecting the antitrust sentiment of the state, frequently sustained the rulings of Heinze's Butte judges.

It was clear by early 1904 that the Heinzes were in full retreat before the burgeoning might of the Amalgamated. The big shutdown of late 1903 had badly tarnished their luster with the public; the "Fair Trials Law" seemed sure to cut away their sway over the Butte courts; and in both the state and federal courts, they faced mounting troubles. But the war still raged on, for Fritz and his brothers yet commanded ample ores, elaborate plant facilities, a mass of threatening litigation, and a fine-tuned political organization. Writing in mid-1904, an official of the federal Bureau of Corporations wrote accurately: "The only line of division here is on the copper question, no parties are known except the Heinze party and the Amalgamated. . . . Montana is an excellent example of the baleful effect of corporations engaging in politics; the perversion of the government for business purposes."[53]

Neither side seemed ready to give an inch. In January 1904, Henry Rogers was quoted: "The flag has never been lowered at 26 Broadway, and I'll drive Heinze out of Montana if it takes ten millions to do it." A month later, he wrote Mark Twain that "we are, I think, gaining slowly" and remarked to a friend of Wall Street insider Clarence

But He Hasn't Got the Chain on---Yet.

From the *Butte Reveille*, October 7, 1904 (courtesy of the Montana Historical Society, Helena)

Barron: "Of course Heinze has got to quit. Why this last decision puts him down and out. The court decided on the apex. Why, Heinze is only a fly on an elephant's trunk compared with Lawson and Rogers." As for Heinze, he seemed anything but intimidated. He boasted to Barron in May that the Montana war was wearing down the trust at the rate of $2,000,000 lost annually and that he would soon force them to sue for peace on his terms: "I know that Rogers is sick of this fight and wants to settle."[54]

With the approach of the 1904 political campaign, F. Augustus Heinze geared up for yet another bout with the trust. He faced a rugged, uphill battle this time, however, for the leadership of both major parties was now more solidly pro-Amalgamated than it had been in 1902. Senator Clark and Governor Joseph Toole held the Democratic Party in a solid anti-Heinze grip. Basking in the glow of Teddy Roosevelt's popularity, the Republicans nonetheless faced severe internal divisions between a progressive younger faction led by fast-rising Congressman Joseph Dixon and a conservative older wing led by Standard Oil ally Thomas Carter. The one issue that seemed to unite all Republicans was their common hatred of Heinze. Both parties froze out the Heinze element, and Fritz found himself hard pressed to put together yet another fusion based upon his old antitrust coalition. He faltered this time, and much of his old Labor-Populist support returned to the ranks of the Democratic party. Some others joined up with the fast-rising and unpredictable Socialists. In desperation, Heinze concentrated his efforts on preserving his hold on Silver Bow County and in searching out candidates wherever he he could find them who would strike an antitrust posture.[55]

The Hand on Guard

WILL THE COILS ENFOLD MONTANA ALSO?

From the *Butte Reveille*, October 1904 (courtesy of the Montana Historical Society, Helena)

Outwardly, Heinze seemed to stage as wild a campaign as ever in 1904, this time comparing his defense of Montana's liberties with the antilabor violence which the Rockefellers and their minions were working in Colorado. In truth, however, the old Heinze magic had lost its effervescence. Fritz seemed played out, dissipated, and desperate. He turned up that autumn at Twin Bridges to campaign against Republican legislative candidate Frank Linderman, complete with a red car, chauffeur, and four banjo-playing black minstrels. Heinze delivered a biting harangue against Linderman as a corporate stooge, but later apologized to him, explaining that he had been drunk at the time. Congressman Dixon years later stated that Heinze had offered him a sizable bribe in return for his support of a friendly GOP nominee to the state supreme court.[56]

Heinze's speeches and his papers hammered away at the old theme of Standard Oil domination, but this time the trust had an effective response—that the self-proclaimed crusader against monopoly was actually negotiating a sellout to his supposed adversary. The *Reveille* angrily denounced the "Persistency of the Sell-Out Lie," but the charges hit home. Desertions from the cause hurt badly, too. Allies of two years before, like Governor Toole and Butte Mayor Mullins, were now lined up with the opposition. In the election of 8 November 1904, the Republicans easily won control of the legislature, which in 1905 would send Heinze's old foe Tom Carter back to the U.S. Senate. And Heinze's main target of abuse, Chief Justice Theodore Brantly, won reelection. In Silver Bow County, Heinze's men suffered some severe losses, most notably the judgeships of William Clancy and Edward Harney. Crowed the *Inter Mountain:* " . . . it is certain that the Napoleon of humbug, and corruption, and fraud, and crime, has met his Waterloo, and that the end of Heinzeism is in sight in the Treasure State."[57]

Heinze's setback of 1904 did not end his political influence overnight; that persisted in diminished form for years afterward. But it did signal the beginning of the end, demonstrating that he could no longer command either Butte itself or a major voice in state affairs. The great Montana mining war was fast approaching its end. Soon after the election, the Heinzes and the Amalgamated either began or resumed secret negotiations for a sellout. F. Augustus and his brothers detested Henry Rogers and disliked William Scallon. They got along nicely, though, with the smooth-talking diplomat John Ryan, whom Otto Heinze, Fritz's brother, later remembered as "an extremely nice man." For fifteen months, first at Butte, then at New York hotels, the secret negotiations continued. "Heinze was mortally afraid," Ryan later recalled, "that the miners in Butte would learn that he was preparing to sell out, as he was loudly promising to fight their battles for them if they would stand by him." The bargainers had to reach accord not only on a price, but also on who and what sort of company would take over the Heinze properties. Fritz would not accept the embarrassment of having them pass directly into Amalgamated, after all his talk of standing off the trust.[58]

WHAT FUSION MEANS IN BUTTE.

INTERMOUNTAIN NOVEMBER 5 1904

From the *Intermountain*, November 5, 1904 (courtesy of the Montana Historical Society, Helena)

In mid-February of 1906, reports of a settlement reached the press, heralding the end of nearly a decade of mining warfare. For a rumored price of $10,500,000–$12,000,000, the Heinzes turned over the bulk of their Montana properties, not directly to Amalgamated, but rather to the Butte Coalition Mining Company, newly incorporated in New Jersey and capitalized at $15 million. Thomas F. Cole of Duluth, a key figure in iron and copper mining who had worked with Ryan in the negotiations, took office as president of the Butte Coalition; and both Ryan and H. U. Broughton, Henry Rogers' son-in-law, sat on the board of directors. The Butte Coalition served as a holding company similar to Amalgamated, with the Heinze properties grouped into its wholly owned subsidiary, the Red Metal Mining Company.[59] Using the Butte Coalition as an Amalgamated-controlled holder of the Heinze operations allowed both the Heinzes and the Amalgamated crowd a semblance of pride, since they both seemed to be dealing with a third party.

The Heinze properties turned over to the Butte Coalition Mining Company included the Montana Ore Purchasing Company, with its elaborate mills, concentrators, and smelters at Meaderville; the Johnstown Mining Company; and a cluster of mining claims including the Rarus, Minnie Healy, Johnstown, Corra and Rock Island, Hypocka, as well as fractional shares in the Tramway, Snohomish, Nipper Consolidated, Pennsylvania, Mountain Chief, and others. Perhaps most significantly, the purchase price involved the dismissal of 110 law suits, which were tying up properties valued at $70–100 million. No doubt with tongue in cheek, the *Reveille* commented: "It Means Peace for Butte. . . . It Does Not Eliminate Heinze." Literally, it did not eliminate Heinze. The brothers still held a lease and bond on the old Lexington Mine and works, a similar lease on the Boston and Bay State works at Basin north of Butte, holdings in the newly formed Davis–Daly Estates Company, which would attempt without much luck to rework some old claims southwest of the city, and several unproven claims. They still held properties in the Trail district of British Columbia and majority control of a new firm in the Bingham Canyon district of Utah, the Ohio Copper Company, which soon prospered. And they retained the over-capitalized United Copper holding company, formed back in 1902, which now looked like a hollow shell, devoid of most of its operating companies.[60]

In reality, the sellout of early 1906 *did* eliminate F. Augustus Heinze as a major factor in Montana mining and politics. And it did indeed signal the end of the battle between the independents and the trust. The war was over. Now, even after seventy-five years, it is difficult to judge Heinze and his motives. He justified his own transgressions by arguing that his Goliath-like enemy forced him to fight dirty, once writing to a troubled parent: "My dear Mother, I cannot fight a band of robbers by singing hymns and sprinkling holy water." Admitting his sins, romantic writers like Joseph Kinsey Howard made him something of an epic hero, a "Robin Hood of copper" who fought the hated Standard Oil behemoth to a standstill.[61] Yet the dispassionate observer must conclude, especially in view of the 1906 sellout, that Heinze had really aimed all along primarily at forcing the trust to pay him an exorbitant price for his holdings. This is not to say that his antitrust crusades were altogether insincere, only that he was an especially virulent example of the ruthless capitalists of his time.

What, after all, did the war of 1898–1906 produce? It yielded some good and necessary results. The consolidation of the Butte hill, so essential to cost efficiency and steady employment, could now be effected. Even the costly litigation led to positive achievements. The courtroom arguments forced both sides to map the district thoroughly. The expensive "litigation drifts," dug to prove or disprove theories as to the courses of veins, sometimes unearthed unsuspected new deposits. Butte mining became less haphazard and wasteful, more scientific and productive. And Butte itself served for a time as the center stage of world metal mining, the training ground for a generation of mining experts who carried their expertise to the corners of the earth. Young Butte men pioneered in copper mining technology for years to come: for instance geologists Reno Sales and Horace Winchell of Amalgamated, or engineers David Brunton of Amalgamated and Cyrus Robinson of the MOP Company, who later became chief engineer for the Guggenheims. Usually forgotten is William Boyce Thompson, one of the giants of the modern copper industry. Thompson grew up at Alder Gulch and at Butte, where he gathered the knowledge which made him a master of mining investment. In 1921 he gathered his holdings into the Newmont Mining Corporation, which is still a major concern.[62]

Beyond any dispute, however, the Heinze-Amalgamated fight left behind a bitter legacy which far outweighed any positive results. The debauchery of a small state by big money horrified the nation and left scars which have persisted to the present day. According to old Wilbur Fisk Sanders, President William McKinley "was shocked at conditions in Montana and had he lived he would have changed the order of things." In Gertrude Atherton's novel *Perch of the Devil*, the Heinze-like hero Gregory Compton says of Montana: "She's been so debauched the last twenty years by open bribery that I doubt if you could lay your hand on a hundred men in her that haven't had a roll anywhere from $500 to $2000 passed to them and pocketed it."[63]

The conservative *Mining and Scientific Press* condemned Heinze as "that Apache of finance," but concluded with "a plague on both parties": "The judiciary of a State has been debauched, its politics mired, its people obsessed, while two parties of mine-owners have twisted our awkward mining laws to the acquirement of territory and the destruction of property." Equally conservative businessmen agreed. John Hays Hammond, the famed mining consultant, reported that J. P. Morgan told him: "It reflects on every business in Wall Street, and it ought to be stopped." Sol Guggenheim commented similarly to Hammond: "I can't understand why Rogers keeps up such a dirty mess. He may get a few million out of it, but he'll only give it right away to charity. Wouldn't you think he'd have more sense than to sacrifice his good name for that? I think it's a damn shame!" Perhaps the progressive *Nation* summed up the attitude of 1906 best: "Nobody comes out of the contest with clean hands, but at any rate there is now hope of ending it."[64]

It need not have been this way. Even considering the size and richness of the Butte district, the bribery, shenanigans, violence, and corruption were not unavoidable. In other great districts, such as Bisbee, Arizona, competing companies formed agreements not to cannibalize one another through the mischievous Apex Law.[65] The trouble at Butte had grown out of a complex and tortured situation. Clark and Daly first fouled the political waters with their venomous personal feud. Then, as fate would have it, an especially mean and ruthless group of Wall Street manipulators took up the lucrative task of building the inevitable consolidation. They failed to reckon with the unscrupulous ingenuity of two local independents, Clark and Heinze, and ended up getting into an eye-gouging, knee-to-the-groin fight before achieving their goal. In the process, they disgraced themselves and injured thousands of people, living and yet unborn.

9. Denouement: The Time of Transition

The years following Heinze's 1906 sellout and the close of the Butte mining war marked a time of transition, an end and a beginning. Old contestants like Clark, Heinze, and Rogers passed from the scene; and newer ones, such as John Ryan and Cornelius Kelley succeeded them, building the corporate structure which would dominate Butte and Montana until past midcentury. The long-sought consolidation of the hill now became a reality, first under the auspices of the Amalgamated Copper Company and then under its chief operating company and successor, Anaconda. In time, the people of the "Treasure State" came to realize that consolidation was a mixed blessing. It brought an end to contention and a new efficiency and a new lease on life to the great old mining "camp." But it also brought to fruition the black legacy of the long and bitter political war of 1888–1906. No longer facing real competition for mastery of the hill, the Amalgamated monolith now bestrode the state like a great, insensate colossus. Montana, it seemed, was the unfortunate fiefdom of an awesomely powerful corporation.

Neither F. Augustus Heinze nor, for that matter, William A. Clark offered any meaningful resistance to the Amalgamated after 1906. Despite his promises to the contrary, Fritz Heinze showed little sign of maintaining his political opposition to the trust after the sellout. He soon closed down the *Reveille*, his vitriolic little political engine, and replaced it with the more sedate *Butte Evening News*, edited by the establishment-oriented Richard Kilroy. His lieutenants, led by John MacGinniss, Peter Breen, and J. M. Kennedy, tried to hold the old organization together. Many of them truly believed in the antitrust cause. The Heinze machine even entered another fusionist slate in the 1906 campaign. As the results of that election indicated, however, the old magic was gone. The once-mighty Heinze organization had fallen apart.[1]

In fact, F. Augustus Heinze was fast losing interest in Montana. With the millions he had won from the sellout to Amalgamated, he set out to establish himself as a genuine Wall Street power, a true equal to the likes of Henry Rogers and the Rockefellers. He took an elaborate double suite of rooms at New York's Waldorf Hotel, the jeweled center of his home city's social life which stood at the present site of the Empire State Building. Although he maintained a handsome office complex nearby on Thirty-Third Street, Heinze used his Waldorf suite as offices in the daytime and as an entertainment center in the evenings. His gala parties, elaborately hosted and enlivened by lovely actresses and the smart set of Manhattan society, made him a big hit here, just as they had back in provincial Butte. Otto Heinze later recalled: "He entertained most lavishly—some forty or fifty men and women at a time. The favors were frequently of gold, the flowers profuse and beautiful, the food excellent and the champagne plentiful. At one dinner given for his Broadway friends and actresses, there was a small envelope at each woman's place with a hundred dollar bill enclosed. These parties usually began late and did not end for many hours. F. A. would often play all night and work all day."[2]

The three Heinze brothers, F. Augustus, Otto, and Arthur, could not come to full agreement in their plans for reinvesting the family fortune; but they loosely cooperated in Fritz's scheme to build a mining-banking empire that would rival that of Standard Oil–Amalgamated. Otto Heinze and Company, the family dry-goods and importing firm, already held a seat on the New York Stock Exchange. They sought now to build up their United Copper holding company by developing new mining operations in Montana, British Columbia, Utah, and Idaho, and by establishing it as a worthy copper rival to Amalgamated. Against the outspoken objections of Otto, a cautious financier by nature, Fritz and his lawyer-brother Arthur chose also to enter the dangerous realm of banking. In the unregulated world of 1906, banks afforded their masters the almost free use of depositors' money for speculation, and the large banks ruled the small. Fritz and Arthur Heinze struck up a fast business friendship with New York plungers E. R. Thomas and Charles W. Morse, the short, squat Maine promoter who had built a monopoly over the city's ice trade and a near monopoly over the East Coast steamship traffic. In partnership with these two magnates, the Heinzes bought the Mercantile National Bank of New York from Edwin Gould for $1,000,000. They then linked the Mercantile National into a highly speculative chain of banks already held by Morse and Thomas.[3]

Fritz Heinze should have listened to brother Otto. In linking up with Morse, he was tying his fate to a man of highly dubious reputation. And in attempting to break into the big leagues of Wall Street banking, a world dominated by the twin citadels of J. P. Morgan and Company and the Rockefeller–National City Bank, the Heinze-Morse-Thomas upstarts were starting a fight which they could not finish. The Morgan and Rockefeller banking interests, along with their establishment allies, controlled the central New York Clearing House, which facilitated the flow of checks and credit between the banks of the city. In these years prior to creation of the Federal Reserve System, the Clearing House served as an instrument by which New York's largest banks could master the smaller ones by controlling their access to credit.

We shall never fully know the extent to which Heinze and his allies caused their own downfall—for Morse had made an enemy of Morgan in his transportation maneuvers—and the extent to which his Standard Oil enemies undercut him. Both factors no doubt combined to destroy him in a spectacular *Gotterdamerung* which set off a brief but sharp nationwide panic. Heinze's troubles began with his shaky United Copper Company, which was vulnerable not only because of its dearth of proven holdings but also because of a tight money market and a skidding copper price. Little more than a near-hollow shell after the 1906 sellout, United Copper was described by the *Copper Handbook*, spokesman for the industry, as a "blind pool," an "exceptionally daring piece of stockjobbery," a pawn of an entrepreneur who "has shown himself utterly rapacious, unscrupulous and conscienceless in his mining and financial operations."[4] United Copper, in short, was overcapitalized and tightly controlled by a group of disingenuous speculators.

From a high of $70 per share on the Paris market in 1906, United Copper stock dropped to $40 by the fall of 1907. Attempting to shore up these losses, Arthur and Fritz Heinze poured over $2,000,000 into mass purchases of United Copper through scattered brokerages, a risky venture which momentarily reversed the downward trend. Then, however, a sudden wave of selling and hurried calls for margin from the brokers forced the Heinzes to the wall by depleting their cash reserves. This led them to believe that the brokers were selling them short. At this point, the Heinzes and their allies made their fateful decision. They determined to create a "corner" in United Copper by calling in their shares, figuring that the brokers held insufficient shares to meet their call and that they would have to bid up the price in a desperate search for them in the open market. The gamble failed, for some party or parties held large enough blocs of the stock to cover the short purchases of the brokers. Receiving their stocks, the Heinzes saw the demand for and the price of their shares suddenly break, while at the same time they had to cough up huge sums to cover the purchases.[5]

On Tuesday, 15 October 1907, United Copper broke from 60 to 36 as the Heinzes desperately sold in an effort to raise enough funds to meet their commitments. On the next day, the price fell to 10. This hemorrhaging of United Copper immediately threw the firm of Otto Heinze and Company and the Mercantile National Bank into jeopardy, for both were large creditors of the stricken copper holding company. Driven to the wall, Otto Heinze and Company was suspended on the New York Exchange. When it became clear that the Mercantile National was in dire straits, a snowballing run on the bank set in as depositors hurriedly pulled out their money. The run rapidly spread to the related Morse-connected banks, like the Trust Company of America and the Knickerbocker Trust, one of the largest financial institutions in America. Fighting for survival, Heinze and Morse came to the Clearing House for aid, and the banking barons of New York now coldly plucked them. The directors of the Clearing House agreed to aid the faltering banks, but only on condition that Heinze, Morse, and the Thomas brothers immediately resign from the boards of all of them. Given no choice, they agreed to do so. The Mercantile National and Morse's Bank of North America weathered the storm; but the great Knickerbocker Trust, badly manipulated and weakened from within, fell. With its fall came a severe, nationwide banking panic.[6]

The so-called Panic of 1907, which arose in large part from the Heinze–Morse fiasco, hit the American economy hard, with teetering banks, plummeting stock values, and a spate of plant closures and layoffs. Only a massive pouring of millions into the banks and the market, orchestrated by J. P. Morgan and Treasury Secretary George Cortelyou, averted a real disaster. As it was, the panic triggered a brief but sharp recession, a recession which clearly demonstrated the awesome power of the Wall Street bankers and underscored the need for closer federal regulation of the financial community. Out of this realization would eventually come the Federal Reserve Act of 1913.[7]

For the Heinzes and their allies, the panic represented a shattering, near-fatal blow. Obviously, they did much to seal their own fate through shady speculations and mismanagement. Yet many observers, such as progressive Senator Robert LaFollette of Wisconsin, believed that the great bankers, led by Morgan and by James Stillman of the National City Bank and of Amalgamated Copper, also had a direct hand in setting off the panic through their efforts to crowd the interlopers out of their domain.[8] The mass sales of United Copper stocks, which destroyed the company's standing, and the horrendous runs on the Heinze-Morse banks look very suspicious. One suspects that the Rogers-Rockefeller-Stillman gang were back to their old tricks, settling some old scores with F. Augustus Heinze.

Amidst the wreckage of his mining and banking empire, Heinze confronted a world of problems. Both he and Charles Morse faced charges of criminal malfeasance. Morse eventually went to prison on convictions of grand larceny. Heinze went to trial in the spring of 1909, charged with granting illegal loans based on insufficient collateral to his brother's business and with other incidents of banking malpractice. He escaped conviction this time, but other charges dogged him during the years which followed. At first, Heinze's troubles seemed not to weigh him down. Still a millionaire and barely forty years of age, he seemed likely to succeed in rebuilding his western mining holdings and his United Copper Company. When he returned to Butte in November of 1909, fresh from his victory in court, the city welcomed him like a returning hero. His followers pulled his hack through the streets by hand, and cheering crowds greeted him with "Oh, you, Heinze." He still cut a wide swath in the social world, too. In 1910, he married the attractive actress Bernice Henderson, amidst much fanfare; and in 1911 she bore him a son, F. Augustus, Jr.[9]

But Heinze's good days were nearly gone. Years of hard drinking and nighttime carousing had taken their toll on his amazingly hearty constitution. Suddenly, he seemed more aged in appearance and more sober in demeanor. Almost overnight, it seemed, his hair turned gray. Tension wracked the married life of Fritz and Bernice Heinze, and they soon separated. Then, tragically, in the spring of 1914, Bernice was stricken by spinal meningitis, and she and Fritz were dramatically reconciled only hours before her death in April. One reversal seemed to follow another. Heinze's efforts to rebuild his mining empire failed. In 1911, with its stock at 80 cents per share, United Copper passed into receivership. Even the brothers themselves, always so close, fell to quarreling and blaming one another for their misfortunes. In October 1914, Fritz suffered a severe setback when a New York court awarded Edwin Gould a $1,200,000 settlement against him for incomplete payment in the earlier purchase of the Mercantile National Bank.[10]

Perhaps his wife's death, followed only months later by this defeat in court, pulled him over the edge. Visibly shaken and dispirited, F. Augustus Heinze traveled upstate to Saratoga, New York, in order to vote on 3 November 1914. He had been suffering for several months from internal bleeding and cirrhosis of the liver; and in the early hours of the next morning, he died suddenly of a massive hemorrhage. Butte and New York noted his passing with considerable interest; but the interest seemed to be historical in tenor, as if recalling a memorable character from the distant past. For Fritz Heinze actually left little behind. Most of his $1,500,000 estate went to his sister, to whom he had entrusted the care of his beloved infant son. Little remained of his once great copper empire. The heart of it now belonged to Amalgamated.[11] A remarkably gifted man, Heinze flew fast and high before his early fall. His tragedy lies in the lost opportunities, in the roads not taken. Had he followed a more constructive and less nihilistic path, F. Augustus Heinze might have been one of the truly great men of his generation. Even as it was, he proved himself a man to reckon with—a major figure in the history of American mining, one of the few men who ever stood off the brigands of Standard Oil.

Neither Heinze nor Daly had lived to savor the fruits of their labors in a ripe old age. By contrast, William Andrews Clark, the most notorious of the Butte mining kings, seemed to live nearly forever, long enough to become a legend in his own time. His 1901 election to the U.S. Senate marked the zenith of an incredible career. He served only one term in the Senate, not even bothering to run again in 1906–7. One suspects that he did not find the demands of the job very appealing, for Clark was not accustomed to catering to constituents. For the rest of his long life, though, he insisted upon the title "Senator." It had, after all, cost him plenty! As a senator, he is remembered as a conservative Democrat, the richest member of the so-called Senate "Millionaires' Club." Predictably, Senator Clark pressed for such typically western causes as opening the Indian reservations and liberalizing the homestead laws. Less predictably, he also opposed the imperialism of Teddy Roosevelt and supported such progressive measures as the Hepburn rail reform act and the Pure Food and Drug Act. Best remembered is his typically western opposition to the Roosevelt conservation measures, well summarized in his remark to the Senate at the close of his term: "In rearing the great structure of empire on this Western Hemisphere we are obliged to avail ourselves of all the resources at our command. The requirements of this great utilitarian age demand it. Those who succeed us can well take care of themselves."[12]

Although he represented Montana in the Senate, W. A. Clark grew increasingly away from the state which had spawned his riches. Following his Senate retirement in 1907, he maintained a close political interest in his home state, and rumors in 1910 even hinted that he might run again for the Senate with company support. He never did. Clark continued over the years to return home for extended visits to his handsome Butte mansion. He enjoyed the annual reunions with his peers in the Society of Montana Pioneers, and he loved to host festivities at the Columbia Gardens—the pleasant little trolley park which he built in the foothills of the continental divide east of town. Clark charged no admission at his park, and he reveled in public adulation there whenever he could. In May of 1907, he chartered special trains to bring in 10,000 children and parents from the surrounding areas, with all the costs on his bill.[13]

In May of 1910, Clark severed his strongest Montana tie by selling his major copper properties to Amalgamated. He was the last great independent to do so. In return for a five-million-dollar settlement, he turned over to the trust a cluster of mining properties which included the Butte Reduction Works, the Colusa-Parrot and the Original Consolidated among others, as well as the Montana Realty Company. Clark kept his Elm Orlu Mine and other zinc claims, along with the concentrator to work them, believing correctly that they promised handsome profits. He also kept numerous town lots and other Butte properties. But his sellout to the trust marked a further milestone on the road toward complete consolidation of the hill, and it closed the process which had begun with his political truce with Amalgamated back in 1901.[14]

During these twilight years, William Andrews Clark continued to pursue what had always been his twin loves, the making and spending of money. Life for the old man was still a battle of will against an adverse world. Even as one of the world's richest men—worth a reputed $50,000,000 in 1900—he drove himself unmercifully hard. Despite the lengthening years, he worked long hours, even when ill, and forced himself to learn French and German in order better to pursue his art collecting. Clark entered whole new fields of investment after he had passed sixty. In each of them, he demonstrated the same fiscal and managerial genius that he had shown as a younger man in Montana.

By 1900 Clark ranked as the world's greatest independent mine-owner. In addition to dozens of other mines in Montana, Arizona, Idaho, Utah, and New Mexico, his fabulous United Verde poured forth millions in new riches each year. He bought extensive planta-tions in Mexico; and, falling in love with southern California, he pur-chased sizable tracts of real estate there, including homes in Los Angeles and Santa Barbara. Convinced of the future of irrigated sugar beet farming, he bought a large farm and refinery near Los Angeles. In his first year at it, he reportedly made a $400,000 profit in sugar beets. Clark purchased the world's largest bronze firm, Henry Bonard and Company of New York, reportedly after convincing himself that the company had overcharged him for some bronze doors for his home.[15]

Clark made his most spectacular move in 1901, when he formed the $25,000,000 San Pedro, Los Angeles, and Salt Lake Railroad to link Utah to the newly dredged harbor of San Pedro. Convinced that such a line could prosper by opening the mining region of southern Utah and by growing with the booming city of Los Angeles, he poured $20,000,000 of his own money into the project. The Salt Lake Line penetrated the empire of E. H. Harriman, master of the Union Pacific–Southern Pacific, and Harriman fought hard to stop it by building competing trackage. In the strategic Meadow Wash Canyon of Nevada, construction crews of both sides raced to preempt each other, sometimes resorting to their fists in the process. In the end, Clark triumphed—one of the few times the tough and wily Harriman ever lost a round—and forced the Union Pacific to buy a half-interest in his line. The road was completed in 1905, linking the "City of the Saints" to the "City of the Angels," as the *Butte Miner* put it. The tracks passed through the sleepy town of Las Vegas, seat of Clark County, Nevada. At both ends of the railroad, Los Angeles and Salt Lake City, Senator Clark became a hero, the man who opened new vistas of commerce and prosperity. Butte watched with interest, too, for the Salt Lake Line gave it a new, alternate freight route to south-ern California and to the slowly building Panama Canal.[16]

So long as he kept to business, W. A. Clark always excelled. His problems persistently arose when his social-political pretensions and his urge to flaunt his wealth got the best of him. Incurably vain, he became more of a rarefied dandy as he grew older. He spent more and more of his time in France and became a conscious Francophile in dress and manner, attiring himself in elegant clothes, fussing over his carefully groomed hair, and parting his graying beard and combing the ends of his mustache meticulously upward. His fondness for the ladies seemed to ripen with the passing years. He set off a sensation in 1904 with the announcement that, back in 1901, he had secretly wed his pretty young ward, Anna LaChapelle, a Butte girl whose education he had been funding in France. According to the carefully worded public statements, she had born him a daughter in 1902, but they had decided to keep the marriage and birth secret so that husband and wife could pursue their careers. The *Butte Miner* rhapsodized about this "very pretty romance"; but naturally enough, it provoked widespread whispers and cackles, calling to mind the song of the time about the "bird in a gilded cage," "whose beauty was sold for an old man's gold." Despite that, the marriage survived and two daughters, the second generation of Clark children, were born to it.[17]

As always, Clark strived for social and cultural recognition. He tried, with mixed success, to marry his daughters into the aristocracy and to push his sons up the business ladder. As the years went by, he devoted more and more of his energies to collecting art. He toured Europe and studied incessantly, and eventually he invested over $1,500,000 in his collection. The heart of the Clark collection, which went finally to the Corcoran Gallery in Washington, D.C., was twenty-two Corot paintings and Rembrandt's *Portrait of a Man*, for which he paid $180,000. It also included works by Turner, DaVinci, Van Dyck, Hogarth, Gainsborough, and Reynolds, as well as many laces and antiques. Some critics scoffed at Clark's tastes, as he mixed the good and bad according to his own predilections; but he took great pride in his art, and he beamed when President Roosevelt asked for and received a personal tour in 1906.[18]

In 1906, Senator Clark began construction of his incredible home on Fifth Avenue in New York City. Completed in 1912 at a reported cost of over $3,000,000, the Clark mansion was rumored to be the most expensive dwelling in the nation. Like California railbuilder Collis Huntington and other western millionaires, the old man evidently felt that he had to have a New York palace as a monument to his success. The huge, scalloped mansion was enormously extravagant, with 131 rooms, 21 of them bathrooms, and 30 of them servants' quarters. Its furnaces burned seventeen tons of coal per day, and its ceilings were timbers cut from Sherwood Forest. New Yorkers considered it an eyesore and a travesty. With a fine display of down-east condescension, one critic described it as "a peerless piece of ludicrous solemnity," "a monument to one of the strangest of millionaires," and "a tribute to the state of Montana." Poet Wallace Irwin immortalized the place in 1911 with these superb lines:

> Senator Copper of Tonopah Ditch
> Made a clean billion in minin' and
>   sich.
> Hiked for New York, where his
>   money he blew,
> Buildin' a palace on Fift' Avenoo.
> 'How,' says the Senator, 'kin I
>   look proudest?
> Build me a house that'll holler the
>   loudest.
> None of your slab-sided, plain
>   mossyleums!
> Gimme the treasures of art an'
>   museums!
> Build it new-fangled,
> Scalloped and angled,
> Fine, like a weddin' cake, gar-
>   nished with pills.
> Gents, do your duty.
> Trot out your beauty.
> Gimme my money's worth—I'll
>   pay the bills.' [19]

For all his success, and for all his efforts to prove to the world that he was a man of culture and refinement, W. A. Clark never really found the acceptance he was seeking. The stigma of bribery and corruption kept returning to haunt him. For instance, after sitting through an insufferable dinner feting Clark in 1907, Mark Twain wrote this scathing assessment:

> He is said to have bought legislatures and judges as other men buy food and raiment. By his example he has so excused and so sweetened corruption that in Montana it no longer has an offensive smell. His history is known to everybody; he is as rotten a human being as can be found anywhere under the flag; he is a shame to the American nation, and no one has helped to send him to the Senate who did not know that his proper place was the penitentiary, with a ball and chain on his legs. To my mind he is the most disgusting creature that the republic has produced since Tweed's time. [20]

He never won respectability, but he certainly won wealth. Like most of America's millionaires, his fortunes surged with the prosperity and inflation of World War I. By the time of his death, his fortune was estimated at over $200,000,000. In today's dollars, he would have been a billionaire. On the floor of the U.S. Senate, Robert LaFollette

described him as one of the 100 men who owned America. He enjoyed the blessings of good health and alertness right to the end and
worked at his offices until only a few days prior to his death. The end
came quickly. Late in February of 1925, the old man, now in his
mid-eighties, contracted a cold which developed into pneumonia. He
died peacefully in his New York mansion on the evening of 2 March.
At Butte, Missoula, and at Jerome, Arizona, his "company town,"
elaborate services were held in his memory. And on 7 March 1925,
his final services were conducted at New York. Over 300 people
attended; and over 400 floral arrangements, including one from President Coolidge, surrounded his casket alongside his masterworks of
art. As the *New York Times* noted: ". . . the faces of Corot could look
down on the end of their great collector. . . ."[21]

Thus ended one of the most remarkable lives that America ever
produced. In the entire history of the West, William Andrews Clark is
the classic rags-to-riches success story, the ultimate embodiment of
the Horatio Alger myth. Yet, following his death, he quickly faded
from memory. This was largely because, unlike Marcus Daly, whose
fine statue by Augustus Saint-Gaudens still faces across the Butte hill,
Clark left no great corporate monument behind. His enormous estate
was immediately divided among his surviving children. Relatively
little of it went to charity, and this too contributed to his eclipse. In
Montana, his Columbia Gardens, along with his other remaining local properties, passed to Anaconda in 1928. The company continued
to operate the popular trolley park until its closure in 1973.

Clark's children eventually contributed some of the family fortune
to worthy causes—founding the Los Angeles Philharmonic Orches-
tra, the William Andrews Clark Memorial Library at UCLA, the law
school library at the University of Virginia—but how little of it went to
the much-abused state which had nurtured the founding father! One
wonders how much better Clark's reputation might have fared had
he stayed out of politics, and had he followed John Neill's advice to
endow a great university at Helena.[22] He did not, however; and so his
place in history, his great achievements in the world of business, are
forever blighted by the aura of scandal and corruption that he
brought down upon himself. Life was good to William A. Clark, but
due to his own excesses, history has been unkind.

One by one, the main contestants in the battle for Butte thus passed
from the scene—Daly in 1900, Heinze in 1914, Clark in 1925. Henry
Huttleston Rogers, the iron-fisted and despotic builder of Amalgamated Copper, died amidst his feverish efforts at Virginia railroad

construction in 1909.[23] Only the corporation endured, seemingly all powerful and omnipresent and impervious to change.

During the years following the close of the copper war, the mining district which sprawled across the great russet hill continued to grow and to thrive. Butte remained, for years to come, America's premier metal mining city. From a total population of 47,635 in 1900, Silver Bow County grew to 56,848 in 1910 and to 60,313 in 1920. The big hill produced, by now, about 30 percent of the United States output of copper, 15 percent of the world output, and more silver than any other district in America. Copper expert Walter Weed reported in 1912: "Its annual production is exceeded in value only by that of the Rand, in South Africa, which was $101,000,000 in 1905 against about $65,000,000 for Butte." With mines valued at $500,000,000, with over 900 miles of underground workings, with a population increasing in numbers and diversity, the camp more than ever before presented a vast spectacle to the eye. It represented the largest and wealthiest concentration of population in a huge area reaching from Minnesota on the east to Spokane on the west, to Salt Lake City on the south.[24] Anyone who knew about the West knew about Butte, fabled for its wealth, its toughness, its sinfulness, and its squalor.

These were years of transition in the history of Butte mining. By 1906 the Amalgamated–Anaconda group of mining companies completely controlled the old four-square-mile heart of the district which centered upon the Anaconda Hill. And by now the company overwhelmingly dominated every aspect of life in Butte. It employed over 12,000 people in western Montana. A number of newer companies sprang up at Butte about this time, but they in no way challenged the trust. Some of them interlocked with Amalgamated, and most of them operated beyond the radius of the company's all-important central sphere. Take, for instance, the North Butte Mining Company, which owned the Speculator and other valuable mines. Employing 1,000 men by 1910, this firm seemed at first glance a budding rival to the trust. Actually, it was just the opposite, for it was controlled by John Ryan and his partner Thomas Cole. Other rising firms, like the East Butte Copper Mining Company, the Butte and Balaklava, and "Captain" A. B. Wolvin's Butte and Superior and Butte and Duluth companies, employed far fewer workers and always followed the lead of Amalgamated in matters relating to general policy. The Butte and Superior Company pioneered large-scale zinc mining at Butte in 1906 with the development of its Black Rock Mine and its air-concentrator and mill. With expanding markets for zinc, W. A. Clark and other operators soon moved into the mining of this metal which lies in such profusion in the zones reaching outward from the central mining district.[25]

Although Butte continued to reign supreme among mining cities of the West, revolutionary new developments in copper mining were even now toppling Montana from the front rank of producing states. Arizona's rich scattering of copper towns, such as Bisbee, Globe, Jerome, Douglas, and Ajo, inexorably pressed that arid and seemingly near-vacant territory into first place. And in the great Bingham Canyon district of Utah, Daniel C. Jackling and his associates were proving out the theory that would transform the mining of the red metal. Jackling demonstrated that, by using the mass-excavation methods of open pit mining, porphyry ore bodies—disseminated deposits of low-grade ore—could be mined profitably. The rise of the Bingham Canyon open-pit mine eventually catapulted Utah to second rank among the copper states, behind Arizona and ahead of Montana. As Michigan meanwhile fell further behind, newer producing regions such as Alaska and Mexico beckoned on the horizon.[26]

These were halcyon days for the American copper miners. Even as Jackling's unlocking of the secrets of mining low-grade ore and as the opening of great new districts in the Southwest provided undreamed-of reserves, the so-called flotation method of concentration revolutionized the process of reduction. In contrast to the cumbersome old mechanical concentrators, flotation removes metal particulate from the crushed ore by dumping it in an oil mixture and forcing air bubbles through the fluid. The bubbles form an oily film around them to which the metal granules adhere, carrying them to the surface and permitting an easy skimming of the concentrates for smelting. Flotation increased the rate of recovery of metals from ore and lowered the cost, thus boosting the efficiency of mining sulfide ores.[27] The earliest flotation patents date back to the 1860s, but the process came into widespread use only at about this time.

Commanding vast reserves of ore, sources of capital, and wondrous new technologies, the American copper men ruled the markets of the world. American copper, efficiently refined and marketed, drove aside the old European companies of Spain and England and retarded the development of potentially great newer mines in Africa and South America. Europe, following the American lead in electrification, now relied overwhelmingly upon American imports for her supply of the vital metal. By 1906 the United States copper companies supplied roughly 60 percent of the world copper output. Following a sag to 11 cents per pound in the wake of the Amalgamated birth pangs, prices held up reasonably well in the range of 13–20 cents, even in the midst of such mushrooming of output.[28]

Of course, the great Amalgamated Copper Company held the dominant position in the turbulent world of red metal mining. But mighty Amalgamated never achieved the monopolistic, price-setting status that its Standard Oil founders seemed to have in mind when they created it back in 1899. It never became the U.S. Steel of copper. The long and costly war with Heinze hamstrung and distracted the Rogers group, and it set back their effort toward a quick consolidation of first Butte and then the entire American industry. And then, by 1906–7, came the real stumbling block to their control of the copper market: the booming mines of the Southwest. With this mounting production, Amalgamated could not secure a large enough share of the market to set the price. It never really came very close. At its peak of influence, the trust's marketing arm, the United Metals Selling Company, sold about 300,000,000 tons yearly, roughly one-half of U.S. output. By the year of Amalgamated's demise, 1915, this share had lapsed by several percentage points.[29]

First under the guidance of Henry Rogers and William Scallon, and then under John Ryan and Cornelius Kelley, the Amalgamated steadily rationalized its collection of operating companies. By 1909 firm control of the company rested in the hands of Ryan, who succeeded Rogers that year as president, and of Kelley, who became general counsel in 1908 and vice president in 1911. Quiet and demure, shrewd and ruthless, Ryan formed a remarkable partnership with his ebullient and fast-rising associate Kelley. Together, they seemed to symbolize the old and the new in America's evolving corporate world: Kelley, the old baronial style of his idol Marcus Daly; Ryan, the cold and impersonal manner of the modern corporate executive. Actually, they had a good deal in common. Both were intelligent, tough, and remorseless in their business dealings; both were Butte men, returning control of the trust to home-state hands; and both were Irish, carrying on the Daly-style Gaelic personality of the company which would persist even beyond the midcentury.[30]

The Amalgamated purchase of the Boston and Montana–Butte and Boston companies in 1901 and the completion of the new reduction works at Anaconda in 1902–3 permitted the centralization of smelting and refining at both Anaconda and at the Boston and Montana works in Great Falls. This allowed the phasing out of most Butte smelting and a fresh breath of air for the "smoky city." The vast increase in roasting at Anaconda, however, intensified the smoke problem there, even after the company built a huge flue-stack structure to carry the noxious gases high into the air in 1903. From 1905 until 1911, the so-called Smoke Cases, instituted against Amalgamated by an association of farmers and ranchers in the upper Deer Lodge Valley, hung fire in the courts. The emission of arsenic and other pollutants caused extremely serious problems, even the death of livestock. The company finally won a dismissal, on the grounds that further abatement of pollution was not practically possible and that a closure would be too injurious to society; but the cases were expensive and distracting.[31]

The grouping of the Amalgamated Butte properties also facilitated the vertical integration of Montana's copper industry, welding the coal, lumber, and water arms of the various companies into a cohesive system. By 1910, the company held more than one million acres of woodlands, feeding its large mill complex at the company town of Bonner in Hellgate Canyon. The directors of the trust paid special heed to electricity; for with the mines of Butte reaching depths of a half-mile, only a cheaper source of power than the old steam plants at the mines could keep them running at cost efficiency into the long-term future. The Amalgamated inherited a close tie to the Great Falls Power Company, which operated the hydroelectric dam at Black Eagle Falls and supplied power to the Boston and Montana plant. Rogers and Ryan also bought into the Missouri River Power Company, organized by Sam Hauser, W. A. Clark, and others, which operated a plant at Canyon Ferry near Helena and sold electricity to the trust. Ryan, Kelley, and their associates John Morony and Max Hebgen soon shouldered aside the oldtimers within the Missouri River Power Company with the plausible threat that they could at any time cancel their contracts and found their own utility. Soon they had control of the firm.[32]

What Ryan and his entourage had in mind was a merger, built around the Helena and Great Falls plants, of the small electric companies of western Montana into a larger, consolidated corporation. This new corporation could not only supply cheap electricity to their mines and mills, but could also sell the surplus for a tidy profit. In 1912–13, they organized the merger of a cluster of small companies: Missouri River Electric and Power, Great Falls Power, Madison River Power, Billings and Eastern Montana Power, Thompson Falls Power, and Butte Electric and Power, which had its plant southwest of Butte on the Big Hole River. The newborn product of this merger was the Montana Power Company, incorporated in New Jersey on 25 October 1912, with a capitalization of $3,900,000.[33]

The infant utility benefited from its close tie to the trust, as did the Amalgamated. Ryan estimated, even in 1912, that the company "is saving today between $1,300,000 and $2,000,000 annually" through its cheap acquisition of hydroelectric power sources. In 1913, the company electrified its Butte, Anaconda and Pacific ore trains, making it the first electrified railroad in the world which carried heavy tonnages of freight. Ryan pulled off a still smarter maneuver that same year when he convinced the Chicago, Milwaukee, St. Paul and Pacific Railroad, of which he was a director, to electrify its tracks across the Rockies from Harlowton, Montana, to Avery, Idaho. This coup not only assured his power company of a lucrative, long-term business; it also garnered $5,000,000 in purchases from his copper company. So it was that the copper trust spawned Montana's major electrical utility. For more than two decades, John Ryan would preside over both corporations, and it is hardly surprising that local folks simply referred to them jointly as "the company." In truth, they were not formally joined, but they might as well have been. The "Montana Twins" shared common legal, publicity, and lobbying teams, shared the same president until 1933, and were joined in a fruitful business embrace.[34] Together, they formed a political alliance of truly awesome might which would persist for many years.

In these and in other ways, the Ryan-Kelley team built their corporation into the world's greatest and most completely integrated copper company. The directors and stockholders formalized this process on 23 March 1910, by voting to group all of the Amalgamated's operating companies into a single corporate entity, Anaconda. The capital stock of the Anaconda Copper Mining Company, Amalgamated's largest component, was increased from $30 million to $150 million and the shares from 1,200,000 to 6,000,000 at $25 apiece. One by one, meetings of stockholders of the lesser Amalgamated companies then voted to transfer their assets to Anaconda. The consolidated Boston companies, the Parrot, Daly's Washoe Copper Company, the Alice, the Colorado, and the others thus all passed into the corpus of Anaconda, which now stood as the Amalgamated holding company's one giant operating firm. The Clark properties, purchased by Amalgamated, were also merged into Anaconda in late May of 1910. And in June of 1911 the Heinze companies, held since 1906 by the Butte Coalition Mining Company, also joined the fold.[35]

The great consolidation of 1910 unified the management of the Butte hill under the auspices of the Anaconda Copper Mining Company. It made of the Amalgamated Copper Company little more than a near-hollow superstructure, a holder of the securities of Anaconda and of a few other scattered operating firms. The company no longer had much reason for being, especially in light of new federal corporate tax laws which threatened to double-tax holding company profits. For a few more years, the Amalgamated lingered on, probably due in large part to a fracas with minority stockholders in settling the affairs of the Parrot and Alice companies. Meanwhile, Ryan continued to pull what remained of the Amalgamated empire into the fattening Anaconda.

In 1914, the latter company absorbed the International Smelting and Refining Company, which the Ryan–Amalgamated group had been developing for some years. This purchase expanded Anaconda's presence into four new states, with smelters at Tooele, Utah and Miami, Arizona, a refinery at East Chicago, Indiana, and refining and marketing facilities at Perth Amboy, New Jersey. Anaconda also inherited other valuable Amalgamated heirlooms. These included a major portion of the trust's profitable marketing arm, the New Jersey-based United Metals Selling Company, which Rogers had kept out of Amalgamated to his own profit; controlling shares in the Greene Cananea Copper Company of northern Mexico, which Ryan and Cole had secured back in 1907 from its colorful founder, Colonel Bill Greene; and the Inspiration Copper Company, with its two low-grade mines at Miami, Arizona.[36]

The final step in this long process came on 9 June 1915, with the dissolution of the Amalgamated Copper Company. Since the holding company's one major remaining asset by now was its possession of 3,327,937 shares of Anaconda stock (55 percent of the total), the stockholders simply voted to exchange their Amalgamated shares for those of Anaconda. John D. Ryan moved over to the presidency of Anaconda, and Cornelius Kelley and Benjamin Thayer became vice presidents. Thus, like a snake molting its skin, the Anaconda Copper Mining Company emerged as an independent corporation. Pronouncing a benediction upon the sixteen-year-old, dead hulk of Amalgamated—the instrument through which Butte had been consolidated—Ryan announced that the defunct trust had earned a total of $113,032,300, of which $91,279,147 had been paid out in dividends and the remainder had been reinvested.[37]

Few wept, or even heeded, the passing of the notorious copper trust. In Montana, it made little difference; for the same mines, mills and managers simply transferred their titles to Anaconda, the name by which most of the trust's operations had generally been known anyway. Regaining the independence she had lost back in 1899, the Anaconda Copper Mining Company reemerged in 1915 as one of America's great corporations, by far the mightiest of world copper companies. The company boasted assets valued in 1915 at $118,000,000 and an annual production capacity of 300,000,000 pounds of copper. With twenty-six major mines on the Butte hill, with vast lumber holdings, coal camps, and supplies of water and power, with new flotation-concentration works at Butte and Anaconda, smelters and refineries at Anaconda and Great Falls, with elaborate East Coast marketing facilities, with all of this and newly added mines and smelters to the southwest and in Mexico, Anaconda was a beautifully integrated company. It controlled its production process from mining ore in the earth to refining copper ready for the market. The company's total debt was a mere $16,000,000.[38]

The new Anaconda stood, therefore, as an impressive corporate monument, the final, well-refined product of the long labors of Daly, Haggin, Hearst, Rogers, Ryan, and the other astute businessmen who fashioned it. In a true sense it represented the melding, as in a carefully alloyed metal, of all the facets of old Butte—from the upstart silver mines of the 1880s, to the big Heinze, Clark, Lewisohn, and Daly corporations of the 1890s—into one finely forged product. Yet this is not the whole story. The new Anaconda was more than a corporation; it was also a social and political organism of enormous weight. The newly consolidated Anaconda embodied not only the many corporate bodies of old Butte, but also many of old Butte's political evils as well.

The change in management which came with the creation of Amalgamated in 1899–1900 had brought with it fundamental changes in corporate attitudes and policies. As seen above, during the 1880s and 1890s the major Butte mining companies operated in the free-wheeling, frontier style of Clark and Daly. Growing up in the local milieu and managed by local men, the companies paid respectable wages and generally treated their workers' families with a sort of baronial benevolence. Strong labor unions arose, but they tended to identify and cooperate with management in a climate of harmony. Even in their political shenanigans, the mining kings had enjoyed the support of their employees, who identified with them and cheered them on. But the rise of Amalgamated changed all of this. As the colorful silver and copper barons left the scene, a new breed of corporate managers, many of them with fewer sensibilities about Butte and her people, took the reins. These men, the Rogers and Rockefellers, kept to the worst of the old ways—strong-arm tactics and political manipulation—but they lacked many of the redeeming features of a Clark or Daly, their loyalties and ties to the community and to the people. At the same time, consolidation gave management the advantage of what mining historian Richard Peterson aptly calls "concentrated power." Without industrial competition, the workers and the people themselves lay at the mercy of a much more powerful and much less sensitive corporation.[39]

The fraying of labor-management relations mirrors this trend exactly. On numerous occasions, the powerful old Butte Miners' Union had demonstrated its clout, as in 1893 when it sponsored creation of the regionwide Western Federation of Miners, or in 1894 when it launched the Montana State Trades and Labor Council. For all its strength, though, the BMU was peculiarly conservative, a result in large part of the shrewd support of it by Marcus Daly and even of outright gifts to its leaders in the form of mining leases and other favors. While the region-wide Western Federation of Miners moved to the left, its number-one local in Butte remained quiet and docile. In sharp contrast to the labor violence in Idaho, Colorado, and Utah, labor harmony prevailed in Montana.

This pattern reversed itself soon after 1900, and not only because of the rise of Amalgamated. After years of deflation and stable living costs, a cycle of inflation set in during the later 1890s, causing the unions to demand an increase in the old $3.50 daily wage. A strong nationwide current of leftist radicalism and socialism, spawned by the fear and exploitation of the new supercorporations and frequently carried by the rising numbers of eastern European immigrants, swept into the mining towns of the Mountain West. In 1905 leaders of the Western Federation of Miners, including some from Butte, played a decisive role in forming the famous Industrial Workers of the World at a Chicago convention. The IWW aimed directly at industrial unionism, at organizing even the poor and illiterate workers into "one big union," and some of its spokesmen directly embraced socialism. Interestingly, C. E. Mahoney and other leaders of the Butte Miners' Union disavowed this leftward turn of the Western Federation and stormily criticized the IWW and the WFM leadership in Denver. Much of the Butte rank and file, however, disagreed with them, cheering the IWW, denouncing the trust, sometimes joining Montana's growing Socialist Party. A chasm thus opened in Butte labor between a radical, anticompany faction and a dominant conservative wing more friendly to management. Predictably, the rebels accused their leaders of being bought off by the company, of "wearing the copper collar."[40]

Things came to a head in 1906–7, when galloping inflation prompted the rank and file of the BMU to demand a raise of 50 cents per day. Ryan countered with an offer of 25 cents, which the union leadership accepted with "thanks," to the anger of many workers. Their anger intensified when the company shut down soon afterward due to mounting copper stockpiles. Once again, the union demanded a $4.00 scale. This time, Ryan won them over to a sliding scale of $4.00 as a maximum when copper prices reached 18 cents a pound. The union accepted this offer through a referendum, but soon afterward the Panic of 1907 sent prices plummeting, depressing the wage and leading to lengthy layoffs as well. These setbacks intensified the mood of bitterness at Butte. So did the company practice, typical of American industry at the time, of importing cheap, often illiterate labor from central and southern Europe. Naturally, the established workers lashed out angrily at the "Wops" and "Bohunks" who competed for their jobs. Even more galling was the company's increasingly systematic use of the hated "rustling card" system, which required all workers to obtain clearance cards for employment from a central "rustling office" and allowed management easily to blacklist troublemakers and radicals.[41]

The eruption of labor violence at Butte, hitherto the peaceful citadel of western mining unionism, began in 1914 and lies beyond the focus of this study. Both the radical IWW itself and the leftist faction of the Butte Miners' Union, which sympathized with it, grew rapidly in numbers after 1906. So did the closely interrelated Socialist party, which thrived in labor towns like Red Lodge, Livingston, and Anaconda, and which garnered enough votes to elect Unitarian minister Lewis Duncan mayor of Butte in 1911. In 1914 the badly divided union would erupt in violence when the radicals attacked their leaders during the festive Miners' Union Day parade and then sacked and blasted the union hall itself. During World War I, the city rocked with labor strife; and a mood of procorporate, antiunion chauvinism set in, with disastrous results for the workers. State and federal troops occupied Butte six different times between 1914 and 1921 in efforts to maintain wartime copper production, keep the peace, and break the radicals. As a result of these turbulent years, unionism in Butte was crushed. Anaconda instituted the open shop during the war, and Montana workers did not regain the closed shop until the New Deal labor euphoria of 1934.[42]

Even more pernicious than its ruthless labor policy was the company's manipulation of the Montana political system. With Heinze's downfall, the Amalgamated and its allies held clear sway over both major parties. The Populists and other Heinze-backed antitrust parties fell into oblivion after 1900, and the Socialists went the same route during the reactionary mood of World War I. Progressive journalist Jerre Murphy wrote bitterly but accurately in his facetiously entitled *Comical History of Montana* that the company and its minions "have better organization and control in both of the principal parties within the state of Montana than either party possesses of and for itself." Gaining a limited victory over Heinzeism in the 1904 election, the company won sweepingly in 1906. For years thereafter, it seldom lost a round. As a Montanan wrote plaintively to Senator Thomas Walsh in 1912, "friends of good government" could only pray for the day of "Montana's redemption from the rottenness of corporate domination."[43]

Montana produced a hearty progressive movement during the years after 1906, led by people like Joseph Dixon and Jeanette Rankin in the Republican party and Thomas Walsh and Burton K. Wheeler among the Democrats. The progressives enacted the same sort of direct democracy and regulatory legislation in Montana that they produced in other states, but they made little real progress in diminishing the hegemony of Anaconda. For, even after the homestead rush of 1909–18 brought a new surge of population into eastern Montana, the Anaconda wielded an economic-political strength which no opposing coterie of groups could match for long. Allying with its Siamese twin Montana Power, with the railroads and other corporations, and with the instinctively conservative stockmen of the plains, it ruled the roost as a giant faction in a small commonwealth—wielding precisely the kind of naked power that James Madison had long ago feared and would now have understood.[44]

Company power loomed openly over its bailiwicks of Butte and Anaconda and was also clearly visible at Missoula and Great Falls. Its legal and lobbying staffs were ubiquitous in political circles, and employees of Montana Power carried the corporate presence far into the hinterland. By the 1920s Anaconda's newspapers, the first of which were acquired in the battles against Clark and Heinze, controlled over half of the state's entire circulation of daily papers. The company owned the *Anaconda Standard* (later the *Montana Standard*) of Butte–Anaconda, the *Butte Daily Post*, the *Daily Missoulian*, the *Missoula Sentinel*, the *Billings Gazette*, the *Helena Independent*, the *Livingston Enterprise*, and from time to time other papers as well. Needless to say, it openly used these papers to protect its interests and to attack its foes.[45]

Anaconda dominated Montana after 1906 like no other single company dominated any other state, with the possible exception of the tiny Dupont satrapy of Delaware. Such had been the high price of industrializing and rationalizing the "richest hill on earth." Arthur Fisher wrote in overly dramatized and Manichaean terms, but nonetheless with considerable accuracy in 1922: "On the one hand, firmly entrenched, stand the ramifying and inter-linked corporate interests centering in the copper industry, now under the leadership of the Anaconda Copper Mining Company. On the other stands the rest of the population which feels it has no stake in the Company's prosperity but suffers from the Company's exploitation of every natural resource and profitable privilege, its avoidance of taxation, and its dominance of the political and educational life of the State."[46]

Epilogue: The Legacy

Seventy-five years have passed since the close of the battle for Butte. And what is the legacy, the historical residue of those remarkable times? At first reckoning, it might seem to be inconsequential. The struggles between Clark and Daly, between Heinze and the Amalgamated, might appear to be only bizarre and colorful frontier conflicts between Gilded Age robber barons—fascinating to observe but of little real relevance in the inevitable march of industrial consolidation. In fact, however, the battle for Butte cast a long historical shadow into the future. For if the outcome of this struggle, consolidation, was inevitable, it is still equally true that its peculiar convolutions were not. In its invasion of related industries like lumber and electricity, and in its contamination of statewide politics and the free press, the battle which closed in 1906 has left a long, bitter, and enduring legacy.

The most visible and concrete legacy of the copper war was, of course, the trust itself, the Anaconda Copper Mining Company. Within Montana, which the company relied upon as its main base of operations for two decades after the fall of Heinze, the Anaconda seemed an all-powerful, unchanging monolith. From the days of Clark and Heinze until the aftermath of World War II, the political constellation in Montana rotated around the polar star of company power. Conservatives in each political party accommodated to that power, and beleaguered progressives and radicals sporadically attacked it. When aroused to the dangers of radicalism, as during World War I, or to the threats of regulation and increased taxation, as in its successful onslaughts against crusading politicians Burton K. Wheeler in 1920, Joseph Dixon in 1924, Wellington Rankin in 1928,

and Jerry O'Connell in 1938, the company reacted like a frightened
and isolated mastodon, attacking whatever approached it.[1]

During the four decades between the Heinze sellout of 1906 and
World War II, Montana was prostrated by a series of droughts, economic collapses, and erosions of its farming and mining population.
These trying years also saw the state's reputation as a sorely abused
corporate bailiwick become even more deeply and lastingly imbedded
in the mind of its own people and of the nation at large. This ugly
image of corporate domination, which reflected a considerable reality, must be counted the most burdensome legacy of the battle for
Butte. It left Montanans with an enervating feeling of apathy and
resignation, a feeling that nothing they cared about or did really
mattered, since the corporate community would in the end always
have its way. Naturally, this mood was most intense at
Butte–Anaconda, but it reached also even into the rural communities
of northern and eastern Montana.

Montanans who doubted such judgments had only to read the
words of prominent national commentators. In 1930 Oswald Garrison
Villard, the widely read liberal spokesman, wrote in The *Nation:* "The
great Commonwealth of Montana is a dual entity. There is the State,
supposedly a free and independent part of the Union, and there is
'the Company,' otherwise the Anaconda Copper Mining Company. It
is not always easy to differentiate between the two, for sometimes
what appears to be the State is the Company and sometimes the
Company seems to be the State. Certainly the influence of the Company runs all through the State of Montana, penetrating every aspect
of its business, social, and political life." At the time of World War II,
Bernard DeVoto, a westerner to whom easterners listened, said much
the same thing: "If you don't know what the Company is, stranger, it
is the Amalgamated Copper Company (later the Anaconda), and it
has usually maintained a more thoroughgoing ownership of Montana's wealth, government, and inhabitants than any other corporation has ever been able to maintain in any other state. It has gutted an
American commonwealth on behalf, if not of its stockholders at least
of its manipulators, through many years." Even after the war, John
Gunther could write these controversial and frequently quoted lines
in *Inside U.S.A.*: "To say that the story of Montana is the story of a
struggle between the people and a corporation, the Anaconda Copper Mining Company, would be to oversimplify . . . [but] Anaconda,
a company aptly named, certainly has a constrictorlike grip on much
that goes on, and Montana is the nearest to a 'colony' of any American state, Delaware alone possibly excepted. . . ."[2]

Like most stereotypes, this image of a big, backward state caught in
the death embrace of a big, backward corporation fell considerably
short of a more complex reality. Anaconda never really ruled supreme or secure. It had of necessity to form fragile and awkward
alliances with other corporate powers and conservative interest
groups, and its liberal foes were neither numerically nor politically
impotent. Relying upon a strong farmer-labor base rooted in the unions of Butte-Anaconda-Great Falls and in the Farmers' Union organizations of northern and eastern Montana, the anticompany liberals
usually lost. But they sometimes won, especially in sending outspoken progressives like Burton K. Wheeler, James E. Murray, and
Lee Metcalf to the U.S. Senate.[3]

Nor was the company itself immune to the forces of history. Gradually, as the years passed, it edged toward the mainstream of modern corporate evolution, breaking one by one the antiquated ties to
the old order. In 1922 the enduring team of John D. Ryan as chairman
of the board and Cornelius Kelley as president engineered the purchase of the American Brass Company, the greatest brass producer in
the world. This purchase, made in order to facilitate the marketing
and pricing of copper (which alloys with zinc to form brass), took the
company directly into the far "downstream" end of production—
fabrication. Acquisition of American Brass gave birth to the company's new slogan, "From Mine to Consumer." It also enhanced the
Anaconda's appetite for the red metal and underscored a painful
reality: that the labor-intensive deep mines of Butte were losing their
competitive edge to the mass-production, open-pit mines of competitors like Kennecott and Phelps Dodge. So in 1923, Anaconda completed purchase of majority control of the Chile Copper Company
from the Guggenheim family for $77,000,000, the largest single
purchase that Wall Street had ever seen. This huge acquisition gave
Anaconda control of the world's greatest copper deposits, most notably the incredible mountain of low-grade ore at Chuquicamata, high
in the Andes Mountains of Chile. Within only a few years, these rich,
low-cost Chilean mines produced two-thirds of Anaconda's copper
and at times three-fourths of its profits.[4] Other burgeoning mines in
Mexico, Arizona, and elsewhere served further to diminish the role of
Montana in the priority scale of company investments.

Especially after the onset of the Great Depression, which devastated the heavily indebted Anaconda, Montanans came to fear that
their distrusted but badly needed homestate corporation might close
down altogether. With each passing year, the ever deeper mines of
Butte lagged further behind the increasingly automated, open-pit

mines of Latin America, Africa, and the southwestern United States in cost efficiency. The only hope for long term future mining lay in the lower-grade disseminated ore bodies which surrounded the worked out veins of the central district. But pit-mining these ores seemed implausible, since it would involve carving up sizable portions of the city itself.

Nevertheless, in 1947 the aging giant of the industry, Cornelius Kelley, returned to his home town to announce the so-called Greater Butte Project, which utilized the technique of "block-caving" to blast and excavate beneath the earth on a massive scale. Although this project failed and was soon abandoned, it still heralded a continuing commitment by the company to its heavy Butte investment.[5] And in 1955, Anaconda took the final logical, if somewhat incongruous, step in its search for an answer to the Butte problem: it began open-pit mining on the hill. Now, after a quarter century of excavation, all of the old deep mines are closed. Most of the great mines of legend, including the entirety of the Anaconda Hill itself, have disappeared along with much of uptown Butte into the yawning cavity of the Berkeley Pit.

These shifts in company direction inevitably brought with them comparable changes in Anaconda's role in the life of the state. Slowly, almost as imperceptibly as a glacier retreats, Anaconda's global expansion eroded its morbid determination to maintain its grasp on political affairs in Montana. During the 1930s and 1940s, the company noticeably inched away from the bare-knuckled attacks upon its foes which it had relied upon previously. Instead, it turned to more subtle and often more effective methods. The company papers, mirroring this trend, turned from pillorying anticorporate politicians to a policy of "Afghanistaning," or ignoring hot issues and their advocates and dwelling instead upon insipid and far-removed topics. As historian Richard Ruetten comments, the Anaconda papers became "monuments of indifference," flatulent sheets which often failed to provide even a basic coverage of statewide issues.[6]

Intelligent younger executives like W. H. Hoover, Al Wilkinson, and William Kirkpatrick introduced more enlightened methods of corporate lobbying and public relations, even as oldtimers like Cornelius Kelley seemed irrevocably wedded to the antiquated, free-swinging ways of the Clark–Daly era. It seems more than mere coincidence that it was only after Con Kelley's retirement in the mid-1950s that Anaconda truly left behind the bad habits it had acquired during the battle for Butte. The company sold its newspapers to the Lee chain of Iowa in 1959. By the early 1960s, evidently due to disagreements about public power and executive conflicts, it had broken away from its longtime, symbiotic relationship to the Montana Power Company. Oldtimers scratched their heads in bewilderment to see one ex-company paper hotly attacking another, or to see Anaconda supporting a political candidate—for example, Senator Lee Metcalf in 1966—while Montana Power vigorously opposed him. By now, Anaconda seemed to differ little from other western resource corporations. It employed deft lobbyists like Al Wilkinson and Glen Carney and closed down the notorious "watering holes" which reputedly had kept some legislators drunk throughout much of their stays in Helena. The company polished its public image and stewed nervously about government environmental regulations. Most experts now agreed that Montana Power wielded greater political clout than did its ex-partner.[7]

During the 1960s and 1970s one sensed that, at last, Montana was emerging from the remarkably extended shadows of the battle for Butte. In the early 1970s, the Chilean Marxist government of Salvador Allende seized and nationalized the company's greatest blue-chip properties. This catastrophe drove the once-mighty Anaconda to the brink of bankruptcy. Forced to cut costs to the bone, the company sold off its lumber operation to Champion International in 1972 and closed down such costly old operations as the last deep mines at Butte and the zinc plants at Anaconda and Great Falls. Anaconda stock fell to such lows that the firm's absorption into a conglomerate corporation became inevitable. In 1976–77, Atlantic Richfield bought the company; and Montana, hopeful of badly needed transfusions of capital, breathed a sigh of relief. They breathed too soon, however, for in the fall of 1980, ARCO announced its decision to close down both the old smelter at Anaconda and the equally old refinery at Great Falls. These drastic cutbacks would cost Montana more than 1,500 jobs. They dealt a heavy blow to the western Montana economy; and, although the company stated its intent to keep open the Butte mines, their future seemed imperiled by the necessity of shipping concentrates to faraway smelters.[8]

As the Anaconda contracted, so too did the city of Butte. A gradual loss of population set in during the years following World War I; and the Depression, World War II, and the intervening years have brought booms, busts, strikes, and severe dislocations. The advent of pit mining and the closure of the deep shafts literally transformed the city and its population. The large armies of colorful ethnic, hard-rock miners gave way to thinning ranks of teamsters, operating engineers, and technicians who dig out and haul the ores and man the giant Clyde Weed concentrator. As the pit widened and deepened, it devoured the eastern reaches of the historic uptown area. Butte's dwindling, increasingly middle-class population moved steadily to the "flats" south of the hill; and the newly consolidated city-county government even pondered the wisdom of relocating the central business district. Meanwhile, Butte saw its statewide hegemony crumble slowly away. Once by far the state's largest city, it was surpassed by Great Falls in the 1940s, Billings in the 1950s, and Missoula in the 1960s. Butte has maintained a fair measure of its age-old political clout through finely tuned Democratic bloc-voting and careful attention to its political interests, and it remains a key Montana center of corporate and labor influence. But Butte no longer cracks the political whip over Montana as it did not so many years ago.

Many times over the years, pundits have pronounced the imminent demise of the great old mining center. Time has always proven them wrong, for technology has again and again provided new methods to reduce Butte's vast reserves of lower-grade ores. Such is the vastness of its wealth, and such are the commitments of its people, that the city will endure into the indefinite future. Indeed, not the least of Butte's resources is its remarkable history. One of America's most intriguing ethnic melting pots, most bizarre corporate battlegrounds, and most interesting historic places, the city savors its past and works increasingly to preserve it. History, however, is more than antiquarian reminiscences of colorful mining kings and of epic doings of yesteryear. Much more weightily, history is the burden of attitudes, mores, prejudices, loves, and hatreds rooted in the economic, social, and political milieu which formed over 100 years ago. Thus the battle for Butte, which ended seventy-five years ago, has colored much of Montana's subsequent history. Beyond a doubt, Anaconda held to its iron-handed, secretive methods for so many years in large part because of the desperate, traumatic battles through which it passed in its formative years. Just as certainly, the company's antediluvian behavior fed the festering Montana mood of anger, radicalism, and despairing resignation which has persisted in weakening form even into the second half of this century.

The battle for Butte was a rich slice of Americana, a classic instance of raw, unrestrained frontier capitalism. It brought great wealth to a handful of willful men, gave employment to thousands more, and brought a quick and peculiar form of industrialization to a remote corner of the Mountain West. It corrupted the political culture of an American state and shocked the sensibilities of a nation that was not easily shocked. It left behind a bitter heritage which took three generations to dissipate. Like the frontier itself, Butte was rich, unabashedly exploited, turbulent—and endlessly fascinating.

Notes

1. Gold Camp

1. From Rossiter W. Raymond, *Statistics of Mines and Mining in the States and Territories West of the Rocky Mountains . . . Fifth Annual Report of . . . Commissioner of Mining Statistics*, p. 225; see also Walter H. Weed, *Geology and Ore Deposits of the Butte District, Montana*, pp. 18–19; James F. Kemp, *The Ore Deposits of the United States and Canada*, 3rd ed., pp. 196–203; M. H. Gidel, "History of Geology and Ore Deposits," in *Seven Talks about Mines*, p. 17.

2. In addition to the sources given in note 1, especially valuable on Butte's geology are Richard N. Miller, ed., *Guidebook for the Butte Field Meeting of Society of Economic Geologists* (n.p.: n.p., 1978); Anaconda Copper Mining Co., *Copper: From Mine to Finished Product*, pp. 7–8; and Eugene S. Perry, *The Butte Mining District, Montana*. A still valuable reference source is Work Projects Administration, Mineral Resources Survey, *Memoir No. 21: Bibliography of the Geology and Mineral Resources of Montana*.

3. See especially, Rodman W. Paul, *California Gold*; and Charles H. Shinn, *Mining Camps: A Study in American Frontier Government*.

4. The best histories of the western mining frontier are Rodman W. Paul, *Mining Frontiers of the Far West*; William S. Greever, *The Bonanza West*; and Otis E. Young, Jr., *Western Mining*. Still valuable, also, is T. A. Rickard, *A History of American Mining*.

5. For descriptions of the Montana mining frontier, see William J. Trimble, *The Mining Advance into the Inland Empire*; Michael P. Malone and Richard B. Roeder, *Montana: A History of Two Centuries*, chap. 4; Clark C. Spence, *Mon-*

tana: A Bicentennial History, chap. 3; Merrill G. Burlingame, *The Montana Frontier*, chap. 4; and for an episodic overview, Dan Cushman, *Montana: The Gold Frontier*.

6. Alan Goddard, *Butte Oldtimers' Handbook*, pp. 5–6; Guy X. Piatt, ed., *The Story of Butte* (special issue of the *Butte Bystander*, 15 April 1897), pp. 8–9; *Butte Daily Inter Mountain*, special ed. of 1890–91, pp. 11–13.

7. Frank Quinn, "Butte: The Rise of a City," *Butte Montana Standard*, 13 June 1954; Kate H. Fogarty, *The Story of Montana*, pp. 152–53; and Fogarty, "Butte in the Sixties," ms. in Kate Hammond Fogarty Papers, Montana Historical Society Library.

8. Dennis Leary to "George," 9 January 1916, copy in W. J. Wilcox ms., in possession of Mrs. Dan Kinsella, Butte; the Wilcox manuscript, a lengthy and carefully done compendium of Butte's early history by one of its most distinguished citizens, is a valuable source; *White Sulphur Springs Rocky Mountain Husbandman*, 23 July 1936.

9. *Butte Montana Standard*, 26 January 1936; 30 September 1973; Fogarty, "Butte in the Sixties"; Quinn, "Butte"; Charles S. Warren, "Historical Address: The Territory of Montana," in *Contributions to the Historical Society of Montana*, 13 vols., 2:61–64.

10. Fogarty, "Butte in the Sixties"; W. R. M. Edwards, "Pioneer Days in German Gulch" (1933), typescript copy in possession of Neil Lynch, Butte.

11. *Deer Lodge New Northwest*, 13 July 1869; 28 January, 8 July 1870; Harry C. Freeman, *A Brief History of Butte, Montana*, pp. 8–9; Tom Stout, *Montana: Its Story and Biography*, 3 vols., 1:371; Michael A. Leeson, *History of Montana*, pp. 916–17.

12. *Virginia City Montana Post*, 7 January 1865; see also the issues of 29 October 1864; 11 February, 11 and 20 March, 9 June 1865; 23 March 1867; 4 January 1868.

13. Warren, "Historical Address," pp. 67–69; Leeson, *History*, pp. 917–18; Stout, *Montana*, 1:371; Joaquin Miller, *An Illustrated History of the State of Montana*, pp. 289–90; Robert G. Raymer, *Montana: The Land and the People*, 3 vols., 1:441; Robert G. Young, *The Public School System of Butte, Montana*, pp. 1, 12, 15.

14. Warren, "Historical Address," p. 66; Freeman, *Brief History*, pp. 11–13; *Deer Lodge New Northwest*, 13 July 1869, 8 July 1870; A. K. McClure, *Three Thousand Miles through the Rocky Mountains*, pp. 307–8.

15. Ralph I. Smith, "History of the Early Reduction Works of Butte, Montana," pamphlet reproduced from *De Re Metallica*, 18 (Butte: Montana School of Mines, 1953), pp. 1–2; Raymer, *Montana*, 1:444; Leeson, *History*, p. 917; Frank T. Larrimore, "Montana's Treasure City," *Harper's Weekly*, 7 June 1913, p. 9.

16. Piatt, *Story*, pp. 19, 27–28; Stout, *Montana*, pp. 371–72; Smith, "History," pp. 1–2; Raymer, *Montana*, 1:444.

17. U.S., Department of the Interior, Office of the Census, *Ninth Census, vol. 1: The Statistics of the Population . . . 1870*, p. 195.

2. Clark, Daly, and the Anaconda

1. Richard H. Peterson, *The Bonanza Kings*, pp. 24–25.
2. *Anaconda Standard*, 12 March 1890; E. G. Leipheimer, *The First National Bank of Butte*, pp. 2–4. On Hauser, see John W. Hakola, "Samuel T. Hauser and the Economic Development of Montana: A Case Study in Nineteenth-Century Frontier Capitalism" (Ph.D. diss., Indiana University, 1961).
3. Leipheimer, *First National Bank*, pp. 5–18; Donald MacMillan, "Andrew Jackson Davis: A Story of Frontier Capitalism, 1864–1890" (M.A. thesis, University of Montana, 1967), pp. 12–24, 53, 70; Hakola, "Hauser," pp. 103–5.
4. The quote is from Warren G. Davenport, *Butte and Montana beneath the X-Ray*, p. 173. For other, similar characterizations of Clark, see Samuel T. Hauser to J. S. M. Neill, 8 January 1906, Neill Papers, Montana Historical Society Archives, Helena; M. G. O'Malley to Herbert Peet, ? December 1938, Peet Collection, bk. 3, Montana Historical Society Archives; and Henry R. Knapp, "William Andrews Clark," *Cosmopolitan*, February 1903, pp. 474, 476.
5. On Clark's work habits, see the obituary remarks of J. L. Dobell in *Butte Miner*, 3 March 1925; Clark's genealogy and earlier years may be briefly studied in *Progressive Men of the State of Montana*, p. 1104; Helen Fitzgerald Sanders, *A History of Montana*, 3 vols., 2:854; and Paul C. Phillips, "William Andrews Clark," *Dictionary of American Biography*, ed. Allen Johnson and Dumas Malone, 20 vols., 4:144; for various newspaper clippings on Clark's career, consult the two Clark folders in the Vertical File, Montana Historical Society Library.
6. Clark recounted these early days many years later, shortly before his death, in a series of addresses to Montana pioneer groups. These reminiscences may be found most conveniently in *Butte Miner*, 3 March 1925; see also the pamphlet, *Montana's Distinguished Pioneer, W. A. Clark, Gives Historical Reminiscences*, Society of Montana Pioneers, Forty-first Annual Convention, Butte, 28–30 August 1924, pp. 1–10. Cited hereafter, regardless of particular source, as *Clark Reminiscences*.
7. *Clark Reminiscences*; C. B. Glasscock, *The War of the Copper Kings*, pp. 46–52. Glasscock's widely read book is heavily anecdotal, but it is still valuable in that it is based largely on 1930s interviews with men who knew Clark personally.
8. On Clark's family, see *Clark Reminiscences*; *Progressive Men*, p. 1108; his returns home are discussed in "Deposition of Anna B. Clark," 22 June 1926, in the case of *Alma E. Clark Hines* et al. v. *Charles W. Clark* et al., File 7594, Silver Bow County Courthouse, Butte.
9. *Clark Reminiscences*; Phillips, "Clark," p. 144; *Progressive Men*, p. 1105; Glasscock, *War*, pp. 53–55; Mary M. Farrell, "William Andrews Clark" (M.A. thesis, University of Washington, 1933), pp. 17–22.
10. *Clark Reminiscences*; Phillips, "Clark," p. 144; Glasscock, *War*, pp. 58–60; Robert G. Raymer, *A History of Copper Mining in Montana*, p. 9.
11. Michael A. Leeson, *History of Montana*, pp. 923, 1334; Harry C. Free-

man, *A Brief History of Butte, Montana*, pp. 14–15; Kate H. Fogarty, *The Story of Montana*, p. 201; *Butte Miner*, 3 June 1876.

12. *Butte Miner*, 3 and 13 June, 26 July, 26 August 1876; 3 July 1877; Leeson, *History*, p. 923.

13. *Butte Miner*, 8 June 1876; 23 January 1877; Work Projects Administration of Montana, Writers' Program, *Copper Camp*, pp. 27–29; Charles S. Warren, "Historical Address: The Territory of Montana," in *Contributions to the Historical Society of Montana*, 13 vols., 2:70.

14. *Butte Miner*, 1 and 3 June, 15 August 1876; 23 January 1877; Leeson, *History*, pp. 923–26; Freeman, *Brief History*, p. 16; *Helena Independent*, 8 and 9 March 1876; Rossiter W. Raymond, *Statistics of Mines and Mining in the States and Territories West of the Rocky Mountains . . . Eighth Annual Report of Commissioner of Mining Statistics*, pp. 252–54.

15. Leeson, *History*, p. 923; Freeman, *Brief History*, p. 16; *Helena Independent*, 6 and 11 May 1876; *Diamond City Rocky Mountain Husbandman*, 27 July 1876.

16. Michael P. Malone and Richard B. Roeder, *Montana As It Was: 1876*, p. 56.

17. *Butte Miner*, 3 July 1877; *Copper Camp*, p. 29.

18. *Butte Miner*, 13 June 1876; 24 April, 9 October 1877; Peterson, *Bonanza Kings*, pp. 24–25. I am indebted to Alan Goddard of Butte for informing me of these accounts of the Clark-Farlin episode, which he has uncovered in his many inquiries into the city's history.

19. Rossiter W. Raymond, *Statistics of Mines and Mining in the States and Territories West of the Rocky Mountains . . . Sixth Annual Report of Commissioner of Mining Statistics*, p. 353.

20. These traits seem to have impressed nearly all who knew and remembered Daly. See the description by K. Ross Toole, based on interviews more than three decades ago with oldtimers who still recalled him: "Marcus Daly: A Study of Business in Politics" (M.A. thesis, University of Montana, 1948), p. 19; for other characterizations, see *Harper's Weekly*, 24 November 1900, p. 1117; and notes on letter from M. G. O'Malley to Herbert Peet of 14 December 1938, Herbert Peet Collection, bk. 6, Montana Historical Society Archives, Helena; *Butte Miner*, 13 November 1900.

21. Paul C. Phillips, "Marcus Daly," *Dictionary of American Biography*, Allen Johnson and Dumas Malone, eds., 20 vols., 5:45; *Progressive Men*, p. 16. In his little booklet study of his distant relative, *Biography of Marcus Daly of Montana*, p. 2, Hugh Daly argues that the Dalys were relatively prosperous. However, as K. Ross Toole notes in his "Marcus Daly," pp. 1–12, this seems doubtful. The one attempt at a major biographical study, H. Minar Shoebotham, *Anaconda: Life of Marcus Daly the Copper King*, leaves much to be desired.

22. Daly quote is in *New York Times*, 13 November 1900, p. 2; W. H. Hoover, *Marcus Daly (1841–1900)—and His Contributions to Anaconda*, pp. 8–9; Walter E. Taylor, "The Rise of a Copper King," newspaper clipping of 16 September 1940 in Daly folder, Vertical File, Montana Historical Society Library.

23. Hoover, *Marcus Daly*, pp. 9–10; see the remarks of Daly's Utah friend Robert C. Chambers in *Anaconda Standard*, 18 November 1900; *Sketches of the Inter-Mountain States*, pp. 103, 345, 347.

24. Isaac F. Marcosson, *Anaconda*, pp. 43–44.

25. This legend has often been repeated. See, for instance, Samuel E. Moffett, "Marcus Daly, Empire Builder," *American Monthly Review of Reviews*, December 1900, pp. 707–8; and Kenneth V. Lottich, ed., "My Trip to Montana Territory, 1879: The Unpretentious Journal of Charles French Kellogg," *Montana: The Magazine of Western History* 15 (Winter 1965): 21. Daly rebutted these tales in *Anaconda Standard*, 3 November 1895.

26. *Butte Miner*, 26 September, 3 and 10 October 1876; *Deer Lodge New Northwest*, 25 August 1876; Hoover, *Marcus Daly*, pp. 10–11.

27. *Butte Weekly Miner*, 24 February 1880; *Butte Miner*, 16 December 1880; Leeson, *History*, p. 953; for a fragmentary look into the Alice's early operations, see Alice Gold and Silver Mining Co. Records, letterpress books in Montana Historical Society Archives; Beverly J. Brothers, *Sketches of Walkerville*, pp. 9–14.

28. A. J. Davis to Samuel T. Hauser, 6 February 1877, Samuel T. Hauser Papers, box 4, Montana Historical Society Archives; K. Ross Toole, "When Big Money Came to Butte," *Pacific Northwest Quarterly* 44 (January 1953): 23–29.

29. Robert G. Athearn, *Union Pacific Country*, pp. 238–52; and Athearn, "Railroad to a Far-Off Country: The Utah and Northern," *Montana: The Magazine of Western History* 18 (Autumn 1968): 2–23.

30. Leeson, *History*, p. 950; Toole, "Big Money," p. 25; MacMillan, "Andrew Jackson Davis," pp. 25–26.

31. *Clark Reminiscences*; Rodman W. Paul, *Mining Frontiers of the Far West*, pp. 123–24; *Denver Evening Post*, 22 May 1900; Joseph E. King, *A Mine to Make a Mine: Financing the Colorado Mining Industry, 1859–1902*, pp. 25–26.

32. *Clark Reminiscences*; *Butte Miner*, 15 August 1879, Holiday ed. of 1888–89, and 3 March 1925; Glasscock, *War*, p. 71; see letterpress books 1, 13 of the Colorado Smelting and Mining Co., Anaconda Copper Mining Co. Records, Montana Historical Society Archives; James E. Fell, Jr., *Ores to Metals*, pp. 51, 140–1, 163–4.

33. On the Lewisohns, consult Geoffrey T. Hellman, "Adolph Lewisohn," *Dictionary of American Biography*, 20 vols., supplement 2, vol. 22, Robert L. Schuyler, ed., pp. 383–84; and Isaac F. Marcosson, *Metal Magic: The Story of the American Smelting and Refining Company* (New York: Farrar, Strauss & Co., 1949), pp. 61ff., and William B. Gates, Jr., *Michigan Copper and Boston Dollars*, p. 71; a valuable description of Meader is in *Anaconda Standard*, 25 November 1900; see, too, Freeman, *Brief History*, pp. 16–17; *Mining and Scientific Press*, 84 (15 February 1902): 86.

34. *Butte Weekly Miner*, 17 February 1880, quoted in Athearn, *Union Pacific*, p. 259; *Butte Weekly Miner*, 16 March, 8 June 1880.

35. Athearn, *Union Pacific*, pp. 259–62; *Butte Daily Miner*, 22 December

1881; Rex C. Myers, "Montana: A State and Its Relationship with Railroads, 1864–1970" (Ph.D. diss., University of Montana, 1972), pp. 57–58.

36. See Hickey's reminiscence, "T'was Christened Anaconda," *Anaconda Standard*, 21 December 1921, 5, p. 8.

37. Ibid.; on Edward Hickey, see Tom Stout, *Montana: Its Story and Biography*, 3 vols., 1:829.

38. Captain John Branagan, "Story of the Anaconda," in John Lindsay, *Amazing Experiences of a Judge*, p. 70. This source may not be entirely reliable. The quote is from a very intriguing but inconclusive letter, Marcus Daly to Patrick Clark, 19 December 1880, unfiled, in the World Museum of Mining Archives, Butte.

39. The most reliable account of the purchase seems to be that in the W. J. Wilcox Papers, this copy in the possession of Neil Lynch, Butte. Wilcox was the chief clerk of the Anaconda Copper Mining Co. and, unlike later historians, may have had some access to full company records. Compare this to the account in Branagan, "Story," pp. 70–71; and the corporate-sponsored Marcosson, *Anaconda*, p. 32.

40. One may draw either conclusion from the letter, Daly to Patrick Clark, 19 December 1880, World Museum of Mining. Al Hooper of Butte pursued the Walker connection several years ago, and distant descendants of Joseph and Samuel Walker in Utah indicated that the family was long embittered at Daly's cutting them out of the Anaconda: interview with Hooper, 28 June 1978. For clear proof of Daly's relationship to George Hearst during the years prior to 1881, see Marcus Daly to Robert C. Chambers, 29 January 1877; Chambers to George Hearst, 8 and 19 February 1877, George Hearst Papers, Chambers File, Phoebe Hearst Collection, Bancroft Library, University of California, Berkeley.

41. Hearst's autobiography, *The Way It Was*, is thin; more revealing are Fremont and Cora Older, *George Hearst: California Pioneer*, 2nd ed.; W. A. Swanberg's biography of his son, *Citizen Hearst*, pp. 3–62 (quote is on p. 3); the obituary in *Engineering and Mining Journal* 51 (7 March 1891): 293; and the clipping files on Hearst and Haggin in the Herbert Peet Collection, bk. 14, Montana Historical Society Archives.

42. "Haggin and Tevis," *Pacific Coast Annual Mining Review and Stock Ledger*, pp. 34–35; *Anaconda Standard*, 13 September 1914; Marcosson, *Anaconda*, pp. 33–35.

43. Marcus Daly to George Hearst, 11 September 1872, Hearst Papers, Daly File; Hearst, *The Way It Was*, pp. 20–21; Older and Older, *Hearst*, pp. 140–49; Shoebotham, *Anaconda*, p. 33; Marcosson, *Anaconda*, pp. 38–39; Joseph H. Cash, *Working the Homestake*, pp. 17–18.

44. Marcosson, *Anaconda*, p. 35; Swanberg, *Citizen Hearst*, pp. 35–62; *Anaconda Standard*, 13 September 1914; P. O. Ray, "James Ben Ali Haggin," and Edgar E. Robinson, "George Hearst," *Dictionary of American Biography*, 8: 83–84, 487–48; Alvin F. Harlow, "Lloyd Tevis," ibid., 18:384–85.

45. C. C. Goodwin, "As I Remember Them—Marcus Daly," *Goodwin's*

Weekly (n.d.), clipping in Daly Folder, Vertical File, Montana Historical Society Library; Hearst, *The Way It Was*, pp. 23–25; Older and Older, *George Hearst*, pp. 162–64. Clark himself always denied ever having had any business dealings with Daly: see *New York Herald*, 23 September 1900.

46. *Butte Daily Miner*, 31 May 1881; Marcosson, *Anaconda*, p. 45; Older and Older, *George Hearst*, pp. 164–65. The percentages of ownership are drawn from what seems the most authoritative source, the *New York Tribune*'s account of 5 July 1896, clipping in J. B. Haggin Papers, Bancroft Library. Hearst's *The Way It Was*, a not very exact reminiscence, places the percentages as: Hearst, 30; Haggin, 27; Daly, 25; and Tevis, 17. Among the various rumor-based accounts of their agreement, see the faulted remembrance by ex-Congressman Martin Maginnis in *Anaconda Standard*, 3 September 1907.

47. *Butte Daily Miner*, 2 June 1881 and 9 June 1882; *Anaconda Weekly Review*, 10 May 1884; T. A. Rickard, *A History of American Mining*, pp. 351–52.

48. See the account of this discovery by Cornelius Kelley in *Anaconda Standard*, 3 September 1907; Marcosson, *Anaconda*, p. 46; Titus Ulke, "The Anaconda Copper Mine and Works," *Engineering Magazine*, July 1897, pp. 512–15.

49. Lindsay, *Amazing Experiences*, pp. 94–95; *Butte Daily Miner*, 9 June 1882.

50. Marcus Daly to J. B. Haggin, 1 January 1887, Haggin Papers; *Engineering and Mining Journal* 70 (17 November 1900): 574–75; C. B. Glasscock picked up much of this lore in his interviews and wrote his account in *War*, pp. 83–84.

51. *Butte Daily Miner*, 11 June 1882 and 30 March 1883; Marcosson, *Anaconda*, p. 47; Rickard, *History*, pp. 352–53; *Anaconda Weekly Review*, 10 May 1884; *A Brief Description of the Anaconda Reduction Works*, p. 6.

52. *Deer Lodge New Northwest*, 2 March 1883; *Butte Daily Miner*, 7 January, 11 March 1883; *Butte Montana Standard*, 13 June 1954, sec. A., p. 26.

53. *Mining and Scientific Press* 48 (22 March 1884): 206; *Anaconda Weekly Review*, 10 May 1884; Marcosson, *Anaconda*, p. 51; Deer Lodge County History Group, "In the Shadow of Mount Haggin" (1975), ms. in Montana Historical Society Library. James B. Allen notes that Anaconda was not a typical company town in *The Company Town in the American West*, pp. 35–36.

54. The quote is from Charles C. Goodwin, *As I Remember Them*, p. 271; *White Sulphur Springs Rocky Mountain Husbandman*, 16 October 1884; *Engineering and Mining Journal* 38 (20 September 1884): 200.

55. *Butte Semi-Weekly Miner*, 16 July and 20 August 1884.

56. *Engineering and Mining Journal*, 38 (4 October 1884): 236; (18 October 1884): 272; (25 October 1884): 288; *Helena Independent*, 16, 23 October 1884; *Brief Description of . . . Anaconda*, p. 6; Rickard, *History*, p. 355; *Butte Daily Miner*, 9 September 1884.

57. *Mining and Scientific Press* 48 (22 March 1884): 206; *Butte Weekly Inter-Mountain*, 3 July 1884; "The Camp of Butte," *West Shore*, August 1885, p. 233.

58. *Mining and Scientific Press*, 48 (12 January 1884): 44; *Butte Weekly Inter-Mountain*, 3 July 1884. A comment on the boom atmosphere at this time may be found in Thomas Buzzy to Benjamin Silliman, 11 April 1883, Silliman Papers, Montana Historical Society Archives.

59. Michael P. Malone and Richard B. Roeder, *Montana: A History of Two Centuries*, pp. 140–47.

60. Ibid.; Rickard, *History*, pp. 349–50; "Camp of Butte," pp. 233–36; *Butte Weekly Inter-Mountain*, 3 July 1884.

3. THE RICHEST HILL ON EARTH

1. A readable introduction is Ira B. Joralemon, *Copper*, 2nd ed.; see also Horace C. Baker, ed., *Copper*.

2. Joralemon, *Copper*, chap. 3; F. Ernest Richter, "The Copper Mining Industry in the United States, 1845–1925," *Quarterly Journal of Economics* 41 (February, 1927): 237, 248–51; William B. Gates, Jr., *Michigan Copper and Boston Dollars*; Arthur W. Thurner, *Calumet Copper and People: History of a Michigan Mining Community, 1864–1970* (Hancock, Mich.: Book Concern, 1974).

3. U.S., Department of Commerce, Bureau of the Census, *Historical Statistics of the United States*, 2 vols., 1:602.

4. The price situation may be traced in ibid., 1:602; on market percentages, see Walter H. Weed, *Geology and Ore Deposits of the Butte District, Montana*, p. 22; also, Horace J. Stevens, *The Copper Handbook* (Marquette, Mich.: Mining Journal Co., 1900); and U.S., Department of the Interior, Geological Survey, *Mineral Resources of the United States . . . 1883–84*, esp. pp. 336–40, and the volumes for subsequent years.

5. Gates, *Michigan Copper*, p. 77; Richter, "Copper Mining," pp. 256–57; K. Ross Toole, "The Anaconda Copper Mining Company: A Price War and a Copper Corner," *Pacific Northwest Quarterly* 41 (October 1950):318–20.

6. *Anaconda Weekly Review*, 19 August (quote), 2 September 1886; *Fort Benton River Press*, 1 September 1886; Toole, "Anaconda," p. 320.

7. *Engineering and Mining Journal* 45 (7 January 1888): 5; Richter, "Copper Mining," pp. 256–57.

8. Toole, "Anaconda," pp. 323–25; Richter, "Copper Mining," pp. 258–59; Gates, *Michigan Copper*, pp. 77–79; also see the data in the Herbert Peet Collection, bk. 14, Montana Historical Society Archives, Helena.

9. Toole, "Anaconda," pp. 324–27; "The Difficulties of the Copper Syndicate," *Commercial and Financial Chronicle* 48 (23 March 1889): 382–83; *Anaconda Weekly Review*, 1 November 1888.

10. *Commercial and Financial Chronicle* 48 (23 March 1889): 382–83; *Engineering and Mining Journal* 67 (23 March 1889): 274; *Mining and Scientific Press*, 58 (23 March 1889): 208; *Helena Daily Herald*, 1 April 1889; Toole, "Anaconda," pp. 328–29; Gates, *Michigan Copper*, pp. 80–83; C. Harry Benedict, *Red Metal: The Calumet and Hecla Story* (Ann Arbor: University of Michigan Press, 1952), pp. 107–8.

11. Ibid.; *Historical Statistics of the United States*, 1:602; *Wall Street Journal*, 11 July 1889, p. 1.

12. *Butte Daily Inter Mountain*, holiday ed. of 1887–88; see also the holiday ed. of 1889–90.

13. *Butte Daily Inter Mountain,* holiday ed. of 1887–88.
14. *Butte Semi-Weekly Miner,* 24 July 1886 and 14 July 1888; Albro Martin, *James J. Hill and the Opening of the Northwest,* pp. 348–49 (Hill quote is on p. 348); James J. Hill to Martin Maginnis, 25 March 1905, Maginnis Papers, box 2, Montana Historical Society Archives.
15. "On the Great Northern," *New York Times,* 26 October 1890, p. 19; for a broader perspective, see "Butte, Montana, at the Dawn of the Twentieth Century," *Western Resources* 134 (June 1901); and *Butte: On Top and Underground.*
16. Isaac F. Marcosson, *Anaconda,* p. 57; the fullest available description of the diverse Anaconda operation of that time is in the W. J. Wilcox manuscript, in the possession of Mrs. Dan Kinsella, Butte.
17. T. A. Rickard, *A History of American Mining,* pp. 354–56; *Butte Montana Standard,* 13 June 1954, sec. A, p. 26; Hubert H. Bancroft, *History of Washington, Idaho, and Montana,* p. 764.
18. "New Reduction Works, Anaconda, Montana," *Mining and Scientific Press* 84 (12 April 1902): 202–3; *Helena Independent,* 30 September 1896; Titus Ulke, "The Anaconda Copper Mine and Works," *Engineering Magazine,* July 1897, pp. 525–27; and Ulke, *Modern Electrolytic Copper Refining,* pp. 89–99.
19. Marcosson, *Anaconda,* pp. 55–56; *Engineering and Mining Journal* 45 (7 April 1888): 258; Anaconda Copper Mining Co. Records, General Letter Book: 3 October 1903–16 March 1904, pp. 236, 260, 277, 353, Montana Historical Society Archives.
20. K. Ross Toole and Edward Butcher, "Timber Depredations on the Montana Public Domain, 1885–1918," *Journal of the West* 7 (July 1968): 353–54; Butcher, "An Analysis of Timber Depredations in Montana to 1900" (M.A. thesis, University of Montana, 1967); Toole, *Montana: An Uncommon Land,* pp. 160–61; Dale L. Johnson, "Andrew B. Hammond: Education of a Capitalist on the Montana Frontier" (Ph.D. diss., University of Montana, 1976).
21. Toole and Butcher, "Timber Depredations," pp. 354–58; W. A. Clark to Martin Maginnis, 11 and 14 December 1878, Maginnis Papers, box 1.
22. *Butte Miner,* 28 and 31 October 1885; *Deer Lodge New Northwest,* 18 September 1885; Marcus Daly to Samuel T. Hauser, 13 November 1885; telegram, Daly, A. J. Davis, and W. A. Clark to Hauser, 10 November 1885, Hauser Papers, box 11, Montana Historical Society Archives.
23. *U.S. v. Clark,* 50 LEd. 613 (1906).
24. *U.S. v. Bitter Root Development Co.,* et al., 133 F. 274 (CCA, 9th Circuit 1904); Johnson, "Hammond," pp. 197–198; Toole and Butcher, "Timber Depredations," pp. 356–60; *New York Times,* 29 June 1901, p. 9. For a revealing insight into the timid federal prosecution, see the correspondence in File 11341–98, especially M. C. Burch to U.S. Solicitor General, 20 December 1906, and box 1266, Department of Justice Year Files: 1901, Records of the Department of Justice, Record Group 60, National Archives, Washington, D.C.
25. *Hammond v U.S.,* 246 F. 40 (CCA, 9th Circuit 1917); C. W. Wilber, "The Way of the Land Transgressor, 6: How Montana Was 'Done,'" *Pacific Monthly),* January 1908, pp. 108–15.

26. Johnson, "Hammond," pp. 188–91; Marcosson, *Anaconda*, p. 55; *Butte Miner*, 12 and 13 August 1898.

27. For a listing of these Anaconda properties, see Wilcox ms.

28. W. A. Swanberg, *Citizen Hearst*, pp. 61–62; *Anaconda Standard*, 20 January 1891; Marcosson, *Anaconda*, p. 57; a copy of the articles of incorporation is in Records of the Bureau of Corporations, File 0–119–2, Numeric File: 1903–14, Record Group 122, National Archives.

29. Swanberg, *Citizen Hearst*, p. 75; James A. Close, "Some Phases of the History of the Anaconda Copper Mining Company" (Ph.D. diss., University of Michigan, 1945), pp. 26–28; K. Ross Toole, "A History of the Anaconda Copper Mining Company," (Ph.D. diss., University of California at Los Angeles, 1954), pp. 80–82; quote is from copy, Hamilton Smith to the Exploration Company, Ltd., ? November 1895, James Ben Ali Haggin Papers, Bancroft Library, University of California, Berkeley; also in this small collection are the 27 August 1890 assessments performed for the Exploration Company by James D. Hague and Henry C. Perkins.

30. Close, "Some Phases," pp. 26–34; Toole, "History," pp. 80–82; *New York Tribune*, 5 July 1896; letter by Marcus Daly in *Anaconda Standard*, 3 November 1895; a copy of the 1895 articles of incorporation is in Records of the Bureau of Corporations, Numeric File: 1903–14, File 0–119–2, National Archives.

31. *The Economist*, 59 (7 December 1901): 1804–5; see also, W. Turrentine Jackson, *The Enterprising Scot*, p. 205; and Clark C. Spence, *British Investments and the American Mining Frontier*, p. 78.

32. *Commercial and Financial Chronicle* 67 (5 November 1898): 953. For a further assessment of Anaconda's mine holdings at this time, see Chief Engineer August Christian's report to Daly of 18 April 1898, Anaconda Copper Mining Co. Records, Small Collection No. 390, Montana Historical Society Archives; also, copy of report, Jones, Caesar & Co. to Anaconda directors, 5 May 1897, Anaconda Copper Mining Co. Records, Letter Box: Incoming Correspondence: February 1896–June 1898.

33. James A. MacKnight, *The Mines of Montana*; pp. 36–39; the records of the Alice Gold and Silver Mining Co., at the World Museum of Mining at Butte, contain some correspondence, most of it routine, between the Butte and Salt Lake City offices of the firm. The annual reports of the Inspector of Mines of the State of Montana for the years 1889–1900 are handily collected in one volume at the Montana Historical Society Library. On a county-by-county basis, the mines of Montana are each thoroughly described.

34. MacKnight, *Mines*, p. 42; Butte Chamber of Commerce, *Resources of Butte*, p. 27; *The Copper Handbook*, 2:333. The Samuel T. Hauser Papers, at the Montana Historical Society Archives, contain much material on the Parrot. See, for instance, W. A. Clark to Hauser, 13 July 1887, box 14.

35. Butte Chamber of Commerce, *Resources*, pp. 29–30; MacKnight, *Mines*, pp. 34, 39–40; Robert G. Raymer, *Montana: The Land and the People*, 3 vols., 1:449; *Engineering and Mining Journal* 45 (12 May 1888): 347; 56 (9 December 1893): 601.

36. P. A. O'Farrell, *Butte: Its Copper Mines and Copper Kings*, pp. 53–55; copies of the articles of incorporation of both firms are in Records of the Bureau of Corporations, Numeric File: 1903–14, File 0–119–3, Record Group 122, National Archives.

37. *The Copper Handbook*, 2:302–3; *Butte Tribune-Review*, 8 February 1902; *Butte Daily and Weekly Inter Mountain*, holiday ed. of 1889–90.

38. *The Copper Handbook*, 2:302–3; *Engineering and Mining Journal*, 46 (15 September 1888): 224, 232; 55 (15 April 1893): 350; Martin, *James J. Hill*, p. 349; MacKnight, *Mines*, pp. 43–47; Butte Chamber of Commerce, *Resources*, p. 26; Raymer, *Montana*, 1:449; Edith R. Maxwell, ed., "*Great Falls Yesterday*" (1939), mimeographed ms. in Montana Historical Society Library.

39. *The Copper Handbook*, 2:305; *Engineering and Mining Journal* 46 (18 September 1888): 224; O'Farrell, *Butte*, pp. 56–58; Butte Chamber of Commerce, *Resources*, p. 28; MacKnight, *Mines*, pp. 40–42; Raymer, *Montana*, 1:455.

40. The quote is in "The Story of Heinze, a Tale of Copper—and Brass," *Current Literature*, January 1907, pp. 34–36; Sarah McNelis, *Copper King at War*, pp. 1–3; Paul C. Phillips, "Frederick Augustus Heinze," *Dictionary of American Biography*, Dumas Malone, ed., 20 vols., 8:507 (An erratum slip in this edition, written by Otto Heinze, Jr., vigorously denies Phillips' assertion that the Heinzes were German Jews.); *Progressive Men of the State of Montana*, p. 1683; *Butte Miner*, 5 November 1914.

41. McNelis, *Copper King*, pp. 2–3.

42. Ibid., pp. 3–9; *Butte Daily Post*, 5 November 1914.

43. Sarah McNelis, "F. Augustus Heinze: An Early Cahpter in the Life of a Copper King," *The Montana Magazine of History* 2 (October 1952): 25–27.

44. McNelis, *Copper King*, pp. 15–16; *Engineering and Mining Journal* 98 (14 November 1914): 880–81.

45. *The Copper Handbook*, 2:326–27; McNelis, "F. Augustus Heinze," pp. 29–32.

46. McNelis, "F. Augustus Heinze," pp. 29–32; O'Farrell, *Butte*, pp. 29–31; William R. Stewart, "Captains of Industry, Part 21: F. Augustus Heinze," *Cosmopolitan*, January 1904, pp. 290–91.

47. Stewart, "Captains," pp. 290–91; *The Copper Handbook*, 2:326–27.

48. McNelis, *Copper King*, chap. 3; John Fahey, *Inland Empire: D. C. Corbin and Spokane*, pp. 148–83.

49. "The Wealth of a Rocky Mountain State," *Review of Reviews*, November 1894, pp. 546–47; the production statistics are in *Engineering and Mining Journal* 65 (25 June 1898): 756; see also ibid. 65 (1 January 1898): 5–6, (29 January 1898): 142, and (14 May 1898): 576.

50. A superb discussion of these developments is F. Ernest Richter, "The Copper-Mining Industry in the United States, 1845–1925," *Quarterly Journal of Economics* 41 (February 1927): 259–72.

51. Michael P. Malone and Richard B. Roeder, *Montana: A History of Two Centuries*, p. 143; *Engineering and Mining Journal* 65 (1 January 1898): 6.

52. Douglas W. Steeples, "The Panic of 1893," *Mid-America* 47 (1965): 155.

53. Thomas A. Clinch, *Urban Populism and Free Silver in Montana*, pp. 85–100; Muriel S. Wolle, *Montana Pay Dirt: A Guide to the Mining Camps of the Treasure State*, pp. 250–52; *Engineering and Mining Journal* 56 (8 July 1893): 38.

54. Clinch, *Urban Populism*, pp. 101–22; James D. Harrington, "'Free Silver,' Montana's Political Dream of Economic Prosperity: 1864–1900" (M.A. thesis, University of Montana, 1969), pp. 93–103.

55. Clinch, *Urban Populism*, pp. 90–93, 105–10; *Helena Independent*, 7 and 23 July, 31 October, 1 November 1893; Daly quote is in letter to Haggin, 14 July 1893, copy in George Hearst Papers, Phoebe Hearst Collection, Bancroft Library, University of California, Berkeley.

56. Clinch, *Urban Populism*, pp. 90–110; *Engineering and Mining Journal* 55 (8 April 1893): 327; 65 (28 May 1898): 636; 65 (4 June 1898): 682; for a silver miner's woes, see Joseph R. Walker's "President's Report," in *Annual Report of the Alice Gold and Silver Mining Company for 1894*, pp. 3–4.

57. Thomas R. Navin, *Copper Mining and Management*, p. 203.

4. Boom Town

1. Joseph Kinsey Howard, *Montana: High, Wide, and Handsome*, p. 85; John K. Hutchens, *One Man's Montana: An Informal Portrait of a State*, chap. 19; Chet Huntley, *The Generous Years: Remembrances of a Frontier Boyhood*, pp. 157–71.

2. Edwards Roberts, "Two Montana Cities," *Harper's New Monthly Magazine*, September 1883, p. 594; see also Julian Ralph "Montana: The Treasure State," ibid., June 1892, pp. 101–4; Ray Stannard Baker, "Butte City: Greatest of Copper Camps," *The Century*, April 1903, pp. 870–75.

3. *Anaconda Standard*, 24 August 1919.

4. Neil J. Lynch, *Butte Centennial Recollections*, p. 1; U.S., Department of the Interior, Office of the Census, *Statistics of the United States at the Tenth Census . . . 1880*, p. 250; *Report of the Population of the United States at the Eleventh Census: 1890*, p. 224; *Twelfth Census of the United States . . . 1900: Population, Part 1*, p. 251; Department of Commerce, Bureau of the Census. *Thirteenth Census of the United States . . . 1910: Vol. 2, Population*, p. 1143; *Montana Standard*, 30 September 1973.

5. These papers, unidentified, are quoted in *Anaconda Standard*, 24 August 1919.

6. *Deer Lodge New Northwest*, 2 June 1882; *Anaconda Standard*, 11 December 1891; *Montana Standard*, 12 January 1936.

7. Harry C. Freeman, *A Brief History of Butte, Montana*, p. 106; Eddie Foy and Alvin F. Harlow, *Clowning through Life*, pp. 185–87; John N. DeHaas, Jr., *Historic Uptown Butte*, offers an interesting, illustrated assessment.

8. Don James, *Butte's Memory Book*, pp. 78–85, 96; Gertrude Atherton, *Perch of the Devil*, pp. 56–57; Writers' Program of the Work Projects Administration in . . . Montana, *Copper Camp*, pp. 267–70. *Copper Camp* is the most valuable and entertaining look into Butte's social history.

9. James, *Butte's Memory Book*, pp. 93–94; Atherton, *Perch*, pp. 56–57; Jacob H. Ostberg, *Sketches of Old Butte*, pp. 23–26; on the disappearance of the old "east side" settlements in modern times, see Frank Quinn in *Montana Standard*, 7 November 1965.

10. Freeman, *Brief History*, pp. 89–105, offers an excellent description of the camp's operations. On the rail-trolley systems, see Ira L. Swett, *Montana's Trolleys—2*, esp. pp. 12, 78–85.

11. Hammett's Butte–Anaconda based novel, *Red Harvest*, is quoted in Edmund Christopherson, "The Cities of America: Butte," *Saturday Evening Post*, 8 December 1951, p. 40; William D. Haywood, *Bill Haywood's Book*, p. 83; Atherton, *Perch*, pp. 56–57.

12. Donald MacMillan, "A History of the Struggle to Abate Air Pollution from the Copper Smelters of the Far West: 1885–1933" (Ph.D. diss., University of Montana, 1973), pp. 16–17; memo, J. B. Steiger to Butte City Council, n.d., in Butte City Government Records, World Museum of Mining, Butte; *Engineering and Mining Journal* 55 (7 January 1893): 1.

13. *Anaconda Standard*, 16 November 1890; MacMillan, "History," pp. 18–19, 33–37, 103–60; *Engineering and Mining Journal* 55 (11 March 1893): 229; 59 (12 January 1895): 38; 66 (24 December 1898): 767; A. M. Wethy to Mayor and Aldermen of Butte, 2 August 1892, Butte City Government Records; Henry Williams to Guy Stapleton, 22 December 1898, Records of the Colorado Smelting and Mining Co., Letter Book: May 1898–December 1899, Anaconda Copper Mining Co. Records, Montana Historical Society Archives, Helena.

14. Mary MacLane, *The Story of Mary MacLane*, pp. 112–14.

15. U.S., Department of the Interior, Office of the Census, *Report on Population of the United States at the Eleventh Census: 1890*, p. 641; Department of Commerce, Bureau of the Census, *Thirteenth Census of the United States, Taken in the Year 1910: Vol. 2, Population, 1910*, p. 1156.

16. *Eleventh Census: 1890*, p. 641; *Twelfth Census . . . 1900 . . . Part 1*, p. 768; for an instance of Daly's hiring preferences, see Mrs. E. M. Banon, comp., *The Diary of Edward M. Banon*, pp. 1–31. Historians of the Irish in America have failed to perceive that remote Butte was one of America's most Irish cities: see William V. Shannon, *The American Irish*, which narrowly focuses, almost exclusively, on the Boston–New York corridor; Lawrence J. McCaffrey, *The Irish Diaspora in America*; and Marjorie R. Fallows, *Irish Americans: Identity and Assimilation*.

17. The quote is from P. J. Brophy to James H. Murphy, 31 December 1912, Brophy Papers, box 4, Montana Historical Society Archives; *Copper Camp*, pp. 6–7, 271; *Bozeman Courier*, 3 September 1937.

18. A. L. Rowse, *The Cousin Jacks: The Cornish in America*, pp. 354–63 (quote on p. 22); John Rowe, *The Hard-Rock Men: Cornish Immigrants and the North American Mining Frontier*, pp. 239–74; the rhymed quote is from Otis E. Young, Jr., *Western Mining*, p. 151.

19. Rowse, *Cousin Jacks*, pp. 354–55; *Butte Montana Standard*, 8 May 1949; 28 May and 25 June 1950; Frank B. Linderman, *Montana Adventure*, pp. 97–98.

20. Rowe, *Hard-Rock Men*, pp. 246–48; for good examples of how management mixed work crews, see W. Reed to the Walker Brothers, 18 July 1878,
Alice Gold and Silver Mining Co. Records, box 7, letterpress book no. 1, p.
580, Montana Historical Society Archives; and Frank Klepetko to G. M.
Hyams, 17 November 1900, Boston and Montana Co. Records, Eastern Correspondence: 1897–1902 letter book, Anaconda Copper Mining Co. Records.
   21. *Copper Camp*, pp. 47–59; *Anaconda Standard*, 6 July 1894; *Butte Bystander*,
7 July 1894; *Butte Montana Standard*, 3 July 1977.
   22. See the census references in note 4; Ostberg, *Sketches of Old Butte*, pp.
53, 83–89, 99; *Bozeman Courier*, 3 September 1937; *Copper Camp*, pp. 109, 121–3;
Christopherson, "Cities," p. 40; A. William Hoglund's *Finnish Immigrants in
America* offers general background but nothing specifically on Butte, see pp.
59–71 on mining.
   23. *Thirteenth Census . . . 1910*, p. 1156; Ostberg, *Sketches of Old Butte*, pp.
95–97.
   24. *Copper Camp*, pp. 107–11; for a general overview, see Gunther Barth,
Bitter Strength: A History of the Chinese in the United States, especially on min-
ing, pp. 113–17; John R. Wunder, "Law and Chinese in Frontier Montana,"
Montana: The Magazine of Western History 30 (Summer 1980): 18–31.
   25. *Bozeman Courier*, 16 April, 3 September 1937; Mrs. J. N. Jackson to Sam
C. Ford, 8 April and 24 May 1917; Ford to Mrs. Jackson, 15 and 16 January, 10
April 1917; W. E. Carroll to Ford, 4 February 1917; Jerre Murphy to Joseph
Jackson, 28 March 1917, Records of the Montana Attorney General, General
Correspondence Files, 1908–20, Montana State Archives, Helena; the news-
paper quotes are from the *Butte Bystander*, 4 and 11 February 1893; Kim
Chung Tai *et al.* to the Mayor and City Council of Butte, 9 February 1900,
Butte City Government Records; *Copper Camp*, pp. 107–21, 215.
   26. *Copper Camp*, pp. 100–7.
   27. *Thirteenth Census . . . 1910*, p. 1156; Helen Fitzgerald Sanders,
"Butte—The Heart of the Copper Industry," *Overland Monthly*, November
1906, p. 382.
   28. *Butte Evening News*, 24 July 1910; *Bozeman Courier*, 3 September 1937;
Ostberg, *Sketches of Old Butte*, pp. 93–94; Atherton, *Perch*, p. 58.
   29. Wayland D. Hand *et al.*, "Songs of the Butte Miners," *Western Folklore* 9
(January 1950): 25–26; see also, Hand's "The Folklore, Customs, and Traditions of the Butte Miner," *California Folklore Quarterly* 5 (1946): 1–25, 153–78.
   30. For a flavorful look into Butte's multinational ancestry, see the remarkably popular *Butte's Heritage Cookbook*, Jean McGrath, ed. (Butte: Butte–Silver
Bow Bicentennial Commission, 1976).
   31. The quotes are, in order, from Charles Sullivan to Mayor and City
Council, 3 March 1894; Carlton V. Jocron to Butte City Council, 16 February
1898; and Anthony Shovlin and William Walsh to Mayor and City Council of
Butte, 13 June 1896, Butte City Government Records.
   32. *Copper Camp*, pp. 59–60; *Bozeman Courier*, 16 April 1937.
   33. *Copper Camp*, pp. 166–72; John F. Davies, *The Great Dynamite Explosions
at Butte, Montana, January 15, 1895*, pp. 16–31; *Butte Daily Inter Mountain*, 18

January 1895; Arnon Gutfeld, "The Speculator Disaster in 1917: Labor Resurgence at Butte, Montana," *Arizona and the West* 2 (Spring 1969): 27–38.

34. Lemuel Eli Quigg in *New York Tribune*, July 1889, quoted in *Butte Montana Standard*, 2 January 1938; see also, Baker, "Butte City," p. 879.

35. Berton Braley, *Pegasus Pulls a Hack*, pp. 51, 57; see also, "Poems by Berton Braley," bound typescript in Montana Case, Montana Historical Society Library.

36. *Copper Camp*, pp. 76–89, 257–58; *Choteau Montanan*, 31 December 1920; Leslie Wheeler, "Montana's Shocking 'Litr'y Lady,'" *Montana: The Magazine of Western History* 27 (Summer 1977): 20–33; and Carolyn J. Mattern, "Mary MacLane: A Feminist Opinion," ibid. 27 (Autumn 1977): 54–63; George W. Davis, *Sketches of Butte*.

37. Lynch, *Butte Centennial Recollections*, p. 22.

38. *Copper Camp*, pp. 89–93; poem is quoted from William S. Greever, *The Bonanza West: The Story of the Western Mining Rushes*, p. 251.

39. Robert G. Young, *The Public School System of Butte, Montana*, p. 20; C. B. Glasscock, *The War of the Copper Kings*, p. 166; *Copper Camp*, p. 4; Archie L. Clark, "The Theater in Butte: A Short History" (1936), typed ms. copy in possession of Neil Lynch, Butte. Warren G. Davenport offers amusing insights into Butte's social life, "from tenderloin to upper tendon," in *Butte and Montana Beneath the X-Ray*, p. 7, *passim*.; and in his paper, the *Butte X-Ray*; see for instance, the issues of 1 August 1907, and 1 January 1908.

40. Alan Goddard in *Montana Standard*, 3 September 1978; Ralph, "Montana: The Treasure State," p. 103; *Copper Camp*, pp. 9, 176, 249–50.

41. Ralph, "Montana: The Treasure State," p. 103; William Scallon et al., to Sheriff John J. Quinn and deputies, 12 April 1906, Manuscript Cases, Montana Historical Society Library.

42. *Copper Camp*, pp. 177–83; Charles Chaplin, *My Autobiography*, p. 128.

43. *Anaconda Standard*, 26 and 27 January 1910; *Copper Camp*, p. 2.

44. Richard E. Lingenfelter, *The Hardrock Miners*; Ronald C. Brown, *Hard-Rock Miners*; Mark Wyman, *Hard Rock Epic*, pp. 91, 99, 115.

45. The best account of early unionism at Butte is Norma Smith, "The Rise and Fall of the Butte Miners' Union, 1878–1914" (M.A. thesis, Montana State University, 1961), pp. 9–11; James L. Macpherson, "Butte Miners' Union: An Analysis of Its Development and Economic Bargaining position" (M.A. thesis, University of Montana, 1949), pp. 1–12; *Butte Weekly Miner*, 18 and 25 June, 9 July 1878; *Butte Montana Standard*, 11 June 1978; W. Read to Walker Brothers, 9, 10, 11, 17, 21, and 30 June, 15 July 1878, Alice Gold and Silver Mining Co. Records, box 7, letterpress book, pp. 480, 485, 502, 513, 534, 575, Montana Historical Society Archives.

46. Smith, "Rise and Fall," pp. 12–16; Lingenfelter, *Hardrock Miners*, pp. 185–87.

47. Haywood, *Bill Haywood's Book*, p. 83; *Butte Montana Standard*, 11 June 1978.

48. Lingenfelter, *Hardrock Miners*, pp. 188–91; *Anaconda Standard*, 10 June 1891; Rowland Berthoff, *British Immigrants in Industrial America*, p. 189.

234 Notes

49. Smith, "Rise and Fall," pp. 17–18; Lingenfelter, *Hardrock Miners*, pp. 194–95; *Engineering and Mining Journal* 51 (14 February 1891): 216.
50. Richard H. Peterson, *The Bonanza Kings*, pp. 76–84.
51. Peterson, *Bonanza Kings*, pp. 68, 75; *Engineering and Mining Journal* 45 (28 April 1888): 310; Richard Smith to Phoebe Hearst, 1 November 1895, 1 June 1904, Phoebe Hearst Collection, Anaconda File, Bancroft Library, University of California, Berkeley; Joseph Cash, *Working the Homestake*, chap. 5–6; Cash wrongly asserts (p. 73) that the Montana mining interests did not reveal the benevolence indicated at Homestake.
52. "Proceedings of the First Annual Convention of the Western Federation of Miners, Held at Butte, Montana, May 15–19, 1893," ms. in File 163a, Western Federation of Miners Papers, Western History Collections, University of Colorado, Boulder; Vernon H. Jensen, *Heritage of Conflict: Labor Relations in the Nonferrous Metals Industry Up to 1930*, pp. 54–56; *Butte Daily Inter Mountain*, 15 May 1893.
53. *Anaconda Standard*, 9 November 1895; Smith, "Rise and Fall," p. 20; Jensen, *Heritage*, p. 56.

5. POLITICS: THE CLARK-DALY FEUD

1. *New York Times*, 13 November 1900, p. 2; on the Daly family, see the memoir of his son-in-law, James W. Gerard, *My First Eighty-three Years in America*, pp. 94–95. Gerard, who married Molly Daly in 1901, was a prominent and wealthy businessman-politician, who served as ambassador to Germany during the Wilson administration.
2. K. Ross Toole, "Marcus Daly: A Study of Business in Politics" (M.A. thesis, University of Montana, 1948), pp. 45–48; Isaac F. Marcosson, *Anaconda*, pp. 53–54.
3. Harriet Miller and Elizabeth Harrison, "Marcus Daly's Western Champions," *The Western Horseman*, March 1958, pp. 26–27; W. H. Gocher, *Fasig's Tales of the Turf*, pp. 163–65; Hugh Daly, *Biography of Marcus Daly of Montana*, pp. 21–30.
4. J. Carl Brogdon, "The History of Jerome, Arizona" (M.A. thesis, University of Arizona, 1952), pp. 20–34; *Clark Reminiscences*, pp. 19–23; *The Copper Handbook*, 3: pp. 529–33; Helen F. Sanders, *A History of Montana*, 3 vols., 2:856–57; *Progressive Men of the State of Montana*, pp. 1105–6; a rare glimpse into Clark's banking firm may be gained from the Alex J. Johnston Papers, Montana Historical Society Archives, Helena, which contains an 1890–98 letterpress book.
5. Deposition of Ella Clark Newell, 22 June 1926, in the case of *Alma E. Clark Hines et al. v. Charles W. Clark et al.*, File 7594, Silver Bow County Courthouse, Butte; *Progressive Men*, p. 1108; Sanders, *History*, 2:860; William D. Mangam, *The Clarks of Montana*, pp. 71–72, 82–83.
6. *Progressive Men*, p. 1107; Clark, "Centennial Address on the Origin, Growth and Resources of Montana," in *Contributions to the Historical Society of*

Montana, 2:45–60; on the Nez Perce War, see James H. Mills to Martin Maginnis, 31 July 1877, Maginnis Papers, box 3, Montana Historical Society Archives; and on the 1884 Constitutional Convention, Margery H. Brown, "Metamorphosis and Revision," *Montana: The Magazine of Western History* 20 (Autumn 1970): 3–17.

7. George Hearst, *The Way It Was*, p. 24; Clark is quoted in *New York Herald*, 23 September 1900, p. 5; for a good example of some of the wilder exaggerations regarding the origins of the feud, see "The Clark-Daly Feud," *Public Opinion*, 15 March 1900, pp. 325–26.

8. B. E. Stack, "Origin of the Clark-Daly Feud," typescript copy (1933) in Daly folder, Vertical File, Montana Historical Society Library; C. B. Glasscock, *The War of the Copper Kings*, pp. 64–65; K. Ross Toole, "The Genesis of the Clark-Daly Feud," *The Montana Magazine of History* 1 (April 1951): 27; *Butte Miner*, 26 September, 3 and 10 October 1876.

9. Toole, "Genesis," pp. 27–28; "Captain" John Branagan, "Story of the Anaconda," in John Lindsay, *Amazing Experiences of a Judge*, p. 72; *New York Times*, 10 September 1893, p. 20.

10. M. G. O'Malley, "Butte Close-ups: Personal Narrative," *The Frontier* 8 (May 1928): 211; notes on a letter of 26 November 1938, from O'Malley by Herbert Peet, Peet Collection, bk. 6, Montana Historical Society Archives.

11. Kenneth N. Owens, "Patterns and Structure in Western Territorial Politics," *Western Historical Quarterly* 1 (October 1970): 377–78; Clark C. Spence, *Territorial Politics and Government in Montana*.

12. *Great Falls Tribune*, 24 September 1889; Ellis Waldron and Paul B. Wilson, *Atlas of Montana Elections: 1889–1976*, p. 8.

13. *Butte Daily Miner*, 8 November 1888; *Ft. Benton River Press*, 28 November 1888; *Helena Independent*, 7 November 1888; "Personal Explanation . . . Speech of Hon. William A. Clark, of Montana, in the Senate of the United States, Tuesday, May 15, 1900," pp. 6–7; Clark Testimony in *Report of the Committee on Privileges and Elections of the United States Senate Relative to the Right and Title of William A. Clark to a Seat as Senator from the State of Montana*, 56th Cong., 1st sess., S. Rept. 1052, 3 vols., 3:1937, hereafter cited as *Report of Committee on Privileges and Elections*.

14. On Carter, see P. C. Phillips, "Thomas Henry Carter," *Dictionary of American Biography*, Allen Johnson, ed., 20 vols., 3:544–55; and "Genealogical Material," Thomas Carter Papers, "Biographical Material" files, box 22, Manuscripts Division, Library of Congress, Washington, D.C.

15. *Anaconda Weekly Review*, 8 November 1888; *Butte Daily Miner*, 4, 5, 6 November 1888.

16. Toole, "Genesis," pp. 28–32; K. Ross Toole, *Montana: An Uncommon Land*, pp. 161–62, 180–82; Dale L. Johnson, "Andrew B. Hammond: Education of a Capitalist on the Montana Frontier" (Ph.D. diss., University of Montana, 1976), chap. 9; K. Ross Toole and Edward Butcher, "Timber Depredations on the Montana Public Domain, 1885–1918," *Journal of the West*, 7 (July 1968): 351–62; Herbert Peet Collection, bks. 11, 28.

17. Clark Testimony in *Report of Committee on Privileges and Elections*, 3:1938;

Clark, "Personal Explanation," p. 7; *Butte Daily Miner*, 7, 10 November 1888; Kenneth V. Lottich, ed., "My Trip to Montana Territory in 1879," *Montana: The Magazine of Western History* 15 (Winter 1965): 21; Ellis L. Waldron, *Montana Politics since 1864: An Atlas of Elections*, p. 48.

18. Daly is quoted in *Report of Committee on Privileges and Elections*, 3:2233; *Butte Daily Inter Mountain*, 7, 8 November 1888; *Anaconda Weekly Review*, 8 November 1888; *Butte Daily Miner*, 9, 10 November 1888; *Helena Independent*, 7 November 1888; *Great Falls Tribune*, 8, 10 November 1888; *Billings Weekly Gazette*, 8 November 1888; "1888—The Campaign Opens," ms. by unidentified author in Carter Papers, box 16; William E. Hall to Joseph R. Walker, 10 November 1888, Alice Gold and Silver Mining Co. Records, box 10, letterpress book, Montana Historical Society Archives.

19. Clark to Martin Maginnis, 10 November, 1888, Maginnis Papers, box 1; Clark Testimony in *Report of Committee on Privileges and Elections*, 3:1938; Clark, "Personal Explanation," p. 7; see also, *Butte Daily Miner*, 25 November 1888; Clark to Joseph K. Toole, 4 February 1889, Toole Papers, Montana Historical Society Archives.

20. Phillips, "Carter," pp. 544–45; "Biography of Thomas H. Carter," unsigned, undated typescript in Carter Papers, box 22; Carter to Benjamin Harrison, 25 October and 4, 8 November 1892; and Harrison to Carter, 15 April 1893, Benjamin Harrison Papers, Library of Congress.

21. Daly to Samuel T. Hauser, 6 January 1889, Hauser Papers, box 24; Hauser to Daly, 8 January 1890, ibid., box 32, Montana Historical Society Archives.

22. Johnson, "Hammond," pp. 124–47; Toole, "Genesis," p. 33; Daly to Samuel T. Hauser, 23 September 1889, Hauser Papers, box 18; A. B. Hammond to T. C. Power, 28 August 1889; Gustavus Moser to Power, 27 August and 3 September 1889, Power Papers, box 1; Hammond to Power, 15 June 1890, ibid., box 23, Montana Historical Society Archives; "The Story of Hammond Lumber Company," ms. in Walter H. McLeod Papers, box 93, University of Montana Archives, Missoula.

23. *Anaconda Standard*, 4 September 1889; John P. Fought, "John Hurst Durston, Editor: The Anaconda Standard in the Clark-Daly Feud" (M.A. thesis, University of Montana, 1959), pp. 9–20; Charles H. Eggleston in *Butte Montana Standard*, 4 September 1929.

24. *Proceedings and Debates of the Constitutional Convention . . . 1889*, pp. 21, 115–16, 172, 475–77; Clark quote is on p. 477; Joseph K. Howard wrote, with more emotion than accuracy, of the "tax conspiracy" of 1889 in *Montana: High, Wide and Handsome*, pp. 61–64; J. W. Smurr offers a convincing rebuttal in "The Montana 'Tax Conspiracy' of 1889," *Montana: The Magazine of Western History* 5 (Spring 1955): 46–53; and (Summer 1955): 47–56; see also, John W. Smurr, "A Critical Study of the Montana Constitutional Convention of 1889" (M.A. thesis, University of Montana, 1951); and Brian Cockhill, "An Economic Analysis of Montana's Constitution" (M.A. thesis, University of Montana, 1968).

25. *Proceedings and Debates*, p. 754.

26. *Butte Semi-Weekly Inter Mountain,* 13 October 1889; Neil J. Lynch, *Montana's Legislature Through the Years,* pp. 38–39; Waldron, *Montana Politics* pp. 54–59.

27. Morton Keller, *Affairs of State: Public Life in Late Nineteenth Century America,* p. 567.

28. James M. Hamilton, *History of Montana,* Merrill G. Burlingame, ed., pp. 561–685; Herbert Peet Collection, bk. 29; W. A. Clark to Samuel T. Hauser, 24 October 1889, Hauser Papers, box 18; *Butte Semi-Weekly Inter Mountain,* 13 October, 10 November 1889.

29. Hamilton, *History of Montana,* pp. 569–79; *Butte Semi-Weekly Miner,* 14 December 1889; 15 March and 19 April 1890; *Ft. Benton River Press,* 26 February, 23 April 1890; *Butte Semi-Weekly Inter Mountain,* 27 November 1889; 9, 12 March 1890; Thomas Carter to T. C. Power, 7 March 1890, Power Papers, box 1; Charles Warren, Lee Mantle *et al.* to Senators W. F. Sanders and T. C. Power and Representative Thomas Carter, 13 April 1890, ibid., box 3; Clark Testimony, *Report of Committee on Privileges and Elections,* 3:1938.

30. The standard, older history of populism is John D. Hicks, *The Populist Revolt* (Minneapolis: University of Minnesota Press, 1931); an appreciative newer study is Lawrence Goodwyn, *Democratic Promise: The Populist Movement in America.*

31. Thomas A. Clinch, *Urban Populism and Free Silver in Montana;* and Clinch, "The Northern Pacific Railroad and Montana's Mineral Lands," *Pacific Historical Review* 34 (August 1965): 323–35.

32. *Anaconda Standard,* 21 January, 17 June 1892; Robert E. Williams, "The Silver Republican Movement in Montana" (M.A. thesis, University of Montana, 1965), pp. 73–75; James D. Harrington, "'Free Silver,' Montana's Political Dream of Economic Prosperity: 1864–1900" (M.A. thesis, University of Montana, 1969), pp. 93–103; Clinch, *Urban Populism,* pp. 47–65.

33. *New York Times,* 10 September 1893, p. 20; *Helena Daily Independent,* 3 March 1893.

34. Daly quote is in *New York Herald,* 23 September 1900, p. 5; Janet C. Thomson, "The Role of Lee Mantle in Montana Politics, 1889–1900: An Interpretation" (M.A. thesis, University of Montana, 1956), pp. 73–80; Herbert Peet Collection, bk. 12; Sanders, *History of Montana,* 2:860–63.

35. Waldron, *Atlas of Montana Elections,* pp. 15–17; *Butte Weekly Miner,* 9 March 1893; *Helena Daily Independent,* 3 March 1893; *Livingston Enterprise,* 29 October 1892.

36. "Montana," *Appleton's Annual Cyclopedia . . . 1893,* pp. 500–2; Clinch, *Urban Populism,* pp. 64–65; J. A. MacKnight, "The Montana Capital Fight," *Harper's Weekly,* 27 October, 1894, p. 1049; *Helena Herald,* 4 March 1893; Jean Schmidt, "Copper Kings, Populists, and Logrollers: The Montana Legislative Session of 1893 (M. A. Thesis, Montana State University, 1980).

37. Christopher P. Connolly, *The Devil Learns to Vote: The Story of Montana,* pp. 100–1; *New York Times,* 10 September 1893, p. 20.

38. *House Journal of the Third Session of the Legislative Assembly of the State of Montana . . . 1893*, pp. 50, 55, 60; Clark Testimony in *Report of Committee on Privileges and Elections*, 3:1939; "Montana," *Appleton's Annual Cyclopedia . . . 1893*, pp. 500–1; *Anaconda Standard*, 19 February 1893.

39. Quote is from L. C. Fisk to Mother, 15 February 1893; see also J. U. Sanders to W. E. Sanders, 17, 20 January 1893, Fisk Family Papers, box 8, Montana Historical Society Archives; for evidence of Daly's use of detectives, see W. A. Pinkerton to Wilbur F. Sanders, 4 March 1893, Wilbur Fisk Sanders Papers, Montana Historical Society Archives; Samuel T. Hauser to Senators Gorman, Carlisle, and (?), January 1893, Hauser Papers, box 32; Connolly, *Devil Learns to Vote*, pp. 100–1.

40. Both quotes are in *Anaconda Standard*, 3 March 1893; *Helena Herald*, 2, 3 March 1893; *House Journal of the Third Session*, p. 375; *Appleton's Annual Cyclopedia . . . 1893*, pp. 500–1.

41. Lee Mantle to T. C. Power, 29 March 1894, Power Papers, box 8; *Butte Weekly Miner*, 9 March 1893; *Butte Semi-Weekly Inter Mountain*, 5 March 1893; *Billings Gazette*, 9 March 1893; *Evening Missoulian*, 2 March 1893; *Helena Daily Independent*, 3 March 1893; *Helena Herald*, 4 March 1893; *Anaconda Standard*, 5 March 1893.

42. U.S., Congress, Senate, 53rd Cong., 1st sess., pt. 1, spec. sess., *Congressional Record*, 25:994–96; *Great Falls Tribune*, 21 August 1893; *Bozeman Chronicle*, 31 August 1893; *Billings Gazette*, 2 September 1893; Telegrams, S. T. Hauser to Lee Mantle, 21, 24 August 1893; Pat Conlon to T. C. Power, 23 August 1893; Power to W. W. Abbott, 11 September 1893; Power to Editor, *Helena Independent*, 6 September 1893, Power Papers, box 8; John Rickards to Power, 27 August 1893, ibid., box 28; Mantle to Power, 24 September, 30 October 1893, ibid., box 6; letter, Rickards to Power, 31 August, 9 September 1893, ibid., box 6; Martin Maginnis et al. to Grover Cleveland, 24 September 1894, Cleveland Papers, Manuscripts Division, Library of Congress.

43. Clinch, *Urban Populism*, pp. 112–18.

44. Connolly, *Devil Learns to Vote*, pp. 103–4; Clark and Daly Testimony, *Report of Committee on Privileges and Elections*, 3:1837–39, 2228–29.

45. MacKnight, "Montana Capital Fight," p. 1049; Thomson, "Lee Mantle," pp. 91–93; *Butte Miner*, 30 October 1894; *Butte Bystander*, 31 October 1894; *Great Falls Daily Tribune*, 1 November 1894; W. A. Clark to S. T. Hauser, 18 October 1894, Hauser Papers, box 23; Julia Anne Carter Lang, "Reminiscences," undated ms. in Carter Papers, box 22.

46. *Butte Miner*, 2, 4 November 1894; *A Monster Monopoly: An Exposition of the Methods of the Anaconda Mining Company*, undated pamphlet in Montana Historical Society Library; *Helena Independent*, 25, 28 October 1894; see also the materials in the Women's Helena for the Capital Club Records, Montana Historical Society Archives.

47. Clinch, "Northern Pacific"; *Anaconda Standard*, 23, 27, 29, 31 October, and 6, 7, 8, 9 November 1894; *Butte Bystander*, 31 October, and 1, 17 Novem-

ber 1894; *Anaconda, Montana, 1894,* pamphlet; John P. Fought, "Editor in the Montana Capital Fight," in *A Century of Montana Journalism,* Warren J. Brier and Nathan B. Blumberg, eds., pp. 41–55.

48. *Billings Gazette,* 3, 10 November 1894; *Great Falls Daily Tribune,* 1, 2, 6, 7, 10 November 1894; *Bozeman Weekly Chronicle,* 1, 8 November 1894.

49 *Daily Missoulian,* 17, 30 October, and 4, 7 November 1894; A. B. Hammond to T. C. Power, 11, 16, 28 May 1894, Power Papers, box 8; Johnson, "Hammond," pp. 164–78; "Story of Hammond Lumber Company," pp. 21–22; A. B. Hammond to C. H. McLeod, 17 December 1894, C. H. McLeod Papers, box 1, University of Montana Archives.

50. Frank B. Linderman, *Montana Adventure,* H. G. Merriam, ed., pp. 95–97; Connolly, *Devil Learns to Vote,* p. 103.

51. Clinch, *Urban Populism,* pp. 112–19; *Butte Miner,* 7 November 1894; *Butte Daily Inter Mountain,* 8 November 1894; *Anaconda Standard,* 9 November 1894; *Helena Independent,* 7 November 1894.

52. Waldron and Wilson, *Atlas,* p. 18.

53. Connolly, *Devil Learns to Vote,* p. 103; Howard, *Montana,* pp. 66–67; Toole, "Marcus Daly," pp. 131–32.

54. *Helena Weekly Independent,* 20 June 1895.

55. Matthew Josephson, *The Politicos,* p. 664; Harrington, "Free Silver," pp. 93–103; Goodwyn, *Democratic Promise,* pp. 389–91; Clinch, *Urban Populism,* pp. 99–94; *Anaconda Standard,* 7 July and 2 August 1893.

56. Goodwyn, *Democratic Promise,* pp. 431–32.

57. Harrington, "Free Silver," pp. 115–17; Williams, "Silver Republican Movement, pp. 49–74; Thomson, "Lee Mantle," p. 111; Clinch, *UrbanPopulism,* pp. 129–30.

58. Among several studies of the 1896 campaign, see especially Robert F. Durden, *The Climax of Populism: The Election of 1896* (Lexington: University of Kentucky Press, 1965).

59. Clinch, *Urban Populism,* pp. 132–41; *Butte Sunday Bystander,* 23 August and 20 September 1896; *Helena Daily Herald,* 3 September 1896; *Daily Missoulian,* 4, 5, September 1896.

60. Clinch, *Urban Populism,* pp. 142–44; *Helena Daily Herald,* 11 September 1896.

61. Clinch, *Urban Populism,* pp. 144–49; *Butte Miner,* 31 October 1896; *Helena Weekly Herald,* 8 October 1896; *Anaconda Standard,* 1, 2 November 1896.

62. Gerard, *My First Eighty-Three Years,* p. 92; Paolo E. Coletta, *William Jennings Bryan: 1, Political Evangelist, 1860–1908* (Lincoln; University of Nebraska Press, 1964), p. 198; *New York World,* 16 October 1896, quoted in *Butte Daily Inter Mountain,* 20 October 1896; Clinch, *Urban Populism,* pp. 147–51.

63. *Butte Daily Inter Mountain,* 20, 21 October 1896; Clinch, *Urban Populism,* pp. 151–52; Stanley L. Jones, *The Presidential Election of 1896* (Madison: University of Wisconsin Press, 1964), p. 302; Josephson, *The Politicos,* p. 664; Goodwyn, *Democratic Promise,* pp. 526–27; Toole, "Marcus Daly," p. 141.

64. Waldron and Wilson, *Atlas*, pp. 19–22; Clinch, *Urban Populism*, pp. 152–54; *Anaconda Standard*, 4 November 1896; *Butte Miner*, 4 November 1896; *Helena Weekly Herald*, 5 November 1896; *Phillipsburg Citizens' Call*, 4, 11 November 1896.

65. *Anaconda Standard*, 13, 14, 15 August 1897; Gerard, *My First Eighty-three Years*, p. 92.

6. MR. CLARK GOES TO WASHINGTON

1. Forrest L. Foor, "The Senatorial Aspirations of William A. Clark, 1898–1901: A Study in Montana Politics" (Ph.D. diss., University of California, Berkeley, 1941).

2. Hauser and Clark Testimony, *Report of the Committee on Privileges and Elections of the United States Senate Relative to the Right and Title of William A. Clark to a Seat as Senator from the State of Montana*, 56th Cong., 1st sess., S. Rept. 1052, 3 vols., 1:306–7; 3:1744–47; hereafter cited as *Report of Committee on Privileges and Elections*.

3. W. A. Clark to J. S. M. Neill, 7 July 1898; Neill to S. T. Hauser, 4 October 1898; Clark to Neill, 18 March 1899; Neill to Clark, 8 April 1899, Samuel T. Hauser Papers, box 26, Montana Historical Society, Helena; *Anaconda Standard*, 22, 23, 25 September 1898; Thomas A. Clinch, *Urban Populism and Free Silver in Montana*, pp. 156–59; *Report of Committee on Privileges and Elections*, 3:1834–35.

4. J. S. M. Neill to Samuel T. Hauser, 4 October 1898, Hauser Papers, box 26; *Butte Daily Inter Mountain*, 9 November 1898; Christopher P. Connolly, *The Devil Learns to Vote*, p. 124.

5. Ellis Waldron and Paul B. Wilson, *Atlas of Montana Elections: 1889–1976*, pp. 23–25; *Great Falls Tribune*, 5 November 1898; *Butte Daily Inter Mountain*, 9 November 1898; *Daily Missoulian*, 9 November 1898; Foor, "Senatorial Aspirations," pp. 39–45.

6. Charlie Clark quote is in Connolly, *Devil Learns to Vote*, p. 125; W. A. Clark quote is legendary and may be apocryphal; Daly quote is in *Miles City Yellowstone Journal*, 6 January 1900.

7. Connolly, *Devil Learns to Vote*, p. 126; see also, *Hamilton Western News*, 18 January 1899.

8. Dorothy M. Johnson, ed., "Three Hundred Grand!" *Montana: The Magazine of Western History* 10 (Winter 1960): 41; Connolly, *Devil Learns to Vote*, pp. 127–28; *Anaconda Standard*, 3 January 1899.

9. Connolly, *Devil Learns to Vote*, pp. 139–47 (quote is on pp. 146–47); Foor, "Senatorial Aspirations," pp. 51–60; Johnson, "Three Hundred Grand!", pp. 40–44; see Senator Clark's (of Madison County) testimony in *Great Falls Tribune*, 25 January 1899; *Helena Herald*, 10 January 1899.

10. *Portland Morning Oregonian*, 11 January 1899, p. 1; *Anaconda Standard*, 11 January 1899; *Butte Miner*, 11 January 1899; *Great Falls Daily Tribune*, 11 Janu-

ary 1899; *Helena Independent,* 12 January 1899; *Kalispell Inter Lake,* 13 January 1899; *Billings Gazette,* 10 January 1899; Foor, "Senatorial Aspirations," p. 85.

11. *Miles City Yellowstone Journal,* 12 January 1900.

12. Foor, "Senatorial Aspirations," pp. 64–69; *Anaconda Standard,* 12 January 1899; *Butte Miner,* 15 January 1899.

13. *Butte Miner,* 13, 14 January 1899.

14. Connolly, *Devil Learns to Vote,* pp. 147–48; *Billings Gazette,* 17, 27 January 1899.

15. *New York Times,* 21 January 1899, p. 1; *Butte Miner,* 27 January 1899; *Anaconda Standard,* 27 January 1899.

16. Whiteside's speech may be found in *Anaconda Standard,* 27 January 1899; and in Connolly, *Devil Learns to Vote,* pp. 158–60; *Butte Miner,* 27 January 1899; Foor, "Senatorial Aspirations," pp. 71–76.

17. *Lewistown Fergus County Argus,* 1 February 1899; Foor, "Senatorial Aspirations," pp. 77–78; Connolly, *Devil Learns to Vote,* pp. 160–61.

18. *Senate Journal of the Sixth Session of the Legislative Assembly of the State of Montana,* pp. 98–113; Foor, "Senatorial Aspirations," pp. 78–79; *New York Times,* 29 January 1899, p. 3; 3 February 1899, p. 5.

19. Telegram, W. A. Clark to S. T. Hauser, 29 January 1899, Hauser Papers, box 26; Connolly, *Devil Learns to Vote,* pp. 164–65; *Helena Independent,* 29 January 1899.

20. *Butte Miner,* 29 January 1899; *Helena Independent,* 29 January 1899; *Great Falls Daily Tribune,* 29 January 1899; *Billings Gazette,* 31 January 1899; *Lewistown Fergus County Argus,* 1 February 1899; *Bozeman Chronicle,* 19 January and 2 February 1899; *Livingston Enterprise,* 4 February 1899; Sanders quoted in *Anaconda Standard,* 29 January 1899; Connolly, *Devil Learns to Vote,* p. 166.

21. *Salt Lake Tribune,* 29 January 1899, pp. 1, 12; 30 January 1899, pp. 1, 4; *Denver Rocky Mountain News,* 27 January 1899, p. 3; 29 January 1899, p. 6; 30 January, p. 4 (quote); *Denver Evening Post,* 27 January 1899, p. 4; 29 January 1899, pp. 1, 4 (quote); *St. Paul Dispatch,* quoted in C. B. Glasscock, *The War of the Copper Kings,* p. 175.

22. *Anaconda Standard,* 5 February 1899.

23. *Butte Daily Inter Mountain,* 30 January 1899; Foor, "Senatorial Aspirations," pp. 114–15; *Report of Committee on Privileges and Elections,* 3:2209, 2220 (Daly quote); *Butte Miner,* 3, 6, 7 March 1899.

24. *Helena Herald,* 2 August 1899; Foor, "Senatorial Aspirations," pp. 124–26; Connolly, *Devil Learns to Vote,* pp. 191–92.

25. "Memoirs of William H. Hunt," pp. 83–84, ms. copy in Hunt Papers, Montana Historical Society Archives; William H. Conrad, ed., "William Henry Hunt: The Montana Years," *Montana: The Magazine of Western History* 30 (Spring 1980): 66; *Report of Committee on Privileges and Elections,* 2:1631–50; 3: 1651–87, 1725–40, 1902–8, 1954–2017, 2025–38; *New York Times,* 2 August 1899, p. 2; *Anaconda Standard,* 24 December 1899; Connolly, *Devil Learns to Vote,* chap. 14; Foor, "Senatorial Aspirations," pp. 126–29; Z. T. Cason to J. B. Root, 8 December 1899, letter in Manuscript Cases, Montana Historical Society Library.

26. The two memorials from Montana are reproduced in *Documents* no. 2 and 3, *Report of Committee on Privileges and Elections*, 1:1–400; S. T. Hauser to W. A. Clark, 19 April 1899, Hauser Papers, box 33; Foor, "Senatorial Aspirations," pp. 135–36.

27. Foor, "Senatorial Aspirations," pp. 137–40; Connolly, *Devil Learns to Vote*, pp. 205–6.

28. *Report of Committee on Privileges and Elections*, 2:1408.

29. Ibid., 3:1742–86, 1822–1901, 1908–41, 2204–39.

30. Ibid., 3:2383–2363; Foor, "Senatorial Aspirations," chap. 5, pp. 154–55.

31. *Report of Committee on Privileges and Elections*, 1:4–6, 481–504, 506–10; 2:920–70, 988–1015.

32. Ibid., 1: 3–6, 400ff.; 2: 822–44, 1271–1304, 1312–91; 3: 2323–46; Connolly, *Devil Learns to Vote*, p. 166; Foor, "Senatorial Aspirations," pp. 145–46.

33. *Report of Committee on Privileges and Elections*, 1:89–244 passim.; 2: 708–30, 1082–1125; Foor, "Senatorial Aspirations," pp. 147–49; *Miles City Yellowstone Journal*, 6, 9, 12, 16 January and 5, 6, 8 (quote), 26, 27 February 1900.

34. *Report of Committee on Privileges and Elections*, 1:1, 15, 21–4; *Miles City Yellowstone Journal*, 5 March 1900.

35. W. A. Clark, *Personal Explanation. Speech of Hon. W. A. Clark of Montana, in the Senate of the United States, Tuesday, May 15, 1900*, pamphlet copy in Montana Historical Society Library; U.S., Congress, Senate, 56th Cong., 1st sess., *Congressional Record*, 33:5531–36; Clark's letter of resignation to Governor Smith, dated May ?, 1900 is in Montana's Governors' Papers, box 33, Montana State Archives, Helena; *Anaconda Standard*, 11 April 1900; *Butte Daily Inter Mountain*, 15 May 1900; *Butte Miner*, 16 May 1900.

36. See the coded telegrams, J. S. M. Neill to S. T. Hauser, 16, 17, 18 April 1900 Hauser Papers, box 26; W. F. Sanders to Senator William E. Chandler, 19 May 1900, Sanders Papers, Montana Historical Society Archives.

37. W. F. Sanders to William E. Chandler, 19 May 1900, Sanders Papers; *Butte Miner*, 16 May 1900; *Butte Daily Inter Mountain*, 15 May 1900; Connolly, *Devil Learns to Vote*, pp. 214–19; Foor, "Senatorial Aspirations," pp. 173–75.

38. *Anaconda Standard*, 16 (Chandler quote), 17 (Smith and Sanders quotes) May 1900; *Butte Daily Inter Mountain*, 16, 18 May 1900.

39. Robert B. Smith to Martin Maginnis, 18 May 1900, Maginnis Papers, box 3, Montana Historical Society Archives; W. A. Clark to S. T. Hauser, 22 May 1900, Hauser Papers, box 26; *Butte Daily Inter Mountain*, 21 May 1900; *Anaconda Standard*, 19, 20, 23 May 1900; *Butte Miner*, 18, 23 May 1900; U.S., Congress, Senate, *Congressional Record*, 56th Cong., 1st sess., 1900, 33, pt. 6:5584, 5738, 5782, 5937, 5950; 2d sess., 34, pt. 29, 58–93, 216–19, 3420–36.

40. *Butte Miner*, 11 June 1900 (Clark quote); *Anaconda Standard*, 11 June 1900 (Chandler quote); Foor, "Senatorial Aspirations," pp. 181–83; Connolly, *Devil Learns to Vote*, pp. 218–19.

41. *Billings Gazette*, 10 April 1900; Foor, "Senatorial Aspirations," pp. 161–62.

42. "The Montana Bribery Scandal," *Public Opinion*, 4 January 1900, p. 8; "The Montana Senatorial Scandal," *Literary Digest*, 20 January 1900, p. 74;

"Senator Clark's Seat Declared Vacant," *Public Opinion*, 19 April 1900, pp. 488–89; *The Nation*, 22 February 1900, p. 138; 19 April 1900, p. 295; "The Contested Senate Seats," *American Monthly Review of Reviews*, June 1900, pp. 649–50; "Mr. Clark's Coup d'Etat," *Public Opinion*, 24 May 1900, pp. 648–49; *Denver Evening Post*, 16 May 1900, p. 1

43. Johnson, "Three Hundred Grand!," p. 47.

7. "CONSOLIDATION": THE AMALGAMATED AND THE INDEPENDENTS

1. Morton Keller, *Affairs of State: Public Life in Late Nineteenth Century America*, pp. 434–51; Thomas C. Cochran and William Miller, *The Age of Enterprise*, pp. 188–92.

2. T. A. Rickard, *A History of American Mining*, pp. 125–27; Isaac F. Marcosson, *Metal Magic: The Story of the American Smelting and Refining Company*, pp. 61–69.

3. F. Ernest Richter, "The Copper Mining Industry in the United States, 1845–1925," *Quarterly Journal of Economics* 41 (February 1927): 272–76; Charles F. Speare, "The Story of Copper," *American Monthly Review of Reviews*, November 1906, pp. 573–74.

4. Thomas R. Navin, *Copper Mining and Management*, p. 115; Louis Filler, *Crusaders for American Liberalism*, pp. 171–76.

5. Thomas W. Lawson, *Frenzied Finance, Vol. 1: The Crime of Amalgamated*, pp. 232–40. (A second volume was never written.)

6. Allan Nevins, *Study in Power: John D. Rockefeller, Industrialist and Philanthropist*, 2 vols., 2:283; Peter Collier and David Horowitz, *The Rockefellers: An American Dynasty*, p. 37.

7. Collier and Horowitz, *The Rockefellers*, p. 37; the nearest approach to a biography of Rogers is Earl J. Dias's uncritical *Henry Huttleston Rogers: Portrait of a "Capitalist"* (Fairhaven, Mass.: Millicent Library, 1974); but see Alvin F. Harlow, "Henry Huttleston Rogers," *Dictionary of American Biography*, Dumas Malone, ed., 22 vols., 16:95–96; "A Chapter in High Finance," *The Nation*, May 1909, pp. 545–46; "The Career of H. H. Rogers," *The Outlook*, 29 May 1909, pp. 257–58; John S. Gregory, "Henry H. Rogers—Monopolist," *The World's Work*, May 1905, pp. 6127–30; Twain is quoted in Samuel L. Clemens, *Mark Twain's Autobiography*, 2 vols., 2:250–51; Lewis Leary, ed., *Mark Twain's Correspondence with Henry Huttleston Rogers: 1893–1909*, pp. v–vi, 555–56.

8. John T. Flynn, *God's Gold: The Story of Rockefeller and His Times*, pp. 344–45; Matthew Josephson, *The Robber Barons*, pp. 394–99; Collier and Horowitz, *The Rockefellers*, pp. 38, 46; Nevins, *Study in Power*, 2:282–87.

9. Lawson, *Frenzied Finance*, pp. 242–80; K. Ross Toole, "When Big Money Came to Butte," *Pacific Northwest Quarterly* 44 (January 1953): 25.

10. Lawson, *Frenzied Finance*, pp. 283–88 (Rogers quote on p. 287); K. Ross Toole, "Marcus Daly: A Study of Business in Politics" (M.A. thesis, Universi-

ty of Montana, 1948), pp. 181–83 (Toole interviewed Alex Leggat); Clarence W. Barron, *More They Told Barron*, Arthur Pound and Samuel T. Moore, eds., pp. 52–53; C. B. Glasscock, *The War of the Copper Kings*, p. 211.

11. *Laws, Resolutions and Memorials of the State of Montana, Passed at the Sixth Regular Session of the Legislative Assembly*, pp. 113–17; Toole, "Big Money," p. 26; Smith quoted in K. Ross Toole, *Montana: An Uncommon Land*, p. 166.

12. *Wall Street Journal*, 25 April 1899, pp. 1, 4; *New York Times*, 12 January 1899, p. 11; *Engineering and Mining Journal* 67 (4 February 1899): 137 (quote); (25 February 1899): 250; (4 March 1899): 281.

13. *New York Times*, 28 April 1899, p. 1; *Commercial and Financial Chronicle*, 19 April 1899, pp. 820–21; *Engineering and Mining Journal* 67 (29 April 1899): 494; (6 May 1899): 547; Isaac F. Marcosson, *Anaconda*, pp. 95–96; *Butte Daily Inter Mountain*, 21 April 1899. Marcus Daly to M. Donahoe, 30 December 1899, Anaconda Copper Mining Co. Records, box 854, Montana Historical Society Records, Helena.

14. Marcosson, *Anaconda*, pp. 95–99; Navin, *Copper Mining and Management*, pp. 206, 310–11.

15. *New York Times*, 28 April 1899, p. 1; 29 April 1899, p. 8; *Engineering and Mining Journal* 67 (13 May 1899): 553; Lawson, *Frenzied Finance*, pp. 370–72.

16. Lawson, *Frenzied Finance*, pp. 353–75; Glasscock, *War of Copper Kings*, pp. 216–17; William S. Greever, *The Bonanza West: The Story of the Western Mining Rushes*, p. 241.

17. Lawson, *Frenzied Finance*, pp. 292–300, 307–11; Navin, *Copper Mining and Management*, pp. 304–5.

18. F. Ernest Richter, "The Amalgamated Copper Company: A Closed Chapter in Corporate Finance," *Quarterly Journal of Economics* 30 (February 1916): 389–90; Speare, "Story of Copper," pp. 573–74; Thomas W. Lawson, "Fools and Their Money," *Everybody's Magazine*, May 1906, pp. 690–95; Lawson, *Frenzied Finance*, pp. 514–21; Glasscock, *War of Copper Kings*, pp. 218–20.

19. *The Miners' Magazine*, April 1900, pp. 39–42; *Engineering and Mining Journal* 68 (29 July 1899): 175 (quote); 79 (8 June 1905): 1097, 1103; second quote is from letter, H. L. Dole to Herbert Knox Smith, 13 May 1901, Records of the Bureau of Corporations, Numeric File: 1903–14, File 4642, Record Group 122, National Archives, Washington, D.C.

20. Lawson, *Frenzied Finance*, pp. 1–48; Nevins, *Study in Power*, 2:343–44; Louis Filler, *Appointment at Armageddon: Muckraking and Progressivism in the American Tradition*, pp. 335–36; Filler, *Crusaders for American Liberalism*, pp. 177–78.

21. Rossiter W. Raymond, "The Law of the Apex," *Engineering and Mining Journal* 38 (2 August 1884): 74–75; (9 August 1884): 89–91; (16 August 1884): 105–6; (20 September 1884): 192–94; (27 September 1884): 212–14; *The Copper Handbook*, 3:111; Richard H. Peterson, *The Bonanaza Kings: The Social Origins and Business Behavior of Western Mining Entrepreneurs*, pp. 53–60.

22. Glasscock, *War of the Copper Kings*, pp. 143–44 (Murray quote); *Engineering and Mining Journal* 55 (28 January 1893): 86; (4 February 1893): 110; 59 (19 January 1895): 61; *Murray v. Heinze*, 17 Mont. 353 (1895).

23. M. G. O'Malley, "Butte Close-ups: Personal Narrative," *The Frontier* 8 (May 1928): 210–11.

24. F. A. Heinze, *The Political Situation in Montana: 1900–1902*, p. 44.

25. Navin, *Copper Mining and Management*, pp. 207–8.

26. Sarah McNelis, *Copper King at War: The Biography of F. Augustus Heinze*, chap. 4–5.

27. *Morse v. Montana Ore Purchasing Co.*, 105 F. 337 (CCD Mont 1900); *Engineering and Mining Journal* 65 (9 April 1898): 441; Robert G. Raymer, *A History of Copper Mining in Montana*, pp. 36–38, 61; McNelis, *Copper King*, pp. 62–63.

28. *Helena Independent*, 23 December 1899; McNelis, *Copper King*, pp. 64–65; Raymer, *History of Copper*, p. 61; George B. Child to John MacGinniss, 10, 19 February 1900; E. L. Whitmore to Child, 31 March 1900; Child to F. A. Heinze, 14 May 1900, Montana Ore Purchasing Co. Records, Montana Historical Society Archives, Helena; Barron, *More They Told Barron*, p. 49; Frank Klepetko to A. S. Bigelow, 29 January 1900, Boston and Montana Consolidated Copper and Silver Mining Co. Records, letter book, Eastern Correspondence, 1897–1902 File, Anaconda Copper Mining Co. Records, Montana Historical Society Archives. See also the correspondence in Eastern Correspondence and General Letter Book, March 1897–March 1898, Records of the Butte and Boston Consolidated Mining Co., Anaconda Copper Mining Co. Records.

29. Christopher P. Connolly, *The Devil Learns to Vote*, pp. 184–90; Daly is quoted in Barron, *More They Told Barron*, p. 53.

30. *Montana Ore Purchasing Co. v. Boston and Montana Co.*, 20 Mont. 528 (1898); there were many subsequent cases; see, for instance, *State v. Montana Ore Purchasing Co.*, 22 Mont. 352 (1899); *Montana Ore Purchasing Co. v. Boston and Montana Co.*, 27 Mont. 536 (1903); Case Files 1559, 1629, 1720, 1756, Montana Supreme Court Records, Montana State Archives, Helena; *Engineering and Mining Journal* 67 (2 September 1898): 329; 68 (30 December 1899): 804; *Anaconda Standard*, 29, 30 December 1899; McNelis, *Copper King*, pp. 56–57; *Montana Ore Purchasing Co. v. Boston and Montana Co.*, 93 F. 274 (CCA, 9th Circuit 1899).

31. *Forrester v. Boston and Montana Co.*, 21 Mont. 544 (1898); Raymer, *History of Copper*, pp. 38–41; Connolly, *Devil Learns to Vote*, pp. 221–22; McNelis, *Copper King*, pp. 41, 66–75.

32. *Butte Miner*, 19 December 1898; 15 April 1899; *State ex. rel. Boston and Montana Co. v. 2nd Judicial District*, 22 Mont. 438 (1899); *Forrester and MacGinniss v. Boston and Montana Co.*, 22 Mont. 430 (1899); 23 Mont. 122 (1899); 24 Mont. 148 (1900); Case Files No. 1385, 1719, Montana Supreme Court Records; *Engineering and Mining Journal* 66 (3 December 1898): 678; (17 December 1898): 737–38; (24 December 1898): 767; 67 (15 April 1899): 450.

33. McNelis, *Copper King*, p. 73.

34. *Butte and Boston Co. v. Montana Ore Purchasing Co.*, 24 Mont. 125 (1900); 25 Mont. 41 (1901); *Talbot v. Heinze*, 25 Mont. 4 (1901); Case File 1460, Montana Supreme Court Records; Raymer, *History of Copper*, pp. 54–55.

35. *State* ex. rel. *Anaconda Copper Mining Co.* v. *2nd Judicial District*, 25 Mont. 504 (1901); *Anaconda Standard*, 21, 22, 23 December 1899; *Engineering and Mining Journal* 79 (2 February 1905): 222–24; McNelis, *Copper King*, pp. 54–56.

36. Marcus Daly to John Durston, 19 January 1900, Daly Papers, Montana Historical Society Archives.

37. Lloyd is quoted in Collier and Horowitz, *The Rockefellers*, p. 29; *Mining and Scientific Press* 81 (20 October 1900): 463.

38. Byron E. Cooney, "Heinze's Cabinet," *Baker Fallon County Times*, 2 January 1928; White Sulphur Springs *Rocky Mountain Husbandman*, 8 September 1938.

39. See n. 38 above; see also Writers' Program of the Work Projects Administration in the State of Montana, *Copper Camp*, p. 43; for an example of the Heinze approach, see William Bartle to F. A. Heinze, 16 June 1900, Montana Ore Purchasing Co. Records, Montana Historical Society Archives.

40. *Butte Miner*, 12 June and 4 July 1900; *Anaconda Standard*, 21 June 1900; W. A. Clark to S. T. Hauser, 23 June 1900, Hauser Papers, box 26, Montana Historical Society Archives; "Montana," *Appleton's Annual Cyclopedia . . . 1900*, pp. 393–94; Forrest L. Foor, "The Senatorial Aspirations of William A. Clark, 1898–1901," (Ph.D. diss., University of California, Berkeley, 1941), pp. 200–15.

41. *The Miners' Magazine*, July 1900, pp. 1–2 (quote); September 1900, pp. 11–12; *Butte Miner*, 14 June 1900.

42. J. H. Calderhead to F. A. Heinze, 13 July 1900; John Bloor to John MacGinniss, 4, 8 August 1900, Montana Ore Purchasing Co. Records; *Butte Miner*, 15 August 1900; Foor, "Senatorial Aspirations," p. 216.

43. *Anaconda Standard*, 6 September 1900; Foor, "Senatorial Aspirations," p. 217; on the Sanders–Carter split, see *Helena Evening Herald*, 12 December 1900; and "An Open Letter to Hon. Wilbur F. Sanders from Thomas H. Carter," December 18, 1900, Thomas H. Carter Papers, box 6, Manuscripts Div., Library of Congress, Washington, D.C.

44. *Butte Miner*, 20, 21, 22, 23 September 1900; Thomas A. Clinch, *Urban Populism and Free Silver in Montana*, pp. 162–64; *Appleton's Annual Cyclopedia . . . 1900*, pp. 393–94; notes of two telephone conversations between W. A. Clark and S. T. Hauser, 19 September 1900, Hauser Papers, box 26; Clark quote is in *New York Herald*, 23 September 1900. He later denied having made it.

45. *Butte Miner*, 2 October 1900; *Anaconda Standard*, 3 October 1900; Clinch, *Urban Populism*, p. 164; *Appleton's Annual Cyclopedia . . . 1900*, p. 394.

46. Clinch, *Urban Populism*, p. 165; *Butte Miner*, 26 October 1900; Foor, "Senatorial Aspirations," chap. 5; *Hamilton Western News*, 9 January 1901. The late Robert Warden, son of O. S. Warden, described to me on various occasions the Clark purchase of the *Great Falls Tribune*.

47. Connolly, *Devil Learns to Vote*, p. 237; McNelis, *Copper King*, p. 95.

48. *Butte Miner*, 26, 27 October and 6 November 1900; *Helena Independent*, 11 October 1900; *Butte Reveille*, 2, 9, 23, 30 October and 3 November 1900.

49. See the collection of Heinze antitrust orations, *The Political Situation in*

Montana, quotes from pp. 10, 47, 61; see also, P. A. O'Farrell, *Butte: Its Copper Mines and Copper Kings*, pp. 61–63; Connolly, *Devil Learns to Vote*, p. 237.

50. Foor, "Senatorial Aspirations," pp. 244–48; *Butte Miner*, 26 October 1900; *The Missoulian*, 3 November 1900.

51. *Anaconda Standard*, 29, 30, 31 October and 4, 5, 7, 8 November 1900; Foor, "Senatorial Aspirations," pp. 263–66.

52. *Butte Reveille*, 13 November 1900; *Butte Miner*, 7 November 1900; Joseph Walker to T. W. Buzzo, 9 November 1900, Alice Gold and Silver Mining Co. Records, box 4, Montana Historical Society Archives; Ellis Waldron and Paul B. Wilson, *Atlas of Montana Elections: 1889–1976*, pp. 26–28.

53. *New York Times*, 13 November 1900, p. 2; *Anaconda Standard*, 13, 16 November 1900; *Butte Miner*, 13 November 1900; Scallon's reminiscences are from an interview by K. Ross Toole in "Marcus Daly," pp. 190–91; ? to M. Donahoe, 17 October 1899, Anaconda Copper Mining Co. Records, box 410.

54. *Butte Miner*, 13 November 1900.

8. The Battle for Butte: 1901–6

1. *House Journal of the Seventh Session of the Legislative Assembly of the State of Montana . . . 1901*, pp. 27–30; *Helena Independent*, 17 January 1901; *Billings Gazette*, 17 January 1901; Forrest L. Foor, "The Senatorial Aspirations of William A. Clark, 1898–1901: A Study in Montana Politics" (Ph.D. dissertation, University of California, Berkeley, 1941), chap. 15.

2. *New York Times*, 17 January 1901; *Helena Independent*, 17 January 1901.

3. *Butte Reveille*, 8 January 1901; Foor, "Senatorial Aspirations," pp. 277–9.

4. *Butte Reveille*, 2, 16 April 1901; *Helena Press*, 13 September, 11, 18 October 1902; "Senator Clark and the Amalgamated Copper Trust," *The Miners' Magazine*, June 1901, pp. 6–8.

5. Foor, "Senatorial Aspirations," pp. 279–83; C. P. Connolly, "Big Business and the Bench," *Everybody's Magazine*, February 1912, pp. 154–55.

6. Joseph K. Howard, *Montana: High, Wide, and Handsome*, p. 69.

7. Lawson is quoted in "The Story of Heinze, A Tale of Copper—and Brass," *Current Literature*, January 1908, p. 36; see also, "Heinze, the Copper King," *American Monthly Review of Reviews*, January 1904, pp. 99–100.

8. John S. M. Neill to S. T. Hauser, 22 April 1901, Hauser Papers, box 27, Montana Historical Society Archives, Helena; *Engineering and Mining Journal* 66 (8 October 1898): 437; 67 (13 May 1899): 569; Robert G. Raymer, *A History of Copper Mining in Montana*, p. 65.

9. W. A. Clark to S. T. Hauser, 14 June 1902; H. H. Rogers to Hauser (quote), 24 September 1902, Hauser Papers, box 27; *New York Times*, 25 September 1902, p. 1; *Helena Press*, 4 October 1902.

10. *Anaconda Standard*, 6 October 1902; *Butte Reveille*, 25 October 1902.

11. The poem is quoted in Warren G. Davenport, *Butte and Montana beneath the X-Ray*, p. 375; *New York Times*, 27 September 1902, p. 14; 30 October 1902, p. 2; *Great Falls Tribune*, 3 November 1902; *Butte Miner*, 3, 4 November 1902;

C. B. Nolan to William Scallon, 9 September 1902; J. G. Morony to Nolan, 12 September 1902, Nolan Papers, Montana Historical Society Archives; *Helena Independent*, 21 October 1902.

12. *Butte Tribune-Review*, 15, 17 October and 8 November 1902; *Butte Reveille*, 7 November 1902; *New York Times*, 2 November 1902, p. 15; *Butte Labor World*, 7 November 1902; *Butte Inter Mountain*, 5, 6 November 1902; *Great Falls Tribune*, 5 November 1902; *Butte Miner*, 7 November 1902; Davenport, *Butte and Montana*, p. 375; Ellis Waldron and Paul B. Wilson, *Atlas of Montana Elections: 1889–1976*, pp. 29–30; for a Republican vantage on the campaign, see the Joseph M. Dixon Papers, box 2, University of Montana Archives, Missoula.

13. *Anaconda Standard*, 28 May 1903; *White Sulphur Springs Rocky Mountain Husbandman*, 8 September 1938; Isaac F. Marcosson, *Anaconda*, pp. 106–8.

14. *The Copper Handbook*, 2:350, 392–93; William B. Gates, Jr., *Michigan Copper and Boston Dollars*, pp. 85–89; *Butte Tribune-Review*, 21 December 1901.

15. Marcosson, *Anaconda*, pp. 77–78; Thomas C. Satterthwaite, "Cornelius Francis Kelley: The Rise of an Industrial Statesman" (M.A. thesis, Montana State University, 1971), pp. 1–66, 129–30.

16. Marcosson, *Anaconda*, p. 76; Jerre C. Murphy, *The Comical History of Montana*, pp. 55–60; *Butte Reveille*, 15 February 1904.

17. B. C. Forbes, *Men Who Are Making the West*, pp. 241–44; Marcosson, *Anaconda*, pp. 99–101; Murphy, *Comical History*, pp. 64–69.

18. Murphy, *Comical History*, pp. 64–65; James A. Close, "Some Phases of the History of the Anaconda Copper Mining Company" (Ph.D. diss., University of Michigan, 1945), pp. 203–6.

19. *Helena Independent*, 21 October 1902; *Butte Reveille*, 12 February 1904; Close, "Some Phases," p. 205.

20. Clarence W. Barron, *More They Told Barron*, Arthur Pound and Samuel T. Moore, eds., pp. 51–52; *Butte American Labor Union Journal*, 29 October 1903; Western Federation of Miners, *Official Proceedings of the Eleventh Annual Convention* (Denver: Western Newspaper Union, 1903), copy in Western Federation of Miners Records, Western History Collections, University of Colorado, Boulder.

21. *Engineering and Mining Journal* 71 (9 February 1901): 171, 195; Clark C. Spence, *Mining Engineers and the American West*, pp. 209, 228–29; C. R. Hillyer to the Commissioner of Corporations, 15 June 1904, Records of the Bureau of Corporations, Numeric File: 1903–14, File 679, Record Group 122, National Archives, Washington, D.C.

22. *Montana Ore Purchasing Co.* v. *Boston and Montana Co.*, 27 Mont. 288 (1902); 27 Mont. 410 (1903); 27 Mont. 431 (1903); 27 Mont. 536 (1903); 47 LEd. 626, 634 (1903); Files 1559, 1629, 1720, 1756, Montana Supreme Court Records, Montana State Archives, Helena.

23. *Heinze* v. *Butte and Boston Co.*, 107 F. 165 (1901); 126 F. 1 (1903); 129 F. 337 (1904).

24. *Parrot Silver and Copper Co.* v. *Heinze*, 24 Mont. 485 (1900); 25 Mont. 139 (1901); *Hickey* v. *Parrot Silver and Copper Co.*, 25 Mont. 164 (1901); *State ex rel.*

Heinze v. *2nd Judicial District,* 28 Mont. 227 (1903); *State* ex rel. *Parrot* v. *2nd Judicial District,* 28 Mont. 528 (1903); File 1569, Montana Supreme Court Records.

25. P. A. O'Farrell, *Butte: Its Copper Mines and Copper Kings,* pp. 44–45; Frank Klepetko to G. M. Hyams, 2, 4 January, 14 March 1901, Records of the Boston and Montana Consolidated Copper and Silver Co., Eastern Correspondence: 1897–1902 letter book, Anaconda Copper Mining Co. Records, Montana Historical Society Archives; *Engineering and Mining Journal* 62 (17 October 1896): 374; Raymer, *History of Copper,* pp. 55–57; *Heinze* v. *Kleinschmidt,* 25 Mont. 89 (1901); *Butte Miner,* 21 April 1905; Sarah McNelis, *Copper King at War: The Biography of F. Augustus Heinze,* pp. 59–60.

26. Raymer, *History of Copper,* p. 57; *Heinze* v. *Boston and Montana Co.,* 26 Mont. 265 (1902); *State* ex rel. *Finlen* v. *2nd Judicial District,* 26 Mont. 372 (1902); *State* ex rel. *Heinze* v. *2nd Judicial District,* 26 Mont. 416 (1902); *Finlen* v. *Heinze,* 27 Mont. 107 (1902); 28 Mont. 549 (1903) (quote).

27. See the depositions of E. L. Waters, 18 July 1901, and J. W. Waters, 6 August 1901, File 7980, Montana Supreme Court Records; Christopher P. Connolly, *The Devil Learns to Vote: The Story of Montana,* pp. 244–49.

28. The "dearie letters" are reproduced in Exhibits C and D, File 7980, Montana Supreme Court Records; and in *Finlen* v. *Heinze,* 28 Mont. 549 (1903); Connolly, *Devil Learns to Vote,* pp. 244–49; K. Ross Toole, *Montana: An Uncommon Land,* pp. 202–4.

29. See the testimony of Harney, Brackett, and Clark reproduced in *Butte Reveille,* 18, 20 August 1901, 25, 28 October 1902, and 20 March 1903; Connolly, *Devil Learns to Vote,* pp. 252–60; *Butte Miner,* 16 January 1904.

30. *Butte Reveille,* 21 November 1902; 2, 16 January and 10 February 1903; *Finlen* v. *Heinze,* 28 Mont. 549 (1903); Connolly, *Devil Learns to Vote,* pp. 260–61; Frank B. Linderman, *Montana Adventure,* H. G. Merriam, ed., pp. 126–31.

31. Reno H. Sales, *Underground Warfare at Butte,* pp. 9–30; Connolly, *Devil Learns to Vote,* pp. 271–72; *Butte Reveille,* 1 January 1904.

32. *MacGinniss* v. *Boston and Montana Co.,* 29 Mont. 428 (1904); *Lamm* et al. v. *Parrot Silver and Copper Co.* et al., 29 Mont. 464 (1904); *Forrester and MacGinniss* v. *Boston and Montana Co.,* 29 Mont. 397 (1904); *MacGinniss* v. *Boston and Montana Co.,* 119 F. 96 (CCA, 9th Circuit 1902); File 2001, Montana Supreme Court Records.

33. William Scallon to C. B. Nolan, 17 November 1902; Nolan to Scallon, 22 November 1902, Nolan Papers, Montana Historical Society Archives; *Anaconda Standard,* 26 August 1903; Connolly, *Devil Learns to Vote,* pp. 283–84.

34. *Butte Inter Mountain,* 22 October 1903; *New York Times,* 23 October 1903, p. 11.

35. *San Francisco Examiner,* 23 October 1903, p. 1; 24 October 1903, p. 4; *New York Times,* 24 October 1903, p. 13; *Engineering and Mining Journal* 76 (31 October 1903): 648.

36. *Butte Reveille,* 23, 28 October 1903; *Butte Inter Mountain,* 23 October 1903; McNelis, *Copper King,* pp. 77–79.

37. *Engineering and Mining Journal* 76 (31 October 1903): 648; *San Francisco Examiner*, 23 October 1903, p. 1, 24 October 1903, p. 4, 25 October 1903, p. 18, 26 October 1903, p. 1, 27 October 1903, p. 1 (quote); *Portland Morning Oregonian*, 23 October 1903, p. 1, 24 October 1903, pp. 2, 8, 26 October 1903, p. 2; *Denver Post*, 24 October 1903, pp. 1, 4 (quote); *Chicago Daily Tribune*, 23 October 1903, p. 1.

38. *New York Times*, 25 October 1903, p. 8; *Butte Inter Mountain*, 24, 25 October 1903; *Butte Miner*, 24, 25 October 1903; Christopher P. Connolly, "The Fight for the Minnie Healy," *McClure's*, July 1907, pp. 329–30.

39. Compare the accounts of Heinze's speech in *Butte Reveille*, 28 October 1903; and Connolly, "Fight for Minnie Healy," pp. 330–31; *Anaconda Standard*, 27 October 1903; *New York Times*, 27 October 1903, p. 1.

40. *Helena Press*, 31 October, 7 November 1903; *Butte Reveille*, 30 October, 4 November 1903; *Butte Inter Mountain*, 31 October 1903; *Anaconda Standard*, 1 November 1903; R. A. O'Hara to Joseph M. Dixon, 10 November 1903, Dixon Papers, box 3.

41. *New York Times*, 29 October 1903, p. 1; *Anaconda Standard*, 2 November 1903; *Butte Miner*, 6 December 1903.

42. E. A. Winstanley to Joseph M. Dixon, 5 November 1903; W. E. Lindenborn to Dixon, 13 November 1903; Dixon to D. B. Price, 28 November 1903, Dixon Papers, box 3; *Anaconda Standard*, 1, 4 (quote), 11 November 1903; *Butte Reveille*, 20 November 1903; *Helena Press*, 21 November 1903; *Miles City Independent*, 12 November 1903 (quote); *Glendive Independent*, 14 November 1903 (quote); *Lewistown Fergus County News*, 4 November 1903; *Fort Benton River Press*, 4 November 1903; see the petitions in Montana Governors' Papers, Legislative Series, box 2, Montana State Archives.

43. "Litigation in Butte, Montana," *Mining and Scientific Press* 87 (31 October 1903): 282; "Industrial War in Montana," *The Outlook*, 5 December 1903, pp. 762–63; *Butte American Labor Union Journal*, 12 November 1903; "Corporations and Montana Justice," *Literary Digest*, 21 November 1903, pp. 692–93 (*Journal of Commerce* quote); "Mining Troubles in Montana," ibid., 14 November 1903, p. 655; for a biased further sampling of nationwide reactions, see *Butte Reveille*, 27 November 1903.

44. *Helena Independent*, 8 December 1903; *Butte Miner*, 8 December 1903; *Helena Press*, 12, 19 December 1903; *Butte Reveille*, 4, 11, 18 December 1903; *Anaconda Standard*, 8 December 1903.

45. *Anaconda Standard*, 11 December 1903; *House Journal of the Second Extraordinary Session of the Eighth Legislative Assembly . . . 1903*, pp. 10–13; *Laws and Resolutions of the State of Montana, Passed at the Second Extraordinary Session of the Eighth Legislative Assembly . . . 1903* (Helena: State Publishing Co., 1903), pp. 8–10; Linderman, *Montana Adventure*, pp. 131–32; Neil J. Lynch, *Montana's Legislature through the Years*, pp. 40–41; interview with Neil J. Lynch, 28 June 1978.

46. Sales, *Underground Warfare*, pp. 31–34.

47. *U.S.* ex rel. *Montana Ore Purchasing Co.* v. *Circuit Court, Ninth Circuit, District of Montana*, 126 F. 169 (1903); *Montana Ore Purchasing Co.* v. *Butte and*

Boston Co., 125 F. 1003 (1903); 126 F. 168 (1903); *U.S.* ex rel. *Johnstown Mining Co.* v. *Circuit Court, Ninth Circuit, District of Montana*, 125 F. 1003 (1903); Sales, *Underground Warfare*, pp. 32–37; Connolly, *Devil Learns to Vote*, pp. 275–77.

48. *In re* Heinze, 127 F. 96 (1904); Sales, *Underground Warfare*, pp. 37–39; Connolly, *Devil Learns to Vote*, pp. 277–78.

49. *Butte Miner*, 2, 3, 5 January 1904.

50. *Butte Reveille*, 1, 8 January, 28 March 1904; Connolly, *Devil Learns to Vote*, pp. 277–82; Sales, *Underground Warfare*, pp. 40–45, 55–74; Ira B. Joralemon, *Copper*, pp. 102–14.

51. *Heinze* v. *Butte and Boston Co.*, 129 F. 274 (1904); *Butte and Boston Co.* v. *Montana Ore Purchasing Co.*, 158 F. 131 (1907); *Anaconda Standard*, 31 March 1904 (Beatty quote); Raymer, *History of Copper*, pp. 61–62.

52. "The Battle for Copper," *Mining and Scientific Press* 77 (6 February 1904): 91; *Engineering and Mining Journal* 77 (4 February 1904): 217; *Butte Reveille*, 21 April 1905; *Butte Miner*, 21 April 1905; *Finlen* v. *Heinze*, 27 Mont. 107 (1903); 29 Mont. 573 (1904); *Forrester and MacGinniss* v. *Boston and Montana Co.*, 29 Mont. 397 (1904); *MacGinniss* v. *Boston and Montana Co.*, 29 Mont. 428 (1904); *Lamm et al.* v. *Parrot Silver and Copper Co.*, 29 Mont. 464 (1904); File 2001, Montana Supreme Court Records.

53. C. R. Hillyer to the Commissioner of Corporations, 15 June 1904, Records of the Bureau of Corporations, Numeric File: 1903–14, File 679, Record Group 122, National Archives.

54. Barron, *More They Told Barron*, pp. 54–56, 82; Lewis Leary, ed., *Mark Twain's Correspondence with Henry Huttleston Rogers*, pp. v–vi, 555–57.

55. Hillyer to Commissioner of Corporations; *Helena Montana Lookout*, 8 August 1908; McNelis, *Copper King*, pp. 116–19.

56. Linderman, *Montana Adventure*, pp. 132–33; Dixon's remark is based on an interview and is discussed in William S. Youngman, Jr., "The Anaconda Copper Mining Company and Some Phases of Its Influence in the Politics of the State of Montana, 1880–1929" (history thesis, Harvard University, 1929), p. 48.

57. Waldron and Wilson, *Atlas*, pp. 31–34; *Butte Inter Mountain*, 9 November 1904; *Butte Reveille*, 7, 17 October, 18 November 1904; *Helena Montana Weekly Record*, 27 October and 10, 17 November 1904.

58. Ryan is quoted in Forbes, *Men Who Are Making the West*, pp. 245–46; Marcosson, *Anaconda*, p. 132; McNelis, *Copper King*, pp. 120–38.

59. *Engineering and Mining Journal* 81 (17 February 1906): 350; *New York Times*, 25 February 1906, p. 20; 28 February 1906, p. 10; *Anaconda Standard*, 14, 15 February 1906; *Butte Miner*, 14, 15 February 1906.

60. McNelis, *Copper King*, pp. 139–50; Marcosson, *Anaconda*, pp. 132–33; *Engineering and Mining Journal* 81 (24 February 1906): 391, (3 March 1906): 438; *Butte Reveille*, 16 February 1906; *Anaconda Standard*, 18 February 1906; Raymer, *History of Copper*, pp. 73–75; see typescript on the Ohio Copper Co., dated November 1906, in Montana Ore Purchasing Co. Records, Montana Historical Society Archives.

61. Heinze is quoted in McNelis, *Copper King*, p. 69; Howard, *Montana*, pp. 83–84.

62. *Engineering and Mining Journal* 98 (14 November 1914): 880–81; Spence, *Mining Engineers*, pp. 228–29; T. A. Rickard, "David W. Brunton: Consulting Engineer," *Mining and Scientific Press* 122 (28 May 1921): 750–51; Thomas R. Navin, *Copper Mining and Management*, pp. 285–96.

63. Wilbur F. Sanders to James Fergus, 9 February 1902, Sanders Papers, Montana Historical Society Archives; Gertrude Atherton, *Perch of the Devil*, p. 155.

64. "The Amalgamated and Mr. Heinze," *Mining and Scientific Press* 92 (17 February 1909): 99; *Engineering and Mining Journal* 98 (14 November 1914): 880–81; *The Autobiography of John Hays Hammond*, 2 vols., 2:524; *The Nation*, 22 February 1906, p. 149.

65. Navin, *Copper Mining and Management*, p. 232.

9. DENOUEMENT: THE TIME OF TRANSITION

1. Richard B. Roeder, "Montana in the Early Years of the Progressive Period" (Ph.D. diss., University of Pennsylvania, 1972), pp. 127–79; Byron E. Cooney, "Heinze's Cabinet," *Baker Fallon County Times*, 2 January 1928; *Butte Inter Mountain*, 7 November 1906; *Butte Evening News*, 26 October 1906.

2. Sarah McNelis, *Copper King at War: The Biography of F. Augustus Heinze*, pp. 176–79.

3. Ibid., pp. 150–53; Frederick Lewis Allen, *The Lords of Creation*, Quadrangle ed., pp. 116–17; "The Story of Morse," *Current Literature*, February 1910, pp. 151–53.

4. *The Copper Handbook*, 8:1354–56.

5. Allen, *Lords of Creation*, pp. 118–20; McNelis, *Copper King*, pp. 156–67.

6. See n. 5 above; see also "A Review of the World," *Current Literature*, December 1907, pp. 585–90; *New York Times*, 5 November 1914, p. 11.

7. Allen, *Lords of Creation*, pp. 112–43; "Review of the World," *Current Literature*, p. 585.

8. "LaFollette's Theory of the Panic," *Literary Digest*, 4 April 1908, p. 470; "Story of Heinze," *Current Literature*, p. 35; McNelis, *Copper King*, pp. 154–66.

9. McNelis, *Copper King*, pp. 167–75, 179–82; *New York Times*, 5 November 1914, p. 11; *Butte Daily Post*, 5 November 1914.

10. McNelis, *Copper King*, pp. 167–75; *Great Falls Tribune*, 5 November 1914; *New York Times*, 19 June 1914, p. 22; 5 October 1914, p. 11.

11. McNelis, *Copper King*, pp. 182–85; *New York Times*, 5 November 1914, p. 11; 8 November 1914, p. 3; *Great Falls Tribune*, 5 November 1914; *Butte Miner*, 5, 8 November 1914; *Anaconda Standard*, 5 November 1914; *Butte Daily Post*, 5 November 1914; *Engineering and Mining Journal* 98 (14 November 1914): 880–81.

12. The quote is from U.S., Congress, Senate, 59th Cong., 2d Sess., 1907,

41, pt. 4:3726, *Congressional Record*, 41:3726; Clayton Farrington, "The Political Life of William Andrews Clark" (M.A. thesis, University of Montana, 1942), pp. 265–313; Mary M. Farrell, "William Andrews Clark" (M.A. thesis, University of Washington, 1933), chap. 5; Paul C. Phillips, "William Andrews Clark," *Dictionary of American Biography*, Allen Johnson and Dumas Malone, eds., 20 vols., 4:145.

13. On the political rumors of 1910, see George Scharsburg to Thomas H. Carter, 6, 29, 30 April, 30 May, and 20 June 1910, Thomas H. Carter Papers, box 10, Manuscripts Division, Library of Congress, Washington, D.C.; on the Columbia Gardens, Frank Quinn, *Memories of Columbia Gardens; Anaconda Standard*, 13 December 1928.

14. W. A. Clark to Samuel T. Hauser, 13 May 1910, Hauser Papers, box 30, Montana Historical Society Archives, Helena; *Report of the Anaconda Copper Mining Company for the Year Ending December 31, 1910.*

15. *New York Times*, 3 March 1925, pp. 1, 7; F. W. Ellis, "The World's Copper King," *Idaho Magazine*, January 1904, pp. 28–32; *Butte Miner*, 3 March 1925.

16. French Strother, "Swinging the March of Empire Southwestward," *World's Work*, January 1906, pp. 7072–81; Glenn Chesney Quiett, *They Built the West: An Epic of Rails and Cities*, pp. 295–97; *Butte Miner*, 7 May 1905.

17. *Butte Miner*, 13 July 1904; *Anaconda Standard*, 13 July 1904; William D. Mangam, *The Clarks of Montana*, pp. 71–76, 82–100. Mangam's little book is an exposé of the Clarks and must thus be used with caution. It seems, however, to be generally accurate.

18. *Illustrated Handbook of the W. A. Clark Collection*, p. 15; *New York Times*, 3 March 1925, pp. 1, 7; *Great Falls Tribune*, 22 January 1928; "Selling Art to Our Millionaires," *Literary Digest*, 23 November 1912, pp. 960–61; James High, "William Andrews Clark, Westerner: An Interpretive Vignette," *Arizona and the West* 2 (Autumn 1960): 260–64; Theodore Roosevelt to Clark, 27 January, 5 February 1906, Roosevelt Papers, Manuscripts Division, Library of Congress.

19. Wallace Irwin, "Senator Copper's House," *New York Times Book Review*, 1 January 1939, p. 15; *New York Times*, 3 March 1925, pp. 1, 7; the quote is from Robert Littell, "The House That Clark Built," *New Republic*, 30 March 1927, pp. 171–72.

20. Mark Twain, "Senator Clark of Montana" (28 January 1907), in *Mark Twain in Eruption*, Bernard DeVoto, ed., pp. 70–73.

21. *New York Times*, 3 March 1925, pp. 1, 7; 7 March 1925, p. 13 (quote); 15 March 1925, sec. 4, p. 3; *Butte Miner*, 3, 7 March 1925; *Anaconda Standard*, 3 March 1925.

22. The Clark will and estate papers are in File 7594, Silver Bow County Courthouse, Butte; the will is reproduced in *Anaconda Standard*, 7 April 1925; *New York Times*, 25 March 1925, p. 1; Mangam, *The Clarks*, pp. 76–80; Neill's suggestion is in a letter of 8 April 1899 to Clark, copy in Hauser Papers, box 26; on the sale of the remaining Clark properties, see *Anaconda Standard*, 22, 23 August 1928.

23. "The Career of H. H. Rogers," *The Outlook*, 29 May 1909, pp. 257–58.

24. Walter H. Weed, *Geology and Ore Deposits of the Butte District, Montana*, p. 22; Helen F. Sanders, *A History of Montana*, 3 vols., 1:735–37; changing county population profiles of Montana are handily profiled in Ellis Waldron and Paul B. Wilson, *Atlas of Montana Elections*, p. 7.

25. Sanders, *History of Montana*, 1:735–77; Al Darr in *Butte Montana Standard*, 10 June 1973; Isaac F. Marcosson, *Anaconda*, pp. 81–82; Muriel S. Wolle, *Montana Pay Dirt: A Guide to the Mining Camps of the Treasure State*, p. 171.

26. Weed, *Geology and Ore Deposits*, p. 22; Ira B. Joralemon, *Copper*, chap. 8; *The Copper Handbook*, 7:1185; F. Ernest Richter, "The Copper Mining Industry in the United States: 1845–1925," *Quarterly Journal of Economics*, 41 (February 1927): 272–77.

27. "The History of the Flotation Process," *The Mining Magazine* 1 (September 1909): 61–64.

28. *Copper Handbook*, 7:1185; *Historical Statistics of the United States*, 2 vols., 1:583–84, 602; "The Price of Copper," *Mining and Scientific Press*, 92 (27 January 1906): 50; Charles F. Speare, "The Story of Copper," *American Monthly Review of Reviews*, November 1906, pp. 561–74.

29. F. Ernest Richter, "The Amalgamated Copper Company: A Closed Chapter in Corporate Finance," *Quarterly Journal of Economics* 30 (February 1916): 405–6; *The Nation*, 22 February 1906, p. 149; Thomas R. Navin, *Copper Mining and Management* pp. 117–21, 207.

30. Marcosson, *Anaconda*, pp. 99–102.

31. Jerre C. Murphy, *The Comical History of Montana*, pp. 201–21; *Engineering and Mining Journal*, 76 (24 December 1903): 926–27; Donald MacMillan, "A History of the Struggle to Abate Air Pollution from the Copper Smelters of the Far West: 1885–1933" (Ph.D. diss., University of Montana, 1973), pp. 109–60.

32. Samuel T. Hauser to Clark, Dodge & Co., 16 April 1901; Hauser to J. S. M. Neill, 2 July 1910, Hauser Papers, box 33; M. G. Gerry to Hauser, 25 February 1905, ibid., box 28; John D. Ryan to Hauser, 23 August 1908; W. A. Clark to Hauser, 10 September 1909, ibid., box 29; Clark to Hauser, 7 August 1910; Clark to Jeremiah Collins, 17 November 1910; Clark to Hauser, 18 January 1911; Neill to Hauser, 4 March 1911, ibid., box 30; see also the George G. E. Neill Papers, Montana Historical Society Archives. Alan S. Newell, "A Victim of Monopoly: Samuel T. Hauser and Hydroelectric Development on the Missouri River, 1898–1912" (M.A. thesis, University of Montana, 1979), pp. 113–23; and *The Montana Power Company: Reclassification of Electric Plant* (Butte: n.p., 1940), pp. 1–92, copy at the company's head offices, Butte.

33. Douglas F. Leighton, "The Corporate History of the Montana Power Company: 1882–1913" (M.A. thesis, University of Montana, 1951), chaps. 1, 3, 5; *Anaconda Standard*, 14 December 1913; depositions of C. F. Kelley and W. D. Thornton before the Public Service Commission, 19 May 1943, Records of the Montana Department of Public Service Regulation, Record Series 107, Montana State Archives, Helena; *Great Falls Tribune*, 17 May 1981.

34. "Report of Lecture by John D. Ryan . . . 42 Broadway, New York," 14 March 1912, copy in Records of the Department of Public Service Regulation,

Record Series 107; Marcosson, *Anaconda*, pp. 144–47; "Anaconda Copper," *Fortune*, December 1936, pp. 91–92; Walter Aikens, "Electric Power for Montana Mines, Mills and Smelters," *Mining and Engineering World* 43 (12 July 1915): 91–96.

35. *Report of the Anaconda Copper Mining Company . . . 1910*, n.p.; Robert G. Raymer, *Montana: The Land and the People*, 3 vols., 1:513–14; Richter, "Amalgamated Copper," pp. 396–99; Marcosson, *Anaconda*, pp. 138–40; *Anaconda Standard*, 24 March 1910.

36. Richter, "Amalgamated Copper," pp. 399–400, 404–5; "Anaconda Copper," *Fortune*, p. 93; Marcosson, *Anaconda*, pp. 143–44; C. L. Sonnichsen, *Colonel Greene and the Copper Skyrocket*, pp. 215–19.

37. Richter, "Amalgamated Copper," pp. 387, 402–6; *Engineering and Mining Journal* 99 (3 April 1915): 625–26; *Mining and Engineering World* 43 (10 July 1915): 90; Joralemon, *Copper*, pp. 167–69.

38. *The New Anaconda*, pamphlet, pp. 1–31; Anaconda Copper Mining Co., *Assessment of Property in Montana for the Years 1915–16*, pamphlet; "Anaconda Copper," *Fortune*, December 1936, pp. 91–93; Richter, "Amalgamated Copper," pp. 404–6; for a valuable overview of the corporate profile of Butte following consolidation, see Walter H. Weed, *The Mines Handbook: An Enlargement of the Copper Handbook*, pp. 977–1021.

39. Richard H. Peterson, *The Bonanza Kings: The Social Origins and Business Behavior of Western Mining Entrepreneurs*, pp. 68, 75–83.

40. Norma Smith, "The Rise and Fall of the Butte Miners' Union, 1878–1914" (M.A. thesis, Montana State University, 1961), pp. 32–36; Vernon H. Jensen, *Heritage of Conflict: Labor Relations in the Nonferrous Metals Industry Up to 1930*, pp. 291–300; Elizabeth Ann Jameson, *Guide to the Archives, Western Federation of Miners and International Union of Mine, Mill and Smelter Workers* (1969), pp. 1–4, ms. in Western Federation of Miners Papers, Western History Collections, University of Colorado, Boulder; *Official Proceedings of the Fourteenth Annual Convention, Western Federation of Miners, 1906* (Denver: Reed Publishing Co., 1906), pp. 180–84, copy in Western Federation of Miners Papers; James Murphy to Charles Moyer, 12 September 1904, ibid., Executive Board Minutes: June 1902–July 1907, pp. 183–85; "The Western Labor Union," *The Miners' Magazine*, January 1900, pp. 24–26; John Stahlberg, "Butte," *Rocky Mountain Cities*, R. B. West, Jr., ed., p. 252; for an interesting glimpse into the Socialists, see Percival J. Cooney to H. L. Duncan, n.d., Montana Socialist Party Papers, Montana Historical Society Archives.

41. Jensen, *Heritage of Conflict*, pp. 302–6; Smith, "Rise and Fall," pp. 41–43; Paul F. Brissenden, "The Butte Miners and the Rustling Card," *American Economic Review* 10 (December 1920): 755–75.

42. Michael P. Malone and Richard B. Roeder, *Montana: A History of Two Centuries*, pp. 205–15; Arnon Gutfeld, *Montana's Agony: Years of War and Hysteria, 1917–1921*, pp. 14–36; K. Ross Toole, *Twentieth-Century Montana*, chap. 5. The soon-to-be-published research of Professor Jerry Calvert of Montana State University will tell us much about the rise of socialism in Montana.

43. Murphy, *Comical History*, pp. 48–49; F. B. Maikland to Senator T. J.

Walsh, 14 November 1912, Walsh Papers, box 363, Manuscripts Division, Library of Congress.

44. Roeder, "Montana in the Early Years"; Richard B. Roeder, "Montana Progressivism: Sound and Fury and One Small Tax Reform," *Montana: The Magazine of Western History* 20 (October 1970): 18–26.

45. Richard T. Ruetten, "Anaconda Journalism: The End of an Era," *Journalism Quarterly* 37 (Winter 1960): 3–12, 104.

46. Arthur Fisher, "Montana: The Land of the Copper Collar," *The Nation*, 26 September 1922, p. 290.

EPILOGUE: THE LEGACY

1. On the company's political role during these years, see Michael P. Malone and Richard B. Roeder, *Montana: A History of Two Centuries*, chap. 11, 15; K. Ross Toole, *Twentieth-Century Montana*, chaps. 6–11; Jules A. Karlin, *Joseph M. Dixon of Montana*, 2 vols.; J. Leonard Bates, "Senator Walsh of Montana, 1918–1924: A Liberal under Pressure" (Ph.D. diss., University of North Carolina, 1952); and Richard T. Ruetten, "Burton K. Wheeler, 1905–1925: An Independent Liberal under Fire" (M.A. thesis, University of Oregon, 1957).

2. Oswald Garrison Villard, "Montana and 'the Company,'" *The Nation*, 9 July 1930, p. 39; DeVoto is quoted in A. G. Mezerik, *The Revolt of the South and the West*, pp. 53–54; John Gunther, *Inside U.S.A.*, p. 155.

3. I have elaborated on this theme in "Montana as a Corporate Bailiwick: An Image in History," in M. P. Malone and P. J. Powell, *Montana: Past and Present*, pp. 55–76.

4. "Anaconda Copper," *Fortune*, December 1936, p. 83; and "Anaconda II," ibid., January 1937, p. 71; Isaac F. Marcosson, *Anaconda*, chaps. 8–9; Thomas R. Navin, *Copper Mining and Management*, pp. 211–14; *Billings Gazette*, 20, 21 April 1980.

5. Joseph K. Howard, "What Happened in Butte," *Harper's*, August 1948, pp. 89–96.

6. Richard T. Ruetten, "Anaconda Journalism: The End of an Era," *Journalism Quarterly* 37 (Winter 1960): 3–12, 104.

7. *Billings Gazette*, 20, 27 August and 3, 10 September 1972; Thomas Payne, "Montana: Politics under the Copper Dome," *Politics in the American West*, Frank H. Jonas, ed., pp. 202–30; Neil R. Peirce, *The Mountain States of America*, pp. 90–119; Malone and Roeder, *Montana*, chaps. 13, 15.

8. *Billings Gazette*, 20, 21, 22, 23 April 1980; *Butte Montana Standard*, 30 September and 1, 2, 3 October 1980.

Selected Bibliography

MANUSCRIPT COLLECTIONS

Berkeley, California. University of California. Bancroft Library. James Ben Ali Haggin Papers.

———. University of California. Bancroft Library. Phoebe Hearst Collection. George Hearst Papers.

Boulder, Colorado. University of Colorado. Western History Collections. Western Federation of Miners Papers.

Butte, Montana. Neil Lynch Collection (in his possession).

———. Silver Bow County Courthouse. File 7594, *Alma E. Clark Hines* et al. v. *Charles W. Clark* et al.

———. W. J. Wilcox Manuscript (in possession of Mrs. Dan Kinsella).

———. World Museum of Mining. Butte City Government Records.

———. World Museum of Mining. Records of the Alice Gold and Silver Mining Company.

Helena, Montana. Montana Historical Society Archives. Alice Gold and Silver Mining Company Records.

———. Montana Historical Society Archives. Anaconda Copper Mining Company Records.

———. Montana Historical Society Archives. P. J. Brophy Papers.

———. Montana Historical Society Archives. Marcus Daly Papers.

———. Montana Historical Society Archives. Fisk Family Papers.

———. Montana Historical Society Archives. Kate Hammond Fogarty Papers.

———. Montana Historical Society Archives. Samuel T. Hauser Papers.

———. Montana Historical Society Archives. William H. Hunt Papers.

———. Montana Historical Society Archives. Alex J. Johnston Papers.

———. Montana Historical Society Archives. Martin Maginnis Papers.

———. Montana Historical Society Archives. Montana Ore Purchasing Company Records.

257

——. Montana Historical Society Archives. Montana Socialist Party Papers.
——. Montana Historical Society Archives. George G. E. Neill Papers.
——. Montana Historical Society Archives. John S. M. Neill Papers.
——. Montana Historical Society Archives. C. B. Nolan Papers.
——. Montana Historical Society Archives. Herbert Peet Collection.
——. Montana Historical Society Archives. T. C. Power Papers.
——. Montana Historical Society Archives. Wilbur Fisk Sanders Papers.
——. Montana Historical Society Archives. Benjamin Silliman Papers.
——. Montana Historical Society Archives. Joseph K. Toole Papers.
——. Montana Historical Society Archives. Women's Helena for the Capital
Club Records.
——. Montana State Archives. Montana Attorney Generals Records.
——. Montana State Archives. Montana Governors Papers.
——. Montana State Archives. Montana Public Service Commission Records.
ords.
——. Montana State Archives. Montana Supreme Court Records.
Missoula, Montana, University of Montana Archives. Joseph M. Dixon Papers.
pers.
——. University of Montana Archives. Walter H. McLeod Papers.
Washington, D.C. Library of Congress. Manuscripts Division. Thomas H.
Carter Papers.
——. Library of Congress. Manuscripts Division. Grover Cleveland Papers.
——. Library of Congress. Manuscripts Division. Benjamin Harrison Papers.
pers.
——. Library of Congress. Manuscripts Division. Theodore Roosevelt Papers.
pers.
——. Library of Congress. Manuscripts Division. Thomas J. Walsh Papers.
——. National Archives. Record Group 122. Records of the Bureau of Corporations.
porations.
——. National Archives. Record Group 60. Records of the Department of
Justice.

PUBLIC AND CORPORATE DOCUMENTS

Alice Gold and Silver Mining Company. *Annual Report* (1894). Salt Lake City:
Salt Lake Lithographing Co., 1895.
Anaconda Copper Mining Company. *Assessment of Property in Montana for the
Years 1915–16*. Pamphlet. Butte: Murphy-Cheely Printing Co., 1916.
——. *Copper: From Mine to Finished Product*. New York: Anaconda Copper
Mining Co., 1920.
——. *The New Anaconda*. Pamphlet. New York: Eugene Meyer, Jr. & Co.,
1916.
——. *Report of the Anaconda Copper Mining Company for the Year Ending December 31, 1910*. Pamphlet. N.p.: n.p., 1911.
cember 31, 1910. Pamphlet. N.p.: n.p., 1911.
Montana. *House Journal of the Second Extraordinary Session of the Eighth Legisla-*

tive Assembly of the State of Montana . . . 1903. Helena: State Publishing Co., 1904.

———. *House Journal of the Seventh Session of the Legislative Assembly of the State of Montana . . . 1901.* Helena: State Publishing Co., 1901.

———. *House Journal of the Third Session of the Legislative Assembly of the State of Montana . . . 1893.* Butte: Inter Mountain Publishing Co., 1893.

———. *Laws, Resolutions and Memorials of the State of Montana, Passed at the Sixth Regular Session of the Legislative Assembly.* Helena: Independent Publishing Co., 1899.

———. *Proceedings and Debates of the Constitutional Convention . . . 1889.* Helena: State Publishing Co., 1921.

———. *Reports of Cases Argued and Determined in the Supreme Court of the State of Montana.* San Francisco: Bancroft-Whitney Co., 1895–1904.

———. *Senate Journal of the Sixth Session of the Legislative Assembly of the State of Montana.* Helena: Independent Publishing Co., 1899.

U.S. Congress, Senate. Committee on Privileges and Elections. *Report of the Committee on Privileges and Elections of the United States Senate Relative to the Right and Title of William A. Clark to a Seat as Senator from the State of Montana.* 56th Cong., 1st sess., 1900. 3 vols.

———. Senate. *Vote on the Motion to Deny a Seat to Lee Mantle of Montana.* 53rd Cong., 1st sess., 28 August 1893. *Congressional Record,* vol. 25.

———. Senate. *Resignation Remarks of Senator W. A. Clark.* 56th Cong., 1st sess., 15 May 1900. *Congresssional Record,* vol. 33.

———. Senate. *Senator Clark Speaking on the National Forest Reserves.* 59th Cong., 2nd sess., 23 February 1907. *Congressional Record,* vol. 41.

U.S. Department of Commerce. Bureau of the Census. *Historical Statistics of the United States.* 2 vols. 1975.

———. Bureau of the Census. *Thirteenth Census of the United States . . . 1910: Population,* vol. 2.

———. Bureau of the Census. *Fourteenth Census of the United States . . . 1920: Population,* vol. 1.

U.S. Department of the Interior. Census Office. *Ninth Census of the United States . . . 1870: Population,* vol. 1.

———. Census Office. *Tenth Census of the United States . . . 1880.*

———. Census Office. *Eleventh Census of the United States . . . 1890.*

———. Census Office. *Twelfth Census of the United States . . . 1900: Population,* part 1.

———. U.S. Geological Survey. *Mineral Resources of the United States . . . 1883–84* (1885).

U.S. Judiciary. *Federal Reporter: Cases Argued and Determined in the Circuit Courts of Appeals and Circuit and District Courts of the United States.* St. Paul: West Publishing Co., 1895–1917.

———. *United States Reports: Cases Adjudged in the Supreme Court.* New York and Albany: Banks and Brothers Law Publishers, 1898–1904.

———. *United States Supreme Court Reports: Cases Argued and Decided in the Supreme Court of the United States.* Rochester: Lawyers' Cooperative Publishing Co., 1898–1904.

PRIMARY SOURCES

Banon, Mrs. E. M., ed. *The Diary of Edward M. Banon . . . 1897.* Newport, R.I.: Ward Printing Co., 1948.

Barron, Clarence W. *More They Told Barron.* Edited by Arthur Pound and Samuel T. Moore. New York: Harper & Brothers, 1931.

Boyce, Edward. "Miners' Union Day at Butte, Montana." *The Miners' Magazine,* April 1900, pp. 39–42.

Braley, Berton. *Pegasus Pulls a Hack.* New York: Milton, Balch & Co., 1934.

Chaplin, Charles. *My Autobiography.* New York: Simon and Schuster, 1964.

Clark, William A. "Centennial Address on the Origin, Growth and Resources of Montana." *Contributions to the Historical Society of Montana,* vol. 2. Helena: State Publishing Co., 1896. Pp. 45–60.

———. *Montana's Distinguished Pioneer, W. A. Clark, Gives Historical Reminiscences.* Addresses presented to the Forty-First Annual Convention of the Society of Montana Pioneers, Butte, 28–30 August 1924. Missoula: Missoulian Publishing Co., 1924.

———. *Personal Explanation . . . Speech of Hon. William A. Clark, of Montana, in the Senate of the United States, Tuesday, May 15, 1900.* Washington: n.p., 1900. Copy in Montana Historical Society Library.

Clemens, Samuel L. *Mark Twain's Autobiography.* 2 vols. New York and London: Harper & Brothers, 1924.

———. *Mark Twain's Correspondence with Henry Huttleston Rogers: 1893–1909.* Edited by Lewis Leary. Berkeley and Los Angeles: University of California Press, 1969.

———. "Senator Clark of Montana (January 28, 1907)." *Mark Twain in Eruption.* Edited by Bernard DeVoto. Reprint ed.; New York: Capricorn Books, 1968. Pp. 70–77.

Foy, Eddie, with Harlow, Alvin F. *Clowning Through Life.* New York: E. P. Dutton & Co., 1928.

Gerard, James W. *My First Eighty-three Years in America.* Garden City, N.Y.: Doubleday & Co., 1951.

Goodwin, Charles C. *As I Remember Them.* Salt Lake City: Salt Lake Commercial Club, 1913.

Hammond, John Hays. *The Autobiography of John Hays Hammond.* 2 vols. New York: Farrar & Rinehart, 1935.

Haywood, William D. *Bill Haywood's Book: The Autobiography of William D. Haywood.* New York: International Publishers, 1929.

Hearst, George. *The Way It Was.* San Francisco: The Hearst Corporation, 1972.

Heinze, F. Augustus. *The Political Situation in Montana: 1900–1902.* Butte: n.p., 1902.

Hickey, Michael. "'Twas Christened Anaconda." *Anaconda Standard,* 21 December 1921.

Huntley, Chet. *The Generous Years: Remembrances of a Frontier Boyhood.* New York: Random House, 1968.

Hutchens, John K. *One Man's Montana: An Informal Portrait of a State.* Philadelphia and New York: J. B. Lippincott, 1964.

Johnson, Dorothy M., ed. "Three Hundred Grand!" *Montana: The Magazine of Western History* 10 (Winter 1960): 40–50.

Lawson, Thomas W. *Frenzied Finance.* Vol. 1: *The Crime of Amalgamated.* New York: The Ridgway-Thayer Co., 1905.

Linderman, Frank B. *Montana Adventure.* Edited by H. G. Merriam. Lincoln: University of Nebraska Press, 1968.

Lindsay, John. *Amazing Experiences of a Judge.* Philadelphia: Dorrance & Co., 1939.

Lottich, Kenneth V., ed. "My Trip to Montana Territory, 1879: The Unpretentious Journal of Charles French Kellogg." *Montana: The Magazine of Western History* 15 (Winter 1965): 12–25.

McClure, A. K. *Three Thousand Miles through the Rocky Mountains.* Philadelphia: J. B. Lippincott & Co., 1896.

MacLane, Mary. *The Story of Mary MacLane.* Chicago: Herbert S. Stone & Co., 1902.

O'Malley, M. G. "Butte Close-ups: Personal Narrative." *The Frontier* 8 (May 1928): 210–11.

Sales, Reno H. *Underground Warfare at Butte.* Caldwell, Ida: Caxton Printers, 1964.

Stack, B. E. "Origin of the Clark-Daly Feud" (1933). Unsigned typescript in Montana Historical Society Library, Helena.

Warren, Charles S. "Historical Address: The Territory of Montana." *Contributions to the Historical Society of Montana,* vol. 2. Helena: State Publishing Co., 1896. Pp. 61–75.

SECONDARY SOURCES

Aikens, Warren. "Electric Power for Montana Mines, Mills and Smelters." *Mining and Engineering World* 43 (17 July 1915): 91–96.

Allen, James B. *The Company Town in the American West.* Norman: University of Oklahoma Press, 1966.

"The Amalgamated and Mr. Heinze." *Mining and Scientific Press* 92 (17 February 1906): 99.

Anaconda, Montana, 1894. Pamphlet, Anaconda: Standard Publishing Co., 1894.

"Anaconda Copper." *Fortune,* December 1936, pp. 82–94, 210, 212, 214, 220; January 1937, pp. 70–77, 134, 136, 138, 143–44, 146, 149.

Athearn, Robert G. "Railroad to a Far-Off Country: The Utah and Northern." *Montana: The Magazine of Western History* 18 (Autumn 1968): 2–23.

———. *Union Pacific Country.* New York: Rand McNally, 1971.

Atherton, Gertrude. *Perch of the Devil.* New York: Frederick A. Stokes Co., 1914.

Baker, Horace C., ed. *Copper.* New York: Charles A. Stoneham & Co., 1915.

Baker, Ray Stannard. "Butte City: Greatest of Copper Camps." *The Century,* April 1903, pp. 870–79.

Bancroft, Hubert H. *History of Washington, Idaho, and Montana*. San Francisco: The History Company, 1890.

Barth, Gunther. *Bitter Strength: A History of the Chinese in the United States: 1850–70*. Cambridge: Harvard University Press, 1964.

Bates, J. Leonard. "Senator Walsh of Montana, 1918–24: A Liberal under Pressure." Ph.D. dissertation, University of North Carolina, 1952.

"The Battle for Copper." *Mining and Scientific Press* 88 (6 February 1904): 91.

Berthoff, Roland. *British Immigrants in Industrial America: 1790–1950*. New York: Russell & Russell, 1953.

Berthold, Mary Paddock. *Including Two Captains: A Later Look Westward*. Detroit: Harlo Press, 1975.

A Brief Description of the Anaconda Reduction Works. Butte: Montana Standard, n.d.

Brissenden, Paul F. "The Butte Miners and the Rustling Card." *American Economic Review* 10 (December 1920): 755–75.

Brogdon, J. Carl "The History of Jerome, Arizona." M.A. thesis, University of Arizona, 1952.

Brothers, Beverly J. *Historical Butte*. Bozeman: Artcraft Printers, 1977.

———. *Sketches of Walkerville: The High and the Mighty*. Butte: Ashton Printing & Engraving, 1973.

Brown, Ronald C. *Hard-Rock Miners: The Intermountain West, 1860–1920*. College Station and London: Texas A&M University Press, 1979.

Burlingame, Merrill G. *The Montana Frontier*. Helena, Mont.: State Publishing Co., 1942.

Butte Chamber of Commerce. *Resources of Butte: Its Mines and Smelters*. Butte: Inter Mountain Printers, 1895.

———. *Seven Talks About Mines*. Butte: Butte Chamber of Commerce, 1939.

"Butte, Montana, at the Dawn of the Twentieth Century." *Western Resources*, June 1901, pp. 1–50.

Butte: "On Top" and Underground. Pamphlet. Butte: Butte Chamber of Commerce, 1928.

"The Camp of Butte." *The West Shore*, August 1885, pp. 233–36.

"The Career of H. H. Rogers." *The Outlook*, 29 May 1909, pp. 257–58.

Cash, Joseph H. *Working the Homestake*. Ames: Iowa State University Press, 1973.

"A Chapter in High Finance." *The Nation*, 27 May 1909, pp. 545–46.

Christopherson, Edmond. "The Cities of America: Butte." *Saturday Evening Post*, 8 December 1951, pp. 40–41, 124, 127, 129.

"The Clark-Daly Feud." *Public Opinion*, 15 March 1900, pp. 325–26.

Clinch, Thomas A. "Coxey's Army in Montana." *Montana: The Magazine of Western History* 15 (Autumn 1965): 2–11.

———. "The Northern Pacific Railroad and Montana's Mineral Lands." *Pacific Historical Review* 34 (August 1965): 323–35.

———. *Urban Populism and Free Silver in Montana*. Missoula: University of Montana Press, 1970.

Cochran, Thomas C., and Miller, William. *The Age of Enterprise*. New York: Macmillan, 1942.

Cockhill, Brian E. "An Economic Analysis of Montana's Constitution." M.A. thesis, University of Montana, 1968.

Close, James A. "Some Phases of the History of the Anaconda Copper Mining Company." Ph.D. dissertation, University of Michigan, 1945.

Collier, Peter, and Horowitz, David. *The Rockefellers: An American Dynasty.* New York: Holt, Rinehart and Winston, 1976.

The Commercial and Financial Chronicle, 1888–99.

Connolly, Christopher P. "Big Business and the Bench." *Everybody's Magazine*, February 1912, pp. 147–60.

———. *The Devil Learns to Vote: The Story of Montana.* New York: Covici Friede, 1938.

"The Contested Senate Seats." *American Monthly Review of Reviews*, June 1900, pp. 649–50.

The Copper Handbook, vols. 2–8. Houghton, Mich.: Horace J. Stevens, 1902–8.

"The Copper Situation." *Mining and Scientific Press* 58 (23 March 1889): 208.

"Corporations and Montana Justice." *Literary Digest*, 21 November 1903, pp. 692–93.

Cushman, Dan. *Montana: The Gold Frontier.* Great Falls: Stay Away, Joe Publishers, 1973.

Daly, Hugh. *Biography of Marcus Daly of Montana.* Butte: Independent Publishers, 1934.

Davenport, Warren G. *Butte and Montana beneath the X-Ray.* Butte: X-Ray Publishing Co., 1909.

Davies, John F. *The Great Dynamite Explosions at Butte, Montana.* Pamphlet. Butte: Butte Bystanders Printers, 1895.

Davis, George W. *Sketches of Butte.* Boston: Cornhill Co., 1921.

Deer Lodge County History Group. "In the Shadow of Mount Haggin" (1975). Bound typescript in Montana Historical Society Library, Helena.

DeHaas, John N., Jr. *Historic Uptown Butte: An Architectural Analysis of the Central Business District of Butte, Montana.* N.p.: n.p., 1977.

"The Difficulties of the Copper Syndicate." *Commercial and Financial Chronicle*, 23 March 1889, pp. 382–83.

Ellis, F. W. "The World's Copper King." *Idaho Magazine*, January 1904, pp. 28–32.

Engineering and Mining Journal, vol. 38 (1884)–vol. 98 (1914).

Fahey, John. *Inland Empire: D. C. Corbin and Spokane.* Seattle: University of Washington Press, 1965.

Fallows, Marjorie R. *Irish Americans: Identity and Assimilation.* Englewood Cliffs, N.J.: Prentice-Hall, 1979.

Farrell, Mary M. "William Andrews Clark." M.A. thesis, University of Washington, 1933.

Farrington, Clayton. "The Political Life of William Andrews Clark." M.A. thesis, University of Montana, 1942.

Fell, James E., Jr. *Ores to Metals: The Rocky Mountain Smelting Industry.* Lincoln: University of Nebraska Press, 1979.

Filler, Louis. *Appointment at Armageddon: Muckraking and Progressivism in the American Tradition.* Westport, Conn.: Greenwood Press, 1976.

——. *Crusaders for American Liberalism*. New York: Harcourt Brace & Co., 1939.

Fisher, Arthur. "Montana: Land of the Copper Collar." *The Nation*, September 1922, pp. 290–92.

Flynn, John T. *God's Gold: The Story of Rockefeller and His Times*. Chautauqua, N.Y.: Chautauqua Press, 1932.

Fogarty, Kate Hammond. *The Story of Montana*. New York and Chicago: A. S. Barnes Co., 1916.

Foor, Forrest L. "The Senatorial Aspirations of William A. Clark, 1898–1901: A Study in Montana Politics." Ph.D. dissertation, University of California, Berkeley, 1941.

Forbes, B. C. *Men Who Are Making the West*. New York: B. C. Forbes Publishing Co., 1923.

Fought, John P. "Editor in the Montana Capital Fight." *A Century of Montana Journalism*. Edited by Warren J. Brier and Nathan B. Blumberg. Missoula: University of Montana Press, 1971.

——. "John Hurst Durston, Editor: The Anaconda Standard in the Clark–Daly Feud." M.A. thesis, University of Montana, 1959.

Freeman, Harry C. *A Brief History of Butte, Montana*. Chicago: Henry O. Shepard Co., 1900.

Gates, William B., Jr. *Michigan Copper and Boston Dollars*. Cambridge: Harvard University Press, 1951.

Gidel, M. H. "History of Geology and Ore Deposits." *Seven Talks about Mines*. Butte: Butte Chamber of Commerce, 1938.

Glasscock, C. B. *The War of the Copper Kings*. New York: Grosset & Dunlap, 1935.

Gocher, W. H. *Fasig's Tales of the Turf*. Hartford, Conn.: W. H. Gocher, 1903.

Goddard, Alan. *Butte Oldtimers' Handbook*. Butte: Bumont Press, 1976.

Goodwyn, Lawrence. *Democratic Promise: The Populist Movement in America*. New York: Oxford University Press, 1976.

Greever, William S. *The Bonanza West: The Story of the Western Mining Rushes, 1848–1900*. Norman: University of Oklahoma Press, 1963.

Gregory, John S. "Henry H. Rogers—Monopolist." *The World's Work*, May 1905, pp. 6127–30.

Gunther, John. *Inside U.S.A.* New York and London: Harper and Row, 1947.

"Haggin and Tevis." *Pacific Coast Annual Mining Review and Stock Ledger*. San Francisco: Francis & Valentine, 1878. Pp. 34–35.

Hakola, John W. "Samuel T. Hauser and the Economic Development of Montana: A Case Study in Nineteenth-Century Frontier Capitalism." Ph.D. dissertation, Indiana University, 1961.

Hamilton, James M. *History of Montana: From Wilderness to Statehood*. Edited by Merrill G. Burlingame. Portland: Binfords & Mort, 1957, 1970.

Hand, Wayland D. *et al.* "Songs of the Butte Miners." *Western Folklore* 9 (January 1950): 1–49.

Harrington, James D. " 'Free Silver,' Montana's Political Dream of Economic Prosperity: 1864–1900." M.A. thesis, University of Montana, 1969.

"Heinze, The Copper King." *American Monthly Review of Reviews*, January 1904, pp. 99–100.

High, James. "William Andrews Clark, Westerner: An Interpretative Vignette." *Arizona and the West* 2 (Autumn 1960): 245–64.

"The History of the Flotation Process." *The Mining Magazine*, September 1909, pp. 61–64.

Hoglund, A. William. *Finnish Immigrants in America: 1880–1920.* Madison: University of Wisconsin Press, 1960.

Hoover, W. H. *Marcus Daly (1841–1900)—and His Contributions to Anaconda.* Pamphlet. New York: Newcomen Society in North America, 1950.

Howard, Joseph Kinsey. *Montana: High, Wide, and Handsome.* New Haven: Yale University Press, 1943.

———. "What Happened in Butte," *Harper's*, August 1948, pp. 89–96.

Illustrated Handbook of the W. A. Clark Collection. Washington: Corcoran Gallery of Art, 1932.

"Industrial War in Montana." *The Outlook*, 5 December 1903, pp. 762–63.

Jackson, W. Turrentine. *The Enterprising Scot: Investors in the American West After 1873.* Edinburgh: Edinburgh University Press, 1968.

James, Don. *Butte's Memory Book.* Caldwell, Id.: Caxton Printers, 1975.

Jensen, Vernon H. *Heritage of Conflict: Labor Relations in the Nonferrous Metals Industry Up to 1930.* Ithaca: Cornell University Press, 1950.

Johnson, Allen, and Malone, Dumas, eds. *Dictionary of American Biography.* 20 vols. New York: Charles Scribner's Sons, 1930.

Johnson, Dale L. "Andrew B. Hammond: Education of a Capitalist on the Montana Frontier." Ph.D. dissertation, University of Montana, 1976.

Joralemon, Ira B. *Copper.* 2nd ed.; Berkeley, California: Howell-North, 1973.

Josephson, Matthew. *The Politicos.* New York: Harcourt, Brace & World, 1938.

———. *The Robber Barons.* New York: Harcourt, Brace & World, 1934.

Karlin, Jules A. *Joseph M. Dixon of Montana.* 2 vols. Missoula: University of Montana Publications in History, 1973.

Keller, Morton. *Affairs of State: Public Life in Late Nineteenth Century America.* Cambridge and London: Harvard University Press, 1977.

Kemp, James F. *The Ore Deposits of the United States and Canada.* 3rd ed. New York and London: The Scientific Publishing Co., 1900.

King, Joseph E. *A Mine to Make a Mine: Financing the Colorado Mining Industry, 1859–1902.* College Station: Texas A&M University Press, 1977.

Knapp, Henry R. "Captains of Industry, Part 10: William Andrews Clark." *Cosmopolitan*, February 1903, pp. 474–76.

Larrimore, Frank T. "Montana's Treasure City." *Harper's Weekly*, 7 June 1913, p. 9.

Lawson, Thomas W. "Fools and Their Money." *Everybody's Magazine*, May 1906, pp. 690–95.

Leeper, Joseph S. "The Changing Urban Landscape of Butte, Montana." Ph.D. dissertation, University of Oregon, 1974.

Leeson, Michael A. *History of Montana: 1739–1885.* Chicago: Warner, Beers & Co., 1885.

Leighton, Douglas F. "The Corporate History of the Montana Power Company: 1882–1913." M.A. thesis, University of Montana, 1951.

Leipheimer, E. G. *The First National Bank of Butte*. St. Paul: Brown & Bigelow, 1952.

Lingenfelter, Richard E. *The Hardrock Miners: A History of the Mining Labor Movement in the American West, 1863–93*. Berkeley and London: University of California Press, 1974.

"Litigation in Butte, Montana." *Mining and Scientific Press* 87 (31 October 1903): 282.

Littell, Robert. "The House That Clark Built." *New Republic*, 30 March 1927, pp. 171–72.

Lynch, Neil J. *Butte Centennial Recollections*. Butte: Pioneer Printing, 1979.

———. *Montana's Legislature Through the Years*. Bozeman: Color World of Montana, 1977.

McCaffrey, Lawrence J. *The Irish Diaspora in America*. Bloomington: Indiana University Press, 1976.

MacKnight, James A. *The Mines of Montana: Their History and Development*. Helena: C. K. Wells, 1892.

———. "The Montana Capital Fight." *Harper's Weekly*, 27 October 1894, p. 1049.

MacMillan, Donald. "Andrew Jackson Davis: A Story of Frontier Capitalism, 1864–90." M.A. thesis, University of Montana, 1967.

———. "A History of the Struggle to Abate Air Pollution from the Copper Smelters of the Far West: 1885–1933." Ph.D. dissertation, University of Montana, 1973.

McNelis, Sarah. *Copper King at War: The Biography of F. Augustus Heinze*. Missoula: University of Montana Press, 1968.

———. "F. Augustus Heinze: An Early Chapter in the Life of a Copper King." *The Montana Magazine of History* 2 (October 1952): 24–32.

Macpherson, James L. "Butte Miners' Union: An Analysis of Its Development and Economic Bargaining Position." M.A. thesis, University of Montana, 1949.

Malone, Michael P. "Montana as a Corporate Bailiwick: An Image in History." *Montana: Past and Present*. By Peter J. Powell and Michael P. Malone. Los Angeles: William Andrews Clark Memorial Library, 1976. Pp. 55–76.

———, and Roeder, Richard B. *Montana: A History of Two Centuries*. Seattle: University of Washington Press, 1976.

———, and Roeder, Richard B. *Montana as It Was: 1876*. Bozeman: Big Sky Books, 1975.

Mangam, William D. *The Clarks of Montana*. Np.: n.p., 1939.

Marcosson, Isaac F. *Anaconda*. New York: Dodd, Mead & Co., 1957.

Martin, Albro. *James J. Hill and the Opening of the Northwest*. New York: Oxford University Press, 1976.

Maxwell, Edith R., ed. "Great Falls Yesterday." Great Falls, 1939 (mimeographed).

Mezerik, A. G. *The Revolt of the South and the West*. New York: Duell, Sloan and Pearce, 1946.

Miller, Harriet, and Harrison, Elizabeth. "Marcus Daly's Western Champions." *The Western Horseman*, March 1958, pp. 26–27.

Miller, Joaquin. *An Illustrated History of the State of Montana*. Chicago: Lewis Publishing Co., 1894.

Mining and Scientific Press, vol. 48 (1884)–vol. 88 (1904).

"Mining Troubles in Montana." *Literary Digest*, 14 November 1900, p. 655.

Moffett, Samuel E. "Marcus Daly, Empire Builder." *American Monthly Review of Reviews*, December 1900, pp. 707–8.

"Money and Senatorships." *The Nation*, 19 April 1900, p. 295.

A Monster Monopoly: An Exposition of the Methods of the Anaconda Mining Company. N.p.: n.p., 1894.

"Montana." *Appleton's Annual Cyclopedia and Register of Important Events of the Year 1893*. New York: D. Appleton & Co., 1894. Pp. 500–2.

"The Montana Bribery Scandal." *Public Opinion*, 4 January 1900, p. 8.

"Montana Politics." *The Miners' Magazine*, July 1900, pp. 1–2.

Montana Power Company: Reclassification of Electric Plant. Butte: n.p., 1940, copy at company's Butte offices.

"The Montana Senatorial Scandal." *Literary Digest*, 20 January 1900, p. 74.

"Morse's Comeback." *Literary Digest*, 28 June 1913, pp. 1438–40.

"Mr. Clark's Coup d'Etat." *Public Opinion*, 24 May 1900, pp. 648–49.

Murphy, Jerre C. *The Comical History of Montana*. San Diego: E. L. Scofield, 1912.

Myers, Rex C. "Montana: A State and Its Relationship with Railroads, 1864–70." Ph.D. dissertation, University of Montana, 1972.

Navin, Thomas R. *Copper Mining and Management*. Tucson: University of Arizona Press, 1978.

Nevins, Allan. *Study in Power: John D. Rockefeller, Industrialist and Philanthropist*. 2 vols. New York and London: Charles Scribner's Sons, 1953.

Newell, Alan S. "A Victim of Monopoly: Samuel T. Hauser and Hydroelectric Development on the Missouri River, 1898–1912." M.A. thesis, University of Montana, 1979.

"New Reduction Works, Anaconda, Montana." *Mining and Scientific Press* 84 (12 April 1902): 202–3.

O'Farrell, P. A. *Butte: Its Copper Mines and Copper Kings*. New York: James A. Rogers, 1899.

Older, Fremont and Cora. *George Hearst: California Pioneer*. 2nd ed. Los Angeles: Westernlore Press, 1966.

Ostberg, Jacob H. *Sketches of Old Butte*. N.p.: n.p., 1972.

Paul, Rodman W. *California Gold: The Beginning of Mining in the Far West*. Cambridge: Harvard University Press, 1967.

———. *Mining Frontiers of the Far West, 1848–1900*. New York: Holt, Rinehart, and Winston, 1963.

Payne, Thomas. "Montana: Politics under the Copper Dome." *Politics in the*

American West. Edited by Frank H. Jonas. Salt Lake City: University of Utah Press, 1969. Pp. 202–30.

Peirce, Neil R. *The Mountain States of America.* New York: W. W. Norton, 1972.

Perry, Eugene S. *The Butte Mining District, Montana.* Washington: Government Printing Office, 1932.

Peterson, Richard H. *The Bonanza Kings: The Social Origins and Business Behavior of Western Mining Entrepreneurs, 1870–1900.* Lincoln: University of Nebraska Press, 1971, 1977.

Piatt, Guy X., ed. *The Story of Butte.* Bound issue of *Butte Bystander,* 15 April 1897, Montana Historical Society Library, Helena.

"The Price of Copper." *Mining and Scientific Press* 92 (27 January 1906): 50.

Progressive Men of the State of Montana. Chicago: A. W. Bowen & Co., 1901.

Quiett, Glenn C. *They Built the West: An Epic of Rails and Cities.* New York and London: D. Appleton-Century Co., 1934.

Quinn, Frank. *Memories of Columbia Gardens.* Butte: Pioneer Printing, 1973.

Ralph, Julian. "Montana: The Treasure State." *Harper's New Monthly Magazine,* June 1892, pp. 101–4.

Raymer, Robert G. *A History of Copper Mining in Montana.* Chicago and New York: Lewis Publishing Co., 1930.

———. *Montana: The Land and the People.* 3 vols. Chicago and New York: Lewis Publishing Co., 1930.

Raymond, Rossiter W. *Statistics of Mines and Mining in the States and Territories West of the Rocky Mountains: Being the Fifth* [Sixth and Eighth] *Annual Report of Rossiter W. Raymond, United States Commissioner of Mining Statistics.* Washington: Government Printing Office, 1873 [1874, 1877].

"Review of the World." *Current Literature,* December 1907, p. 585.

Richter, F. Ernest. "The Amalgamated Copper Company: A Closed Chapter in Corporation Finance." *Quarterly Journal of Economics* 30 (February 1916): 387–407.

———. "The Copper-Mining Industry in the United States, 1845–1925." *Quarterly Journal of Economics* 41 (February 1927): 236–91.

Rickard, T. A. "David W. Brunton: Consulting Engineer." *Mining and Scientific Press* 122 (28 May 1921): 745–56.

———. *A History of American Mining.* New York and London: McGraw-Hill, 1932.

Roberts, Edwards. "Two Montana Cities." *Harper's New Monthly Magazine,* September 1888, pp. 585–96.

Roeder, Richard B. "Montana in the Early Years of the Progressive Period." Ph.D. dissertation, University of Pennsylvania, 1972.

———. "Montana Progressivism: Sound and Fury and One Small Tax Reform." *Montana: The Magazine of Western History* 20 (October 1970): 18–26.

Rowe, John. *The Hard-Rock Men: Cornish Immigrants and the North American Mining Frontier.* New York: Barnes & Noble, 1974.

Rowse, A. L. *The Cousin Jacks: The Cornish in America.* New York: Charles Scribner's Sons, 1969.

Ruetten, Richard T. "Burton K. Wheeler, 1905–25: An Independent Liberal under Fire." M.A. thesis, University of Oregon, 1957.

———. "Burton K. Wheeler of Montana: A Progressive Between the Wars." Ph.D. dissertation, University of Oregon, 1961.

Sanders, Helen Fitzgerald. "Butte—The Heart of the Copper Industry." *Overland Monthly,* November 1906, pp. 367–84.

———. *A History of Montana.* 3 vols. Chicago and New York: Lewis Publishing Co., 1913.

Satterthwaite, Thomas C. "Cornelius Francis Kelley: The Rise of an Industrial Statesman." M.A. thesis, Montana State University, 1971.

Schmidt, Jean. "Copper Kings, Populists, and Logrollers: The Montana Legislative Session of 1893." M.A. thesis, Montana State University, 1980.

"Selling Art to Our Millionaires." *Literary Digest,* 23 November 1912, pp. 960–61.

"Senator Clark and the Amalgamated Copper Trust." *The Miners' Magazine,* June 1901, pp. 6–8.

Shannon, William V. *The American Irish.* New York: Macmillan, 1963.

Shinn, Charles H. *Mining Camps: A Study in American Frontier Government.* New York: Harper & Row, 1965.

Shoebotham, H. Minar. *Anaconda: Life of Marcus Daly the Copper King.* Harrisburg: The Stackpole Co., 1956.

Sketches of the Inter-Mountain States. Salt Lake City: Salt Lake Tribune, 1909.

Smith, Duane A. *Rocky Mountain Mining Camps: The Urban Frontier.* Bloomington: Indiana University Press, 1967.

Smith, Norma. "The Rise and Fall of the Butte Miners' Union, 1878–1914." M.A. thesis, Montana State University, 1961.

Smurr, John W. "The Montana 'Tax Conspiracy' of 1889." *Montana: The Magazine of Western History* 5 (Spring 1955): 46–53, and (Summer 1955): 47–56.

Speare, Charles F. "The Story of Copper." *American Monthly Review of Reviews,* November 1906, pp. 561–74.

Spence, Clark C. *British Investments and the American Mining Frontier: 1860–1901.* Ithaca: Cornell University Press, 1958.

———. *Mining Engineers and the American West: The Lace-Boot Brigade, 1849–1922.* New Haven and London: Yale University Press, 1970.

———. *Montana: A Bicentennial History.* New York: W. W. Norton, 1978.

———. *Territorial Politics and Government in Montana: 1864–1889.* Urbana: University of Illinois Press, 1975.

Stahlberg, John. "Butte." *Rocky Mountain Cities.* Edited by Ray B. West, Jr. New York: W. W. Norton, 1949. Pp. 248–64.

Stewart, John A. "William A. Clark." *American Review of Reviews,* April 1925, pp. 422–23.

Stewart, William R. "Captains of Industry, Part 21: F. Augustus Heinze." *Cosmopolitan,* January 1904, pp. 189–92.

"The Story of Heinze, a Tale of Copper—and Brass." *Current Literature,* January 1907, pp. 34–36.

"The Story of Morse." *Current Literature*, February 1910, pp. 151–53.
Stout, Tom. *Montana: Its Story and Biography*. 3 vols. Chicago and New York: American Historical Society, 1921.
Strother, French. "Swinging the March of Empire Southwestward." *The World's Work*, January 1906, pp. 7072–81.
Swanberg, W. A. *Citizen Hearst*. New York: Charles Scribner's Sons, 1961.
Swett, Ira L. *Montana's Trolleys—2: Butte, Anaconda, Butte, Anaconda & Pacific*. Southgate, Cal.: Interurbans Magazine, 1970.
Thomson, Janet C. "The Role of Lee Mantle in Montana Politics, 1889–1900: An Interpretation." M.A. thesis, University of Montana, 1956.
Toole, K. Ross. "The Anaconda Copper Mining Company: A Price War and a Copper Corner." *Pacific Northwest Quarterly* 41 (October 1950): 312–29.
————. "The Genesis of the Clark-Daly Feud." *The Montana Magazine of History* 1 (April 1951): 21–33.
————. "A History of the Anaconda Copper Mining Company: A Study in the Relationships Between a State and Its People and a Corporation: 1880–1950." Ph.D. dissertation, University of California, Los Angeles, 1954.
————."Marcus Daly: A Study of Business in Politics." M.A. thesis, University of Montana, 1948.
————. *Montana: An Uncommon Land*. Norman: University of Oklahoma Press, 1959.
————."When Big Money Came to Butte." *Pacific Northwest Quarterly* 44 (January 1953): 23–29.
————, and Butcher, Edward. "Timber Depredations on the Montana Public Domain, 1885–1918." *Journal of the West* 7 (July 1968): 351–62.
Trimble, William J. *The Mining Advance into the Inland Empire*. Madison: University of Wisconsin Press, 1914.
Ulke, Titus. "The Anaconda Copper Mine and Works." *Engineering Magazine*, July 1897, pp. 512–34.
————. *Modern Electrolytic Copper Refining*. New York: John Wiley & Sons, 1907.
Villard, Oswald Garrison. "Montana and 'the Company.'" *The Nation*, 9 July 1930, pp. 39–45.
Waldron, Ellis L. *Montana Politics since 1864: An Atlas of Elections*. Missoula: University of Montana Press, 1958.
————, and Wilson, Paul B. *Atlas of Montana Elections: 1889–1976*. Missoula: University of Montana Publications in History, 1978.
"The Wealth of a Rocky Mountain State." *Review of Reviews*, November 1894, pp. 546–47.
Weed, Walter H. *Geology and Ore Deposits of the Butte District, Montana*. Washington: Government Printing Office, 1912.
————. *The Mines Handbook*, vol. 12. New York: Stevens Copper Handbook Co., 1916.
————. *The Mines Handbook*, vol. 13. New York: W. H. Weed, 1918.
"The Western Labor Union." *The Miners' Magazine*, January 1900, pp. 24–26.

Wheeler, Leslie A. "Montana and the Lady Novelist." *Montana: The Magazine of Western History* 27 (Winter 1977): 40–51.
———. "Montana's Shocking 'Litr'y' Lady." *Montana: The Magazine of Western History* 27 (Summer 1977): 20–33.
Wilber, C. W. "The Way of the Land Transgressor, 6: How Montana Was 'Done.'" *Pacific Monthly*, January 1908, pp. 108–15.
Williams, Robert E. "The Silver Republican Movement in Montana." M.A. thesis, University of Montana, 1965.
Wolle, Muriel S. *Montana Pay Dirt: A Guide to the Mining Camps of the Treasure State.* Chicago: Sage Books, 1963.
Work Projects Administration of Montana. Mineral Resources Survey. *Memoir No. 21: Bibliography of the Geology and Mineral Resources of Montana.* Butte: Montana School of Mines, 1942.
———. Writers' Program. *Copper Camp.* New York: Hastings House, 1943.
Wunder, John R. "Law and Chinese in Frontier Montana." *Montana: The Magazine of Western History* 30 (Summer 1980): 18–31.
Wyman, Mark. *Hard Rock Epic: Western Miners and the Industrial Revolution, 1860–1910.* Berkeley and Los Angeles: University of California Press, 1979.
Young, Otis E., Jr. *Western Mining.* Norman: University of Oklahoma Press, 1970.
Young, Robert G. *The Public School System of Butte, Montana.* N.p.: n.p., 1904.
Youngman, William S., Jr. "The Anaconda Copper Mining Company and Some Phases of Its Influence in the Politics of the State of Montana, 1880–1929." Honors thesis, Harvard University, 1929.

NEWSPAPERS

Anaconda Standard
Anaconda Weekly Review
Baker Fallon County Times
Billings Gazette
Bozeman Courier
Butte American Labor Union Journal
Butte Bystander
Butte Daily Post
Butte Evening News
Butte Daily Inter Mountain, Butte Weekly Inter Mountain
Butte Labor World
Butte Miner, Butte Daily Miner, Butte Weekly Miner
Butte Semi-Weekly Miner
Butte Montana Standard
Butte Reveille
Butte Tribune-Review
Chicago Daily Tribune
Choteau Montanan

Denver Post
Denver Rocky Mountain News
Deer Lodge New Northwest
Fort Benton River Press
Great Falls Tribune
Hamilton Western News
Havre Plaindealer
Helena Herald, Helena Daily Herald
Helena Independent
Helena Montana Lookout
Helena Press
Kalispell Inter Lake
Lewistown Fergus County Argus
Livingston Enterprise
Miles City Independent
Miles City Yellowstone Journal
Missoula Missoulian
New York Herald
New York Tribune
New York Times
New York Wall Street Journal
Portland Oregonian
Salt Lake Tribune
San Francisco Examiner
Spokane Spokesman-Review
Virginia City Montana Post
White Sulphur Springs Rocky Mountain Husbandman

Index

Acquisition Mine, 48
Addicks, John "Gas," 129, 134
Agassiz, Alexander, 35
Alder Gulch, 4, 6, 7
Aldrich, Nelson, 90
Alice Mine (Alice Gold and Silver Mining Co.), 16, 17, 20, 32, 47, 54, 61, 76, 83, 205, 206
Allende, Salvador, 216
Allie Brown Mine, 20
Allison, William, 7, 8
Allport, John, 169
Amalgamated Copper Co., 148, 149, 159, 161, 162, 190, 191, 194, 195, 196, 201–4 passim, 207, 208, 209, 213; creation of, 137–43; in 1900 campaign, 151–56; struggles with F. A. Heinze, 163–89; dissolution of, 205–6
American Bimetallic League, 106
American Brass Co., 214
American Labor Union Journal: quoted, 178
American Smelting and Refining Co., 132
American Protective Association, 66, 98
American Tobacco Co., 132
Anaconda, 41, 81; foundation of, 30; in capital fight, 93–105
Anaconda Copper Mining Co. (Anaconda Co., Anaconda Mining Co.), 53, 112, 136, 141, 149, 157, 166, 167, 190, 200; beginnings, 27–31; price war with Michigan mines, 36–37; and world copper industry, 37–39; 1880s–1890s development, 41–45; 1890 incorporations, 45–47; absorption into Amalgamated Copper Co., 137; reorganization of,

205–7; and labor, 207–8; and politics, 209–16; development after 1915, 212–17
Anaconda Hill, 4, 24, 61, 201, 215
Anaconda Mine, 24, 25, 32, 33, 41, 105–6, 147, 148; development of, 27–31
Anaconda Standard, 114, 124; formation of, 88–89; quoted, 97, 100, 115–16, 118, 127, 147, 155, 163, 177, 182, 210
Anaconda syndicate, 25–31, 36, 37, 45, 78
Anaconda Weekly Review: quoted, 36
Ancient Order of Hibernians, 66
"A.P.A. Riot" (1894), 66, 70
Apex Law, 140–41, 147, 189
Archbold, John, 134
Atherton, Gertrude: quoted, 61, 62, 69, 188
Atlantic Richfield Co., 216

Badger State Mine, 49
Baker, "Diamond Tooth," 71–72
Baker, Ray S.: quoted, 57–58
Bannack, 6
Barron, Clarence, 167, 182–83; quoted, 136, 143
Batterman, C. H., 142
Bay, Harvey, 10
Beasley, W. W., 120, 124
Beatty, James H., 180; quoted, 181
Becker, William, 91
Bell Mine, 23, 33
Belle of Butte Mine, 32, 49
Belmont Mine, 163
Berkeley Pit, 61, 215
Bernhardt, Sarah, 73
Bessemer Process, 21, 53

273

135, 207; characterized, 25–26; and creation of Anaconda Co., 27–31; death of, 45–46
Hearst, Phoebe, 45, 46, 109
Hearst, William R., 25, 45, 46
Hearst estate, 109, 137
Hebgen, Max, 204
Hedges, W. A., 119
Heimendinger, H. M., 170
Heinze, Arthur, 51, 142, 147, 172, 191
Heinze, Bernice Henderson, 194
Heinze, Eliza, 50
Heinze, F. Augustus, 78, 109, 159, 160, 161, 190, 200, 205, 207, 209, 210, 212, 213; characterization and early career, 49–53; litigation with Amalgamated Copper Co. and Boston companies, 141–48; and 1900 campaign, 148–56; "war" with Amalgamated, 162–89; post-1906 career, 191–95; death and assessment, 195
Heinze, F. Augustus, Jr., 194
Heinze, Otto, Sr. 50, 51
Heinze, Otto Charles, 51, 142, 144, 185, 191, 192
Heinze, Otto, and Co., 191, 193
Heinze v. Butte and Boston Co., 180
Helena: in capital fight, 94–104; loyalty to W. A. Clark in 1899–1900 Senate contest, 114, 117, 118, 120
Helena Independent, 111, 121, 154, 161, 210; quoted, 87, 116, 120, 143
Hendrie, Charles, 10
Hendrie Mill, 16
Hennessy, Dan J., 44, 59, 88, 163, 165, 167
Hennessy's Department Store, 59, 150, 167
Hepburn Act, 195
Hickey, Edward, 24, 29, 150
Hickey, Michael, 24, 25
High Ore Mine, 41
Hill, Ben, 117, 125
Hill, James J., 40, 49, 73, 81, 177
Hill, Nathaniel P., 22, 47, 82
Hinds, Thomas, 127, 146, 147, 150
Hoar, George, 123; quoted, 125
Hobson, Simeon S., 119, 125
Hogan, T. S., 107, 153
Hogan, "General" William, 55
Holloway, William, 64
Holmes, Oliver Wendell, Jr., 44
Holter, Anton, 21
Homestake Mine (South Dakota), 26, 27, 78, 131
Hoover, W. H., 215

House Bill 132, 136, 146
How, John, 16
Howard, Joseph K., 188; quoted, 57, 162
Humphreys, G. O., 7, 8
Hunt, William: quoted, 122
Huntington, Collis, 198
Huntley, Chet, 57
Hutchens, John K., 57
Hyams, G. M., 154
Hypocka Mine, 187

Idaho: mining in, 6
Indians of Butte, 68
Industrial Workers of the World, 79, 208, 209
Inspiration Copper Co., 206
International Harvester Co., 132
International Smelting and Refining Co., 206
International Steamship Co., 132
Irish of Butte, 64–65; political power, 85
Irvine, Caleb, 7
Irwin, Wallace: quoted, 198
Italians of Butte, 69

Jackling, Daniel C., 202
Jews of Butte, 67
Johnstown Mine (Johnstown Mining Co.), 52, 144, 163, 168, 172, 173, 179, 180, 181, 187
Jones, "Fat Jack," 72, 109, 165
Jones, John P., 128
Josephson, Matthew, 109
July, Jimmy, 68

Kalispell Inter Lake: quoted, 116
Kelley, Cornelius, 19, 167, 173, 190, 203, 204, 205, 214, 215; characterized, 166
Kelley, Jeremiah, 19, 166
Kennecott Copper Co., 214
Kennedy, J. M., 190
Ketchell, Stanley, 74
Kilroy, Richard, 190
Kirkpatrick, William, 215
Klepetko, Frank, 42
Knickerbocker Trust Co., 193
Knights of Labor, 76
Knowles, Hiram, 143, 179, 180

Labor: solidarity with management, 55, 77–78; rise of, at Butte, 75–79; deterioration of Butte position, 207–9
LaFollette, Robert, 194, 199
Lamar, Lucius Q. C., 86
Lamm, Daniel, 172, 173, 176

90–91; of 1893, 94–98; of 1899, 111–20; of 1901, 151, 160; special session of Dec., 1903, 178–79
Montana Ore Purchasing Co., 142, 144, 146, 147, 149, 162, 170, 172, 180, 181, 187, 188; formation of, 51–52
Montana Power Co., 210, 216; creation of, 204–5
Montana Realty Co., 196
Montana Supereme Court, 144–48 passim, 169, 170, 177, 180, 182
Montana Trades and Labor Council, 79, 208
Montana Union Railroad, 40, 41
Morgan, J. P., 73, 192, 193; quoted, 189
Morony, John, 204
Morse, Charles W., 191–94 passim
Moulton Mine (Moulton Mining and Reduction Works), 20, 32, 47, 54
Mountain Chief Mine, 15, 16, 187
Mountain Consolidated Mine, 41
Mountain View Mine, 49, 181
Mullins, Pat, 150, 164, 185
Murphy, Jerre, 166; quoted, 167, 209
Murray, James, 51, 141
Murray, James E., 214
Murray, Thomas, 18
Myers, Henry L., 114, 115, 116

The Nation: quoted, 129, 189
Nation, Carrie, 75
Navin, Thomas R., 142
Neill, John S. M., 111, 151, 200; quoted, 112, 161
Nettie Mine, 32, 48
Neversweat Mine, 29, 41, 61, 148
Nevins, Allan: quoted, 134
Newmont Mining Corporation, 188
New York Clearing House, 192, 193
New York Journal of Commerce: quoted, 178
New York Press: quoted, 129
New York Times: quoted, 138, 160, 200
New York World: quoted, 108–9
Nipper Mine, 29, 163, 168, 176, 182, 187
Nolan, C. B., 118; quoted, 122
North Butte Mining Co., 201
Northern Pacific Railroad, 21, 24, 29, 32, 40, 42, 49, 93, 99, 100
Norwegians of Butte, 67
Noyes, John, 8

O'Connell, Jerry, 213
O'Connor, Burdette, 147, 148
Odin Mine, 48
O'Farrell, Pat, 149, 169
Ohio Copper Co., 187

Olin, Giles, 16, 17
Olson, Sam, 180
O'Malley, M. G., 84, 141
Omnibus States, 90
Ontario Mine (Utah), 26, 27
Original Mine, 15, 22, 196
Oro Butte Mine, 48
Orphan Girl Mine, 41
Outlook Magazine: quoted, 178
Owen, John, 7
Owens, Kenneth, 84
Owsley, William, 68

Panama Canal, 197
Panic of 1873, 7, 11, 21
Panic of 1893, 54–56, 106
Panic of 1907, 193, 209
Parker, Bud (Budd), 7
Parks, Billy, 9, 10, 16, 17
Parnell, Charles, 81
Parrot Mine (Parrot Silver and Copper Co.), 17, 21, 33, 47, 53, 137, 149, 169, 172, 174, 196, 205, 206
Pennsylvania cases, 143–47
Pennsylvania Mine, 49, 144, 168, 172, 179, 181, 187
Penrose, W. J., 77
Peterson, Richard H., 11, 77, 207
Pettit, B., 17
Pettus, E. W., 126
Phelps Dodge Co., 214
Piccolo Mine, 169
Pigott, William, 122
Pimps, 74
Plummer, Henry, 13
Populism (Populist party), 55, 94, 98, 104–12 passim, 150–53 passim, 156, 163, 209; described, 92–93
Porter, Charles, 9
Porter, Henry, 8
Power, T. C., 84, 90, 98
Precinct 34 controversy, 91
Progressive movement, 210
Prostitution: in Butte, 74–75
Pure Food and Drug Act, 195

Quartz mining: Butte beginnings, 9
Quary, Matthew, 129
Quigg, Lemuel E.: quoted, 71
Quinn, Jack, 150

Ralph, Julian: quoted, 74
Ramsdell, Joseph, 9
Rankin, Wellington, 212
Rarus Mine, 52, 142, 143, 144, 162, 169, 171, 172, 179, 187